Integral Transforms for Engineers and Physicists

Integral Transforms for Engineers and Physicists

Dr. P. K. Mittal
M.Sc. (Maths, Physics), Ph.D.
P.L.M.S. Govt. P.G. College
Rishikesh, U.P.

Revised Edition: 2011

Published by Ashok Gosain and Ashish Gosain for:
HAR-ANAND PUBLICATIONS PVT LTD
E-49/3, Okhla Industrial Area, Phase-II, New Delhi-110020
Tel.: 41603490 Fax: 011-41708607
E-mail: info@haranandpublications.com
Website: www.haranandpublications.com

Printed in India at Saujanya Printing Press

Preface

This Book has been written with an intention of introducing the students of engineering and physics the integral transform methods which are very powerful tools in solving the problems of theoretical physics and other technical sciences. The present book has been prepared with the needs of modern scientists and engineers in mind and since mathematics is not their practical subject, the book has been presented in such a way that it may be studied with a minimum amount of guidance.

In preparing the present book, a number of standard books in physics and mathematics have freely been consulted. The author will remain thankful to the authors and publishers of these books.

The author shall highly appreciate any comments, criticism and suggestions for the further improvement of the book. My sincere thanks are due to my publisher Mr. Ashok Gosain of Har-Anand Publications for bringing out the book in a very short time.

P.K. Mittal

Contents

1

The Laplace Transforms

1.1 INTRODUCTION

The students are already familiar with some operators which transform a function into another function. Differential operator D and integral operator D^{-1} are the examples. *Laplace transform* or *Laplace transformation* is a method for solving linear differential equation arising in physical sciences and Engineering. It reduces the problem of solving a differential equation to an algebraic problem. Here we shall consider the Laplace Transformation and its properties.

1.2 PIECE-WISE OR SECTIONALLY CONTINUOUS FUNCTION

A function $f(x)$ is said to be sectionally continuous in a closed interval $a \le t \le b$ if that interval can be subdivided into a finite number of intervals such that in each of which the function is continuous and has finite right and left hand limits. In the diagram $f(x)$ has discontinuities at x_1, x_2, x_3, x_4 but is sectionally continuous in the interval (a, b).

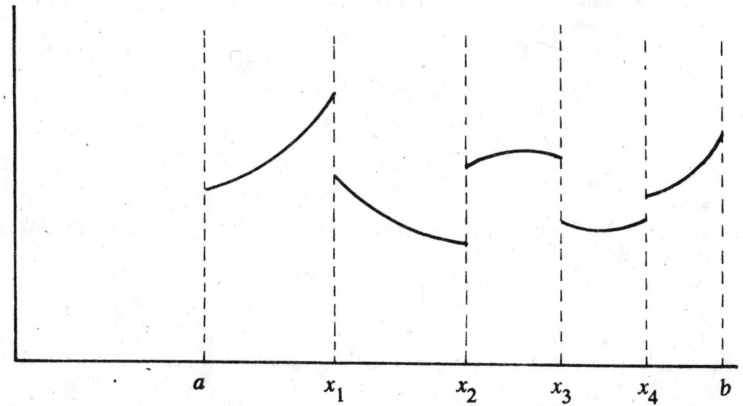

(i) Here $f(x)$ is continuous in the open intervals

$$a < x < x_1, \quad x_1 < x < x_2, \quad x_3 < x < x_4, \quad x_4 < x < b.$$

(ii) The right hand and left hand limits at x_1 are

$$\lim_{\varepsilon \to 0} f(x_1 + \varepsilon) \text{ and } \lim_{\varepsilon \to 0} f(x_1 - \varepsilon)$$

which exist as is evident from the diagram.

1.3 FUNCTIONS OF EXPONENTIAL ORDER

A function $f(x)$ is said to be exponential order b as $x \to \infty$ if there exists a positive constant M, a number b and a finite number x_0 such that

$$|f(x)| < M e^{bx}, \text{ for } x \geq x_0.$$

Sometimes we write

$$f(x) = 0(e^{bx}), \; x \to \infty$$

and read it as "$f(x)$ is of exponential order b, as $t \to \infty$".

Note. If a function is of exponential order b, it is also of order a such that $a > b$.

Example 1. *Show that x^n is of exponential order as $x \to \infty$, n being any positive integer.*

Solution. $\lim_{x \to \infty} e^{-ax} x^n, \; a > 0$

$$= \lim_{x \to \infty} \frac{x^n}{e^{ax}} \qquad \left[\text{form } \frac{\infty}{\infty}\right]$$

$$= \lim_{x \to \infty} \frac{n!}{a^n e^{ax}} \text{ by L. Hospital's rule}$$

$$= \frac{n!}{\infty} = 0$$

$\therefore \lim_{x \to \infty} e^{-ax} x^n = 0 =$ finite number. Consequently x^n is of exponential order as $x \to \infty$.

Example 2. *Show that $F(x) = e^{x^2}$ is not of exponential order as $n \to \infty$.*

Solution. We have

$$\lim_{x \to \infty} e^{-ax} \cdot e^{x^2}$$

$$= \lim_{x \to \infty} \frac{e^{x^2}}{e^{ax}} \qquad \left[\text{form } \frac{\infty}{\infty}\right]$$

$$= \lim_{x \to \infty} e^{x^2 - ax}$$

Case I. If $a \leq 0$, this limit is infinite.

Case II. If $a > 0$, $\lim_{x \to \infty} e^{x(x-a)} = \infty$.

Thus whatever be the value of a, this limit is not finite, hence we can not find a number M such that

$$e^{x^2} < M e^{bx}.$$

1.4 FUNCTION OF CLASS A

A function which is sectionally continuous over every finite interval in the range $x \geq 0$, and is of exponential order as $x \to \infty$ is termed as '*a function of class A*'.

1.5 THE TRANSFORM CONCEPT

An improper integral of the form

$$\int_{-\infty}^{\infty} K(p, t)\, F(t)\, dt$$

is called *integral transform* of $F(t)$ if it is convergent. Sometimes it is denoted by $f(p)$ or $T\{F(t)\}$. Thus

$$f(p) = T\{F(t)\} = \int_{-\infty}^{\infty} K(p, t)\, F(t)\, dt \qquad \ldots\text{(i)}$$

The function $K(p, t)$ appearing in the integrand is called *Kernel* of the transform. Here p is a parameter and is independent of t, p may be real or complex number.

1.6 LAPLACE TRANSFORM (DEFINITION)

If the kernel $K(p, t)$ is defined as

$$K(p, t) = \begin{cases} e^{-pt}, & t \geq 0 \\ 0, & t < 0 \end{cases}$$

Then (i) becomes

$$f(p) = T\{F(t)\} = \int_0^\infty F(t)\, e^{-pt}\, dt \qquad \ldots\text{(ii)}$$

This transform is known as *Laplace transform* of the function $F(t)$ and is also denoted by $\tilde{F}(p)$.

Hence *Laplace transform* is a function of a new variable (or parameter) p given by (ii). The parameter p is real or complex number. In general, the parameter p is taken to be a real positive number.

The Laplace transform is said to exist if the integral (ii) is convergent for some value of p.

The operation of multiplying $F(t)$ by e^{-pt} and integrating from 0 to ∞ is called *Laplace transformation*.

1.7 NOTATION

We follow two types of notations:

(i) Functions are denoted by capital letters

$$F(t), G(t), H(t), \ldots.$$

and their Laplace transforms are denoted by corresponding lower case letters $f(p), g(p), h(p), \ldots.$ or by $f(s), g(s), h(s), \ldots.$

(ii) Functions are denoted by lower case letters

$$f(t), g(t), h(t) \ldots.$$

and their Laplace transforms are denoted by

$$\tilde{f}(p), \tilde{g}(p), \tilde{h}(p), \ldots. \text{ or } \tilde{f}(s)$$

$$\tilde{g}(s), \tilde{h}(s), \ldots. \text{ respectively.}$$

1.8 EXISTENCE OF LAPLACE TRANSFORM

Theorem. *If $F(t)$ is piecewise continuous in every finite interval and is of exponential order a as $t \to \infty$, then $f(p)$ exists $\forall\ p > a$, i.e., Laplace transform exists.*

or

If $F(t)$ is a function of class A, then Laplace transform of $F(t)$ exists for all $p > a$.

Proof. We have

$$L\{F(t)\} = \int_0^\infty e^{-pt} F(t)\, dt$$

$$= \int_0^{t_0} e^{-pt} F(t)\, dt + \int_{t_0}^\infty e^{-pt} F(t)\, dt \qquad \ldots\text{(i)}$$

The integral $\int_0^{t_0} e^{-pt} F(t)\, dt$ exists since $F(t)$ is piecewise continuous on every finite interval $0 \leq t \leq t_0$.

Now, $$\left| \int_{t_0}^{\infty} e^{-pt} F(t)\, dt \right| \leq \int_{t_0}^{\infty} | e^{-pt} F(t) |\, dt$$

$$\leq \int_{t_0}^{\infty} e^{-pt} M e^{at}\, dt$$

since $F(t)$ is exponential order a as $t \to \infty$

$$= \int_{t_0}^{\infty} e^{-(p-a)t} M\, dt$$

$$= \frac{M e^{-(p-a)t_0}}{p-a},\ p > a$$

$$\therefore \quad \left| \int_{t_0}^{\infty} e^{-pt} F(t)\, dt \right| \leq \frac{M e^{-(p-a)t_0}}{p-a},\ p > a.$$

But $\dfrac{Me^{-(p-a)t_0}}{p-a}$ can be made as small as we please by taking t_0 sufficiently large.

Hence from (i), we conclude that $L\{F(t)\}$ exists for all $p > a$.

Note. Conditions in the theorem of § 1.8 are sufficient but not necessary for the existence of the Laplace transform. If these conditions are satisfied, the Laplace transform must exist. If these conditions are not satisfied, the Laplace transform may or may not exist.

1.9 LAPLACE TRANSFORMS OF ELEMENTARY FUNCTIONS

Transforms of some of the elementary functions can easily be found. The process of finding these may be clear from following examples:

ILLUSTRATIVE EXAMPLES

Example 1. *Find the Laplace transform of the function $F(t) = 1$.*

Solution. We have $L\{F(t)\} = \int_0^{\infty} e^{-pt} \cdot F(t)\, dt$

$$\therefore \quad L\{1\} = \int_0^\infty e^{-pt} \cdot 1\, dt$$

$$= \left[-\frac{e^{-pt}}{p} \right]_0^\infty = \frac{1}{p}, \; p > 0.$$

Since the integral is convergent if $p > 0$ and divergent if $p \le 0$, hence the condition $p > 0$ is necessary.

Example 2. *Find* $L\{t\}$.

Solution. $$L\{t\} = \int_0^\infty e^{-pt} \cdot t\, dt$$

$$= \left[-\frac{1}{p} t\, e^{-pt} \right]_0^\infty + \frac{1}{p} \int_0^\infty e^{-pt}\, dt$$

$$= \frac{1}{p^2}, \; p > 0.$$

Example 3. *Find* $L\{t^n\}$, *n is a positive integer.*

Solution. $$L\{t^n\} = \int_0^\infty e^{-pt} \cdot t^n\, dt$$

$$= \int_0^\infty e^{-u}\, u^n\, du \cdot p^{-n-1}, \text{ where } pt = u$$

$$= \frac{\Gamma(n+1)}{p^{n+1}} \qquad \left[\because \int_0^\infty e^{-u}\, u^n\, du = \Gamma(n+1) \right]$$

$$= \frac{n!}{p^{n+1}}, \; p > 0.$$

Example 4. *Find* $L\{e^{at}\}$.

Solution. $$L\{e^{at}\} = \int_0^\infty e^{-pt} \cdot e^{at}\, dt$$

$$= \int_0^\infty e^{-(p-a)t}\, dt.$$

If $p \leq a$, integral diverges. For $p > a$, the integral converges. Hence for $p > a$

$$L\{e^{at}\} = \int_0^\infty e^{-(p-a)t}\,dt$$

$$= \left[\frac{-e^{-(p-a)t}}{p-a}\right]_0^\infty = 0 + \frac{1}{p-a}$$

$$= \frac{1}{p-a} \quad p > a.$$

Example 5. *Find L {sin at}.*

Solution. $L\{\sin at\} = \int_0^\infty e^{-pt} \sin at\,dt.$

$$= \left[\frac{e^{-pt}(-p\sin at - a\cos at)}{p^2+a^2}\right]_0^\infty$$

$$= \frac{a}{p^2+a^2},\ p > 0.$$

Example 6. *Find L {cos at}.*

Solution. Using the formula

$$\int e^{ax}\cos bx\,dx = \frac{e^{ax}(a\cos bx + b\sin bx)}{a^2+b^2}$$

We have

$$L\{\cos at\} = \int_0^\infty e^{-pt}\cos at\,dt$$

$$= \left[\frac{e^{-pt}(-p\cos at + a\sin at)}{a^2+p^2}\right]_0^\infty$$

$$= \frac{p}{p^2+a^2},\ p > 0.$$

Example 7. *Obtain (i) L {sinh at}.*

(ii) L {cosh at}.

Solution. (i) $L\{\sinh at\} = L\left\{\dfrac{e^{at}-e^{-at}}{2}\right\}$

$$= \frac{1}{2}L\{e^{at}\} - \frac{1}{2}L\{e^{-at}\}$$

$$= \frac{1}{2}\cdot\frac{1}{p-a} - \frac{1}{2}\cdot\frac{1}{p+a}$$

$$= \frac{a}{p^2-a^2}.$$

(ii) Proceed similarly as in part (i)

$$L\{\cosh at\} = \frac{p}{p^2-a^2}.$$

The Laplace transforms of the above cases can be tabulated as given below:

	$F(t)$	$I\{F(t)\}$
1.	1	$\frac{1}{p}$, $p > 0$
2.	t	$\frac{1}{p^2}$, $p > 0$
3.	t^n (n is a positive integer)	$\frac{n!}{p^{n+1}}$, $p > 0$
4.	t^a $(a > -1)$	$\frac{\Gamma a+1}{p^{a+1}}$ $p > 0$
5.	e^{at}	$\frac{1}{p-a}$, $p > a$
6.	$\sin at$	$\frac{a}{p^2+a^2}$, $p > 0$
7.	$\cos at$	$\frac{p}{p^2+a^2}$, $p > 0$
8.	$\sinh at$	$\frac{a}{p^2-a^2}$, $p > \lvert a\rvert$
9.	$\cosh at$	$\frac{p}{p^2-a^2}$, $p > \lvert a\rvert$

If we know that Laplace transforms in the above table then nearly all the transforms can be obtained by using the general theorems which we shall consider in the following discussions.

1.10 LINEARITY PROPERTY OF LAPLACE TRANSFORMS

Theorem. *The Laplace transformation is a linear transformation*, i.e.,*

$$L\{c_1 F_1(t) \pm c_2 F_2(t)\} = c_1 L\{F_1(t)\} \pm c_2 L\{F_2(t)\}$$
$$= c_1 f_1(p) \pm c_2 f_2(p)$$

where $L\{F_1(t)\} = f_1(p)$, $L\{F_2(t)\} = f_2(p)$ *and* c_1, c_2 *are constants.*

Proof. We have

$$L\{F(t)\} = \int_0^\infty e^{-pt} F(t)\, dt$$

$\therefore$ $L\{c_1 F_1(t) \pm c_2 F_2(t)\}$

$$= \int_0^\infty e^{-pt} [c_1 F_1(t) \pm c_2 F_2(t)]\, dt$$

$$= c_1 \int_0^\infty e^{-pt} F_1(t)\, dt \pm c_2 \int_0^\infty e^{-pt} \cdot F_2(t)\, dt$$
$$= c_1 L\{F_1(t)\} \pm c_2 L\{F_2(t)\}$$
$$= c_1 f_1(p) \pm c_2 f_2(p).$$

1.11 FIRST TRANSLATION OR SHIFTING PROPERTY

Theorem. *If* $L\{F(t)\} = f(p)$, *then* $L\{e^{at} F(t)\} = f(p - a)$.

Proof. We have, by definition of Laplace transform

$$L\{F(t)\} = f(p) = \int_0^\infty e^{-pt} F(t)\, dt$$

Then $\quad L\{e^{at} F(t)\} = \int_0^\infty e^{-pt} \cdot e^{at} F(t)\, dt$

---

* A transformation T is said to be *linear* if for every pair of functions $F_1(t)$ and $F_2(t)$ and for every pair of constants c_1 and c_2, we have

$$T\{c_1 F_1(t) \pm c_2 F_2(t)\} = c_1 T\{F_1(t)\} \pm c_2 T\{F_2(t)\}$$

$$= \int_0^\infty e^{-(p-a)t} \cdot F(t)\, dt$$

$$= \int_0^\infty e^{-ut} F(t)\, dt$$

where $\quad u = p - a > 0$

$$= f(u) = f(p-a).$$

Note. This theorem can also be stated as given below:

If $f(p)$ is the Laplace transform of $F(t)$ and a is any number real or complex, then $f(p+a)$ is the Laplace transform of $e^{-at} F(t)$.

1.12. SECOND TRANSLATION OR HEAVISIDE'S SHIFTING THEOREM

Theorem. *If $L\{F(t)\} = f(p)$ and*

$$G(t) = \begin{cases} F(t-a), & t > a \\ 0, & t > a, \end{cases}$$

then $\quad L\{G(t)\} = e^{-ap} f(p)$

or $\quad L[F(t-a)\, H(t-a)] = e^{-ap} F(p).$

Proof. Let $L\{F(t)\} = f(p)$ and

$$G(t) = \begin{cases} F(t-a) & \text{if } t > a \\ 0 & \text{if } t < a \end{cases}$$

Then $\quad L\{G(t)\} = \int_0^\infty e^{-pt} G(t)\, dt$

$$= \int_0^a e^{-pt} G(t)\, dt + \int_a^\infty e^{-pt} G(t)\, dt$$

$$= \int_0^a e^{-pt} \cdot 0\, dt + \int_a^\infty e^{-pt} F(t-a)\, dt$$

$$= 0 + \int_a^\infty e^{-pt} F(t-a)\, dt.$$

Let $\quad t - a = u$, so that $dt = du$

If $t = a$, then $u = t - a = a - a = 0$

If $t = \infty$, then $s = \infty - a = \infty$

$$\therefore \quad L\{G(t)\} = \int_0^\infty e^{-pt(u+a)} F(u)\, du$$

$$= e^{-pa} \int_0^\infty e^{-pu} F(u)\, du$$

$$= e^{-pa} f(p).$$

Another Form. *If $F(p)$ is the Laplace transform of $F(t)$, and $c > 0$, then $e^{-cp} f(p)$ is the Laplace transform of $F(t-c)\, H(t-c)$, where*

$$H(t) = \begin{cases} 1 & \text{if } t > 0 \\ 0 & \text{if } t < 0 \end{cases}$$

Proof. Suppose $f(p) = L\{F(t)\}$ and $c > 0$.

Also, $H(t) = \begin{cases} 1 & \text{if } t > 0 \\ 0 & \text{if } t < 0 \end{cases}$

Then $L\{F(t-c)\, H(t-c)\} = \int_0^\infty e^{-pt} F(t-c)\, H(t-c)\, dt$

Let $t - c = x$, so that $dt = dx$

$t - c = x, \quad t = 0 \quad \Rightarrow x = -c$

$t - c = x, \quad t = \infty \quad \Rightarrow x = \infty$

Thus $L\{F(t-c)\, H(t-c)\} = \int_{-c}^\infty F(x)\, H(x) \cdot e^{-p(c+x)}\, dx$

$$= \int_{-c}^0 F(x)\, H(x)\, e^{-p(c+x)}\, dx + \int_0^\infty F(x)\, H(x)\, e^{-p(c+x)}\, dx$$

$$= \int_{-c}^0 F(x) \cdot 0 \cdot e^{-p(c+x)}\, dx + \int_0^\infty F(x) \cdot 1 \cdot e^{-p(c+x)}\, dx$$

$$= 0 + \int_0^\infty F(t) \cdot e^{-pc} \cdot e^{-px}\, dx$$

$$= e^{-pc} \int_0^\infty F(t)\, e^{-pt}\, dt \qquad \left[\because \int_a^b f(x)\, dx = \int_a^b f(t)\, dt\right]$$

$$= e^{-pc} f(p).$$

1.13 CHANGE OF SCALE PROPERTY

Theorem. *If $L\{F(t)\} = f(p)$, then $L\{F(at)\} = \frac{1}{a} f\left(\frac{p}{a}\right)$.*

Proof. By definition

$$
\begin{aligned}
L\{F(at)\} &= \int_0^\infty e^{-pt} F(at)\,dt \\
&= \int_0^\infty \cdot e^{-pu/a} F(u)\frac{du}{a} \qquad \text{if } at = u \\
&= \frac{1}{a}\int_0^\infty e^{-pu/a}\, F(u)\,du \\
&= \frac{1}{a}\int_0^\infty e^{-st} F(t)\,dt, \qquad s = \frac{p}{a} \\
&= \frac{1}{a} f(s) = \frac{1}{a} f\left(\frac{p}{a}\right).
\end{aligned}
$$

ILLUSTRATIVE EXAMPLES

Example 1. *Find Laplace transform of*

$$3e^{3t} + 5t^4 - 4\cos 3t + 3\sin 4t.$$

Solution. $L\{3e^{3t} + 5t^4 - 4\cos 3t + 3\sin 4t\}$

$$
\begin{aligned}
&= 3L\{e^{3t}\} + 5L\{t^4\} - 4L\{\cos 3t\} + 3L\{\sin 4t\} \\
&= 3\cdot\frac{1}{p-3} + 5\cdot\frac{4!}{p^5} - 4\cdot\frac{p}{p^2+9} + 3\cdot\frac{4}{p^2+16} \\
&= \frac{3}{p-3} + \frac{120}{p^5} - \frac{4p}{p^2+9} + \frac{12}{p^2+16}, \quad p > 3.
\end{aligned}
$$

Example 2. *Find* $L\{\cos^2 at\}$.

Solution. We have $\cos^2 at = \frac{1}{2}(1 + \cos 2at)$

$$
\begin{aligned}
\therefore \qquad L\{\cos^2 at\} &= \frac{1}{2} L\{1 + \cos 2at\} \\
&= \frac{1}{2}[L\{1\} + L\{\cos 2at\}] \\
&= \frac{1}{2}\left[\frac{1}{p} + \frac{p}{p^2+4a^2}\right], \quad p > 0 \\
&= \frac{p^2 + 2a^2}{p(p^2+4a^2)}, \quad p > 0.
\end{aligned}
$$

Example 3. *Find* $L\{t^3 e^{2t}\}$.

Solution. We have $L\{t^3\} = \frac{3!}{p^4} = \frac{6}{p^4}$.

Then by first shifting property

$$L\{t^3 e^{2t}\} = \frac{6}{(p-2)^4}.$$

Example 4. *Find* $L\{e^{-3t} \sin 2t\}$.

Solution. We have $L\{\sin 2t\} = \frac{2}{p^2+4}$.

Then by first shifting property

$$L\{e^{-3t} \sin 2t\} = \frac{2}{(p+3)^2+4} = \frac{2}{p^2+6p+13}.$$

Example 5. *Find (i)* $L\{\sin kt \sinh kt\}$

(ii) $L\{\cos kt \sinh kt\}$

Solution. We have

$$L\{\sinh kt\} = \frac{k}{p^2-k^2} = f(p) \text{ say,}$$

$$L\{e^{ikt} \sinh kt\} = f(p-ik)$$

$$= \frac{k}{(p-ik)^2-k^2}$$

$$= \frac{k}{(p^2-2k^2)-2ipk}$$

$$= \frac{k\,[p^2-2k^2+2ipk]}{(p^2-2k^2)^2+4p^2k^2}$$

Equating real and imaginary parts

$$L\{\cos kt \sinh kt\} = \frac{(p^2-2k^2)\,k}{p^4+4k^4}$$

and $$L\{\sin kt \sinh kt\} = \frac{2pk^2}{p^4+4k^4}$$

Example 6. *Find $L\{F(t)\}$ if*

$$F(t) = \begin{cases} \sin\left(t - \frac{\pi}{3}\right), & t > \frac{\pi}{3} \\ 0, & t < \frac{\pi}{3}. \end{cases}$$

Solution. By definition,

$$L\{F(t)\} = \int_0^\infty e^{-pt} F(t)\, dt$$

$$= \int_0^{\pi/3} e^{-pt} F(t)\, dt + \int_{\pi/3}^\infty e^{-pt} F(t)\, dt$$

$$= 0 + \int_{\pi/3}^\infty e^{-pt} \sin\left(t - \frac{\pi}{3}\right) dt$$

$$= \int_0^\infty e^{-p(u+\pi/3)} \sin u\, du, \text{ if } t - \frac{\pi}{3} = u$$

$$= e^{-p(\pi/3)} \int_0^\infty e^{-pu} \sin u\, du$$

$$= e^{-p(\pi/3)} \cdot L\{\sin t\}$$

$$= e^{-p(\pi/3)} \cdot \frac{1}{p^2+1}$$

Example 7. *Find $L\{\cos 3t\}$.*

Solution. We have

$$L\{\cos t\} = \frac{p}{p^2+1}, \; p > 0$$

Then by change of scale property

$$L\{\cos 3t\} = \frac{1}{3} \cdot \frac{p/3}{(p/3)^2+1} = \frac{p}{p^2+9}.$$

Example 8. *If $L\left\{\frac{\sin t}{t}\right\} = \tan^{-1}\left(\frac{1}{p}\right)$, find $L\left\{\frac{\sin 3t}{t}\right\}$.*

Solution. $L\left\{\frac{\sin 3t}{t}\right\} = 3\,L\left\{\frac{\sin 3t}{3t}\right\}$

$$= 3 \cdot \frac{1}{3} \tan^{-1} \left\{ \frac{1}{p/3} \right\}$$

$$= \tan^{-1} \left(\frac{3}{p} \right).$$

EXERCISE 1(A)

Find the Laplace Transforms of each of the following functions:

1. (a) $5t - 2$; (b) $2e^{5t}$; (c) $e^{3t} + 5e^{t}$; (d) $e^{-3t} + 5e^{-t}$; (e) $e^{at} - e^{bt}$.
2. (a) $4 \cos 7t$; (b) $6 \sin 2t - 5 \cos 2t$; (c) $a + bt + ct^2$; (d) $9 \cos^2 3t$.
3. (a) $3t^2 + 6t + 4$; (b) $(t^2 + 1)^2$; (c) $3 \cosh 5t - 4 \sinh 4t$; (d) $(5e^{2t} - 3)^2$.
4. (a) $7e^{2t} + 9e^{-2t} + 5 \cos t + 7t^3 + 5 \sin 3t + 2$.
   (b) $4e^{-3t} - 2 \sin 5t + 3 \cos 2t - 2t^3 + 3t^4$.
5. (a) te^{2t}; (b) $t^3 e^{-3t}$.
6. (a) $e^{-2t} \sin 4t$; (b) $e^{-t} \cos 2t$; (c) $2e^{3t} \sin 4t$; (d) $e^{4t} \cosh 5t$.
7. (a) $e^{-2t} (3 \cos 6t - 5 \sin 6t)$;
   (b) $e^{-t} (3 \sinh 2t - 5 \cosh 2t)$.
8. $\dfrac{e^{-at}\, t^{n-1}}{(n-1)!}$
9. If $L\{F(t)\} = \dfrac{p^2 - p + 1}{(2p+1)^2 \cdot (p-1)}$,

   Show that

   $$L\{F(2t)\} = \frac{p^2 - 2p + 4}{4(p+1)^2 (p-2)}.$$

10. Evaluate $L\{F(t)\}$, if

    $$F(t) = \begin{cases} (t-1)^2, & t > 1 \\ 0, & 0 < t < 1 \end{cases}.$$

11. Find $L\{F(t)\}$, where

    $$F(t) = \begin{cases} \cos\left(t - \frac{2}{3}\pi\right), & t > \frac{2\pi}{3} \\ 0, & 5 < \frac{2\pi}{3} \end{cases}.$$

12. (a) $\sin^2 at$

(b) $\sin at \cos at$

(c) $(\sin t - \cos t)^2$

(d) $\cosh^2 4t$.

ANSWERS

1. (a) $\dfrac{5-2p}{p^2}$, $p > 0$; (b) $\dfrac{2}{p-5}$, $p > 3$;

(c) $\dfrac{2(3p-8)}{(p-1)(p-3)}$, $p > 3$; (d) $\dfrac{2(3p+8)}{(p+1)(p+3)}$, $p > -1$;

(e) $\dfrac{a-b}{(p-a)(p-b)}$, $p > a, p > b$.

2. (a) $\dfrac{4p}{p^2+49}$, $p > 0$; (b) $\dfrac{12-5p}{p^2+4}$, $p > 0$;

(c) $\dfrac{ap^2+bp+2c}{p^3}$, $p > 0$; (d) $\dfrac{9(p^2+18)}{p(p^2+36)}$.

3. (a) $\dfrac{6+6p+4p^2}{p^3}$, $p > 0$; (b) $\dfrac{p^4+4p^2+24}{p^5}$, $p > 0$;

(c) $\dfrac{3p}{p^2-25} - \dfrac{16}{p^2-16}$, $p > 5$; (d) $\dfrac{25}{p-4} - \dfrac{30}{p-2} + \dfrac{9}{p}$, $p > 4$.

4. (a) $\dfrac{16p-4}{p^2-4} + \dfrac{5p}{p^2+1} + \dfrac{42+2p^3}{p^4} + \dfrac{15}{p^2+9}$,

(b) $\dfrac{4}{p+3} - \dfrac{10}{p^2+25} + \dfrac{3p}{p^2+4} - \dfrac{12}{p^4} + \dfrac{72}{p^5}$.

5. (a) $\dfrac{1}{(p-2)^2}$; (b) $\dfrac{6}{(p+3)^4}$.

6. (a) $\dfrac{4}{p^2+4p+20}$; (b) $\dfrac{p+1}{p^2+2p+5}$;

(c) $\dfrac{8}{p^2-6p+25}$; (d) $\dfrac{p-4}{p^2-8p-9}$.

7. (a) $\dfrac{3p-24}{p^2+4p+40}$; (b) $\dfrac{1-5p}{p^2+2p-3}$.

8. $\dfrac{1}{(p+a)^n}$. **10.** $\dfrac{2}{p^3}e^{-p}$.

11. $\dfrac{p\,e^{-(2/3)\,\pi\,p}}{p^2+1}$

12. (a) $\dfrac{2a^2}{p\,(p^2+4a^2)}$, $p > 0$; (b) $\dfrac{a}{p^2+4a^2}$, $p > 0$;

(c) $\dfrac{p^2-2p+4}{p\,(p^2+4)}$, $p > 0$; (d) $\dfrac{p^2-32}{p\,(p^2-64)}$.

1.14 LAPLACE TRANSFORMS OF DERIVATIVES

Theorem. *Let $F(t)$ be continuous for all $t \geq 0$ and be of exponential order as $t \to \infty$ and if $F(t)$ is of class A, the Laplace Transform of the derivative $F(t)$ exists when $p > a$, and*

$$L\{F(t)\} = p\,L\{F(t)\} - F(0)$$

Proof. By definition, we have

$$L\{F(t)\} = \int_0^\infty e^{-pt}\,F(t)\,dt$$

$$= \left[e^{-pt}\,F(t)\right]_0^\infty + p\int_0^\infty e^{-pt}\,F(t)\,dt$$

[Integrating by parts]

$$= -F(0) + p\,L\{F(t)\}, \text{ as } \lim_{t \to \infty} e^{-pt}\,F(t) = 0$$

$$= p\,f(p) - F(0) \text{ if } L\{F(t)\} = f(p)$$

Corollary. Similarly

$$L\{F'(t)\} = p\,L\{F(t)\} - F(0)$$

$$= p\,[p\,L\{F(t)\} - F(0)] - F(0)$$

$$= p^2\,L\{F(t)\} - p\,F(0) - F(0)$$

$$= p^2\,f(p) - p\,F(0) - F(0).$$

1.15 LAPLACE TRANSFORM OF THE *n* TH ORDER DERIVATIVE OF *F*(t)

Theorem. *If $F(t), F(t), \ldots F^{n-1}(t)$ are continuous for $t \geq 0$ and of exponential order as $t \to \infty$ and if $F^n(t)$ is of class A*, and if $L\{F(t)\} = f(p)$, *then*

$$L\{F^{(n)}(t)\} = p^n f(p) - \sum_{r=0}^{n-1} p^{n-1-r} F^{(r)}(0)$$

$$= p^n f(p) - p^{n-1} F(0) - p^{n-2} F(0) - \ldots - p F^{(n-2)} 0 - F^{(n-1)}(0).$$

Proof. From the theorem of § 1.14 we have

$$L\{F(t)\} = p\, L\{F(t)\} - F(0) \qquad \ldots (i)$$

Similarly, from the Corollary § 1.14 we have

$$L\{F'(t)\} = p^2 L\{F(t)\} - p\, F(0) - F(0) \qquad \ldots (ii)$$

Again applying (i) to the third order derivative $F''(t)$, we have

$$L\{F''(t)\} = p\, L\{F'(t)\} - F'(0)$$

$$= p\,[p^2 L\{F(t)\} - p\, F(0) - F(0)] - F'(0)$$

$$= p^3 L\{F(t)\} - p^2 F(0) - p\, F(0) - F'(0)$$

Proceeding similarly, we have

$$L\{F^n(t)\} = p^n L\{F(t)\} - p^{n-1} F(0) - p^{n-2} F(0) - \ldots - F^{n-1}(0)$$

or

$$L\{F^n(t)\} = p^n L\{F(t)\} - \sum_{r=0}^{n-1} p^{n-1-r} F^r(0).$$

1.16. DERIVATIVE OF LAPLACE TRANSFORMS

Theorem I. *If $F(t)$ is a function of class A and if $L\{F(t)\} = f(p)$ then $L\{t\, F(t)\} = -f'(p)$.*

Proof. We have

$$f(p) = L\{F(t)\} = \int_0^\infty e^{-pt} F(t)\, dt$$

$$\therefore \quad f'(p) = \frac{d}{dp}\int_0^\infty e^{-pt} F(t)\, dt$$

$$= \int_0^\infty \frac{\partial}{\partial p}\{e^{-pt} F(t)\}\, dt$$

[By Leibnitz's rule for differentiating under the sign of integral]

$$= -\int_0^\infty t\, e^{-pt} F(t)\, dt$$

$$= -\int_0^\infty e^{-pt}\{t\,F(t)\}\cdot dt$$

$$= -L\{t\,F(t)\}.$$

$$\therefore \quad L\{t\,F(t)\} = -f'(p).$$

Theorem II. *If $F(t)$ is a function of class A and if*

$$L\{F(t)\} = f(p),$$

then $$L\{t^n F(t)\} = (-1)^n \frac{d^n}{dp^n} f(p),$$

where $n = 1, 2, 3, \ldots.$

Proof. We shall prove this theorem by mathematical induction method. From Theorem I,

$$L\{t\,F(t)\} = (-1)^1 \frac{d}{dp} f(p),$$

i.e., the theorem is true for $n = 1$.

Now, let us assume that the theorem is true for a particular value of n say r. Then, we have

$$L\{t^r F(t)\} = (-1)^r \frac{d^r}{dp^r} f(p)$$

or $$\int_0^\infty e^{-pt}\, t^r F(t)\, dt = (-1)^r \frac{d^r}{dp^r} f(p)$$

Now, differentiating both side w.r.t. p, we have

$$\frac{d}{dp}\int_0^\infty e^{-pt}\, t^r F(t)\, dt = (-1)^r \frac{d^{r+1}}{dp^{r+1}} f(p)$$

or $$\int_0^\infty \frac{\partial}{\partial p}\{e^{-pt}\, t^r F(t)\}dt = (-1)^r \frac{d^{r+1}}{dp^{r+1}} f(p)$$

[By Leibnitz' rule for differentiating under the sign of integration]

or $$-\int_0^\infty e^{-pt}\cdot t^{r+1} F(t)\, dt = (-1)^r \frac{d^{r+1}}{dp^{r+1}} f(p)$$

or $$\int_0^\infty e^{-pt}\cdot \{t^{r+1} F(t)\}\, dt = (-1)^{r+1} \frac{d^{r+1}}{dp^{r+1}} f(p)$$

or $$L\{t^{r+1}F(t)\} = (-1)^{r+1}\frac{d^{r+1}}{dp^{r+1}}f(p)$$

which shows that if the theorem is true for any particular value of n, it is true for the next value of n. But it is also true for $n = 1$. Hence by the method of mathematical induction it is true for every positive integral value of n.

1.17 LAPLACE TRANSFORM OF INTEGRALS

Theorem. *If with necessary conditions* $L\{F(t)\} = f(p)$, *then*

$$L\left\{\int_0^t F(u)\,du\right\} = \frac{1}{p}f(p).$$

Proof. Let $G(t) = \int_0^t F(u)\,du$, then $G'(t) = F(t)$

and $$G(0) = \int_0^0 F(u)\,du = 0,$$

Then, by § 1.14,

$$L\{G'(t) = pL\{G(t)\} - G(0)$$

$$= pL\{G(t)\} \qquad [\because\ G(0) = 0]$$

$$= L\{F(t)\} = f(p), \text{ given.}$$

Then $$L\{G(t)\} = \frac{1}{p}L\{G'(t)\}$$

$$= \frac{1}{p}L\{F(t)\}$$

$$= \frac{1}{p}\cdot f(p),$$

i.e., $$L\left\{\int_0^t F(u)\,du\right\} = \frac{1}{p}f(p).$$

1.18 INTEGRATION OF LAPLACE TRANSFORM

Theorem. *If* $L\{F(t)\} = f(p)$, *then*

$$L\left\{\frac{F(t)}{t}\right\} = \int_p^\infty f(x)\,dx,$$

provided that $\lim\limits_{t \to \infty}\frac{F(t)}{t}$ *exists.*

Proof. Let $G(t) = \frac{1}{t} F(t)$

i.e., $F(t) = t\, G(t)$

$\therefore \quad L\{F(t) = L\{t\, G(t)\}\}$

$$= -\frac{d}{dp} L\{G(t)\} \qquad \text{[by the theorem of § 1.14]}$$

or $$f(p) = -\frac{d}{dp} L\{G(t)\}$$

Integrating both sides w.r.t. p, we have

$$L\{G(t)\} = -\int_{\infty}^{p} f(p)\, dp = \int_{p}^{\infty} f(x)\, dx$$

or $$L\left\{\frac{1}{t} F(t)\right\} = \int_{p}^{\infty} f(x)\, dx$$

The constant of integration is chosen such that

$$\lim_{p \to \infty} L\{G(t)\} = 0.$$

ILLUSTRATIVE EXAMPLES

Example 1. *Obtain* $L\{t\, e^{2t}\}$.

Solution. We have

$$L\{e^{2t}\} = \frac{1}{p-2}$$

$$\therefore \quad L\{t\, e^{2t}\} = -\frac{d}{dp}\left(\frac{1}{p-2}\right) = \frac{1}{(p-2)^2}.$$

Example 2. *Obtain* $L\{t^2 e^{2t}\}$.

Solution. We have

$$L\{e^{2t}\} = \frac{1}{p-2}$$

$$\therefore \quad L\{t^2 e^{2t}\} = (-1)^2 \frac{d^2}{dp^2} \cdot \frac{1}{(p-2)}$$

$$= \frac{2}{(p-2)^3}.$$

Example 3. *Fing L {t sin at}*

Solution. We have

$$L\{\sin at\} = \frac{a}{p^2+a^2}$$

$$\therefore \quad L\{t \sin at\} = -\frac{d}{dp}\left(\frac{a}{p^2+a^2}\right) = \frac{2ap}{(p^2+a^2)^2}.$$

Example 4. *Show that* $L\{t^3 \cos t\} = \dfrac{6p^4 - 36p^2 + 6}{(p^2+1)^4}$

Solution. We have $L\{\cos t\} = \dfrac{p}{p^2+1}$, $p > 0$

$$\therefore \quad L\{t^3 \cos t\} = (-1)^3 \frac{d^3}{dp^3}\left(\frac{p}{p^2+1}\right) = \frac{6p^4 - 36p^2 + 6}{(p^2+1)^4}$$

Example 5. *Show that* $\displaystyle\int_0^\infty \frac{\sin t}{t}\, dt = \frac{\pi}{2}$

Solution. Let $F(t) = \sin t$

$$\therefore \quad L\{F(t)\} = f(p) = \frac{1}{p^2+1}$$

Then $\displaystyle\int_0^\infty \frac{\sin t}{t}\, dt = \int_0^\infty \frac{dy}{y^2+1} = \left[\tan^{-1} y\right]_0^\infty = \frac{\pi}{2}.$

Example 6. *Obtain* $L\left\{\dfrac{\sin t}{t}\right\}$

Solution. We have $L\{\sin t\} = \dfrac{1}{p^2+1}$

and $\quad L\left\{\dfrac{F(t)}{t}\right\} = \displaystyle\int_p^\infty f(y)\, dy$

Provided $\lim\limits_{t \to \infty} \dfrac{F(t)}{t}$ exists, we have $\lim\limits_{t \to \infty} \dfrac{\sin t}{t} = 1$.

$$\therefore \quad L\left\{\frac{\sin t}{t}\right\} = \int_p^{\infty} \frac{dy}{y^2+1} = \left[\tan^{-1} y\right]_p^{\infty}$$

$$= \frac{\pi}{2} - \tan^{-1} p = \frac{\pi}{2} - \cot^{-1}\frac{1}{p}$$

$$= \tan^{-1}\frac{1}{p} = \cot^{-1} p.$$

Example 7. *Show that* $\int_0^{\infty} \frac{F(t)}{t}\, dt = \int_0^{\infty} f(x)\, dx$, *assuming that the integrals converge and* $L\{F(t)\} = f(p)$, *and hence prove that*

$$\int_0^{\infty} \frac{\sin t}{t}\, dt = \frac{\pi}{2}.$$

Solution. We know that

$$L\left\{\frac{F(t)}{t}\right\} = \int_p^{\infty} f(x)\, dx$$

or $$\int_0^{\infty} e^{-pt}\frac{F(t)}{t}\, dt = \int_p^{\infty} f(x)\, dx$$

$$= \int_p^{0} f(x)\, dx + \int_0^{\infty} f(x)\, dx.$$

Taking $p \to 0$, we get

$$\int_0^{\infty} \frac{1 \cdot F(t)}{t}\, dt = 0 + \int_0^{\infty} f(x)\, dx$$

or $$\int_0^{\infty} \frac{F(t)}{t}\, dt = \int_0^{\infty} f(x)\, dx.$$

Second Part. We know that

$$L\{\sin t\} = \frac{1}{p^2+1}.$$

$\therefore$ By first part

$$\int_0^{\infty} \frac{F(t)}{t}\, dt = \int_0^{\infty} f(x)\, dx$$

or $$\int_0^\infty \frac{\sin t}{t}\,dt = \int_0^\infty \frac{dx}{x^2+1} = \left[\tan^{-1} x\right]_0^\infty$$

$$= \tan^{-1}\infty - \tan^{-1} 0 = \frac{\pi}{2} - 0 = \frac{\pi}{2}.$$

EXERCISE 1(B)

Find:

1. $L\{t \cos at\}$.
2. $L\{(\sin at - at \cos at)\}$.
3. (i) $L\{t^2 \sin at\}$.
   (ii) $L\{t^2 \sin 3t\}$.
4. Show that

$$L\{t^2 \cos at\} = \frac{2p\,(p^2 - 3a^2)}{(p^2 + a^2)^3}, \quad p > 0.$$

5. Show that

$$L\{t\,(3 \sin 2t - 2 \cos 2t)\} = \frac{8 + 12p - 2p^2}{(p^2 + 4)^2}.$$

6. Show that

$$L\{t^n e^{at}\} = \frac{n\,!}{(p - a)^{n+1}}, \quad p > a.$$

7. Evaluate:
   (a) $L\{t \sinh 2t\}$.
   (b) $L\{t \cosh 3t\}$
   (c) $L\{t^2 - 3t + 2\} \sin 3t$.

ANSWERS

1. $\dfrac{p^2 - a^2}{(p^2 + a^2)^2}$. 2. $\dfrac{2a^3}{(p^2 + a^2)^2}$.

3. (i) $\dfrac{2a\,(3p^2 - a^2)}{(p^2 + a^2)^3}$, $p > 0$. (ii) $\dfrac{6\,(3p^2 - 9)}{(p^2 + 9)^3}$, $p > 0$

7. (a) $\dfrac{4p}{(p^2 - 4)^2}$. (b) $\dfrac{p^2 + 9}{(p^2 - 9)^2}$.

(c) $\dfrac{6p^4 - 18p^3 + 126p^2 - 162p + 432}{(p^2+9)^3}$

1.19 PERIODIC FUNCTIONS

Theorem. *Let a Function $F(t)$ be periodic with period ω, so that*

$$F(t + n\omega) = F(t) \text{ for } n = 1, 2, 3, \ldots.$$

Then $$L\{F(t)\} = \frac{1}{1 - e^{-p\omega}} \int_0^{\omega} e^{-pt} F(t)\, dt.$$

Proof. We have $$L\{F(t)\} = \int_0^{\infty} e^{-pt} F(t)\, dt$$

$$= \int_0^{\omega} e^{-pt} F(t)\, dt + \int_{\omega}^{2\omega} e^{-pt} F(t)\, dt + \ldots + \int_{n\omega}^{(n+1)\omega} e^{-pt} F(t)\, dt + \ldots$$

$$= \sum_{n=0}^{\infty} \int_{n\omega}^{(n+1)\omega} e^{-pt} F(t)\, dt$$

$$= \sum_{n=0}^{\infty} \int_0^{\omega} e^{-p(x+n\omega)} F(x + n\omega)\, dx$$

where $t = x + n\omega$

$$= \sum_{n=0}^{\infty} \int_0^{\omega} e^{-px} e^{-np\omega} F(x)\, dx$$

$\because$ $F(x + n\omega) = F(x)$ for $n = 0, 1, 2, \ldots$

$$= \sum_{n=0}^{\infty} e^{-np\omega} \int_0^{\omega} e^{-px} F(x)\, dx$$

$$= (1 + e^{-p\omega} + e^{-2p\omega} + \ldots) \int_0^{\omega} e^{-px} F(x)\, dx$$

$$= \frac{1}{1 - e^{-p\omega}} \int_0^{\omega} e^{-px} F(x)\, dx, \qquad \because e^{-p\omega} < 1$$

1.20. INITIAL-VALUE THEOREM

Theorem. *If $F(t)$ be continuous for all $t \geq 0$ and be of exponential order as $t \to \infty$ and if $F(t)$ is of class A, then*

$$\lim_{t \to 0} F(t)\, dt = \lim_{p \to \infty} p L\{F(t)\}.$$

Proof. By the theorem of § 1.14, we have

$$L\{F(t)\} = \int_0^\infty e^{-pt} F(t)\, dt$$

$$= p L\{F(t) - F(0). \qquad \ldots \text{(i)}$$

Since $F(t)$ is sectionally continuous and of exponential order,

$$\therefore \qquad \lim_{p \to \infty} \int_0^\infty e^{-pt} F(t)\, dt = 0.$$

Taking limit as $p \to \infty$ in (i), we have

$$0 = \lim_{p \to \infty} p L\{F(t)\} - F(0)$$

or $$F(0) = \lim_{p \to \infty} p L\{F(t)\}$$

or $$\lim_{t \to 0} F(t) = \lim_{p \to \infty} p L\{F(t)\}.$$

1.21 FINAL VALUE THEOREM

Theorem. *If $F(t)$ be continuous for all $t \geq 0$ and be of exponential order as $t \to \infty$ and if $F(t)$ is of class A, then*

$$\lim_{t \to \infty} F(t) = \lim_{p \to 0} p L\{F(t)\}.$$

Proof. By the theorem of § 1.14, we have

$$L\{F(t)\} = \int_0^\infty e^{-pt} F(t)\, dt$$

$$= p L\{F(t)\} - F(0) \qquad .\text{(i)}$$

Taking limit as $p \to 0$ in (i), we get

$$\lim_{p \to 0} \int_0^\infty e^{-pt} F(t)\, dt = \lim_{p \to 0} [p L\{F(t)\} - F(0)]$$

or $$\int_0^\infty F(t)\, dt = \lim_{p \to 0} p L\{F(t)\} - F(0)$$

or $$[F(t)]_0^{\infty} = \lim_{p \to 0} pL\{F(t)\} - F(0)$$

or $$\lim_{t \to \infty} F(t) - F(0) = \lim_{p \to 0} pL\{F(t)\} - F(0)$$

or $$\lim_{t \to \infty} F(t) = \lim_{p \to 0} pL\{F(t)\}.$$

1.22 LAPLACE TRANSFORM OF THE LAPLACE TRANSFORM

We have

$$L[L\{F(t)\}] = L\left\{\int_0^{\infty} e^{-pt} F(t)\, dt\right\}$$

$$= \int_0^{\infty} e^{-up}\, dp \int_0^{\infty} e^{-pt} F(t)\, dt.$$

The area of integration being the whole positive quadrant. Now, changing the order of integration, we get

$$L[L\{F(t)\}] = \int_0^{\infty} f(t)\, dt \int_0^{\infty} e^{-p(t+u)}\, dp$$

$$= \int_0^{\infty} f(t)\, dt \left[\frac{e^{-p(t+u)}}{-(t+u)}\right]_{p=0}^{\infty}$$

$$= \int_0^{\infty} \frac{f(t)}{t+u}\, du.$$

MISCELLANEOUS ILLUSTRATIVE EXAMPLES

Example 1. *Find the Laplace transform of* $\frac{\sin at}{t}$*. Does the transform of* $\frac{\cos at}{t}$ *exist?*

Solution. We have

$$L\{e^{iat}\} = \int_0^{\infty} e^{-pt} \cdot e^{iat}\, dt$$

$$= \int_0^{\infty} e^{-(p-ia)t}\, dt$$

$$= -\left[\frac{e^{-(p-ia)t}}{p-ia}\right]_{t=0}^{\infty} = \frac{1}{(p-ia)}$$

or $$L\{\cos at + i \sin at\} = \frac{p+ia}{(p-ia)(p+ia)}$$

or $$L\{\cos at\} + i\,L\{\sin at\} = \frac{p}{p^2+a^2} + i\frac{a}{p^2+a^2}.$$

Equating real and imaginary parts

$$L\{\cos at\} = \frac{p}{p^2+a^2},\quad L\{\sin at\}\ \frac{a}{p^2+a^2}$$

by § 1.18,

$$L\left\{\frac{\sin at}{t}\right\} = \int_p^{\infty} f(x)\,dx$$

$$= \int_p^{\infty} L\{\sin at\}\,dx$$

$$= \int_p^{\infty} \frac{a\,dx}{x^2+a^2}$$

$$= \left[\tan^{-1}\frac{x}{a}\right]_p^{\infty} = \tan^{-1}\infty - \tan^{-1}\frac{p}{a}$$

$$= \frac{\pi}{2} - \tan^{-1}\left(\frac{p}{a}\right) = \cot^{-1}\left(\frac{p}{a}\right).$$

$$L\left\{\frac{\cos at}{t}\right\} = \int_p^{\infty} L\{\cos at\}\,dx = \int_p^{\infty} \frac{x}{x^2+a^2}\,dx$$

$$= \frac{1}{2}\left[\log(x^2+a^2)\right]_p^{\infty}$$

$$= \frac{1}{2}\left[\lim_{x\to\infty} \log(x^2+a^2) - \log(p^2+a^2)\right]$$

which does not exist.

For $\lim\limits_{x\to\infty} \log(x^2+a^2)$ is infinite.

Hence $L\left\{\dfrac{\cos at}{t}\right\}$ does not exist.

Example 2. *Prove that*

$$\int_0^\infty \frac{e^{-t}\sin t}{t}\,dt = \frac{\pi}{4}.$$

Solution. As in the previous example

$$L\left\{\frac{\sin at}{t}\right\} = \cot^{-1}\frac{p}{a}$$

i.e.,
$$\int_0^\infty e^{-pt}\frac{\sin at}{t}\,dt = \cot^{-1}\left(\frac{p}{a}\right)$$

Taking $a = 1, p = 1,$

$$\int_0^\infty e^{-t}\frac{\sin t}{t}\,dt = \cot^{-1}(1) = \frac{\pi}{4}.$$

Example 3. *Find the Laplace transform of*

(*i*) $\sin\sqrt{t}$.

(*ii*) $\dfrac{\cos\sqrt{t}}{\sqrt{t}}$

Solution. (i) We know that

$$\sin\theta = \theta - \frac{\theta^3}{3!} + \frac{\theta^5}{5!} - \frac{\theta^7}{7!} + \ldots.$$

$$\therefore \quad \sin\sqrt{t} = \sqrt{t} - \frac{t^{3/2}}{3!} + \frac{t^{5/2}}{5!} - \frac{t^{7/2}}{7!} + \ldots.$$

We have $L\{t^n\} = \dfrac{\Gamma(n+1)}{p^{n+1}}$,

$$\Gamma(n+1) = n\,\Gamma(n) \quad \text{and} \quad \Gamma\left(\frac{1}{2}\right) = \sqrt{\pi}.$$

$$\therefore \quad L\{\sin\sqrt{t}\} = \frac{\Gamma(3/2)}{p^{3/2}} - \frac{\Gamma(5/2)}{p^{5/2}\cdot(3)!} + \frac{\Gamma(7/2)}{p^{7/2}\cdot(5)!} - \frac{\Gamma(9/2)}{p^{9/2}\cdot(7)!} + \ldots$$

$$= \frac{\sqrt{\pi}}{p^{3/2}}\left[\frac{1}{2} - \frac{1}{3!}\cdot\frac{3}{2}\cdot\frac{1}{2}\cdot\frac{1}{p} + \frac{1}{5!}\cdot\frac{5}{2}\cdot\frac{3}{2}\cdot\frac{1}{2}\cdot\frac{1}{p^2} - \frac{1}{7!}\cdot\frac{7}{2}\cdot\frac{5}{2}\cdot\frac{3}{2}\cdot\frac{1}{2}\cdot\frac{1}{p^3} + \ldots\right]$$

$$= \frac{1}{2p}\left(\frac{\pi}{p}\right)^{1/2}\left[1 - \frac{1}{2^2 p} + \frac{1}{(2^2 p)^2\cdot 2!} - \frac{1}{(2^2 p)^3\cdot 3!} + \ldots\right]$$

$$= \frac{1}{2p}\left(\frac{\pi}{p}\right)^{1/2} [e^{-1/2^2} P]$$

$$= \frac{1}{2p}\left(\frac{\pi}{p}\right)^{1/2} e^{-1/4p}.$$

(ii) Let $L\{F(t)\} = L\{\sin\sqrt{t}\}$

$$= \frac{\sqrt{\pi}\, e^{-1/ap}}{2p^{1/2}} = f(p),$$

$$F(0) = \sin 0 = 0$$

$$F(t) = \frac{d}{dt}(\sin\sqrt{t}) = \left(\frac{1}{2\sqrt{t}}\cos\sqrt{t}\right)$$

$$= \frac{1}{2}\left(\frac{\cos\sqrt{t}}{\sqrt{t}}\right).$$

We have

$$L\{F(t)\} = pf(p) - F(0)$$

$$= pf(p) - 0 = pf(p)$$

$$= \frac{\sqrt{\pi}}{2p^{1/2}} e^{-1/4p}$$

or $$\frac{1}{2} L\left\{\frac{\cos\sqrt{t}}{\sqrt{t}}\right\} = \frac{1}{2}\left(\frac{\pi}{p}\right)^{1/2} e^{-1/4p}$$

or $$L\left\{\frac{\cos\sqrt{t}}{\sqrt{t}}\right\} = \left(\frac{\pi}{p}\right)^{1/2} e^{-1/4p}.$$

Example 4. *Find* $L\left\{\int_0^t \frac{\sin x}{x}\, dx\right\}$

Solution. We know that

$$L\left\{\int_0^t F(x)\, dx\right\} = \frac{1}{p} f(p)$$

and $$L\{\sin at\} = \frac{a}{p^2 + a^2},$$

$\therefore$ $$L\{\sin t\} = \frac{1}{1 + p^2}$$

$$L\left\{\frac{\sin t}{t}\right\} = \int_p^\infty L\{\sin t\}\, dp$$

$$= \int_p^\infty \frac{1}{1+p^2}\, dp = [\tan^{-1} p]_p^\infty$$

$$= \frac{\pi}{2} - \tan^{-1} p = \cot^{-1} p,$$

$$\therefore \quad L\left\{\int_0^t \frac{\sin t}{t}\, dt\right\} = \frac{1}{p}\cot^{-1} p.$$

Example 5. *Prove that* $\int_0^\infty J_0(t)\, dt = 1.$

Solution. We know that

$$J_n(x) = \frac{x^n}{2^n \Gamma[(n+1)]}\left[1 - \frac{x^2}{2(2n+2)} + \frac{x^4}{2\cdot 4(2n+2)(2n+4)} - \ldots\right]$$

Putting $n = 0$ and noting that

$$x^0 = 2^0 = 1, \Gamma(1) = 1$$

We get $J_0(x) = \left\{1 - \dfrac{x^2}{2\cdot 2} + \dfrac{x^4}{2\cdot 4\cdot 2\cdot 4} - \ldots\right\}$

Also, we know that

$$L\{t^n\} = \frac{n!}{p^{n+1}}, n = 0, 1, 2, \ldots$$

$$\therefore \quad L\{J_0(t)\} = \left\{\frac{1}{p} - \frac{2!}{2^2\cdot p^3} + \frac{4!}{2^2\cdot 4^2\cdot p^5} - \ldots\right\}$$

$$= \frac{1}{p}\left\{1 - \frac{1}{2\cdot p^2} + \frac{(3/2)(1/2)}{2!}\left(\frac{1}{p^2}\right)^2 - \ldots\right\}$$

$$= \frac{1}{p}\left\{\left(1 + \frac{1}{p^2}\right)^{-1/2}\right\}$$

$$= \frac{1}{p}\cdot\left(\frac{p^2+1}{p^2}\right)^{-1/2} = \frac{1}{\sqrt{[(p^2+1)]}}$$

or $$\int_0^\infty e^{-pt} J_0(t)\, dt = \frac{1}{(p^2+1)^{1/2}}$$

Putting $p = 0$, we get

$$\int_0^\infty J_0(t)\, dt = 1.$$

Example 6. Find $L\{t J_0(at)\}$

Solution. From Example 5, we have

$$L\{J_0(t) = \frac{1}{\sqrt{[(p^2+1)]}}$$

By change of scale property, we have

$$L\{J_0(at)\} = \frac{1}{a}\frac{1}{\sqrt{[\{(p/a)^2+1\}]}}$$

$$= \frac{1}{\sqrt{\{(p^2+a^2)\}}}$$

$$\therefore \quad L\{t J_0(at)\} = (-1)^1 \frac{d}{dp} L\{J_0(at)\}$$

$$= -\frac{d}{dp}\left\{\frac{1}{\sqrt{[(p^2+a^2)]}}\right\}$$

$$= \frac{p}{(p^2+a^2)^{3/2}}.$$

Example 7. *Find the Laplace transform of $F(t)$, where*

$$F(\mathrm{t}) = \begin{cases} t/T & 0 < t < T \\ 1 & t > T \end{cases}$$

Solution. We have

$$L\{F(t)\} = \int_0^\infty e^{-pt} F(t)\, dt$$

$$= \int_0^T e^{-pt} F(t)\, dt + \int_T^\infty e^{-pt} F(t)\, dt$$

$$= \int_0^T \frac{t}{T} e^{-pt}\, dt + \int_T^\infty 1 \cdot e^{-pt}\, dt$$

$$= \frac{1}{T}\left[\left(\frac{t\,e^{-pt}}{-p}\right) - \frac{1}{p^2}e^{-pt}\right]_0^T - \frac{1}{p}\left[e^{-pt}\right]_T^\infty$$

$$= \frac{1}{T}\left[\left(\frac{T\,e^{-pT}}{-p} - 0\right) - \frac{1}{p^2}(e^{-pT} - 1)\right] + \frac{e^{-pT}}{p}$$

$$= \frac{1}{p^2\,T}(1 - e^{-pT})$$

Example 8. *Prove that* $L\{H(t)\} = \dfrac{2(1 - e^{-\pi p})}{p^2 + 4}$

where $H(t) = \begin{cases} \sin 2t, & 0 < t < \pi \\ 0, & t > \pi \end{cases}$

Solution. $L\{H(t)\} = \int_0^\infty e^{-pt}\,H(t)\,dt$

$$= \int_0^\pi e^{-pt}\,H(t)\,dt + \int_\pi^\infty e^{-pt}\,H(t)\,dt$$

$$= \int_0^\pi e^{-pt}\sin 2t\,dt + \int_\pi^\infty e^{-pt}\cdot 0\cdot dt$$

$$= \left[e^{-pt}\frac{(-p\sin 2t - 2\cos 2t)}{p^2 + 4}\right]_0^\pi$$

$$= \frac{2(1 - e^{-\pi p})}{p^2 + 4}.$$

Example 9. *Prove that* $\int_0^\infty t^3\,e^{-t}\sin t\,dt = 0.$

Solution. We know that $L\{e^{at}\} = \dfrac{1}{p - a}$

$$\therefore \quad L\{e^{i\,at}\} = \frac{1}{p - ia} = \frac{p + ia}{p^2 + a^2}$$

Equating imaginary parts from both sides,

$$L\{\sin at\} = \frac{a}{p^2 + a^2}$$

By § 1.15

$$L\{t^3 \sin at\} = (-1)^3 \frac{d^3}{dp^3} L\{\sin at\}$$

$$= -\frac{d^3}{dp^3}\left(\frac{a}{p^2+a^2}\right)$$

$$\therefore \quad L\{t^3 \sin t\} = -\frac{d^3}{dp^3}\left(\frac{1}{p^2+1}\right)$$

$$= -\frac{d^2}{dp^2}\left[\frac{-2p}{(p^2+1)^2}\right]$$

$$= 2\frac{d}{dp}\left[\frac{1-3p^2}{(1+p^2)^3}\right]$$

$$= \frac{2 \cdot 12p\,(1-p^2)}{(1+p^2)^4}$$

$$= \frac{24p\,(1-p^2)}{(1+p^2)^4}$$

By definition

$$\int_0^\infty e^{-pt}\, t^3 \sin t\, dt = \frac{24p\,(1-p^2)}{(1+p^2)^4}$$

Putting $p = 1$, we get

$$\int_0^\infty e^{-t}\, t^3 \sin t\, dt = \frac{24\,(1-1)}{(1+1)^4} = 0.$$

Example 10. *Evaluate:* $\displaystyle\int_0^\infty \frac{e^{-t} - e^{-3t}}{t}\, dt.$

Solution. Let $F(t) = e^{-t} - e^{-3t}$

We know that $L\{e^{at}\} = \dfrac{1}{p-a}$

$$\therefore \quad L\{F(t)\} = L\{e^{-t} - e^{-3t}\} = \frac{1}{p+1} - \frac{1}{p+3}$$

We also know that

$$L\left\{\frac{F(t)}{t}\right\} = \int_p^{\infty} F(x)\,dx, \text{ where } f(p) = L\{F(t)\}$$

$$\therefore \quad L\left\{\frac{e^{-t} - e^{-3t}}{t}\right\} = \int_p^{\infty} \left(\frac{1}{x+1} - \frac{1}{x+3}\right) dx$$

$$= \left[\log\left(\frac{x+1}{x+3}\right)\right]_p^{\infty}$$

$$= -\log\left(\frac{p+1}{p+3}\right)$$

Hence, by definition,

$$\int_0^{\infty} e^{-pt} \cdot \frac{e^{-t} - e^{-3t}}{t}\,dt = -\log\left(\frac{p+1}{p+3}\right)$$

Putting $p = 0$, we get

$$\int_0^{\infty} \frac{e^{-t} - e^{-3t}}{t}\,dt = -\log\left(\frac{0+1}{0+3}\right)$$

$$= -\log\frac{1}{3} = \log 3.$$

Example 11. *Find the Laplace Transform of H (t) defined as*

$$H(t) = \begin{cases} t+1, & 0 \le t \le 2 \\ 3, & t > 2. \end{cases}$$

Also determine L {H′ (t)}.

Solution. $L\{H(t)\} = \int_0^{\infty} e^{-pt} H(t)\,dt$

$$= \int_0^{2} e^{-pt} H(t)\,dt + \int_2^{\infty} e^{-pt} H(t)\,dt$$

$$= \int_0^{2} e^{-pt} (t+1)\,dt + \int_2^{\infty} e^{-pt} \cdot 3dt$$

$$= \int_0^{2} t\,e^{-pt}\,dt + \left[\frac{e^{-pt}}{-p}\right]_0^2 + \left[\frac{3e^{-pt}}{-p}\right]_2^{\infty}$$

$$= \left[\frac{e^{-pt} \cdot t}{-p}\right]_0^2 - \left[\frac{e^{-pt}}{p^2}\right]_0^2 + \frac{1}{p}\left[1 - e^{-2p} + 3e^{-2p}\right]$$

$$= -\frac{2}{p}e^{-2p} - \frac{1}{p^2}(e^{-2p} - 1) + \frac{1}{p}(1 + 2e^{-2p})$$

$$= -\frac{1}{p^2}(e^{-2p} - 1) + \frac{1}{p}$$

$$= \frac{1}{p^2}[p + 1 - e^{-2p}].$$

Now, let $L\{H(t)\} = \frac{1}{p^2}(p + 1 - e^{-2p}) = h(p)$

$$H(0) = [t + 1]_{t=0} = 1.$$

Now, by § 1.14

$$L\{H'(t)\} = ph(p) - H(0)$$

$$= p\left[\frac{p + 1 - e^{-2p}}{p^2}\right] - 1$$

$$= \frac{1 - e^{-2p}}{p}.$$

Example 12. *Show that* $L\{F(t)\}$ *is*

$$\left(\frac{1}{p^2} + \frac{1}{p}\right)e^{-p} - \left(\frac{1}{p^2} + \frac{2}{p}\right)e^{-2p}$$

where $F(t) = \begin{cases} 0, & 0 < t < 1 \\ t, & 1 < t < 2 \\ 0, & t > 2. \end{cases}$

Solution. We have

$$L\{F(t)\} = \int_0^\infty e^{-pt} F(t)\, dt$$

$$= \int_0^1 e^{-pt} \cdot F(t)\, dt + \int_1^2 e^{-pt} F(t)\, dt + \int_2^\infty e^{-pt} F(t)\, dt$$

$$= \int_0^1 e^{-pt} \cdot 0 \cdot dt + \int_1^2 e^{-pt} \cdot t\, dt + \int_2^\infty e^{-pt} \cdot 0 \cdot dt$$

$$= \int_1^2 e^{-pt}\, t\, dt = \left[\frac{e^{-pt} \cdot t}{-p}\right]_1^2 - \int_1^2 \frac{e^{-pt}}{-p}\, dt$$

$$= \frac{1}{p}(e^{-p} - 2e^{-2p}) - \frac{1}{p^2}\left[e^{-pt}\right]_1^2$$

$$= \frac{1}{p}(e^{-p} - 2c^{-2p}) - \frac{1}{p^2}(e^{-2p} - e^{-p})$$

$$= e^{-p}\left(\frac{1}{p} + \frac{1}{p^2}\right) - e^{-2p}\left(\frac{2}{p} + \frac{1}{p^2}\right).$$

Example 13. *Find Laplace transform of*

$$\int_0^t \left(\frac{1 - e^{-2x}}{x}\right) dx$$

Solution. If $L\{F(t)\} = f(p)$, then we have

$$\frac{f(p)}{p} = L\left[\int_0^1 F(u)\, du\right] \qquad \ldots \text{(i)}$$

and
$$\int_p^\infty f(x)\, dx = L\left\{\frac{F(t)}{t}\right\} \qquad \ldots \text{(ii)}$$

$$L\{1 - e^{-2t}\} = L\{1\} - L\{e^{-2t}\} = \frac{1}{p} - \frac{1}{p+2}$$

$$\therefore \quad L\left\{\frac{1 - e^{-2t}}{t}\right\} = \int_p^\infty \left(\frac{1}{p} - \frac{1}{p+2}\right) dp$$

$$= \left[\log p - \log(p+2)\right]_0^\infty$$

$$= -\left[\log\left(\frac{p+2}{p}\right)\right]_p^\infty = \left[-\log\left(1 + \frac{2}{p}\right)\right]_p^\infty$$

$$= -\left[\log 1 - \log\left(1 + \frac{2}{p}\right)\right]$$

$$= \log\left(1 + \frac{2}{p}\right)$$

$\therefore$ by (i)

$$L\int_0^1 \left[\frac{1 - e^{-2x}}{x}\right] dx = \frac{1}{p}\log\left(1 + \frac{2}{p}\right).$$

Example 14. *If* $E(t) = \int_t^\infty \frac{e^{-x}}{x}\,dx$, *[Exponential integral function]*

then show that $L\{E(t)\} = \frac{\log(p+1)}{p}$.

Solution. Let $E(t) = F(t) = \int_t^\infty \frac{e^{-x}}{x}\,dx$,

then $\lim_{t \to \infty} F(t) = 0$ and $F(t) = -\int_\infty^t \frac{e^{-x}}{x}\,dx$

so that $F'(t) = -\frac{e^{-t}}{t}$

or $tF'(t) = -e^{-t}$

or $L\{tF'(t)\} = -L\{e^{-t}\}$

or $-\frac{d}{dp}\{pf(p) - F(0)\} = -\frac{1}{p+1}$

$$\left[\because L\{tF(t)\} = -\frac{d}{dp}f(p) \text{ and } L\{F'(t)\} = pf(p) - F(0)\right]$$

or $\frac{d}{dp}\{pf(p)\} = \frac{1}{p+1}$, as $F(0)$ = const.

Integrating

$$pf(p) = \log(p+1) + C$$

Making $p \to 0$

$$\lim_{p \to 0} pf(p) = \lim_{p \to 0} \log(p+1) + C$$
$$= 0 + C$$

or $\lim_{t \to \infty} F(t) = C$

For $\lim_{t \to \infty} F(t) = \lim_{s \to 0} pf(p)$, by final value problem

or $0 = C$.

Hence, (i) becomes

$$pf(p) = \log(p+1), \text{ or } f(p) = \frac{\log(p+1)}{p}$$

Example 15. *If* $C(t) = \int_t^\infty \frac{\cos x}{x}\,dx$ *(cosine integral function), then show that*

$$L\{C(t)\} = \frac{\log(p^2+1)}{2p}.$$

Solution. Let $F(t) = \int_t^\infty \frac{\cos x}{x}\,dx$

Then $\lim_{t \to \infty} F(t) = 0.$

Also $F(t) = -\int_\infty^t \frac{\cos x}{x}\,dx$

Hence, $F'(t) = -\frac{\cos t}{t}$

or $t F'(t) = -\cos t$

or $L\{t F'(t)\} = L\{-\cos t\}$

or $-\frac{d}{dp}\{p f(p) - F(0)\} = -\frac{p}{p^2+1}$ $[\because L\{F'(t)\} = pf(p) - F(0)]$

or $\frac{d}{dp}\{p f(p)\} = \frac{p}{p^2+1}$, As $F(0)$ = constant.

On integration, we get

$$p f(p) = \frac{1}{2}\log(p^2+1) + C \quad \ldots(i)$$

or $\lim_{p \to 0} p\, f(p) = \lim_{p \to 0} \frac{1}{2}\log(p^2+1) + C$

$= 0 + C$

or $\lim_{t \to \infty} F(t) = 0 + C$ by final value problem.

or $0 = 0 + C$

or $C = 0$

Hence (i) becomes

$$p f(p) = \frac{1}{2}\log(p^2+1)$$

or $f(p) = \frac{1}{2p}\log(p^2+1)$

or $$L\{C(t)\} = \frac{\log(p^2+1)}{2p}.$$

Example 16. *The error function is defined as*

$$erf(t) = \frac{2}{\sqrt{x}} \int_0^t e^{-x^2}\, dx,$$

then show that

$$L\{erf(\sqrt{t})\} = \frac{1}{p\sqrt{(p^2+1)}}.$$

Solution. We have

$$erf(\sqrt{t}) = \frac{2}{\sqrt{\pi}} \int_0^{\sqrt{t}} e^{-x^2}\, dx$$

$$= \frac{2}{\sqrt{\pi}} \int_0^{\sqrt{t}} \left(1 - x^2 + \frac{x^4}{2\,!} - \frac{x^5}{3\,!} + \ldots \, dx\right)$$

$$= \frac{2}{\sqrt{\pi}} \left[x - \frac{x^3}{3} + \frac{x^5}{5 \cdot 2\,!} - \frac{x^7}{7 \cdot 3\,!} + \ldots\right]_0^{\sqrt{t}}$$

$$= \frac{2}{\sqrt{\pi}} \left[t^{1/2} - \frac{t^{3/2}}{3} + \frac{t^{5/2}}{5 \cdot 2\,!} - \frac{t^{7/2}}{7 \cdot 3\,!} + \ldots\right]$$

Taking Laplace transform of both the sides, we get

$$L\{erf(\sqrt{t})\} = \frac{2}{\sqrt{\pi}} \left[\frac{\Gamma(3/2)}{p^{3/2}} - \frac{\Gamma(5/2)}{3p^{5/2}} + \frac{\Gamma(7/2)}{5 \cdot 2\,!\, p^{7/2}} - \frac{\Gamma(9/2)}{7 \cdot 3\,!\, p^{9/2}} + \ldots\right]$$

$$= \frac{1}{p^{3/2}} \left[1 - \frac{1}{2} \cdot \frac{1}{p} + \frac{1.3}{2.4} \cdot \frac{1}{p^2} - \frac{1.3.5}{2.4.6} \frac{1}{p^3} + \ldots\right]$$

$$= \frac{1}{p^{3/2}} \left(1 + \frac{1}{p}\right)^{-1/2} = \frac{1}{p(p+1)^{1/2}}.$$

EXERCISE 1(C)

Find the Laplace transform of the following functions:

1. $F(t) = \begin{cases} (t-1)^2, & t > 1 \\ 0, & 0 < t < 1. \end{cases}$

2. $\dfrac{e^{-at} - e^{-bt}}{t}$.

3. Show that

$$\int_0^\infty \frac{e^{-6t} - e^{-3t}}{t}\, dt = \log \frac{1}{2}.$$

4. Prove that:

$$L\{t\, e^{at} \sin at\} = \frac{2a(p-a)}{(p^2 - 2ap + 2a^2)^2}.$$

5. $L\{G(t)\} = \dfrac{1}{p} + \dfrac{e^{-2p}}{p} + \dfrac{e^{-2p}}{p^2}$

where $G(t) = \begin{cases} 1, & 0 < t < 2 \\ t & t > 2 \end{cases}$

6. Compute $L\{F(t)\}$, if

$$F(t) = \begin{cases} \sin t, & 0 < t < \pi \\ 0, & \pi < t < 2\pi \end{cases}$$

where $F(t)$ has period 2π.

7. Find $L(\sin t - \cos t)^2$

8. Evaluate $L\{F(t)\}$, where

$$F(t) = \begin{cases} 0, & 0 < t < 1 \\ 1, & 1 < t < 2 \\ 2, & t > 2. \end{cases}$$

9. Find Laplace transform of $F(t)$, where

$$F(t) = \begin{cases} t, & 0 \le t \le \frac{1}{2}, \\ t - 1, & \frac{1}{2} \le t \le 1, \\ 0, & t > 1. \end{cases}$$

10. Evaluate

$$L\{F(t)\} \text{ if } F(t) = \begin{cases} \sin(t - \pi/3), & t > \pi/3 \\ 0, & t < \pi/3 \end{cases}$$

11. Evaluate $L\{\sin(at) - at\cos(at)\}$.

12. Prove that

$$L\{\sin \lambda t \cdot \cos \lambda t\} = \frac{\lambda}{p^2 + 4\lambda^2},\ p > 0.$$

13. Evaluate $(t + 3)^2 e^t$.

14. Prove that

$$L\{e^{3t} \, erf \sqrt{t}\} = \frac{1}{(p-3)\sqrt{(p-2)}}.$$

15. Sine integral function is defined as

$$S(t) = \int_0^t \frac{\sin x}{x} \, dx,$$

then prove that

$$L\{S(t)\} = \frac{1}{p} \tan^{-1}\left(\frac{1}{p}\right).$$

ANSWERS

1. $\dfrac{2e^{-p}}{p^3}$;

2. $\log\left(\dfrac{p+b}{p+a}\right)$;

6. $\dfrac{1}{(1+p^2)(1-e^{-\pi p})}$;

7. $\dfrac{p^2 - 2p + 4}{p(p+4)}$.

8. $\dfrac{1}{p}[e^{-2p} + e^{-p}]$;

9. $\dfrac{1}{p^2}[1 - p\,e^{-p/2} - e^{-p}]$;

10. $e^{-p\pi/3}/(p^2+1), p > 0$;

11. $2a^3/(p^2 + a^2)^2$;

13. $\dfrac{2}{(p+1)^3} + \dfrac{9}{(p-1)} + \dfrac{6}{(p-1)^2}$.

1.23. TABLE OF LAPLACE TRANSFORM THEOREM

No.	*Operation*	$F(t)$	$L\{F(t)\} = f(p)$
1.	Linearity Property	$c_1 F_1(t) \pm c_2 F_2(t)$	$c_1 L\{F_1(t)\} \pm c_2 L\{F_2(t)\}$
2.	First translation or shifting theorem	$e^{at} F(t)$	$f(p-a)$
3.	Second translation or shifting theorem	$G(t) = \begin{cases} F(t-a), & t > a \\ 0, & t < a \end{cases}$	$e^{-ap} f(p)$
4.	Change of scale property	$F(at)$	$\frac{1}{a} f(p/a)$
5.	Differentiation theorems	$F'(t)$	$pf(p) - F(0)$
		$F^n(t)$	$p^n f(p) - \sum_{r=0}^{n-1} p^{n-1-r} F^r(0)$
6.	Differentiation of Laplace transform	$t F(t)$	$-f'(p)$
		$t^n F(t)$	$(-1)^n \frac{d^n}{dp^n} f(p)$
7.	Integral theorem	$\int_0^1 F(x)\, dx$	$\frac{1}{p} f(p)$

1.23. TABLE *(CONTD.)*

No.	*Operation*	$F(t)$	$L\{F(t)\} = f(p)$
8.	Integration of Laplace Transform	$\frac{1}{t} F(t)$	$\int_p^\infty f(x)\, dx$
9.	Initial Value Theorem	$\lim_{t \to 0} F(t) = \lim_{p \to \infty} p\, L\{F(t)\}$	
10.	Final Value Theorem	$\lim_{t \to \infty} F(t) = \lim_{p \to 0} p\, L\{F(t)\}$	
11.	Fundamental theorem for Periodic Functions	$L\{F(t)\} = \frac{\int_0^\infty e^{-pt} F(t)\, dt}{1 - e^{-p\omega}}$ $F(t)$ is periodic function of period ω.	
12.	Laplace transform of the Laplace transform	$L\{L f(t)\} = \int_0^\infty \frac{f(t)}{t+u}\, dt.$	

2

The Inverse Laplace Transform

2.1 INVERSE LAPLACE TRANSFORM [DEFINITION]

If $L\{F(t)\} = f(p)$, then $F(t)$ is called on inverse Laplace Transform of $f(p)$ and we write

$$F(t) = L^{-1}\{f(p)\}.$$

Here L^{-1} is called the *inverse Laplace Transformation operator.*

Thus $\quad L^{-1}\left\{\frac{1}{p^2}\right\} = t, \quad L^{-1}\left\{\frac{a}{p^2 + a^2}\right\} = \sin at.$

2.2 NULL FUNCTION

If $N(t)$ is a function of t such that

$$\int_0^t N(t)\, dt = 0$$

for all positive values of t, then $N(t)$ is called a *null function.*

2.3 UNIQUENESS OF INVERSE LAPLACE TRANSFORMS

Since the Laplace Transform of null function is zero and hence if

$$L\{F(t)\} = f(p),$$

then $\quad L\{F(t) + N(t)\} = f(p)$

Obviously,

$$L^{-1}\{f(p)\} = F(t)$$

$$L^{-1}\{f(p)\} = F(t) + N(t)$$

This implies that we can have two different functions, with the same Laplace Transform. As a result of which the inverse Laplace transform of a function is not unique, if we allow null functions. Hence the inverse Laplace transform of a function is unique if we do not allow null function which do not appear in cases of physical interest. This result is explained by Lerch's theorem.

Lerch's Theorem. If $F_1(t)$ and $F_2(t)$ are two functions having the same Laplace transform $f(p)$, then

$$F_1(t) - F_2(t) = N(t)$$

where $N(t)$ is a null function for all $t > 0$.

From this it follows that, an inverse Laplace transform is unique except for the addition of a null function.

If we restrict ourselves to functions $F(t)$ which are sectionally continuous in every finite interval $0 \le t \le t_0$ and of exponential order for $t > t_0$, then the inverse Laplace transform of $f(p)$ is unique.

2.4 TABLE OF INVERSE LAPLACE TRANSFORMS

	$f(p)$	$L^{-1}\{f(p)\} = F(t)$
1	$1/p$	1
2	$1/p^2$	t
3	$\dfrac{1}{p^{n+1}}$	$\dfrac{t^n}{\Gamma(n+1)}$
4	$\dfrac{1}{p-a}$	e^{at}
5	$\dfrac{a}{p^2+a^2}$	$\sin at$
6	$\dfrac{p}{p^2+a^2}$	$\cos at$
7	$\dfrac{a}{p^2-a^2}$	$\sinh at$
8	$\dfrac{p}{p^2-a^2}$	$\cosh at$

2.5 LINEARITY PROPERTY

Theorem. *Let $f_1(p)$ and $f_2(p)$ be the Laplace transforms of functions $F_1(t)$ and $F_2(t)$ respectively, then*

$$L^{-1}\{c_1 f_1(\text{p}) \pm c_2 f_2(\text{p})\} = c_1 L^{-1}\{f_1(\text{p})\} \pm c_2 L^{-1}\{f_2(\text{p})\}$$

$$= c_1 F_1(\text{t}) + c_2 F_2(\text{t})$$

where c_1, c_2 are two constants.

Proof. We have

$$L\{c_1 F_1(t)\} \pm c_2 L\{F_2(t)\}$$

$$= c_1 L\{F_1(t)\} \pm c_2 L\{F_2(t)\}$$

$$= c_1 f_1(p) \pm c_2 f_2(p)$$

$$\therefore \quad L^{-1}\{c_1 f_1(p) \pm c_2 f_2(p)\}$$

$$= c_1 F_1(t) \pm c_2 F_2(t).$$

ILLUSTRATIVE EXAMPLES

Example 1. *Find (i)* $L^{-1}\left\{\frac{1}{p^4}\right\}$, *(ii)* $L^{-1}\left\{\frac{4}{p-2}\right\}$, *(iii)* $L^{-1}\left\{\frac{1}{\sqrt{p}}\right\}$ *and (iv)* $L^{-1}\left\{\frac{1}{p^{7/2}}\right\}$.

Solution. (i) $L^{-1}\left\{\frac{1}{p^4}\right\} = \frac{t^{4-1}}{3!} = \frac{t^3}{6}.$

(ii) $L^{-1}\left\{\frac{4}{p-2}\right\} = 4L^{-1}\left\{\frac{1}{p-2}\right\} = 4e^{2t}.$

(iii) $L^{-1}\left\{\frac{1}{\sqrt{p}}\right\} = \frac{t^{1/2-1}}{\Gamma\left(\frac{1}{2}\right)} = \frac{t^{-1/2}}{\sqrt{\pi}} = \frac{1}{\sqrt{(\pi t)}}.$

(iv) $L^{-1}\left\{\frac{1}{p^{7/2}}\right\} = \frac{t^{7/2-1}}{\Gamma\left(\frac{7}{2}\right)} = \frac{t^{5/2}}{\frac{5}{2}\cdot\frac{3}{2}\cdot\frac{1}{2}\sqrt{\pi}} = \frac{8}{15}t^2\sqrt{\left(\frac{t}{\pi}\right)}$

Example 2. *Evaluate:* $L^{-1}\left\{\frac{p}{p^2+2}+\frac{6p}{p^2-16}+\frac{3}{p-3}\right\}$.

Solution. $L^{-1}\left\{\frac{p}{p^2+2}+\frac{6p}{p^2-16}+\frac{3}{p-3}\right\}$

$$= L^{-1}\left\{\frac{p}{p^2+(\sqrt{2})^2}\right\}+6L^{-1}\left\{\frac{p}{p^2-4^2}\right\}+3L^{-1}\left\{\frac{1}{p-3}\right\}$$

$$= \cos\sqrt{2}\,t + 6\cosh 4t + 3e^{3t}.$$

Example 3. *Find* $L^{-1}\left\{\frac{3}{p^2-3}+\frac{3p+2}{p^3}-\frac{3p-27}{p^2+9}+\frac{6-30\sqrt{p}}{p^4}\right\}$.

Solution. $L^{-1}\left\{\frac{3}{p^2-3}+\frac{3p+2}{p^2}-\frac{3p-27}{p^2-9}+\frac{6-30\sqrt{p}}{p^4}\right\}$

$$= L^{-1}\left\{\frac{3}{p^2-3}\right\}+L^{-1}\left\{\frac{3}{p^2}\right\}+L^{-1}\left\{\frac{2}{p^3}\right\}-L^{-1}\left\{\frac{3p}{p^2+9}\right\}+L^{-1}\left\{\frac{27}{p^2+9}\right\}$$

$$+L^{-1}\left\{\frac{6}{p^4}\right\}-L^{-1}\left\{\frac{30}{p^{7/2}}\right\}$$

$$= 3L^{-1}\left\{\frac{1}{p^2-(\sqrt{3})^2}\right\}+3L^{-1}\left\{\frac{1}{p^2}\right\}+2L^{-1}\left\{\frac{1}{p^3}\right\}-3L^{-1}\left\{\frac{p}{p^2+3^2}\right\}$$

$$+27L^{-1}\left\{\frac{1}{p^2+3^2}\right\}+6L^{-1}\left\{\frac{1}{p^4}\right\}-30L^{-1}\left\{\frac{1}{p^{7/2}}\right\}$$

$$= 3\cdot\frac{1}{\sqrt{3}}\sinh\sqrt{3}\,t+3\cdot\frac{t^{2-1}}{(2-1)!}+2\cdot\frac{t^{3-1}}{(3-1)!}-3\cdot\cos 3t+\frac{27}{3}\sin 3t$$

$$+6\cdot\frac{t^{4-1}}{(4-1)!}-30\cdot\frac{t^{7/2-1}}{\Gamma(7/2)}$$

$$-\sqrt{3}\sinh\sqrt{3}\,t+3t+t^2-3\cos 3t+9\sin 3t+t^3-16t^2\sqrt{(t/\pi)}.$$

EXERCISE 2(A)

Find the Inverse Laplace Transforms for each of the following functions:

1. (i) $\frac{1}{p-3}$; (ii) $\frac{7}{p-4}$; (iii) $\frac{1}{p^3}$; (iv) $\frac{1}{p^4}$.

2. (i) $\dfrac{p}{p^2+2}$; (ii) $\dfrac{5}{p^2-9}$; (iii) $\dfrac{1}{p^2-5}$.

3. (i) $\dfrac{1}{p^{n+1}}$; (ii) $\dfrac{1}{\sqrt{p}}$; (iii) $\dfrac{1}{p^{3/2}}$.

4. $\dfrac{3}{p-3}+\dfrac{5p}{p^2+36}$.

5. $\dfrac{3p+2}{p^3}-\dfrac{3p-27}{p^2+9}+\dfrac{6-30\sqrt{p}}{p^4}$.

6. $\dfrac{1}{p^{7/2}}+\dfrac{p+1}{p^{4/3}}+\dfrac{-6}{p^2+4}+\dfrac{2p-5}{p^2-9}$.

ANSWERS

1. (i) e^{3t}; (ii) $7e^{4t}$; (iii) $\dfrac{1}{2}t^2$; (iv) $\dfrac{1}{6}t^3$.

2. (i) $\cos\sqrt{2}\,t$ (ii) $\dfrac{5}{3}\sinh 3t$; (iii) $\dfrac{\sinh\sqrt{5}\,t}{\sqrt{5}}$

3. (i) $\dfrac{t^n}{\Gamma(n+1)}$; (ii) $\dfrac{1}{\sqrt{(\pi t)}}$; (iii) $2\sqrt{\dfrac{t}{\pi}}$

4. $3e^{3t}+5\cos 6t$.

5. $3t+t^2-3\cos 3t+9\sin 3t+t^3-\dfrac{16t^{5/2}}{\sqrt{\pi}}$.

6. $\dfrac{8t^{3/2}}{15\sqrt{\pi}}+\dfrac{1}{\Gamma\left(\dfrac{1}{3}\right)}(t^{-2/3}+3t^{1/3})+3\sin 2t+2\cosh 3t-\dfrac{5}{3}\sinh 3t$.

2.6 FIRST TRANSLATION OR SHIFTING THEOREM

Theorem. *If* $\{L^{-1}\{f(p)\}=F(t)$, *then* $L^{-1}\{f(p-a)\}=e^{at}F(t)\}$.

Proof. We have

$$f(p)=\int_0^\infty e^{-pt}F(t)\,dt$$

$$\therefore \quad f(p-a)=\int_0^\infty e^{-(p-a)t}F(t)\,dt$$

$$=\int_0^\infty e^{-pt}\{e^{at}F(t)\}\,dt$$

$$= L\{e^{at} F(t)\}$$

$$\therefore \quad L^{-1}\{f(p-a)\} = e^{at} F(t).$$

Note. The result of this theorem is also expressible as:

$$L^{-1}\{f(p)\} = e^{-at} L^{-1}\{f(p-a)\}$$

Also

$$L^{-1}\{f(p)\} = e^{at} L^{-1}\{f(p+a)\}.$$

2.7 SECOND TRANSLATION OR SHIFTING THEOREM

Theorem. *If* $L^{-1}\{f(p)\} = F(t)$,

then $L^{-1}\{e^{-ap} f(p)\} = G(t)$,

where $G(t) = \begin{cases} F(t-a), & t > a \\ 0, & t < a \end{cases}$

Proof. We have, $L\{G(t)\} = \int_0^\infty e^{-pt} G(t)\, dt$

$$= \int_0^a e^{-pt} G(t)\, dt + \int_a^\infty e^{-pt} G(t)\, dt$$

$$= \int_0^a e^{-pt}\, 0\, dt + \int_a^\infty e^{-pt} F(t-a)\, dt$$

$$= 0 - \int_a^\infty e^{-pt} F(t-a)\, dt$$

$$= \int_0^\infty e^{-p(a+u)} F(u)\, du, \text{ if } t - a = u$$

$$= \int_0^\infty e^{-pa} e^{-pu} F(u)\, du$$

$$= e^{-ap} \int_0^\infty e^{-pu} F(u)\, du$$

$$= e^{-ap} L\{F(t)\} = e^{-ap} f(p)$$

Thus, $L\{G(t)\} = e^{-ap} f(p)$

$$\therefore \quad G(t) = L^{-1}\{e^{-ap} f(p)\}.$$

Note. This result is also expressible as

$$L^{-1}\{e^{-ap}f(p)\} = \begin{cases} F(t-a), & \text{if } t > a \\ 0, & \text{if } t < a \end{cases}$$

or $$L^{-1}\{e^{-ap}f(p)\} = F(t-a)\,H(t-a)$$

where $H(t-a)$ is Heaviside unit step function.

2.8 CHANGE OF SCALE PROPERTY

Theorem. *If $f(p) = L\{F(t)\}$ denotes the Laplace transform of the function $F(t)$, prove that*

$$L^{-1}\{f(ap)\} = \frac{1}{a}F\left(\frac{t}{a}\right), \quad a > 0.$$

Proof. We have

$$f(p) = \int_0^{\infty} e^{-pt}F(t)\,dt$$

$$f(ap) = \int_0^{\infty} e^{-apt}F(t)\,dt$$

$$= \int e^{-pu}F\left(\frac{u}{a}\right)\frac{du}{a}; \quad at = u$$

$$= \frac{1}{a}\int_0^{\infty} e^{-pu}F\left(\frac{u}{a}\right)du$$

$$= \frac{1}{a}\int_0^{\infty} e^{-pt}F\left(\frac{t}{a}\right)dt$$

$$= \frac{1}{a}L\left\{F\left(\frac{t}{a}\right)\right\}$$

Because

$$\int_a^b f(u)\,du = \int_a^b f(t)\,dt$$

$$\therefore \quad L^{-1}\{f(ap)\} = \frac{1}{a}F\left(\frac{t}{a}\right).$$

ILLUSTRATIVE EXAMPLES

Example 1. *Find* $L^{-1}\left\{\frac{p-2}{(p-2)^2+5^2} + \frac{p+4}{(p+4)^2+9^2} + \frac{1}{(p+2)^2+3^2}\right\}$.

Solution. $L^{-1}\left\{\frac{p-2}{(p-2)^2+5^2} + \frac{p+4}{(p+4)^2+9^2}\right\} + \left\{\frac{1}{(p+2)^2+3^2}\right\}$

$$= L^{-1}\left\{\frac{p-2}{(p-2)^2+5^2}\right\} + L^{-1}\left\{\frac{p+4}{(p+4)^2+9^2}\right\} + L^{-1}\left\{\frac{1}{(p+2)^2+3^2}\right\}$$

$$= e^{2t} L^{-1}\left\{\frac{p}{p^2+5^2}\right\} + e^{-4t} L^{-1}\left\{\frac{p}{p^2+9^2}\right\} + e^{-2t} L^{-1}\left\{\frac{1}{p^2+3^2}\right\}$$

$$= e^{2t}\cos 5t + e^{-4t}\cos 9t + \frac{e^{-2t}}{3}\sin 3t.$$

Example 2. *Evaluate* $L^{-1}\left\{\frac{p+1}{p^2+6p+25}\right\}$.

Solution. We have $L^{-1}\left\{\frac{p+1}{p+6p+25}\right\} = L^{-1}\left\{\frac{(p+3)-2}{(p+3)^2+16}\right\}$

$$= e^{-3t} L^{-1}\left\{\frac{p-2}{p^2+4^2}\right\}$$

$$= e^{-3t}\left[L^{-1}\left\{\frac{p}{p^2+4^2}\right\} - \frac{1}{2}L^{-1}\left\{\frac{4}{p^2+4^2}\right\}\right]$$

$$= e^{-3t}\left[\cos 4t - \frac{1}{2}\sin 4t\right].$$

Example 3. *Find the inverse Laplace transform of* $\frac{e^{-\pi p}}{p^2+1}$.

Solution. We have, $L^{-1}\left\{\frac{1}{p^2+1}\right\} = \sin t = F(t)$ (say)

By second shifting theorem

$$L^{-1}\left\{\frac{e^{-\pi p}}{p^2+1}\right\} = \begin{cases}\sin(t-\pi), & \text{if } t > \pi\\ 0, & \text{if } t < \pi\end{cases}$$

$$= \sin(t-\pi)\, H(t-\pi)$$

$$= -\sin t \cdot H(t-\pi)$$

Example 4. *Find the inverse Laplace transform of*

$$\frac{p\,e^{-ap}}{p^2-\omega^2},\quad a > 0.$$

Solution. Let $\dfrac{p}{p^2 - \omega^2} = f(p)$, then

$$L^{-1}\{f(p)\} = \cosh \omega t = F(t), \quad \text{say.}$$

Then by second shifting theorem

$$L^{-1}\left\{\frac{p\,e^{-ap}}{p^2 - \omega^2}\right\}$$

$$= \begin{cases} \cosh \omega (t - a), & \text{if } t > a \\ 0, & \text{if } t < a \end{cases}$$

$$= \cosh \omega (t - a)\, H(t - a).$$

Example 5. *Find* $L^{-1}\left\{\dfrac{(p+1)\,e^{-\pi p}}{p^2 + p + 1}\right\}$

Solution. We have $L^{-1}\left\{\dfrac{p+1}{p^2+p+1}\right\} = L^{-1}\left\{\dfrac{(p+\frac{1}{2}) + \frac{1}{2}}{\left(p+\frac{1}{2}\right)^2 + \frac{3}{4}}\right\}$

$$= e^{-t/2}\, L^{-1}\left\{\frac{p + \frac{1}{2}}{p^2 + (\sqrt{3}/2)^2}\right\}$$

$$= e^{-t/2}\left[\cos\frac{t\sqrt{3}}{2} + \frac{1}{2}\cdot\frac{2}{\sqrt{3}}\sin\frac{t\sqrt{3}}{2}\right]$$

Let $\quad f(p) = \dfrac{p+1}{p^2+p+1}$

Then $\quad L^{-1}\{f(p)\} = F(t)$

$$= e^{-t/2}\left[\cos\frac{t\sqrt{3}}{2} + \frac{1}{\sqrt{3}}\sin\frac{t\sqrt{3}}{2}\right]$$

By second shifting theorem,

$$L^{-1}\{f(p)\,e^{-\pi p}\} = \begin{cases} F(t-\pi), & \text{if } t > \pi \\ 0, & \text{if } t < \pi \end{cases}$$

$$= \begin{cases} e^{-1/2(t-\pi)}\left[\cos (t-\pi)\dfrac{\sqrt{3}}{2} + \dfrac{1}{\sqrt{3}}\sin (t-\pi)\dfrac{\sqrt{3}}{2}\right] & \text{if } t > \pi \\ 0 & \text{if } t < \pi \end{cases}$$

$$= e^{-1/2(t-\pi)}\left[\cos(t-\pi)\frac{\sqrt{3}}{2} + \frac{1}{\sqrt{3}}\sin(t-\pi)\frac{\sqrt{3}}{2}\right] H(t-\pi)$$

Example 6. *Prove that*

$$L^{-1}\left\{\frac{P}{p^4+p^2+1}\right\} = \frac{2}{\sqrt{3}}\sinh\frac{t}{2}\sin\frac{t\sqrt{3}}{2}.$$

Solution. We have

$$L^{-1}\left\{\frac{P}{(p^4+p^2+1)}\right\} = L^{-1}\left\{\frac{P}{(p^2+1)^2-p^2}\right\}$$

$$= L^{-1}\left\{\frac{P}{(p^2+p+1)(p^2-p+1)}\right\}$$

$$= L^{-1}\left\{\frac{1}{2(p^2-p+1)} - \frac{1}{2(p^2+p+1)}\right\}$$

$$= L^{-1}\left\{\frac{1}{2\left[\left(p-\frac{1}{2}\right)^2+\frac{3}{4}\right]} - \frac{1}{2\left[\left(p+\frac{1}{2}\right)^2+\frac{3}{4}\right]}\right\}$$

$$= \frac{e^{t/2}}{2}L^{-1}\left\{\frac{1}{p^2+\frac{3}{4}}\right\} - \frac{e^{-t/2}}{2}L^{-1}\left\{\frac{1}{p^2+\frac{3}{4}}\right\}$$

$$= \frac{e^{t/2}}{2}\cdot\frac{2}{\sqrt{3}}\sin\frac{t\sqrt{3}}{2} - \frac{e^{-t/2}}{2}\cdot\frac{2}{\sqrt{3}}\sin\frac{t\sqrt{3}}{2}$$

$$= \frac{2}{\sqrt{3}}\sin\frac{t\sqrt{3}}{2}\cdot\frac{e^{t/2}-e^{-t/2}}{2}$$

$$= \frac{2}{\sqrt{3}}\sin\frac{t\sqrt{3}}{2}\cdot\sinh\frac{t}{2}.$$

Example 7. *If* $L^{-1}\left[\frac{e^{-1/p}}{\sqrt{p}}\right] = \frac{\cos 2\sqrt{t}}{\sqrt{(\pi t)}}$, *then find* $L^{-1}\{e^{-a/p}/p^{1/2}\}$.

Solution. Since $L^{-1}\{f(ap)\} = \frac{1}{a}\cdot F(t/a)$

Hence $L^{-1}\left[\dfrac{e^{-1/p}}{\sqrt{p}}\right]=\dfrac{\cos(2\sqrt{t})}{\sqrt{(\pi t)}}$

gives $L^{-1}\left[\dfrac{e^{-1/pk}}{\sqrt{(pk)}}\right]=\dfrac{1}{k}\dfrac{(\cos 2\sqrt{t/k})}{\sqrt{(\pi t/k)}}$

or, $L^{-1}\left[\dfrac{e^{-1/pk}}{\sqrt{p}}\right]=\dfrac{\cos 2(t/k)^{1/2}}{(\pi t)^{1/2}}$

Putting $k=1/a$, we get

$$L^{-1}\left[\frac{e^{-a/p}}{\sqrt{p}}\right]=\frac{\cos\{2(at)^{1/2}\}}{(\pi t)^{1/2}}$$

EXERCISE 2(B)

1. Evaluate $L^{-1}\left[\dfrac{1}{(p-4)^5}+\dfrac{5}{(p-2)^2+5^2}+\dfrac{p+2}{(p+3)^2+6^2}\right]$

2. Evaluate $L^{-1}\left[\dfrac{1}{(p-4)^5}+\dfrac{5}{(p-2)^2+5^2}\right]$

3. Evaluate $L^{-1}\left[\dfrac{e^{-3p}}{(p-4)^2}\right]$

4. Find $L^{-1}\left[\dfrac{e^{-5p}}{(p-2)^4}\right]$

5. Find $L^{-1}\left[\dfrac{3p+1}{(p+1)^4}\right]$

6. Prove that $L^{-1}\left[\dfrac{e^{-p\pi}}{(p^2+1)}\right]=-\sin t\, H(t-\pi)$

7. Prove that $L^{-1}\left\{\dfrac{p\, e^{-2p\pi/3}}{p^2+9}\right\}=\cos 3\left(t-\dfrac{2\pi}{3}\right)H\left(t-\dfrac{2\pi}{3}\right)$

8. Find $L^{-1}\left[\dfrac{e^{-ap}}{p^2}\right]$, $a>0$

9. Find $L^{-1}\left[\dfrac{p}{(p+3)^{7/2}}\right]$

10. (a) Find $L^{-1}\left[\dfrac{p}{2p^2 - 8}\right]$

(b) Find $L^{-1}\left\{\dfrac{3p+2}{4p^2 + 12p + 9}\right\}$

ANSWERS

1. $e^{4t} \cdot \dfrac{t^4}{24} + e^{2t} \cdot \sin 5t + e^{-3t} \cos 6t - \dfrac{1}{6} e^{-3t} \sin 6t.$

2. $e^{4t} \cdot \dfrac{t^4}{24} + e^{2t} \sin 5t.$ **3.** $(t-3)\, e^{4(t-3)}\, H(t-3).$

4. $\dfrac{(t-5)^3}{6} e^{2(t-5)} \cdot H(t-5).$ **5.** $e^{-t}\left(\dfrac{3}{2}t^2 - \dfrac{t^3}{3}\right).$

8. $(t-a)$ when $t > a$ and 0 otherwise.

9. $\dfrac{e^{-3t}}{\sqrt{\pi}}\left[\dfrac{4}{3}t^{3/2} - \dfrac{8}{5}t^{5/2}\right].$

10. (a) $\dfrac{1}{2}\cosh 2t$ (b) $\dfrac{1}{8} e^{-(3/2)t}(6 - 5t).$

2.9 USE OF PARTIAL FRACTIONS

If $f(p)$ is of the form $\dfrac{\phi(p)}{\psi(p)}$, where ϕ and ψ are polynomials in p, then break $f(p)$ into partial fractions and manipulate term by term.

ILLUSTRATIVE EXAMPLES

Example 1. *Find the inverse Laplace transform of*

$$\frac{3p+7}{p^2 - 2p - 3}.$$

Solution. Let $\dfrac{3p+7}{p^2 - 2p - 3} = \dfrac{3p+7}{(p-3)(p+1)}$

$$= \frac{A}{p-3} + \frac{B}{p+1}$$

or $$3p + 7 = A(p+1) + B(p-3)$$

Putting $p = 3$, $A = 4$ and $p = -1$, $B = -1$

$$\therefore \quad \frac{3p+7}{p^2-2p-3} = \frac{4}{p-3} - \frac{1}{p+1}$$

$$\therefore \quad L^{-1}\left[\frac{3p+7}{(p^2-2p-3)}\right] = 4L^{-1}\left[\frac{1}{p-3}\right] - L^{-1}\left[\frac{1}{p+1}\right]$$

$$= 4e^{3t} - e^{-t}.$$

Example 2. *Find the inverse Laplace transform of*

$$\frac{1+2p}{(p+2)^2(p-1)^2}.$$

Solution. Let $\dfrac{1+2p}{(p+2)^2(p-1)^2} = \dfrac{A}{(p+2)} + \dfrac{B}{(p+2)^2} + \dfrac{C}{(p-1)} + \dfrac{D}{(p-1)^2}$

or $\quad 1 + 2p \equiv A(p+2)(p-1)^2 + B(p-1)^2 + C(p-1)(p+2)^2 + D(p+2)^2$

Putting $p = 1$, we get $D = \dfrac{1}{3}$,

Putting $p = -2$, we get $B = -\dfrac{1}{3}$

Putting $p = 0$, $1 = 2A + B - 4C + 4D$

or $\quad A - 2C = 0$

Again putting $p = -1$, we get

$$-1 = 4A + 4B - 2C + D$$

$2A - C = 0$ which yield $A = 0$, $C = 0$

$$\therefore \quad \frac{1+2p}{(p-2)^2(p-1)^2} = \frac{1}{3}\left[\frac{1}{(p-1)^2} - \frac{1}{(p+2)^2}\right]$$

$$\therefore \quad L^{-1}\left\{\frac{1+2p}{(p-2)^2(p-1)^2}\right\} = \frac{1}{3}\left[L^{-1}\left\{\frac{1}{(p-1)^2}\right\} - L^{-1}\left\{\frac{1}{(p+2)^2}\right\}\right]$$

$$= \frac{1}{3}\left[e^t L^{-1}\left(\frac{1}{p^2}\right) - e^{-2t} L^{-1}\left(\frac{1}{p^2}\right)\right]$$

$$= \frac{1}{3}[e^t \cdot t - e^{-2t} \cdot t]$$

$$= \frac{t}{3}(e^t - e^{-2t}).$$

Example 3. *Find the inverse Laplace transform of*

$$\frac{5p+3}{(p-1)(p^2+2p+5)}.$$

Solution. Let $\dfrac{5p+3}{(p-1)(p^2+2p+5)} = \dfrac{A}{p-1} + \dfrac{Bp+C}{p^2+2p+5}$

$\therefore$ $5p+3 \equiv A(p^2+2p+5) + (Bp+C)(p-1)$

when $p = 1$, $8 = 8A$ $\therefore$ $A = 1$.

when $p^2 = -2p-5$,

$$5p+3 = B(-2p-5) - Bp + Cp - C$$
$$= (-3B+C)p - 5B - C$$

$\therefore$ $-3B + C = 5$

$-5B - C = 3$

or, $B = -1, C = 2$

$$\therefore \frac{5p+3}{(p-1)(p^2+2p+5)} = \frac{1}{p-1} + \frac{2-p}{p^2+2p+5}$$

$$= \frac{1}{p-1} - \left\{\frac{p+1}{(p+1)^2+4} - \frac{3}{(p+1)^2+4}\right]$$

$$\therefore L^{-1}\left[\frac{5p+3}{(p-1)(p^2+2p-5)}\right]$$

$$= L^{-1}\left[\frac{1}{(p-1)} - \frac{p+1}{(p+1)^2+2^2} + \frac{3}{(p+1)^2+2^2}\right]$$

$$= e^t - e^{-t} L^{-1}\left(\frac{p}{p^2+2^2}\right) + 3e^{-t} L^{-1}\left(\frac{1}{p^2+2^2}\right)$$

$$= e^t - e^{-t}\cos 2t + 3e^{-t}\frac{\sin 2t}{2}$$

$$= e^t - e^{-t}\left(\cos 2t - \frac{3}{2}\sin 2t\right).$$

Example 4. *Find the inverse Laplace transform of*

$$\frac{2p^2+5p-4}{p^3+p^2-2p}.$$

Solution. $$\frac{2p^2 + 5p - 4}{p^3 + p^2 - 2p} = \frac{2p^2 + 5p - 4}{p\,(p^2 + p - 2)}$$

$$= \frac{1}{p}\left[2 + \frac{3p}{(p + 2)\,(p - 1)}\right]$$

$$= \frac{2}{p} + \frac{1}{p - 1} - \frac{1}{p + 2}$$

By breaking into partial fractions.

$$\therefore \qquad L^{-1}\left[\frac{2p^2 + 5p - 4}{p^3 + p^2 - 2p}\right] = L^{-1}\left[\frac{2}{p} + \frac{1}{p - 1} - \frac{1}{p + 2}\right]$$

$$= 2.1 - e^{-2t} + e^{t}$$

$$= 2 + e^{t} - e^{-2t}.$$

Example 5. *Find* $L^{-1}\left[\dfrac{1}{(p - 1)^5\,(p + 2)}\right]$.

Solution. $$L^{-1}\left[\frac{1}{(p - 1)^5\,(p + 2)}\right]$$

$$= e^{t}\,L^{-1}\left[\frac{1}{p^5\,(p + 3)}\right] \qquad \ldots\text{(i)}$$

To break $\dfrac{1}{p^5\,(p + 3)}$ into partial fractions we divide 1 by $3 + p$ as follows:

	$\frac{1}{3} - \frac{p}{9} + \frac{p^2}{27} - \frac{p^3}{81} + \frac{p^4}{243}$
$3 + p$	1 $1 + \frac{p}{3}$ $- \quad -$
	$-\frac{p}{3}$ $-\frac{p}{3} - \frac{p^2}{9}$ $+ \quad +$

$$\frac{p^2}{9}$$

$$\frac{p^2}{9} + \frac{p^3}{27}$$

$$- \quad -$$

$$-\frac{p^3}{27}$$

$$-\frac{p^3}{27} - \frac{p^4}{81}$$

$$+ \quad +$$

$$\frac{p^4}{81}$$

$$\frac{p^4}{81} + \frac{p^4}{243}$$

$$- \quad -$$

$$-\frac{p^4}{243}$$

$$\therefore \quad \frac{1}{p^5(p+3)} = \frac{1}{p^5}\left[\frac{1}{3} - \frac{p}{9} + \frac{p^2}{27} - \frac{p^3}{81} + \frac{p^4}{243} - \frac{p^5}{243(p+3)}\right]$$

$$= \frac{1}{3p^5} - \frac{1}{9p^4} + \frac{1}{27p^3} - \frac{1}{81p^2} + \frac{1}{243p} - \frac{1}{243(p+3)}$$

$$L^{-1}\left[\frac{1}{p^5(p+3)}\right] = \frac{1}{3}\cdot\frac{t^4}{4!} - \frac{1}{9}\cdot\frac{t^3}{3!} + \frac{1}{27}\cdot\frac{t^2}{2!} - \frac{1}{81}\cdot\frac{t}{1!} + \frac{1}{243}\cdot\frac{t^0}{0!} - \frac{1}{243}e^{-3t}$$

$\therefore$ From (i), we get

$$L^{-1}\left[\frac{1}{(p-1)^5(p-2)}\right]$$

$$= \frac{e^t}{72}\left(t^4 - \frac{4}{3}t^3 + \frac{5}{3}t^2 - \frac{8}{9}t + \frac{8}{27}\right) - \frac{e^{-3t}}{243}.$$

EXERCISE 2(C)

1. (a) Evaluate $L^{-1}\left[\frac{p^2}{(p^2+a^2)(p^2+b^2)}\right]$ (b) Find $L^{-1}\frac{1}{p(p+1)}$

2. Find $L^{-1}\left[\dfrac{3p+1}{(p-1)^2(p^2+1)}\right]$

3. Evaluate $L^{-1}\left[\dfrac{p^2-2p+3}{(p-1)^2(p+1)}\right]$

4. Evaluate $L^{-1}\left[\dfrac{2p-1}{p^3-p}\right]$

5. Prove that $L^{-1}\left[\dfrac{1}{p^2-6p+10}\right] = e^{3t}\sin t$

6. Prove that $L^{-1}\left[\dfrac{p-1}{(p+3)(p^2+2p+2)}\right] = -\dfrac{4}{5}e^{-3t} + \dfrac{e^{-t}}{5}(4\cos t - 3\sin t)$

7. Prove that

$$L^{-1}\left[\frac{3p-5}{p^2-4p+20}\right] = 3e^{2t}\cos 4t + \frac{1}{4}e^{2t}\sin 4t.$$

ANSWERS

1. (a) $\dfrac{a\sin at - b\sin bt}{a^2-b^2}$ if $a^2 - b^2, ab \neq 0$. (b) $(1-e^{-t})$

2. $-\dfrac{1}{2}e^t + 2te^t + \dfrac{1}{2}\cos t - \dfrac{3}{2}\sin t.$

3. $\left(t-\dfrac{1}{2}\right)e^t + 3/2\, e^{-t}$ **4.** $1 - \dfrac{3}{2}e^{-t} + \dfrac{1}{2}e^t.$

2.10 INVERSE LAPLACE TRANSFORM OF DERIVATIVES

Theorem. *If* $L^{-1}\{f(p)\} = F(t)$

then $L^{-1}\{f^{(n)}(p)\} = (-1)^n t^n F(t).$

Proof. We have from the property of Laplace transform

$$L\{t^n F(t)\} = (-1)^n f^{(n)}(p)$$

$$\therefore \quad t^n F(t) = L^{-1}\{(-1)^n f^{(n)}(p)\}$$

$$= (-1)^n L^{-1}\{f^{(n)}(p)\}$$

or $$L^{-1}\{f^{(n)}(p)\} = (-1)^n t^n F(t).$$

2.11 DIVISION BY P

Theorem. *If* $L^{-1}\{f(p)\} = F(t)$,

then $$L^{-1}\left[\frac{f(p)}{p}\right] = \int_0^t F(u)\,du.$$

Proof. From the property of Laplace transform we know that

$$\frac{f(p)}{p} = L\left[\int_0^t F(u)\,du\right]$$

$$\therefore \quad L^{-1}\left[\frac{f(p)}{p}\right] = \int_0^t F(u)\,du.$$

2.12 MULTIPLICATION BY POWERS OF P

Theorem. *If* $L^{-1}\{f(p)\} = F(t)$ *and* $F(0) = 0$, *then*

$$L^{-1}\{p f(p)\} = F'(t).$$

Proof. Since we have

$$L\{F'(t)\} = p\,L\{F(t)\} - F(0)$$

$$= p f(p) \qquad [\because F(0) = 0]$$

$$\therefore \quad L^{-1}\{p f(p)\} = F'(t)$$

2.13 INVERSE LAPLACE TRANSFORM OF INTEGRALS

Theorem. *If* $L^{-1}\{f(p)\} = F(t)$, *then*

$$L^{-1}\left[\int_p^\infty f(x)\,dx\right] = \frac{F(t)}{t}.$$

Proof. Since, we have

$$L\{t^n F(t)\} = (-1)^n \frac{d^n}{dp^n} f(p)$$

$$= (-1)^n f^n(p)$$

$$\therefore \quad L^{-1}\{f^n(p)\} = L^{-1}\left[\frac{d^n}{dp^n} f(p)\right]$$

$$= (-1)^n t^n F(t).$$

2.14 CONVOLUTION (DEFINITION)

Theorem. *Let $F(t)$ and $G(t)$ be two functions of class A, then the convolution of the two functions $F(t)$ and $G(t)$ denoted by $F^{*}G$ is defined by the relation*

$$F^{*}G = \int_0^t F(x)\, G(t-x)\, dx.$$

The relation $F^{*}G$ is also called the resultant or Falting of F and G.

(*i*) *$F^{*}G$ is commutative i.e., $F^{*}G = G^{*}F$.*

Proof. $F^{*}G = \int_0^t F(x)\, G(t-x)\, dx$

If we put $t - x = y$, so that $dx = -dy$, then

$$F^{*}G = \int_0^t G(y)\, F(t-y)\, dy = G^{*}F$$

(ii) $F^{*}G$ is associative, *i.e.*, $(F^{*}G)^{*} H = F^{*} (G^{*}H)$.

(iii) $F^{*}G$ is distributive with respect to addition, *i.e.*,

$$F^{*} (G + H) = F^{*}G + F^{*}H$$

2.15 CONVOLUTION THEOREM

Theorem. *If $F(t)$ and $G(t)$ be two functions of class A and if $L^{-1}\{f(p)\} = F(t)$ and $L^{-1}\{g(p)\} = G(t)$, then*

$$L^{-1}\{f(p)\, g(p)\} = \int_0^t F(x)\, G(t-x)\, dx$$

$$= F^{*}G.$$

Proof. Let $\int_0^t F(x)\, G(t-x)\, dx = H(t)$

Then $\quad L\{H(t)\} = \int_0^\infty e^{-pt} H(t)\, dt$

$$= \int_0^\infty e^{-pt} \left[\int_0^t F(x)\, G(t-x)\, dx\right] dt$$

$$= \int_0^\infty \left[\int_0^t e^{-pt} F(x)\, G(t-x)\, dx\right] dt$$

the integration being first with respect to u and then t.

The above integration (i) is within the region lying below the line OP whose equation is $x = t$ and above OT, t being taken along OT and x along OX, with O as the origin, the axes being perpendicular to each other. If the order of integration is changed, the strip will be taken parallel to OT so that the limits of t are from x to ∞ and of x from 0 to ∞.

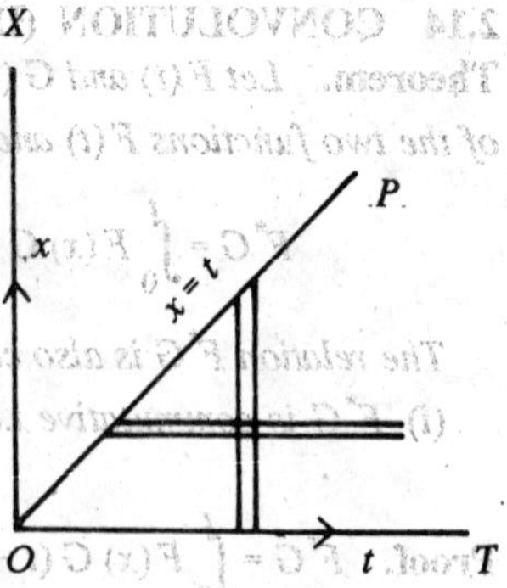

$$\therefore \quad L\{H(t)\} = \int_0^\infty dx \int_x^\infty e^{-pt} F(x)\, G(t-x)\, dt$$

$$= \int_0^\infty e^{-px} F(x)\, dx \int_x^\infty e^{-p(t-x)} G(t-x)\, dt$$

Putting $t - x = \theta$, we have

$$dt = d\theta.$$

$$\therefore \quad L\{H(t)\} = \int_0^\infty e^{-px} F(x) \int_0^\infty e^{-p\theta} G(\theta)\, d\theta\, dx$$

$$= \int_0^\infty e^{-px} F(x)\, g(p)\, dx$$

$$= f(p)\, g(p)$$

Putting the value of $H(t)$, we get

$$L\left\{\int_0^t F(x)\, G(t-x)\, dx\right\} = f(p)\, g(p) \qquad \ldots\text{(ii)}$$

or

$$\int_0^t F(x)\, G(t-x)\, dx = L^{-1}\{f(p)\, g(p)\}$$

$$= F^* G.$$

2.16 TABLE OF INVERSE LAPLACE TRANSFORM THEOREMS

No.	Operation	$f(p)$	$L^{-1}\{f(p)\} = F(t)$
1.	Linearity Property	$c_1 f_1(p) \pm c_2 f_2(p)$	$c_1 L^{-1}\{f_1(p)\} \pm c_2 L^{-1}\{f_2(p)\}$
2.	First translation or shifting theorem	$f(p-a)$	$e^{at} L^{-1}\{f(p)\}$

3.	Second translation or shifting theorem	$e^{-ap} f(p)$	$G(t) = \begin{cases} F(t-a), & t > a \\ 0, & t > a \end{cases}$
4.	Change of Scale Property	$f(ap)$	$\frac{1}{a} F\left(\frac{t}{a}\right)$
5.	Differentiation theorem	$f^n(p)$	$(-1)^n t^n F(t)$
6.	Integral theorem	$\int_p^\infty f(x)\, dx$	$\frac{1}{t} F(t)$
7.	Multiplication theorem	$p f(p)$ $p^n f(p)$	$F'(t)$ $F^n(t)$
8.	Division theorems	$\frac{f(p)}{p}$ $\frac{f(p)}{p^n}$	$\int_0^t F(x)\, dx$ $\int_0^t \int_0^t \cdots \int_0^t F(t) \cdot (dt)^n$
9.	Convolution theorem	$f(p) \cdot g(p)$	$\int_0^t F(x) \cdot G(t-x)\, dx$ $= F^* G.$

ILLUSTRATIVE EXAMPLES

Example 1. *Evaluate* $L^{-1}\left\{\log\left(\frac{p+3}{p+2}\right)\right\}$

Solution. Let $f(p) = \log\left(\frac{p+3}{p+2}\right) = \log(p+3) - \log(p+2)$.

Then $\quad f'(p) = \frac{d f(p)}{dp} = \frac{1}{p+3} - \frac{1}{p+2}$

$$\therefore \quad L^{-1}\{f'(p)\} = L^{-1}\left\{\frac{1}{p+3}\right\} - L^{-1}\left\{\frac{1}{p+2}\right\}$$

$$= e^{-3t} - e^{-2t}$$

But $\quad L^{-1}\{f'(p)\} = (-1)^1 t^1 L^{-1}\{f(p)\}$

$$= -t\, L^{-1}\{f(p)\}$$

or
$$L^{-1}\{f(p)\} = -1/t\, L^{-1}\{f'(p)\}$$
$$= -1/t\,(e^{-3t} - e^{-2t})$$
$$= 1/t\,(e^{-2t} - e^{-3t})$$

Example 2. *Find* $L^{-1}\left[\dfrac{p}{(p^2+a^2)^2}\right]$.

Solution. We have $L\{\sin at\} = \dfrac{a}{(p^2+a^2)}$

$$\therefore \quad L^{-1}\left[\frac{1}{p^2+a^2}\right] = \frac{\sin at}{a}$$

$$L^{-1}\left[\frac{d}{dp}\left(\frac{1}{p^2+a^2}\right)\right] = (-1)^1\frac{t\sin at}{a}$$

or
$$L^{-1}\left[-\frac{2p}{(p^2+a^2)^2}\right] = -\frac{t}{a}\sin at$$

or
$$L^{-1}\left[\frac{p}{(p^2+a^2)}\right] = \frac{1}{2a}\,t\sin at.$$

Example 3. *Find* $L^{-1}\left[\dfrac{1}{p^2(p+1)^2}\right]$.

Solution. We know that

$$L\{e^{at}\} = \frac{1}{p-a}$$

$$\therefore \quad L\{e^{-at}\} = \frac{1}{p+a}$$

or
$$L^{-1}\left[\frac{1}{p+a}\right] = e^{-at}$$

or
$$L^{-1}\left[\frac{1}{p+1}\right] = e^{-t}$$

or
$$L^{-1}\left[\frac{d}{dp}\left(\frac{1}{p+1}\right)\right] = (-1)^1 t^1 e^{-t} = -t\,e^{-t}$$

or $$L^{-1}\left[-\frac{1}{(p+1)^2}\right] = -t\,e^{-t}$$

or $$L^{-1}\left[\frac{1}{(p+1)^2}\right] = t\,e^{-t}$$

Then by § 2.11, we get

$$L^{-1}\left[\frac{1}{p\,(p+1)^2}\right] = \int_0^t x\,e^{-x}\,dx$$

$$= \left[-x\,e^{-x} + \int e^{-x}\,dx\right]_0^t = \left[-e^{-x}\,(x+1)\right]_0^t$$

$$= 1 - e^{-t}\,(t+1)$$

$$\therefore \quad L^{-1}\left[\frac{1}{p^2\,(p+1)^2}\right] = \int_0^t [1 - e^{-x}\,(x+1)]\,dx$$

$$= \left[x + e^{-x}\,(x+1) + e^{-x}\right]_0^t$$

$$= t + e^{-t} + e^{-t}\,(t+1) - (1+1)$$

$$= t\,e^{-t} + 2e^{-t} + t - 2.$$

Example 4. *Prove that the inverse Laplace transform of*

$$\frac{1}{p^3\,(p^2+1)} \text{ is } \frac{t^2}{2} + \cos t - 1.$$

Solution. We know that

$$L^{-1}\left(\frac{a}{p^2+a^2}\right) = \sin at$$

and $$L^{-1}\left(\frac{f(p)}{p}\right) = \int_0^t F(u)\,du,$$

$$L\,\{F(t)\} = f(p)$$

$$\therefore \quad L^{-1}\left(\frac{1}{p^2+1}\right) = \sin t$$

and $$L^{-1}\left(\frac{1}{p\,(p^2+1)}\right) = \int_0^t \sin u\,du$$

$$= (-\cos u)_{u=0}^{t} = 1 - \cos t$$

$$L^{-1}\left(\frac{1}{p^2(p^2+1)}\right) = \int_0^t (1 - \cos u)\, du$$

$$= (u - \sin u)_0^t = t - \sin t$$

and $$L^{-1}\left[\frac{1}{p^3(p^2-1)}\right] = \int_0^t (u - \sin u)\, du$$

$$= \left[\frac{u^2}{2} + \cos u\right]_0^t$$

$$= \frac{t^2}{2} + \cos t - 1$$

Example 5. *Find* $L^{-1}\left[\frac{e^{-\sqrt{p}}}{p}\right]$ *and hence deduce that*

$$L^{-1}\left[\frac{e^{-\sqrt{p}}}{p}\right] = erfc\left(\frac{x}{2\sqrt{t}}\right).$$

Solution. Let $f(p) = e^{-\sqrt{p}} = L\{F(t)\}$

Then $$F(t) = L^{-1}\{e^{-\sqrt{p}}\}$$

$$= L^{-1}\left(1 - p^{1/2} + \frac{p}{2!} - \frac{p^{3/2}}{3!} + \frac{p^2}{4!} - \frac{p^{5/2}}{5!} + \ldots\right) \qquad \ldots\text{(i)}$$

Since $$L^{-1}\{p^{(n+1/2)}\} = L^{-1}\frac{1}{p^{-n-(3/2)+1}}$$

$$= \frac{t^{-n-3/2}}{\Gamma\left(-n-\frac{3}{2}\right)} = \frac{t^{-n-3/2}}{\Gamma\left(-n-\frac{1}{2}-1\right)}$$

$$= \frac{(-1)^{n+1}}{\sqrt{\pi}}\cdot\frac{1}{2}\cdot\frac{3}{2}\cdot\frac{5}{2}\cdots\left(\frac{2n+1}{2}\right)\cdot t^{-n-(3/2)}$$

and $L^{-1}\{p^n\} = 0$, if n is a positive integer.

From (i)

$$F(t) = \frac{(1)\,t^{3/2}}{\sqrt{n}}\cdot\frac{1}{2} - \frac{1}{3!}\frac{(-1)^2}{\sqrt{\pi}}\cdot\frac{1}{2}\cdot\frac{3}{2}t^{-5/2} - \frac{1}{5!}\frac{(-1)^3}{\sqrt{\pi}}\cdot\frac{1}{2}\cdot\frac{3}{2}\cdot\frac{5}{2}\cdot t^{-7/2} + \ldots$$

$$= \frac{1}{2t^{3/2}\sqrt{\pi}}\left[1 - \frac{1}{4t} + \frac{1}{2!}\left(\frac{1}{4t}\right)^2 - \frac{1}{3!}\left(\frac{1}{4t}\right)^3 + \dots\right]$$

or $$F(t) = \frac{1}{2t^{3/2}\sqrt{\pi}} e^{-1/4t} \qquad \dots\text{(ii)}$$

Since $$L^{-1}\left[\frac{f(p)}{p}\right] = \int_0^t F(x)\,dx$$

$$\therefore \quad L^{-1}\left[\frac{e^{-\sqrt{p}}}{p}\right] = \int_0^t \frac{1}{2\sqrt{\pi}\,x^{3/2}} e^{-1/4x}\,dx$$

$$= -\frac{2}{\sqrt{\pi}}\int_{\infty}^{1/(2\sqrt{t})} e^{-y^2}\,dy,$$

$$x = \frac{1}{4y^2},\ dx = -\frac{dy}{2y^3}$$

$$= \frac{2}{\sqrt{\pi}}\int_{1/(2\sqrt{t})}^{\infty} e^{-y^2}\,dy$$

$$= erfc\left(\frac{1}{2\sqrt{t}}\right)$$

$$\therefore \quad L^{-1}\left[\frac{e^{-\sqrt{p}}}{p}\right] = erfc\left(\frac{1}{2\sqrt{t}}\right)^*$$

We know that

$$erfc\,(t) = 1 - erf\,(t) = 1 - \frac{2}{\sqrt{\pi}}\int_0^t e^{-x^2}\,dx$$

$$= \frac{2}{\sqrt{\pi}}\int_t^{\infty} e^{-x^2}\,dx.$$

Deduction

From above, we have

$$L^{-1}\left[\frac{e^{-\sqrt{p}}}{p}\right] = erfc\left(\frac{1}{2\sqrt{t}}\right)$$

---

* $erfc\,(t) = \frac{2}{\sqrt{\pi}}\int_1^{\infty} e^{-y^2}\,dy$ is called complementary error function.

$$\therefore \quad L^{-1}\left[\frac{e^{-\sqrt{(x^2 p)}}}{x^2 p}\right] = \frac{1}{x^2}\, erfc\left[\frac{1}{2\sqrt{(t/x^2)}}\right]$$

by change of scale property

$$\text{or} \quad L^{-1}\left\{\frac{e^{-x\sqrt{p}}}{p}\right\} = erfc\left(\frac{x}{2\sqrt{t}}\right)$$

Example 6. *Find* $L^{-1}\left\{\dfrac{p+1}{(p^2+2p+2)^2}\right\}$

Solution. $L^{-1}\left\{\dfrac{p+1}{(p^2+2p+2)^2}\right\} = L^{-1}\left\{\dfrac{p+1}{[(p+1)^2+1]^2}\right\}$

$$= e^{-t} L^{-1}\left[\frac{p}{(p^2+1)^2}\right]$$

$$\therefore \quad L^{-1}\left[\frac{p+1}{(p^2+2p+2)^2}\right] = e^{-t} L^{-1}\left[\frac{p}{(p^2+1)^2}\right]^{-1} \quad \ldots(i)$$

Let $f(p) = \dfrac{1}{p^2+1} = L\{F(t)\}$

Then $F(t) = \sin t.$

$$f'(p) = -\frac{2p}{(p^2+1)^2}$$

$$\therefore \quad L^{-1}\{f'(p)\} = L^{-1}\left\{\frac{-2p}{(p^2+1)^2}\right\}$$

$$\text{or} \quad (-1)^1 t^1 L^{-1}\{f(p)\} = L^{-1}\left\{\frac{-2p}{(p^2+1)^2}\right\}$$

By putting this in (i), we get

$$L^{-1}\left\{\frac{p+1}{(p^2+2p+2)^2}\right\} = e^{-t}\cdot\frac{1}{2}\, t\sin t.$$

Example 7. *Show that*

$$L^{-1}\left(\frac{p^2}{p^4+4a^4}\right) = \frac{1}{2a}(\cosh at \sin at + \sinh at \cos at)$$

Solution. We have,

$$\frac{p^2}{p^4+4a^4} = \frac{p^2}{(p^2+2a^2)^2-(2ap)^2}$$

$$= \frac{p^2}{(p^2-2ap+2a^2)(p^2+2ap+2a^2)}$$

$$= \frac{1}{4a}\left(\frac{p}{p^2-2ap+2a^2} - \frac{p}{p^2+2ap+2a^2}\right)$$

$$= \frac{1}{4a}\left\{\frac{(p-a)+a}{(p-a)^2+a^2} + \frac{(p+a)-a}{(p+a)^2+a^2}\right\}$$

or $$L^{-1}\left(\frac{p^2}{p^4+4a^4}\right) = \frac{1}{4a}\left\{e^{at}L^{-1}\left(\frac{p+a}{p^2+a^2}\right) - e^{-at}L^{-1}\left(\frac{p-a}{p^2-a^2}\right)\right\}$$

$$= \frac{1}{4a}\left[e^{at}\left\{L^{-1}\left(\frac{p}{p^2+a^2}\right) + L^{-1}\left(\frac{a}{p^2+a^2}\right)\right\}\right.$$

$$\left. - e^{-at}\left\{L^{-1}\left(\frac{p}{p^2+a^2}\right) - L^{-1}\left(\frac{a}{p^2+a^2}\right)\right\}\right]$$

$$= \frac{1}{4a}\left[e^{at}(\cos at + \sin at) - e^{-at}(\cos at - \sin at)\right]$$

$$= \frac{1}{2a}\left\{\cos at\left(\frac{e^{at}-e^{-at}}{2}\right) + \sin at\left(\frac{e^{at}+e^{-at}}{2}\right)\right\}$$

$$= \frac{1}{2a}[\cos at \cdot \sinh at + \sin at \cdot \cosh at]$$

Example 8. *Use convolution theorem to find*

$$L^{-1}\left\{\frac{p}{(p^2+a^2)^2}\right\}.$$

Solution. We have $L^{-1}\left\{\frac{p}{p^2+a^2}\right\} = \cos at$ and

$$L^{-1}\left(\frac{1}{p^2+a^2}\right) = \frac{1}{a}\sin at$$

$\therefore$ By convolution theorem,

$$L^{-1}\left\{\frac{p}{(p^2+a^2)}\cdot\frac{1}{(p^2+a^2)}\right\}$$

$$=\int_0^t \cos au \cdot \frac{1}{a}\sin a(t-u)\,du$$

$$=\frac{1}{a}\int_0^t (\cos au \cdot \sin at \cdot \cos au - \cos au \cdot \cos at \sin au)\,du$$

$$=\frac{1}{a}\int_0^t \left[\sin at\left(\frac{1+\cos 2au}{2}\right)-\frac{1}{2}\cos at \cdot \sin 2au\right]du$$

$$=\frac{1}{a}\left[\frac{1}{2}\sin at\left(u+\frac{1}{2a}\sin 2au\right)_0^t+\frac{1}{4a}\cos at\left(\cos 2au\right)_0^t\right]$$

$$=\frac{1}{a}\left[\frac{1}{2}t\sin at+\frac{1}{4a}(\sin at \cdot \sin 2at+\cos at \cdot \cos 2at)-\frac{1}{4a}\cos at\right]$$

$$=\frac{1}{a}\left[\frac{1}{2}t\sin at+\frac{1}{4a}\cos(2at-at)-\frac{1}{4a}\cos at\right]$$

$$=\frac{1}{2a}t\sin at.$$

Example 9. *Apply convolution theorem to prove that*

$$B(m,n) = \int_0^1 x^{m-1}(1-x)^{n-1}\,dx$$

$$= \frac{\Gamma(m)\Gamma(n)}{\Gamma(m+n)},\ (m>0,\ n>0)$$

Hence deduce that $\int_0^{\pi/2} \sin^{2m-1}\theta \cos^{2n-1}\theta\, d\theta$

$$=\frac{1}{2}B(m,n)=\frac{\Gamma(m)\Gamma(n)}{2\Gamma(m+n)}.$$

Solution. Let $F(t)=\int_0^t x^{m-1}(t-x)^{n-1}\,dx$ ...(i)

where $F_1(x)=x^{m-1}, F_2(x)=x^{n-1}.$

Then $F(t) = \int_0^t F_1(x)F_2(t-x)\,dx$

$$= F_1(x)^* F_2(x)$$

Hence, by convolution theorem

$$L\{F(t)\} = [L\{F_1(t)\}^* F_2(t)\}]$$

$$= L(F_1) \cdot L(F_2) = L(t^{m-1}) \cdot L(t^{n-1})$$

$$= \frac{(m-1)!}{p^m} \cdot \frac{(n-1)!}{p^n} = \frac{\Gamma(m)\Gamma(n)}{p^{m+n}}$$

or $$F(t) = \Gamma(m)\Gamma(n) L^{-1}\left(\frac{1}{p^{m+n}}\right)$$

$$= \Gamma(m) \cdot \Gamma(n) \cdot \frac{t^{m+n-1}}{(m+n-1)!}$$

$$= \frac{\Gamma(m) \cdot \Gamma(n)}{\Gamma(m+n)} t^{m+n-1}$$

$\therefore$ $$F(1) = \frac{\Gamma(m)\Gamma(n)}{\Gamma(m+n)} \cdot 1^{m+n-1}$$

or $$F(1) = \frac{\Gamma(m) \cdot \Gamma(n)}{\Gamma(m+n)}. \qquad \text{...(ii)}$$

Putting $t = 1$ in (i), we get

$$F(1) = \int_0^1 x^{m-1}(1-x)^{n-1}\,dx = B(m, n)$$

Putting this in (ii), we get

$$B(m, n) = \frac{\Gamma(m)\Gamma(n)}{\Gamma(m+n)} = \int_0^1 x^{m-1}(1-x)^{n-1}\,dx \qquad \text{...(iii)}$$

Deduction. Putting $x = \sin^2\theta$, $dx = 2\sin\theta\cos\theta\,d\theta$

$\therefore$ $$B(m, n) = \int_0^{\pi/2} (\sin\theta)^{2m-2}(\cos\theta)^{2n-2} \cdot 2\sin\theta\cos\theta\,d\theta$$

or $$\frac{1}{2}B(m, n) = \int_0^{\pi/2} (\sin\theta)^{2m-1}(\cos\theta)^{2n-1}\,d\theta \qquad \text{...(iv)}$$

Combining (iii) and (iv), we get the required result.

Example 10. *Show that*

$$1^* 1^* 1^* \ldots {}^* 1 \text{ (n times)} = \frac{t^{n-1}}{(n-1)!}$$

Solution. By convolution theorem,

$$1^* 1 = \int_0^t 1.1\, dx = t$$

$$1^* 1^* 1 = t^* 1 = \int_0^t x \cdot 1\, dx = \frac{t^2}{2}$$

$$1^* 1^* 1^* 1 = \frac{t^2}{2} {}^* 1 = \int_0^t \frac{x^2}{2} \cdot 1\, dx = \frac{t^3}{6} = \frac{t^3}{3!}$$

Thus $\quad 1^* 1^* \ldots {}^* 1 \text{ (4 times)} = \dfrac{t^3}{3!}$

Generalising this, we get

$$1^* 1^* 1^* \ldots {}^* 1 \; (n \text{ times}) = \frac{t^{n-1}}{(n-1)!}.$$

EXERCISE 2(D)

1. Find the value of $L^{-1}\left[\dfrac{1}{(p-a)^3}\right]$.

2. Find inverse Laplace transform of

   (i) $\dfrac{1}{p\,(p^2+2p+2)}$, (ii) $\dfrac{2p^3+2p^2+4p+1}{(p^2+1)\,(p^2+p+1)}$.

3. Find inverse Laplace transform of

   (i) $\dfrac{3p+1}{(p-1)\,(p^2+1)}$. (ii) $\dfrac{3p^3-3p^2-40p+36}{(p^2-4)^2}$

4. Find $L^{-1}\left[\dfrac{1}{(p+1)\,(p^2+1)}\right]$.

5. (a) Find $L^{-1}\left[\dfrac{1}{(p^2+1)^2}\right]$ (b) Find $L^{-1}\left[\dfrac{1}{p\,(p^2+9)}\right]$.

6. Find $L^{-1}\left[\dfrac{a^2}{p\,(p+a)^2}\right]$

7. Find $L^{-1}\left[\dfrac{1}{p}\log\dfrac{p+2}{p+1}\right]$

8. Prove that $L^{-1}\left[\dfrac{4p+5}{(p-1)^2(p+2)}\right]$

$$= 3t\,e^t + \frac{1}{3}e^t - \frac{1}{3}e^{-2t}.$$

9. By using convolution theorem, find the value of

$$L^{-1}\left[\frac{1}{(p+1)(p^2+1)}\right].$$

10. Use convolution theorem to find

(i) $L^{-1}\left[\dfrac{p^2}{(p^2+4)^2}\right]$

(ii) $L^{-1}\left(\dfrac{p}{(p^2+4)^3}\right)$

(iii) $L^{-1}\left[\dfrac{1}{(p^2+4)(p+2)}\right]$

11. Find $L^{-1}\left(\dfrac{1}{p^2(p+1)^2}\right)$

12. Find the inverse Laplace transforms of

$$\frac{1}{p^2(p^2-a^2)},$$

by using the convolution theorem.

ANSWERS

1. $\dfrac{t^2}{2}e^{at}$.

2. (i) $\dfrac{1}{2}[1-(\sin t+\cos t)\,e^{-t}]$

(ii) $\cos t + 2\sin t + e^{-t/2}\left[\cos\left(\dfrac{t\sqrt{3}}{2}\right) - \left(\dfrac{\sqrt{3}}{2}\right)\sin\left(\dfrac{t\sqrt{3}}{2}\right)\right]$

3. (i) $2e^t - 2\cos t + \sin t$; (ii) $(5t+3)\,e^{-2t} - 2t\,e^{2t}$

4. $\dfrac{1}{2}[e^{-t} - \cos t + \sin t]$

5. (a) $\dfrac{1}{2}[-t\cos t + \sin t]$ (b) $\dfrac{1}{9}(1-\cos 3t)$

6. $[1 - e^{-at}(at + 1)]$ 7. $\int_0^t \left(\frac{e^{-x} - e^{-2x}}{x}\right) dx.$

9. $\frac{1}{2}[e^{-t} + \sin t - \cos t]$ 10. (i) $\frac{1}{2}\left[t \cos 2t + \frac{1}{2}\sin 2t\right]$

(ii) $\frac{t}{64}[\sin 2t - 2t \cos 2t]$; (ii) $\frac{1}{8}[(\sin 2t - \cos 2t) + e^{-2t}]$

11. $(t + 2)e^{-t} + t - 2.$ 12. $\frac{1}{a^3}[-at \sinh at]$.

2.17 THE HEAVISIDE EXPANSION FORMULA

Theorem. *If $F(p)$ and $G(p)$ are polynomials in p*, the degree of $F(p)$ being less than that of $G(p)$, and if

$$G(\mathrm{p}) = (p - \alpha_1)(p - \alpha_2)\ldots(p - \alpha_n),$$

where $\alpha_1, \alpha_2, \ldots \alpha_n$ are distinct constants real or complex, then

$$L^{-1}\left[\frac{F(p)}{G(p)}\right] = \sum_{r=1}^{n} \frac{F(\alpha_r)}{G'(\alpha_r)} e^{\alpha_r t}$$

Proof. By the method of partial fractions let

$$\frac{F(p)}{G(p)} = \frac{A_1}{p - \alpha_1} + \frac{A_2}{p - \alpha_2} + \ldots + \frac{A_r}{p - \alpha_r} + \ldots + \frac{A_n}{p - \alpha_n}$$

Multiplying both the sides by $(p - \alpha_r)$ and taking the limit $p \to \alpha_r$, we obtain

$$A_r = \lim_{p \to \alpha_r} \frac{F(p)(p - \alpha_r)}{G(p)}$$

$$= \lim_{p \to \alpha_r} F(p) \cdot \lim_{p \to \alpha_r} \frac{p - \alpha_r}{G(p)}$$

$$= \lim_{p \to \alpha_r} F(p). \lim_{p \to \alpha_r} \frac{1}{G'(p)} \qquad \text{[by L' Hospital's rule]}$$

$$= \frac{F(\alpha_r)}{G'(\alpha_r)}$$

$$\therefore \quad \frac{F(p)}{G(p)} = \frac{F(\alpha_1)}{G'(\alpha_1)} \cdot \frac{1}{p - \alpha_1} + \frac{F(\alpha_2)}{G'(\alpha_2)} \cdot \frac{1}{p - \alpha_2} + \ldots + \frac{F(\alpha_r)}{G'(\alpha_r)} \cdot \frac{1}{p - \alpha_r}$$

$$+ \ldots + \frac{F(\alpha_n)}{G'(\alpha_n)} \frac{1}{p - \alpha_n}$$

$$\therefore \quad L^{-1}\left[\frac{F(p)}{G(p)}\right] = \frac{F(\alpha_1)}{G'(\alpha_1)} e^{\alpha_1 t} + \frac{F(\alpha_2)}{G'(\alpha_2)} e^{\alpha_2 t} + \ldots + \frac{F(\alpha_r)}{G'(\alpha_r)} e^{\alpha_r t}$$

$$+ \ldots + \frac{F(\alpha_n)}{G'(\alpha_n)} e^{\alpha_n t}$$

$$= \sum_{r=1}^{n} \frac{F(\alpha_r)}{G'(\alpha_r)} e^{\alpha_r t}.$$

ILLUSTRATIVE EXAMPLES

Example 1. *Using Heaviside's expansion formula, find*

$$L^{-1}\left(\frac{2p^2 + 5p - 4}{p^3 + p^2 - 2p}\right)$$

Solution. Let $F(p) = 2p^2 + 5p - 4,$

$$G(p) = p^3 + p^2 - 2p = p(p^2 + p - 2)$$

$$= p(p+2)(p-1)$$

and $\quad G'(p) = 3p^2 + 2p - 2.$

Evidently, we have $\alpha_1 = 0, \alpha_2 = \pm 1, \alpha_3 = -2.$

By Heavi side's expansion formula

$$L^{-1}\left[\frac{F(p)}{G(p)}\right] = \sum_{r=1}^{n} \frac{F(\alpha_r)}{G'(\alpha_r)} e^{\alpha_r t}$$

$$= \frac{F(\alpha_1)}{G'(\alpha_1)} e^{\alpha_1 t} + \frac{F(\alpha_2)}{G'(\alpha_2)} e^{\alpha_2 t} + \frac{F(\alpha_3)}{G'(\alpha_3)} e^{a_3 t}$$

$$= \frac{F(0)}{G'(0)} e^{0 \cdot t} + \frac{F(1)}{G'(1)} e^{1 \cdot t} + \frac{F(-2)}{G'(-2)} e^{-2t}$$

$$= \frac{-4}{-2} + \frac{3}{3} e^{t} + \frac{(-6)}{6} e^{-2t}$$

$$= 2 + e^{t} - e^{2t}.$$

Example 2. *Applying Heaviside's expansion formula, prove that*

$$L^{-1}\left(\frac{1}{p^3+1}\right)=\frac{1}{3}\left[e^{-t}-e^{t/2}\left(\cos\frac{\sqrt{3}t}{2}-\sqrt{3}\sin\sqrt{3}\frac{t}{2}\right)\right]$$

Solution. Here, $F(p) = 1$ and $G(p) = p^3 + 1$

$$= (p+1)(p^2 - p + 1),$$

$$G'(p) = 3p^2$$

Clearly, $\alpha_1 = -1,\ \alpha_2 = \frac{1}{2} + \frac{\sqrt{3}}{2}i,\ \alpha_3 = \frac{1}{2} - \frac{\sqrt{3}}{2}i.$

$\therefore$ By the Heaviside's expansion formula, we get

$$L^{-1}\left(\frac{1}{p^3+1}\right) = \frac{F(-1)}{G'(-1)}e^{-t} + \frac{F\left(\frac{1+\sqrt{3}i}{2}\right)}{G'\left(\frac{1+\sqrt{3}i}{2}\right)}e^{\left(\frac{1+\sqrt{3}i}{2}\right)t} + \frac{F\left(\frac{1-\sqrt{3}i}{2}\right)}{G'\left(\frac{1-\sqrt{3}i}{2}\right)}e^{\left(\frac{1-\sqrt{3}i}{2}\right)t}$$

$$= \frac{1}{3}e^{-t} + \frac{1}{3\left(\frac{1+\sqrt{3}i}{2}\right)^2}e^{\left(\frac{1+\sqrt{3}i}{2}\right)t} + \frac{1}{3\left(\frac{1-\sqrt{3}i}{2}\right)^2}e^{\left(\frac{1-\sqrt{3}i}{2}\right)t}$$

$$= \frac{1}{3}e^{-t} + \frac{2(\sqrt{3}i+1)}{3(\sqrt{3}i-1)(\sqrt{3}i+1)}e^{\left(\frac{1+\sqrt{3}i}{2}\right)t} + \frac{2(\sqrt{3}i-1)}{-3(\sqrt{3}i+1)(\sqrt{3}i-1)}e^{\left(\frac{1-\sqrt{3}i}{2}\right)t}$$

$$= \frac{1}{3}e^{-t} - \frac{1}{6}e^{t/2}\left[(\sqrt{3}i+1)e^{\sqrt{3}i\,t/2} - (\sqrt{3}i-1)e^{-\sqrt{3}i\,t/2}\right]$$

$$= \frac{1}{3}e^{-t} - \frac{1}{6}e^{t/2}\left[\sqrt{3}i\left(e^{\sqrt{3}i\,t/2} - e^{\sqrt{3}i\,t/2}\right) + \left(e^{\sqrt{3}i\,t/2} + e^{-\sqrt{3}i\,t/2}\right)\right]$$

$$= \frac{1}{3}\left[e^{-t} - e^{t/2}\left(-\sqrt{3}\sin\frac{\sqrt{3}t}{2} + \cos\sqrt{3}\,t/2\right)\right]$$

$$= \frac{1}{3}\left[e^{-t} - e^{t/2}\left(\cos\frac{\sqrt{3}t}{2} - \sqrt{3}\sin\frac{\sqrt{3}t}{2}\right)\right].$$

EXERCISE 2(E)

Using Heaviside's expansion formula find:

1. $L^{-1}\left[\dfrac{p^2-6}{p^3+4p^2+3p}\right]$

2. $L^{-1}\left[\dfrac{3p+1}{(p-1)(p^2+1)}\right]$

3. $L^{-1}\left[\dfrac{2p^2-6p+5}{p^3-6p^2+11p-6}\right]$

4. $L^{-1}\left[\dfrac{p+5}{(p+1)(p^2+1)}\right]$

5. $L^{-1}\left[\dfrac{19p+37}{(p+1)(p-2)(p+3)}\right]$.

ANSWERS

1. $-2+\dfrac{5}{2}e^{-t}+\dfrac{1}{2}e^{-3t}$

2. $2e^{t}+\sin t-2\cos t$

3. $\dfrac{1}{2}e^{t}-e^{2t}+\dfrac{5}{2}e^{3t}$

4. $2e^{-t}+3\sin t-2\cos t$

5. $5e^{2t}-3e^{-t}-2e^{-3t}$.

MISCELLANEOUS ILLUSTRATIVE EXAMPLES

Example 1. *Establish the reciprocity between the following pair of Laplace transforms:*

$$f(t)=\frac{e^{at}-1}{a},\quad F(p)=\frac{1}{p(p-a)}.$$

Solution. We have

$$\begin{aligned}
L\{f(t)\} &= L\left(\frac{e^{at}-1}{a}\right)\\
&= \frac{1}{a}[L\{e^{at}\}-L\{1\}]\\
&= \frac{1}{a}\left[\frac{1}{p-a}-\frac{1}{p}\right]\\
&= \frac{1}{a}\cdot\frac{a}{p(p-a)}=\frac{1}{p(p-a)}\\
&= F(p)
\end{aligned}$$

$\therefore \qquad L\{f(t)\} = F(p)$

This is required relation between $f(t)$ and $F(p)$.

Example 2. *Show that* $\int_0^\infty \cos x^2 \, dx = \frac{1}{2}\sqrt{\left(\frac{\pi}{2}\right)}$.

Solution. Let $F(t) = \int_0^\infty \cos(t x^2)\, dx$

Then
$$L\{F(t)\} = \int_0^\infty e^{-pt} F(t)\, dt$$
$$= \int_0^\infty e^{-pt}\left[\int_0^\infty \cos(t x^2)\, dx\right] dt$$
$$= \int_0^\infty \left[\int_0^\infty e^{-pt} \cos(t x^2)\, dt\, dx\right]$$
$$= \int_0^\infty L\{\cos t x^2\}\, dx$$
$$= \int_0^\infty \frac{p}{p^2 + x^4}\, dx \qquad \left[\because L\{\cos at\} = \frac{p}{p^2 + a^2}\right]$$

Let $x = \sqrt{(p \tan \theta)}$, so that $dx = \dfrac{p \sec^2 \theta \, d\theta}{2\sqrt{(p \tan \theta)}}$

then
$$L\{F(t)\} = \int_0^{\pi/2} \frac{1}{2\sqrt{(p \tan \theta)}}\, d\theta$$
$$= \frac{1}{2\sqrt{(p)}} \int_0^{\pi/2} (\sin \theta)^{-1/2} (\cos \theta)^{1/2}\, d\theta$$
$$= \frac{1}{2\sqrt{(p)}} \cdot \frac{\Gamma\left(\frac{1}{4}\right)\Gamma\left(\frac{3}{4}\right)}{2\Gamma(1)} = \frac{\Gamma\left(\frac{1}{4}\right)\left(1 - \frac{1}{4}\right)}{4\sqrt{(p)}}$$
$$= \frac{1}{4\sqrt{(p)}} \cdot \frac{\pi}{\sin(\pi/4)} \qquad \left[\because \Gamma(n)\Gamma(1-n) = \frac{\pi}{\sin n\pi},\ 0 < n < 1\right]$$
$$= \frac{\pi}{2\sqrt{(2)}} \cdot \frac{1}{\sqrt{(p)}}$$

$$\therefore \qquad F(t) = \frac{\pi}{2\sqrt{2}} L^{-1}\left(\frac{1}{\sqrt{p}}\right) = \frac{\pi}{2\sqrt{2}} \cdot \frac{1}{\sqrt{\pi t}}$$

$$= \frac{1}{2}\left(\frac{\pi}{2t}\right)^{1/2}$$

or $$\int_0^\infty \cos(t x^2)\, dx = \frac{1}{2}\left(\frac{\pi}{2t}\right)^{1/2}.$$

Putting $t = 1$, we get

$$\int_0^\infty \cos x^2\, dx = \frac{1}{2}\sqrt{\left(\frac{\pi}{2}\right)}.$$

Example 3. *Prove that* $L^{-1}\left[\frac{f(p)}{p^2}\right] = \int_0^t dv \int_0^v F(u)\, du.$

Solution. We know that

$$L^{-1}\left(\frac{f(p)}{p}\right) = \int_0^t F(u)\, du = G(t) \quad \text{say} \qquad \ldots\text{(i)}$$

Then $$L\{G(t)\} = g(p) = \frac{f(p)}{p} \qquad \ldots\text{(ii)}$$

$$\therefore \qquad G(t) = \int_0^t F(u)\, du \qquad \ldots\text{(iii)}$$

By equation (i),

$$L^{-1}\left[\frac{g(p)}{p}\right] = \int_0^t G(v)\, dv$$

$$= \int_0^t dv \left[\int_0^v F(u)\, du\right] \qquad \text{by (iii)}$$

Using (ii), we get

$$L^{-1}\left(\frac{f(p)}{p^2}\right) = \int_0^t dv \int_0^v F(u)\, du.$$

Example 4. *Show that* $L^{-1}\left(\tan^{-1}\frac{1}{p}\right) = \frac{\sin t}{t}.$

Solution. Prove as in Example 4 before exercise 2 (D), that

$$L\left(\frac{\sin t}{t}\right) = \cot^{-1} p = \tan^{-1}\left(\frac{1}{p}\right)$$

$$\therefore \quad \frac{\sin t}{t} = L^{-1}\left[\tan^{-1}\left(\frac{1}{p}\right)\right]$$

Example 5. *Find* $L^{-1}\left[\log\left(1+\frac{1}{p^2}\right)\right]$ *and hence deduce the value of*

$$L^{-1}\left[\frac{1}{p}\log\left(1+\frac{1}{p^2}\right)\right].$$

Solution. Let $f(p) = \log\left(1+\frac{1}{p^2}\right) = L\{F(t)\}$.

Then $$f'(p) = \frac{-2/p^3}{\left(1+\frac{1}{p^2}\right)} = -\frac{2}{p(p^2+1)} \qquad \ldots\text{(i)}$$

Now, $$L^{-1}\left(\frac{1}{p^2+1}\right) = \sin t$$

$$\therefore \quad L^{-1}\left[\frac{1}{p(p^2+1)}\right] = \int_0^t \sin x\, dx$$

$$= [-\cos x]_0^t = 1 - \cos t$$

From (i), $$L^{-1}\{f'(p)\} = -2L^{-1}\left[\frac{1}{p(p^2+1)}\right]$$

$$= -2(1-\cos t).$$

But $L^{-1}\{f'(p)\} = (-1)^1 t^1 F(t)$

Hence, $-t\,F(t) = -2(1-\cos t)$

or $$F(t) = \frac{2(1-\cos t)}{t}.$$

Deduction. From above, we have

$$L^{-1}\left[\log\left(1+\frac{1}{p^2}\right)\right] = \frac{2(1-\cos t)}{t}$$

$$\therefore \quad L^{-1}\left[\frac{1}{p}\log\left(1+\frac{1}{p^2}\right)\right]$$

$$= L^{-1}\left[\frac{f(p)}{p}\right] = \int_0^t F(x)\,dx$$

$$= \int_0^t \frac{2(1-\cos x)}{x}\,dx.$$

Example 6. *If* $L\{f(t)\} = f(p)$ *and* $a > 0$*, then show that* $L^{-1}\{f(ap+b)\}$

$$= \frac{1}{a}e^{-bt/a} f(t/a).$$

Solution. We have

$$L\{f(t)\} = f(p)$$

or
$$\int_0^\infty e^{-pt} f(t)\,dt = f(p)$$

Replacing p by $ap + b$, we get

$$\int_0^\infty e^{-(ap+b)t} f(t)\,dt = f(ap+b)$$

or
$$f(ap+b) = \int_0^\infty e^{-(ap+b)t} f(t)\,dt$$

$$= \int_0^\infty e^{-(ap+b)u/a} f\left(\frac{u}{a}\right)\frac{du}{a},$$

where $at = u$

$$= \int_0^\infty e^{-pu} \cdot e^{-bu/a} f\left(\frac{u}{a}\right)\frac{du}{a}$$

$$= \int_0^\infty e^{-pt}\left[\frac{e^{-bt/a}}{a} f\left(\frac{t}{a}\right)\right] dt \qquad \left[\because \int_0^b f(x)\,dx = \int_0^b f(t)\,dt\right]$$

$$= L\left[\frac{e^{-bt/a}}{a} f\left(\frac{t}{a}\right)\right]$$

or
$$L^{-1}\{f(ap+b)\} = \frac{1}{a}e^{-bt/a} f\left(\frac{t}{a}\right).$$

Example 7. *Evaluate* $\int_0^t J_0(u)\,J_0(t-u)\,du.$

Solution. Let $L\{F(t)\} = L\{J_0(t)\} = \dfrac{1}{(p^2+1)^{1/2}} = f(p)$

Then $\int_0^t F(u)\,F(t-u)\,du = L^{-1}\{f(p)\cdot f(p)\}$

or $\int_0^t J_0(u)\,J_0(t-u)\,du = L^{-1}\left[\dfrac{1}{(p^2+1)^{1/2}(p^2+1)^{1/2}}\right]$

$$= L^{-1}\left(\frac{1}{(p^2+1)}\right) = \sin t.$$

Example 8. *Find* $L^{-1}\left(\dfrac{e^{-1/p}}{p}\right)$.

Solution. We have

$$\frac{e^{-1/p}}{p} = \frac{1}{p}\left[1 - \frac{1}{p} + \frac{1}{p^2\cdot 2!} - \frac{1}{p^3\cdot 3!} + \ldots\right]$$

$$= \frac{1}{p} - \frac{1}{p^2} + \frac{1}{2!\,p^3} - \frac{1}{3!\,p^4} + \ldots$$

Taking inverse Laplace transform of both sides, we get

$$L^{-1}\left(\frac{e^{-1/p}}{p}\right) = 1 - t + \frac{1}{2!}\cdot\frac{t^2}{2!} - \frac{1}{3!}\cdot\frac{t^3}{3!} + \ldots$$

$$= 1 - t + \frac{t^2}{2^2} - \frac{t^3}{(3!)^2} + \ldots$$

$$= 1 - \frac{(2\sqrt{t})^2}{2^2} + \frac{(2\sqrt{t})^4}{2^2\cdot 4^2} - \frac{(2\sqrt{t})^6}{2^2\cdot 4^2\cdot 6^2} + \ldots$$

$$= J_0(2\sqrt{5}).$$

Example 9. *Prove that*

$$L^{-1}\left(\tan^{-1}\frac{2}{p^2}\right) = \frac{2}{t}\sin t\cdot\sinh t.$$

Solution. Let $f(p) = \tan^{-1}\dfrac{2}{p^2}$.

Then $$f'(p) = -\left(\frac{4}{p^3}\right)\cdot\frac{1}{1+\dfrac{4}{p^4}} + \frac{-4p}{p^4+4}$$

$$\therefore \quad L^{-1}\{f'(p)\} = -4L^{-1}\left(\frac{p}{p^4+4}\right) \qquad \ldots\text{(i)}$$

We have

$$\frac{p}{p^4+4} = \frac{p}{(p^2+2)^2-(2p^2)^2} = \frac{p}{(p^2-2p+2)(p^2+2p+2)}$$

$$= \frac{1}{4}\left[\frac{1}{p^2-2p+2} - \frac{1}{p^2+2p+2}\right]$$

$$= \frac{1}{4}\left[\frac{1}{(p-1)^2+1} - \frac{1}{(p+1)^2+1}\right]$$

$$\therefore \quad 4L^{-1}\left(\frac{p}{p^4+4}\right) = L^{-1}\left[\frac{1}{(p-1)^2+1}\right] - L^{-1}\left[\frac{1}{(p+1)^2+1}\right]$$

$$= e^t L^{-1}\left(\frac{1}{p^2+1}\right) - e^{-t}L^{-1}\left(\frac{1}{p^2+1}\right)$$

$$= (e^t - e^{-t})\sin t = 2\sin t \sinh t.$$

Hence (i) becomes

$$L^{-1}\{f'(p)\} = -2\sin t\cdot\sinh t$$

But $$L^{-1}\{f'(p)\} = (-1)^1\, t\, L^{-1}\{f(p)\}$$

or $$-2\sin t\cdot\sinh t = -t\,L^{-1}\{f(p)\}$$

or $$L^{-1}\{f(p)\} = L^{-1}\left(\tan^{-1}\frac{2}{p^2}\right)$$

$$= \frac{2}{t}\sin t\cdot\sinh t.$$

Example 10. *Prove that* $\int_0^\infty e^{-x^2}\,dx = \dfrac{\sqrt{\pi}}{2}$.

Solution. Let $F(t) = \int_0^\infty e^{-tx^2}\,dx$.

Then $$L\{F(t)\} = \int_0^\infty e^{-pt}F(t)\,dt$$

$$= \int_0^\infty e^{-pt} \left[\int_0^\infty e^{-tx^2}\, dx \right] dt$$

$$= \int_0^\infty \left[\int_0^\infty e^{-pt} \cdot e^{-tx^2}\, dt \right] dx$$

$$= \int_0^\infty L\, \{e^{-tx^2}\}\, dx$$

$$= \int_0^\infty \frac{dx}{p + x^2} \qquad \left[\because\ L\,\{e^{at}\} = \frac{1}{p-a} \right]$$

$$= \left[\frac{1}{\sqrt{p}} \tan^{-1} \frac{x}{\sqrt{p}} \right]_0^\infty = \frac{\pi}{2\sqrt{p}}$$

$$\therefore \qquad F(t) = \frac{\pi}{2} L^{-1} \left(\frac{1}{\sqrt{p}} \right)$$

$$= \frac{\pi}{2} \cdot \frac{1}{\sqrt{(\pi\, t)}} = \frac{1}{2} \left(\frac{\pi}{t} \right)^{1/2}$$

or

$$\int_0^\infty e^{-tx^2}\, dx = \frac{1}{2} \left(\frac{\pi}{t} \right)^{1/2}$$

Putting $t = 1$, we get

$$\int_0^\infty e^{-x^2}\, dx = \frac{1}{2} \sqrt{\pi}.$$

3

Application of Laplace Transform to Solution of Differential Equations

3.1 SOLUTION OF ORDINARY DIFFERENTIAL EQUATIONS WITH CONSTANT COEFFICIENTS

The Laplace transform is very useful in solving ordinary linear differential equations with constant coefficients.

Let us consider a linear differential equation with constant coefficients

$$\frac{d^n y}{dt^n} + A_1 \frac{d^{n-1} y}{dt^{n-1}} + \ldots + A_{n-1} \frac{dy}{dt} + A_n t = F(t) \qquad \ldots \text{(i)}$$

where $F(t)$ is a function of the independent variable t.

Let $\quad y(0) = c_1, \quad y'(0) = c_2, \ldots y^{n-1}(0) = c_{n-1} \qquad \ldots$(ii)

be the given initial or boundary conditions where $c_1, c_2, \ldots, c_{n-1}$ are constants. On taking the Laplace transform of both sides of equation (i) and using conditions (ii) we obtain an algebraic equation known as *subsidiary equation* from which $y(p) = L\{y(t)\}$ is determined. The required solution is then obtained by finding the inverse Laplace transform of $y(p)$.

ILLUSTRATIVE EXAMPLES

Example 1. *Solve* $\frac{d^2y}{dt^2} + y = 0$ *under the conditions that* $y = 1, \frac{dy}{dt} = 0$ *when* $t = 0$.

Solution. The given differential equation is

$$\frac{d^2y}{dt^2} + y = 0$$

Taking the Laplace transform of both sides, we get

$$L\{y''\} + L\{y\} = 0$$

or $$p^2 L\{y\} - py(0) - y'(0) + L\{y\} = 0$$

or $$p^2 L\{y\} - p \cdot 1 - 0\, L\{y\} = 0$$

[from given conditions]

or $$L[y] = \frac{p}{p^2+1}$$

$\therefore$ $$y = L^{-1}\left(\frac{p}{p^2+1}\right) = \cos t$$

which is the required solution.

Example 2. *Solve* $(D^2 + m^2)\,x = a\cos nt,\ t > 0,\ x,\ Dx$ *equal to* x_0 *and* x_1 *when* $t = 0,\ n \neq m$.

Solution. Taking Laplace transform of both the sides of given equation, we get

$$L\{x''\} + m^2 L\{x\} = a\,L\{\cos nt\}$$

or $$p^2 L\{x\} - px(0) - x'(0) + m^2 L\{x\} = \frac{ap}{p^2+n^2}$$

or $$(p^2+m^2)\,L\{x\} = px_0 + x_1 + \frac{ap}{p^2+n^2}$$

or $$L\{x\} = x_0 \cdot \frac{p}{p^2+m^2} + x_1 \cdot \frac{1}{p^2+m^2} + \frac{ap}{(p^2+m^2)(p^2+n^2)}$$

$$= x_0 \cdot \frac{p}{p^2+m^2} + x_1 \cdot \frac{1}{p^2+m^2} + \frac{a}{(m^2-n^2)}\left(\frac{p}{p^2+n^2} - \frac{p}{p+m^2}\right)$$

Taking the inverse transform, we get

$$x = x_0 \cdot L^{-1}\left(\frac{p}{p^2+m^2}\right) + x_1 \cdot L^{-1}\left(\frac{1}{p^2+m^2}\right)$$

$$+ \frac{a}{(m^2-n^2)}\left[L^{-1}\left(\frac{p}{p^2+n^2}\right) - L^{-1}\left(\frac{p}{p^2+m^2}\right)\right]$$

$$= x_0 \cos mt + \frac{x_1}{m}\sin mt + \frac{a}{(m^2-n^2)}(\cos nt - \cos mt).$$

This is the required solution.

Example 3. *Solve* $(D^2 + 4D + 4)\, x = \sin \omega t,\ t > 0$ *with* x_0 *and* x_1 *for values of* x *and* Dx *when* $t = 0$.

Solution. Taking the Laplace transform of both sides of the given equation, we get

$$L\{D^2 x\} + 4L\{Dx\} + 4L\{x\} = L\{\sin \omega t\}$$

or
$$p^2 L\{x\} - px(0) - x'(0) + 4[pL\{x\} - x(0)] + 4 \cdot L\{x\} = \frac{\omega}{p^2 + \omega^2}$$

or
$$(p^2 + 4p + 4)\, L\{x\} = px_0 + x_1 + 4x_0 + \frac{\omega}{p^2 + \omega^2}$$

or
$$L\{x\} = \frac{px_0}{(p+2)^2} + \frac{(x_1 + 4x_0)}{(p+2)^2} + \frac{\omega}{(p+2)^2 (p^2 + \omega^2)}$$

$$\therefore\quad x = x_0 L^{-1}\left(\frac{(p+2) - 2}{(p+2)^2}\right) + (x_1 + 4x_0)\, L^{-1}\left(\frac{1}{(p+2)^2}\right)$$

$$+ w\, L^{-1}\left\{\frac{1}{(4 + \omega^2)(p+2)^2} + \frac{4}{(4 + \omega^2)^2 (p+2)} + \frac{-4p + 4 - \omega^2}{(4 + \omega^2)^2 (p^2 + \omega^2)}\right]$$

$$= x_0 e^{-2t} L^{-1}\left\{\frac{p-2}{p^2}\right\} + (x_1 + 4x_0)$$

$$e^{-2t} L^{-1}\left\{\frac{1}{p^2}\right\} + \frac{\omega e^{-2t}}{(4 + \omega^2)} L^{-1}\left\{\frac{1}{p^2}\right\} + \frac{4\omega e^{-2t}}{(4 + \omega^2)^2} L^{-1}\left\{\frac{1}{p}\right\} - \frac{4\omega}{(4 + \omega^2)^2}$$

$$L^{-1}\left\{\frac{p}{p^2 + \omega^2}\right\} + \frac{(4 - \omega^2)\,\omega}{(4 + \omega^2)^2} L^{-1}\left\{\frac{1}{p^2 + \omega^2}\right\}$$

$$= e^{-2t}\left[x_0 (1 - 2t) + (x_1 + 4x_0)\, t + \frac{\omega}{(4 + \omega^2)} t + \frac{4\omega}{(4 + \omega^2)^2}\right]$$

$$- \frac{4\omega}{(4 + \omega^2)^2} \cos \omega t + \frac{4 - \omega^2}{(4 + \omega^2)^2} \sin \omega t$$

This is the required solution.

Example 4. *Solve* $(D^2 + 9)\, y = \cos 2t$, *if* $y(0) = 1,\ y\left(\frac{\pi}{2}\right) = -1$.

Solution. Taking the Laplace transform for both sides of the given equation, we have

$$L\{y''\} + 9L\{y\} = L\{\cos 2t\}$$

or $$p^2 L\{y\} - p\,y(0) - y'(0) + 9L\{y\} = \frac{p}{p^2+4}$$

or $$(p^2+9)\,L\{y\} - p - A = \frac{p}{p^2+4}$$

where $y'(0) = A$.

or $$L\{y\} = \frac{p+A}{p^2+9} + \frac{p}{(p^2+9)(p^2+4)}$$

$$= \frac{p}{p^2+9} + \frac{A}{p^2+9} + \frac{p}{5(p^2+4)} - \frac{p}{5(p^2+9)}$$

$$\therefore \quad y = L^{-1}\left\{\frac{p}{p^2+9}\right\} + A\,L^{-1}\left\{\frac{1}{p^2+9}\right\} + \frac{1}{5}L^{-1}\left\{\frac{p}{p^2+4}\right\} - \frac{1}{5}L^{-1}\left\{\frac{p}{p^2+9}\right\}$$

$$= \cos 3t + \frac{A}{3}\sin 3t + \frac{1}{5}\cos 2t - \frac{1}{5}\cos 3t$$

$$= \frac{4}{5}\cos 3t + \frac{A}{3}\sin 3t + \frac{1}{5}\cos 2t.$$

Now, it is given that $y\left(\frac{\pi}{2}\right) = -1$

$$\therefore \quad -1 = \frac{4}{5}\cos\frac{3\pi}{2} + \frac{A}{3}\sin\frac{3\pi}{2} + \frac{1}{5}\cos\pi$$

or $$-1 = -\frac{A}{3} - \frac{1}{5}$$

or $$A = \frac{12}{5}.$$

Hence the required solution will be

$$y = \frac{4}{5}\cos 3t + \frac{4}{5}\sin 3t + \frac{1}{5}\cos 2t.$$

Example 5. *Solve* $(D^2 + 1)\,y = t\cos 2t$, $y = 0$, $\frac{dy}{dt} = 0$ *when* $t = 0$.

Solution. Taking the Laplace transform of the both sides of the given equation, we get

$$L[y''] + L[y] = L[t\cos 2t]$$

or $$p^2 L[y] - p\,y(0) - y'(0) + L[y] = -\frac{d}{dp}[L\{\cos 2t\}].$$

or $$(p^2+1)\,L\,[y] = -\frac{d}{dp}\left(\frac{p}{p^2+4}\right) = -\frac{1}{p^2+4} + \frac{2p^2}{(p^2+4)^2}$$

or $$L\,[y] = \frac{p^2-4}{(p^2+1)(p^2+4)^2}$$

$$= -\frac{5}{9(p^2+1)} + \frac{5}{9(p^2+4)} + \frac{8}{3(p^2+4)^2}$$

$\therefore$ $$y = -\frac{5}{9}L^{-1}\left\{\frac{1}{p^2+1}\right\} + \frac{5}{9}L^{-1}\left\{\frac{1}{p^2+4}\right\} + \frac{8}{3}L^{-1}\left\{\frac{1}{(p^2+4)^2}\right\}$$

$$= -\frac{5}{9}\sin t + \frac{5}{18}\sin 2t + \frac{8}{3}\int_0^t \frac{1}{2}\sin 2x\,\frac{1}{2}\sin 2(t-x)\,dx$$

by the convolution theorem, since

$$L^{-1}\left\{\frac{1}{p^2+4}\right\} = \frac{1}{2}\sin 2t$$

$$= -\frac{5}{9}\sin t + \frac{5}{18}\sin 2t + \frac{1}{3}\int_0^t [\cos 2(t-2x) - \cos 2t]\,dx$$

$$= -\frac{5}{9}\sin t + \frac{5}{18}\sin 2t + \frac{1}{3}\left[-\frac{1}{4}\sin 2(t-2x) - x\cos 2t\right]_0^t$$

$$= -\frac{5}{9}\sin t + \frac{5}{18}\sin 2t + \frac{1}{12}\sin 2t - \frac{t}{3}\cos 2t + \frac{1}{12}\sin 2t$$

$\therefore$ $$y = -\frac{5}{9}\sin t + \frac{4}{9}\sin 2t - \frac{t}{3}\cos 2t$$

This is the required solution.

Example 6. *Solve* $(D^2+1)\,y = \sin t \sin 2t,\ t > 0$ *if* $y = 1,\ Dy = 0$ *when* $t = 0$.

Solution. The given equation is

$$(D^2+1)\,y = \sin t \sin 2t = \frac{1}{2}(\cos t - \cos 3t)$$

$\therefore$ $$L\,\{y''\} + L\,\{y\} = \frac{1}{2}L\,\{\cos t\} - \frac{1}{2}L\,\{\cos 3t\}$$

or $$p^2 L\,\{y\} - p\,y\,(0) - y'\,(0) + L\,\{y\}$$

$$= \frac{p}{2(p^2+1)} - \frac{p}{2(p^2+9)}$$

or $$(p^2+1)L\{y\} - p = \frac{p}{2(p^2+1)} - \frac{p}{2(p^2+9)}$$

or $$L\{y\} = \frac{p}{p^2+1} + \frac{p^2}{2(p^2+1)^2} - \frac{p}{2(p^2+1)(p^2+9)}$$

$$= \frac{p}{p^2+1} - \frac{1}{4}\left\{\frac{d}{dp}\frac{1}{(p^2+1)}\right\} - \frac{p}{16(p^2+1)} + \frac{p}{16(p^2+9)}$$

or $$y = L^{-1}\left\{\frac{p}{p^2+1}\right\} - \frac{1}{4}L^{-1}\left\{\frac{d}{dp}\frac{1}{p^2+1}\right\} - \frac{1}{16}L^{-1}\left\{\frac{p}{p^2+1}\right\} + \frac{1}{16}L^{-1}\left\{\frac{p}{p^2+9}\right\}$$

$$= \cos t + \frac{t}{4}L^{-1}\left\{\frac{1}{p^2+1}\right\} - \frac{1}{16}\cos t + \frac{1}{16}\cos 3t$$

$\therefore$ $$y = \frac{15}{16}\cos t + \frac{t}{4}\sin t + \frac{1}{16}\cos 3t.$$

This is the required solution.

Example 7. *Solve $(D^3 - D^2 - D + 1)\,y = 8te^{-t}$, if $y = D^2y = 0$, $Dy = 1$, when $t = 0$.*

Solution. Taking the Laplace transform of both sides of the given equation, we get

$$L[y'''] - L[y''] - L[y'] + L[y]$$
$$= 8L[t\,e^{-t}]$$

or $$p^3 L[y] - p^2 y(0) - py'(0) - y''(0) - [p^2 L(y) - py(0) - y(0)]$$
$$- [pL(y) - y(0)] + L(y) = -8\frac{d}{dp}[L(e^{-t})]$$

or $$(p^3 - p^2 - p + 1)L[y] - p + 1 = -8\frac{d}{dp}\left(\frac{1}{p+1}\right)$$

or $$(p-1)^2(p+1)L[y] = p - 1 + \frac{8}{(p+1)^2}$$

or $$L[y] = \frac{1}{(p-1)(p+1)} + \frac{8}{(p-1)^2(p+1)^2}$$

$$= \frac{1}{2}\left(\frac{1}{p-1} - \frac{1}{p+1}\right) - \frac{3}{2(p-1)} + \frac{1}{(p-1)^2} + \frac{3}{2(p+1)} + \frac{2}{(p+1)^2} + \frac{2}{(p+1)^3}$$

$$= -\frac{1}{p-1} + \frac{1}{p+1} + \frac{1}{(p-1)^2} + \frac{2}{(p+1)^2} + \frac{2}{(p+1)^3}$$

$$\therefore \quad y = -L^{-1}\left\{\frac{1}{p-1}\right\} + L^{-1}\left\{\frac{1}{p+1}\right\} + L^{-1}\left\{\frac{1}{(p-1)^2}\right\} + 2 \cdot L^{-1}\left\{\frac{1}{(p+1)^2}\right\} 2L^{-1}\left\{\frac{1}{(p+1)^3}\right\}$$

$$= -e^t + e^{-t} + e^t L^{-1}\left\{\frac{1}{p^2}\right\} + 2e^{-t} L^{-1}\left\{\frac{1}{p^2}\right\} + 2e^{-t} L^{-1}\left\{\frac{1}{p^3}\right\}$$

$$= -e^t + e^{-t} + e^t \cdot t + 2e^{-t} \cdot t + 2e^{-t} \cdot \frac{t^2}{2!}$$

$$\therefore \quad y = (1 + 2t + t^2)\, e^{-t} - (1 - t)\, e^{-t}.$$

This is the required solution.

Example 8. *Solve* $\dfrac{d^2y}{dt^2} - 2k\dfrac{dy}{dt} + k^2\, y(t) = F(t).$

Solution. Taking Laplace transform of both sides of the given equation, we get

$$L[y''] - 2k\, L[y'] + k^2 L[y] = L[F(t)]$$

or $\quad p^2 L\{y\} - py(0) - y'(0) - 2k[pL\{y\} - y(0)] + k^2 L\{y\} = L\{F(t)\}$

or $\quad (p^2 - 2kp + k^2)\, L\{y\} - pA - B + 2kA = f(p)$

where $\quad y(0) = A, \;\; y'(0) = B \;$ and $\; L\{F(t)\} = f(p)$

or $\quad L\{y\} = \dfrac{pA + B - 2kA - f(p)}{(p-k)^2}$

$$= \frac{A}{(p-k)} + \frac{(B - kA)}{(p-k)^2} + \frac{1}{(p-k)^2} f(p)$$

$$\therefore \quad y = AL^{-1}\left\{\frac{1}{p-k}\right\} + (B - kA)\, L^{-1}\left\{\frac{1}{(p-k)^2}\right\} + L^{-1}\left\{\frac{1}{(p-k)^2} \cdot f(p)\right\}$$

$$= Ae^{kt} + (B - kA)\, te^{kt} + (te^{kt})\, F(t).$$

$$\left[\because\; L^{-1}\left\{\frac{1}{(p-k)}\right\} = e^{kt}, \quad L^{-1}\left\{\frac{1}{(p-k)^2}\right\} = te^{kt}\right]$$

$$= Ae^{kt} + (B - kA)\, te^{kt} + \int_0^t (t-x)\, e^{k(t-x)}\, F(x)\, dx$$

[by the convolution theorem]

or $$e^{-kt}\, y(t) = A + ct + \int_0^t (t-x)\, e^{-kx}\, F(x)\, dx$$

where A and c are arbitrary constants. This is the required solution.

EXERCISE 3(A)

Solve the following differential equations by means of the Laplace transform:

1. $\dfrac{dy}{dt} + y = 1$, given that $y = 2$ when $t = 0$.
2. $(D + 1)\, y = 0$, $t > 0$, if $y = y_0$ when $t = 0$.
3. $(D^2 + m^2)\, y = a \cos nt$, $t > 0$, if $y = 0$, $Dy = 0$ when $t = 0$.
4. $(D^2 - D - 6)\, y = 2$, $t > 0$, if $y = 1$, $Dy = 0$ when $t = 0$.
5. $(D^2 + 1)\, y = 6 \cos 2t$, if $y = 3$, $Dy = 1$ when $t = 0$.
6. $(D^2 + 6D + 9)\, y = \sin t$, where $y(0) = 1$, $y'(0) = 0$.
7. $(D + 2)^2\, y = 4e^{-2t}$, $y(0) = -1$ and $y'(0) = 4$.
8. $(D^2 + 3D + 2)\, y = 0$, $y = y_0$ and $Dy = y_1$ at $t = 0$.
9. $(D + 1)^2\, y = t$; given that $y = -3$, when $t = 0$ and $y = -1$, when $t = 1$.
10. $(D^2 + 2D + 1)\, y = 5te^{-1}$, $t > 0$, subject to the conditions, $y = 4$, $Dy = 2$, when $t = 0$.
11. $(D^2 - 3D + 2)\, y = 1 - e^{2t}$, $y = 1$, $Dy = 0$, when $t = 0$.
12. $(D^4 - 1)\, y = 1$, $y = Dy = D^2y = D^3y = 0$ at $t = 0$.
13. $(D^3 - 2D^2 + 5D)\, y = 0$, if $y(0) = 0$, $y'(0) = 1$, $y(\pi/8) = 1$.
14. $[D^4 + 2D^2 + 1]\, y = 0$, where $y(0) = 0$, $y'(0) = 1$, $y''(0) = 2$ and $y'''(0) = -3$.
15. $\dfrac{d^2x}{dt^2} + x = f(t)$, if $x = x' = 0$ for $t = 0$.

ANSWERS

1. $y = 1 + e^{-t}$.
2. $y = y_0\, e^{-t}$.

3. $y = \frac{a}{(m^2 - n^2)}(-\cos mt + \cos nt)$.
4. $y = -\frac{1}{3} + \frac{8}{15}e^{3t} + \frac{4}{3}e^{-2t}$.
5. $y = 5\cos t - 2\cos 2t + \sin t$
6. $y = \frac{1}{50}[(53 + 155x)]\, e^{-3x} - (3\cos x - 4\sin x)$.
7. $y = e^{-2t}(2t^2 + 2t - 1)$.
8. $y = (2y_0 + y_1)e^{-t} - (y_0 + y_1)e^{-2t}$.
9. $y = -2 + t - e^{-t} + te^{-t}$.
10. $y = \frac{1}{2}e^{-t}t^3 + 4e^{-t} + 6te^{-t}$.
11. $y = \frac{1}{2} + \frac{1}{2}e^{2t} - te^{2t} + \frac{t^2}{2}e^{2t}$.
12. $y = -1 + \frac{1}{2}\cosh t + \frac{1}{2}\cos t$.
13. $y = 1 + e^t(\sin 2t - \cos 2t)$.
14. $y = t(\sin t + \cos t)$.
15. $x = \int_0^t \sin(t - x)\cdot f(x)\, dx$.

3.2 SOLUTION OF ORDINARY DIFFERENTIAL EQUATIONS WITH VARIABLE COEFFICIENTS

The Laplace transform technique is very useful in solving the equations with variable coefficients. The method is found useful in case of the equations having the terms of the form $t^m y^n(t)$ whose Laplace transform is

$$(-1)^m \frac{d^m}{dp^m} L\{y^n(t)\}.$$

ILLUSTRATIVE EXAMPLES

Example 1. *Solve $ty'' + y' + 4ty = 0$, if $y(0) = 3$, $y'(0) = 0$.*

Solution. Taking the Laplace transform of both sides of the given equation, we get

$$L\{ty''\} + L\{y'\} + 4L\{ty\} = 0$$

or
$$-\frac{d}{dp}L\{y''\} + L\{y'\} + 4(-1)\frac{d}{dp}L\{y\} = 0$$

or
$$-\frac{d}{dp}[p^2 L\{y\} - py(0) - y'(0)] + [pL\{y\} - y(0)] - 4\frac{d}{dp}L\{y\} = 0$$

or
$$\frac{d}{dp}(p^2 z - 3p) + (pz - 3) - 4\frac{dz}{dp} = 0$$

where
$$z = L\{y\}$$

or $$-(p^2+4)\frac{dz}{dp}-pz=0$$

or $$\frac{dz}{z}+\frac{p}{p^2+4}dp=0$$

Integrating, we get

$$\log z+\frac{1}{2}\log(p^2+4)=\log c_1$$

or $$z=\frac{c_1}{\sqrt{(p^2+4)}}$$

or $$L\{y\}=\frac{c_1}{\sqrt{(p^2+4)}}$$

$\therefore$ $$y=c_1L^{-1}\left\{\frac{1}{\sqrt{(p^2+4)}}\right\}$$

or $$y=c_1J_0(2t).$$

Since $y(0)=3 \quad \therefore \quad 3=c_1J_0(0)=c_1$ $\qquad [\because J_0(0)=1]$

$\therefore$ $$y=3J_0(2t).$$

This is the required solution.

Example 2. *Solve* $[tD^2+(1-2t)D-2]y=0$, *if* $y(0)=1$, $y'(0)=2$.

Solution. The given equation can be written as

$$ty''+y'-2ty'-2y=0$$

Taking Laplace transform of both sides, we get

$$L\{ty''\}+L\{y'\}-2L\{ty'\}-2L\{y\}=0$$

or $$-\frac{d}{dp}L\{y''\}+L\{y'\}+2\frac{d}{dp}L\{y'\}-2L\{y\}=0$$

or $$-\frac{d}{dp}[p^2L\{y\}-py(0)-y'(0)]+[pL\{y\}-y(0)]$$
$$+2\frac{d}{dp}[pL\{y\}-y(0)]-2L\{y\}=0$$

or $$-\frac{d}{dp}(p^2z-p-2)+(pz-1)+2\frac{d}{dp}(pz-1)-2z=0$$

where $\quad L\{y\} = z$

or $$-(p^2 - 2p)\frac{dz}{dp} - pz = 0$$

or $$\frac{dz}{z} + \frac{1}{p-2}\,dz = 0.$$

Integrating, we get

$$\log z + \log(p-2) = \log c_1$$

or $$z = \frac{c_1}{p-2}$$

or $$L\{y\} = \frac{c_1}{(p-2)}$$

$\therefore$ $$y = c_1 L^{-1}\left\{\frac{1}{p-2}\right\} = c_1 e^{2t}$$

But $\quad y(0) = 1 \quad \therefore \quad 1 = c_1$

$\therefore$ $$y = e^{2t}.$$

This is the required solution.

Example 3. *Solve* $t\,y''(t) + (2t+3)\,y'(t) + (t+3)\,y(t) = a\,e^{-1}$, *if* $y(t)$ *and its derivatives have transform.*

Solution. Taking Laplace Transform of both sides of the given equation we have

$$L\{ty''\} + 2L\{ty'\} + 3L\{y'\} + L\{ty\} + 3L\{y\} = aL\{e^{-t}\}$$

or $$-\frac{d}{dp}[L\{y''\}] - 2\frac{d}{dp}L\{y'\} + 3L\{y'\} - \frac{d}{dp}L\{y\} + 3L\{y\} = \frac{a}{p+1}$$

or $$-\frac{d}{dp}[p^2z - pz(0) - y'(0)] - 2\frac{d}{dp}[pz - y(0)]$$

$$+ 3[pz - y(0)] - \frac{dz}{dp} + 3z = \frac{a}{p+1} \quad \text{where } L\{y\} = z$$

or $$-\frac{d}{dp}[p^2z - pA - B] - 2\frac{d}{dp}[pz - A] + 3[pz - A] - \frac{dz}{dp} + 3z = \frac{a}{p+1},$$

since $\quad y(0) = A$ and $y'(0) = B$.

or $$-p^2\frac{dz}{dp} - 2pz + A - 2p\frac{dp}{dz} - 2z + 3pz - 3A - \frac{dz}{dp} + 3z = \frac{a}{p+1}$$

or $$-(p^2 + 2p + 1)\frac{dz}{dp} + (p+1)z = 2A + \frac{a}{p+1}$$

or $$\frac{dz}{dp} - \frac{1}{(p+1)}z = -\frac{2A}{(p+1)^2} - \frac{a}{(p+1)^2} \quad \ldots\text{(i)}$$

This is a linear equation of the first order.

Integrating factor $= e^{-\int \{1/(p+1)\}\, dp}$

$$= e^{-\log(p+1)} = \frac{1}{p+1}$$

$\therefore$ Solution of equation (i) is

$$z \cdot \frac{1}{p+1} = B - 2A\int \frac{dp}{(p+1)^3} - a\int \frac{dp}{(p+1)^4}$$

$$= B + \frac{A}{(p+1)^2} + \frac{a}{3(p+1)^3}$$

or $$z = L\{y\} = B(p+1) + \frac{A}{p+1} + \frac{a}{3(p+1)^2}$$

where B is constant of integration. But B must vanish if $z(p)$ is a transform since $z(p)$ must vanish as p tends to infinity.

$\therefore$ $$L\{y\} = \frac{A}{p+1} + \frac{a}{3(p+1)^2}$$

or $$y = A\,L^{-1}\left\{\frac{1}{p+1}\right\} + \frac{a}{3}L^{-1}\left\{\frac{1}{(p+1)^2}\right\}$$

$$= A\,e^{-t} + \frac{a}{3}e^{-t}L^{-1}\left\{\frac{1}{p^2}\right\}$$

$$= \left(A + \frac{at}{3}\right)e^{-t}$$

This is the required solution.

Example 4. *Solve $y'' - t\,y' + y = 1$, if $y(0) = 1$, $y'(0) = 2$.*

Solution. Taking the Laplace transform of both sides of the given equation, we get

$$L\{y''\} - L\{t\,y'\} + L\{y\} = L\{1\}$$

or $$p^2 L\{y\} - p\,y(0) - y'(0) + \frac{d}{dp}[L\{y'\}] + L\{y\} = \frac{1}{p}$$

or $$p^2 L\{y\} - p - 2 + \frac{d}{dp}[pL\{y\} - y(0)] + L\{y\} = \frac{1}{p}$$

or $$p^2 z - p - 2 + \frac{d}{dp}(pz - 1) + z = \frac{1}{p}, \text{ where } z = L\{y\}$$

or $$p\frac{dz}{dp} + (p^2 + 2)z = p + 2 + \frac{1}{p}$$

or $$\frac{dz}{dp} + \left(p + \frac{2}{p}\right)z = 1 + \frac{2}{p} + \frac{1}{p^2}$$

which is linear.

$$\therefore \quad \text{I.F.} = e^{\int (p + 2/p)\,dp} = e^{\left(\frac{1}{2}p^2 + 2\log p\right)}$$

$$= p^2 e^{p^2/2}$$

$$\therefore \quad p^2 e^{p^2/2} z = c_1 + \int\left(1 + \frac{2}{p} + \frac{2}{p^2}\right)p^2 e^{p^2/2}\,dp$$

$$= c_1 + \int (p^2 + 2p + 1)e^{p^2/2}\,dp$$

$$= c_1 + \int (p^2 + 1)e^{p^2/2}\,dp + 2\int p\,e^{p^2/2}\,dp$$

$$= c_1 + \int (2v + 1)e^v \cdot \frac{dv}{\sqrt{(2v)}} + 2\int \sqrt{(2v)}\,e^v \frac{dv}{\sqrt{(2v)}},$$

putting $\frac{p^2}{2} = v$, so that

$$p\,dp = dv \quad \text{or} \quad dp = \frac{dv}{\sqrt{(2v)}}$$

$$= c_1 + \int \sqrt{(2v)}\,e^v\,dv + \int \frac{e^v}{\sqrt{(2v)}}\,dv + 2\int e^v\,dv$$

$$= c_1 + \sqrt{(2v)}\,e^v + 2e^v$$

$$= c_1 + p\,e^{p^2/2} + 2e^{p^2/2}$$

or $$z = L\{y\} = \frac{c_1}{p^2}e^{-p^2/2} + \frac{1}{p} + \frac{2}{p^2}$$

$$= \frac{c_1}{p^2}\left(1 - \frac{p^2}{2} + \frac{p^4}{4.2!} - \ldots\right) + \frac{1}{p} + \frac{2}{p^2}$$

$$= \frac{(2 + c_1)}{p^2} - \frac{c_1}{2} + \frac{c_1}{8}p^2 - \ldots + \frac{1}{p}$$

$$\therefore \quad y = (2 + c_1) L^{-1}\left\{\frac{1}{p^2}\right\} - \frac{c_1}{2} L^{-1}\{1\} + \frac{c_1}{8} L^{-1}\{p^2\} + \ldots + L^{-1}\left\{\frac{1}{p}\right\}$$

$$= (2 + c_1)\, t + 1, \quad \text{since } L^{-1}\{p^n\} = 0, n = 0, 1, 2, \ldots$$

But since $y'(0) = 2$.

$$\therefore \quad 2 = c_1 + 2 \text{ or } c_1 = 0.$$

Hence $y = 2t + 1$.

Hence is the required solution.

EXERCISE 3(B)

1. Solve the differential equation
   $$t\, y''(t) + y'(t) + t\, y(t) = 0$$
   under the conditions that $y(0) = 1$ and $y(t)$ and its derivatives have transforms.
2. Using Laplace transform method, solve $y''(t) + y(t) = t$, given that $y'(0) = 1 \cdot y(\pi) = 0$.
3. Solve $ty'' + (t - 1)y' - y = 0$, given that $y(0) = 5, y(\infty) = 0$.
4. $y''(t) + at\, y(t) - 2at(t) = 0$, if $y(0) = 5, y(\infty) = 0$.

ANSWERS

1. $y(t) = J_0(t)$.
2. $y = \pi \cos t + t$.
3. $y(t) = 5e^{-t}$.
4. $y = \frac{1}{2} t^2$.

3.3 SOLUTION OF SIMULTANEOUS ORDINARY DIFFERENTIAL EQUATIONS

The Laplace transform method can also be used in solving two or more simultaneous ordinary differential equations.

ILLUSTRATIVE EXAMPLES

Example 1. *Solve*

$$(D^2 - 1)\, x + 5\, Dy = t$$

$$-2Dx + (D^2 - 4)\, y = -2$$

if $\quad x = 0 = Dx = y = Dy$ *when* $t = 0$.

Solution. Taking Laplace transform of both sides of the two equations, we get

$$L\{x''\} - L\{x\} + 5L\{y'\} = L\{t\}$$

and $$-2L\{x'\} + L\{y''\} - 4L\{y\} = -2L\{1\}$$

or $$p^2\bar{x} - p\,x(0) - x'(0) - \bar{x} + 5\,[p\bar{y} - y(0)] = \frac{1}{p^2}$$

and $$-2\,\{p\,\bar{x} - x(0)\} + p^2\,\bar{y} - py(0) - y'(0) - 4\bar{y} = -\frac{2}{p}$$

where $\bar{x} = L\{x\}$ and $\bar{y} = L\{y\}$

or $$(p^2 - 1)\,\bar{x} - 5p\,\bar{y} = \frac{1}{p^2}$$

and $$-2p\,\bar{x} + (p^2 - 4)\,\bar{y} = -\frac{2}{p}$$

Solving for $\bar{x}$ and $\bar{y}$, we get

$$\bar{x} = \frac{11p^2 - 4}{p\,(p^2+1)\,(p^2+4)} = -\frac{1}{p^2} + \frac{5}{p^2+1} - \frac{4}{p^2+4}$$

and $$\bar{y} = \frac{-2p^2 + 4}{p\,(p^2+1)\,(p^2+4)} = \frac{1}{p} - \frac{2p}{p^2+1} + \frac{p}{p^2+4}$$

$\therefore$ $$x = -L^{-1}\left\{\frac{1}{p^2}\right\} + 5L^{-1}\left\{\frac{1}{p^2+1}\right\} - 4L^{-1}\left\{\frac{1}{p^2+4}\right\}$$

$$= -t + 5\sin t - 2\sin 2t$$

and $$y = L^{-1}\left\{\frac{1}{p}\right\} - 2L^{-1}\left\{\frac{p}{p^2+1}\right\} + L^{-1}\left\{\frac{p}{p^2+4}\right\}$$

$$= 1 - 2\cos t + \cos 2t.$$

Example 2. *Solve*

$$(D^2 - 3)\,x - 4y = 0$$

$$x + (D^2 + 1)\,y = 0, \quad t > 0$$

if $x = y = Dy = 0,\ \ Dx = 2$ *when* $t = 0$.

Solution. Taking the Laplace transform of both sides of the two equations, we get

$$L\{x''\} - 3L\{x\} - 4L\{y\} = 0$$

and $$L\{x\} + L\{y''\} + L\{y\} = 0$$

or $\quad p^2 \tilde{x} - p\,x(0) - x'(0) - 3\tilde{x} - 4\tilde{y} = 0$

and $\quad \tilde{x} + p^2 \tilde{y} - py(0) - y'(0) + \tilde{y} = 0$

where $\quad \tilde{x} = L\{x\}$ and $\tilde{y} = L\{y\}$

or $\quad (p^2 - 3)\,\tilde{x} - 4\tilde{y} = 2$

and $\quad \tilde{x} + (p^2 + 1)\,\tilde{y} = 0$

solving for $\tilde{x}$ and $\tilde{y}$, we get

$$\tilde{x} = \frac{2(p^2+1)}{(p^2-1)^2} = \frac{1}{(p^2-1)^2} + \frac{1}{(p+1)^2}$$

and
$$\tilde{y} = \frac{-2}{(p+1)^2(p-1)^2} = \frac{1}{2}\left[-\frac{1}{p+1} + \frac{1}{p-1} - \frac{1}{(p+1)^2} - \frac{1}{(p-1)^2}\right]$$

$\therefore$
$$x = L^{-1}\left\{\frac{1}{(p-1)^2}\right\} + L^{-1}\left\{\frac{1}{(p+1)^2}\right\}$$
$$= e^t L^{-1}\left\{\frac{1}{p^2}\right\} + e^{-t} L^{-1}\left\{\frac{1}{p^2}\right\}$$
$$= (e^t + e^{-t})\,t$$

and
$$y = \frac{1}{2}\left[-L^{-1}\left\{\frac{1}{p+1}\right\} + L^{-1}\left\{\frac{1}{p-1}\right\} - L^{-1}\left\{\frac{1}{(p+1)^2}\right\} - L^{-1}\left\{\frac{1}{(p-1)^2}\right\}\right]$$
$$= \frac{1}{2}\left[-e^{-t} + e^t - te^{-t} - te^t\right]$$
$$= \frac{1}{2}(1-t)\,e^t - \frac{1}{2}(1+t)\,e^{-t}.$$

Example 3. *Solve* $Dx + Dy = t$

$$D^2x - y = e^{-t}$$

if $\quad x(0) = 3, \quad x'(0) = -2, \quad y(0) = 0.$

Solution. Taking Laplace transform of both sides of the given equations, we get

$$L\{x'\} + L\{y'\} = L\{t\}$$

and $\quad L\{x''\} - L\{y\} = L\{e^{-t}\}$

or
$$p\tilde{x} - x(0) + p\tilde{y} - y(0) = \frac{1}{p^2}$$

and $$p^2\tilde{x} - px(0) - x'(0) - \tilde{y} = \frac{1}{p+1}$$

or $$\tilde{px} + \tilde{py} = 3 + \frac{1}{p^2}$$

and $$p^2\tilde{x} - \tilde{y} = 3p - 2 + \frac{1}{p+1}$$

Solving for $\tilde{x}$ and $\tilde{y}$, we get

$$\tilde{x} = \frac{3p^2+1}{p^3(1+p^2)} + \frac{3p}{1+p^2} - \frac{2}{1+p^2} - \frac{1}{(p+1)(p^2+1)}$$

$$= \frac{1}{p^3}\left(1 + 2p^2 - \frac{2p^4}{1+p^2}\right) + \frac{3p}{1+p^2} - \frac{2}{1+p^2} + \frac{1}{2(p+1)} - \frac{p}{2(p^2+1)} + \frac{1}{2(p^2+1)}$$

$$= \frac{2}{p} + \frac{1}{p^3} + \frac{1}{2(p+1)} + \frac{p}{2(1+p^2)} - \frac{3}{2(p^2+1)} \qquad \ldots\text{(i)}$$

and $$\tilde{y} = \frac{1}{p(p+1)(p^2+1)} + \frac{2}{p^2+1}$$

$$= \frac{1}{p} - \frac{1}{2(p+1)} - \frac{p}{2(p^2+1)} - \frac{1}{2(p^2+1)} + \frac{2}{p^2+1}$$

$$= \frac{1}{p} - \frac{1}{2(p+1)} - \frac{p}{2(p^2+1)} + \frac{3}{2(p^2+1)} \qquad \ldots\text{(ii)}$$

Taking inverse transforms of (i) and (ii), we get

$$x = 2L^{-1}\left\{\frac{1}{p}\right\} + L^{-1}\left\{\frac{1}{p^3}\right\} + \frac{1}{2}L^{-1}\left\{\frac{1}{p+1}\right\} + \frac{1}{2}L^{-1}\left\{\frac{p}{p^2+1}\right\} - \frac{3}{2}L^{-1}\left\{\frac{1}{p^2+1}\right\}$$

$$= 2 + \frac{1}{2}t^2 + \frac{1}{2}e^{-t} + \frac{1}{2}\cos t - \frac{3}{2}\sin t$$

and $$y = L^{-1}\left\{\frac{1}{p}\right\} - \frac{1}{2}L^{-1}\left\{\frac{1}{p+1}\right\} - \frac{1}{2}L^{-1}\left\{\frac{p}{p^2+1}\right\} + \frac{3}{2}L^{-1}\left\{\frac{1}{p^2+1}\right\}$$

$$= 1 - \frac{1}{2}e^{-t} - \frac{1}{2}\cos t + \frac{3}{2}\sin t.$$

Example 4. *Solve*

$$(D-2)x - (D+1)y = 6e^{3t}$$

$$(2D-3)\,x+(D-3)\,y=6e^{3t}$$

if $\quad x=3,\ y=0$ *when* $t=0$.

Solution. Taking the Laplace transform of both sides of the two given equations, we get

$$L\{x'\}-2L\{x\}-L\{y'\}-L\{y\}=6L\{e^{3t}\}$$

and
$$2L\{x'\}-3L\{x\}+L\{y'\}-3L\{y\}=6L\{e^{3t}\}$$

or
$$p\tilde{x}-x(0)-2\tilde{x}-\{p\tilde{y}-y(0)\}-\tilde{y}=\frac{6}{p-3}$$

and
$$2\{p\tilde{x}-x(0)\}-3\tilde{x}+p\tilde{y}-3\tilde{y}=\frac{6}{p-3}$$

or
$$(p-2)\,\tilde{x}-(p+1)\,\tilde{y}=3+\frac{6}{p-3}=\frac{3p-3}{p-3}$$

and
$$(2p-3)\,\tilde{x}+(p-3)\,\tilde{y}=6+\frac{6}{p-3}=\frac{6p-12}{p-3}$$

Solving for $\tilde{x}$ and $\tilde{y}$, we get

$$\tilde{x}=\frac{3p^2-6p-1}{(p-3)(p-1)^2}=\frac{1}{p-1}+\frac{2}{(p-1)^2}+\frac{2}{p-3} \qquad \text{...(i)}$$

and
$$\tilde{y}=\frac{-3p+5}{(p-3)(p-1)^2}=\frac{1}{p-1}-\frac{1}{(p-1)^2}-\frac{1}{p-3} \qquad \text{...(ii)}$$

Taking inverse transforms for equations (i) and (ii), we get

$$x=L^{-1}\left\{\frac{1}{p-1}\right\}+2L^{-1}\left\{\frac{1}{(p-1)^2}\right\}+2L^{-1}\left\{\frac{1}{p-3}\right\}$$

$$=e^t+2t\,e^t+2e^{3t}$$

and
$$y=L^{-1}\left\{\frac{1}{p-1}\right\}-L^{-1}\left\{\frac{1}{(p-1)^2}\right\}-L^{-1}\left\{\frac{1}{p-3}\right\}$$

$$=e^t-t\,e^t-e^{3t}.$$

EXERCISE 3(C)

1. Solve $(D^2+2)\,x-Dy=1$, $Dx+(D^2+2)\,y=0$, with $t>0$, $x=0$, $Dx=0=y=Dy$, when $t=0$, x and y both are functions of t.

2. Solve $\dfrac{d^2x}{dt^2} + \dfrac{dy}{dt} + 3x = 15e^{-t}$, $\dfrac{d^2y}{dt^2} - 4\dfrac{dx}{dt} + 3y = 15 \sin 2t$ if $x(0) = 35$, $x'(0) = -48$, $y(0) = 27$, $y'(0) = -55$.
3. Using Laplace transform method, solve $(D^2 - 2)x - 3y = e^{2t}$, $(D^2 + 2)y + x = 0$ satisfying the conditions $x = 1, y = 1, Dx = Dy = 0$ when $t = 0$.
4. Using Laplace transforms, solve the equations $\dfrac{dx}{dt} + \dfrac{dy}{dt} = t$, $\dfrac{d^2y}{dt^2} - y = e^{-t}$ given that $x(0) = 0$, $y(0) = 0$, $\dfrac{dx}{dt} = 0$ if $t = 0$.

ANSWERS

1. $x = \dfrac{1}{2} - \dfrac{1}{2}\cos t - \dfrac{1}{6}\cos 2t,\ y = -\dfrac{1}{3}\sin t + \dfrac{1}{6}\sin 2t.$
2. $x = 30\cos t - 15\sin 3t + 3e^{-t} + 2\cos 2t,$

   $y = 30\cos 3t - 60\sin t - 3e^{-t} + \sin 2t.$
3. $x = \dfrac{3}{4}e^{t} + \dfrac{7}{4}e^{-t} + \dfrac{2}{5}e^{2t} + \dfrac{1}{10}(2\sin t - 19\cos t),$

   $y = \dfrac{19}{10}\cos t - \dfrac{1}{5}\sin t - \dfrac{1}{15}e^{2t} - \dfrac{1}{4}e^{t} + \dfrac{7}{12}e^{-t}.$
4. $x = \dfrac{1}{2}(e^{-t} - \cos t + \sin t) + \dfrac{t^2}{2} + \cos t - 1,\ y = 1 - \dfrac{1}{2}(e^{-t} + \cos t - \sin t).$

3.4 SOLUTION OF PARTIAL DIFFERENTIAL EQUATIONS

Theorem. *If $y = y(x, t)$, then*

(*i*) $L\left(\dfrac{\partial y}{\partial t}\right) = p\tilde{y}(x, p) - y(x, 0)$

(*ii*) $L\left(\dfrac{\partial^2 y}{\partial t^2}\right) = p^2\tilde{y}(x, p) - py(x, 0) - y_t(x, 0)$

(*iii*) $L\left(\dfrac{\partial y}{\partial x}\right) = \dfrac{d\tilde{y}}{dx}$

(*iv*) $L\left(\dfrac{\partial^2 y}{\partial x^2}\right) = \dfrac{d^2\tilde{y}}{dx^2}$

Where $L\{y(x,t)\} = \tilde{y}(x,p),\ y_t(x,0) = \left[\frac{\partial y}{\partial t}\right]_{t=0}$

Proof.

(i) $$L\left(\frac{\partial y}{\partial t}\right) = \int_0^\infty e^{-pt}\frac{\partial y}{\partial t}\,dt$$

$$= \lim_{a\to\infty}\int_0^a e^{-pt}\frac{\partial y}{\partial t}\,dt$$

$$= \lim_{a\to\infty}\left[\left\{e^{-pt}\,y(x,t)\right\}_0^\infty + p\int_0^a e^{-pt}\,y(x,t)\,dt\right]$$

$$= -y(x,0) + p\int_0^\infty e^{-pt}\,y\,dt$$

$$= p\tilde{y}(x,p) - y(x,0).$$

(ii) Let $v = \frac{\partial y}{\partial t} = y_t$. Then

$$L\left\{\frac{\partial^2 y}{\partial t^2}\right\} = L\left\{\frac{\partial v}{\partial t}\right\}$$

$$= p\tilde{v}(x,p) - v(x,0) \qquad \text{[by (i)]}$$

$$= p\,L\{v\} - y_t(x,0)$$

$$= p\,L\left\{\frac{\partial y}{\partial t}\right\} - y_t(x,0)$$

$$= p\,[p\,y(x,p) - y(x,0)] - y_t(x,0) \qquad \text{[by (i)]}$$

$$= p^2\tilde{y}(x,p) - py(x,0) - y_t(x,0)$$

(iii) $$L\left\{\frac{\partial y}{\partial x}\right\} = \int_0^\infty e^{-pt}\frac{\partial y}{\partial x}\,dt$$

$$= \frac{d}{dx}\int_0^\infty e^{-pt}\,y\,dt = \frac{d\tilde{y}}{dx}.$$

(iv) $$L\left\{\frac{\partial^2 y}{\partial x^2}\right\} = L\left\{\frac{\partial u}{\partial x}\right\},\quad \text{where } u = \frac{\partial y}{\partial x} = \frac{d\tilde{y}}{dx} \qquad \text{[from (iii)]}$$

$$= \frac{d}{dx}L\{u\} = \frac{d}{dx}L\left\{\frac{\partial y}{\partial x}\right\}$$

$$= \frac{d}{dx}\left(\frac{d\tilde{y}}{dx}\right), \qquad \text{[by (iii)]}$$

$$= \frac{d^2\tilde{y}}{dx^2}.$$

ILLUSTRATIVE EXAMPLES

Example 1. *Apply Laplace transform to solve*

$$\frac{\partial y}{\partial x} = \frac{\partial y}{\partial t} + 1 - e^{-t},\ 0 < x < 1,\ t > 0 \textit{ given that } y(x, 0) = x.$$

Solution. Let $y = y(x, t)$, and $L\{y(x, t)\} = \tilde{y}(x, p)$.

Taking Laplace transform of the given equation, we get

$$\frac{d\tilde{y}}{dx} - [p\tilde{y} - y(x, 0)] = \frac{1}{p} - \frac{1}{p+1}$$

or
$$\frac{d\tilde{y}}{dx} - p\tilde{y} = \frac{1}{p(p+1)} - x$$

It is linear equation.

Hence I.F. $= e^{\int p\,dx} = e^{-\int p\,dx} = e^{-px}$

Hence the solution of (i) will be

$$\tilde{y}\,e^{-px} = c + \int\left[\frac{1}{p(p+1)} - x\right]e^{-px}\,dx$$

or
$$\tilde{y}\,e^{-px} = c + \frac{1}{p(p+1)}\left[\frac{e^{-px}}{-p}\right] + \frac{(-x)\,e^{-px}}{-p} - \int\frac{1}{p}\,e^{-px}\,dx$$

or
$$\tilde{y} = ce^{px} + \frac{x}{p} + \frac{1}{p(p+1)}$$

As y is bounded, hence $\tilde{y}$ is bounded, which mean y is finite as $x \to \infty$.

$\therefore \quad c = 0$

$$\therefore \quad \tilde{y} = \frac{x}{p} + \frac{1}{p(p+1)} = \frac{x}{p} + \frac{1}{p} - \frac{1}{p+1}$$

Taking inverse Laplace transform,

$$y = x + 1 + e^{-t}.$$

Example 2. *Solve* $\frac{\partial y}{\partial t} = 2\frac{\partial^2 y}{\partial x^2}$ *if* $y(0, t) = 0 = y(5, t)$, $y(x, 0) = 10 \sin 4\pi x$.

Solution. Taking Laplace transform of the given equation,

$$2L\left\{\frac{\partial y}{\partial t}\right\} = 2L\left\{\frac{\partial^2 y}{\partial x^2}\right\}$$

or $$p\tilde{y} - y(x, 0) = 2\frac{\partial^2 \tilde{y}}{dx^2}.$$

Putting the value of $y(x, 0)$, we get

$$p\tilde{y} - 10 \sin 4\pi x = 2\frac{d^2\tilde{y}}{dx^2}$$

or $$\frac{d^2\tilde{y}}{dx^2} - \frac{p}{2}\tilde{y} = -5 \sin 4\pi x.$$

The general solution of this is

$$\tilde{y} = A\, e^{x\sqrt{(p/2)}} + B\, e^{-x\sqrt{(p/2)}} + \frac{-5 \sin 4\pi x}{-(4\pi)^2 - p/2}$$

or $$\tilde{y} = A\, e^{x\sqrt{(p/2)}} + B\, e^{-x\sqrt{(p/2)}} + \frac{10 \sin 4\pi x}{32\pi^2 + p} \qquad \text{...(i)}$$

Subjecting this to the conditions

$$\tilde{y}(0.t) = 0, \tilde{y}(5, t) = 0$$

we get $$A + B = 0$$

$$0 = A\, e^{5\sqrt{(p/2)}} + B\, e^{-5\sqrt{(p/2)}} + \frac{10 \sin 20\pi}{32\pi^2 + p}$$

From which, $A + B = 0$

$$A^{10\sqrt{(p/2)}} + B = 0$$

which give $A = 0, B = 0$

∴ From (i)

$$\tilde{y} = \frac{10 \sin 4\pi x}{32\,\pi^2 + p}.$$

Applying inverse Laplace transform, we get

$$y = 10\, e^{-32\,\pi^2 t} \sin 4\pi x.$$

Example 3. *Find the bounded solution of*

$$\frac{\partial y}{\partial x} = 2\frac{\partial y}{\partial t} + y$$

if $$y(x, 0) = 6e^{-3x}.$$

Solution. Let $L\{y\} = \tilde{y}$. Taking Laplace transform of the given equation, we get

$$\frac{d\tilde{y}}{dx} = 2[p\,\tilde{y}(x,p) - y(x,0)] + \tilde{y}$$

or $$\frac{d\tilde{y}}{dx} = 2p\,\tilde{y} - 2 \times 6\,e^{-3x} + \tilde{y}$$

or $$\frac{d\tilde{y}}{dx} - (1 + 2p)\,\tilde{y} = -12e^{-3x} \qquad \ldots\text{(i)}$$

$$\text{I.F.} = e^{\int P\,dx} = e^{-\int (1+2p)\,dx} = e^{-(1+2p)x}.$$

$\therefore$ Solution of (i) will be

$$\tilde{y}\,e^{-(1+2p)x} = c + \int -12e^{-3x} \cdot e^{-(1+2p)x}\,dx$$

or $$\tilde{y}\,e^{-(1+2p)x} = c - 12\int e^{-(2p+4)}\,dx$$

$$= c + \frac{6e^{-(2p+4)}}{p+2}$$

or $$\tilde{y} = c\,e^{(1+2p)x} + \frac{6e^{-3x}}{p+2} \qquad \ldots\text{(ii)}$$

Since $y(x, t)$ bounded for every value of x and hence $\tilde{y}(x, p)$ is bounded for every x and every $p > 0$.

Consequently $c = 0$. For $\tilde{y}$ = finite quantity as $x \to \infty$.

$\therefore$ From (ii)

$$\tilde{y} = \frac{6e^{-3x}}{p+2}$$

$\therefore$ $$y = 6e^{-3x}\,L^{-1}\left\{\frac{1}{p+2}\right\}$$

or $$y = 6e^{-3x} \cdot e^{-2t} = 6e^{-(2t+3x)}.$$

Example 4. *Find the solution of*

$$\frac{\partial^2 u}{\partial x^2} - \frac{\partial^2 u}{\partial t^2} = xt$$

i.e., $\tilde{y}\left(\frac{\pi}{2}, p\right) = 0$

Now, from (i)

$$\frac{d\tilde{y}}{dx} = \sqrt{\left(\frac{p}{3}\right)}\left[A\, e^{x\sqrt{(p/3)}} - B\, e^{-x\sqrt{(p/3)}}\right] - \frac{150 \sin 5x}{75 + p}$$

By $\frac{d\tilde{y}}{dx} = 0$ at $x = 0$, we get

$$0 = \sqrt{(p/3)}\,[A - B] - 0$$

or $A = B.$

Now, (i) becomes

$$\tilde{y} = A\left[e^{x\sqrt{(p/3)}} + e^{-x\sqrt{p/3}}\right] + \frac{30 \cos 5x}{75 + p} \qquad \text{...(ii)}$$

By the condition $\tilde{y}\left(\frac{\pi}{2}, p\right) = 0,$

$$0 = A\left[e^{\pi/2\sqrt{(p/3)}} + e^{-\pi/2\sqrt{(p/3)}}\right] + \frac{30 \cos (5\pi/2)}{75 + p}$$

or

$$0 = 2A \cosh\left[\frac{\pi}{2}\sqrt{(p/3)}\right]$$

which gives $A = 0.$

Now, (ii) becomes

$$\tilde{y} = \frac{30 \cos 5x}{75 + p}$$

Taking inverse Laplace transform, we get

$$y = 30e^{-75t} \cos 5x.$$

EXERCISE 3(D)

Solve the following partial differential equations:

1. $\frac{\partial y}{\partial t} = \frac{\partial^2 y}{\partial x^2} - 4y$, if $y = (0, t) = 0,\ y(\pi, t) = 0.$
2. $\frac{\partial^2 y}{\partial t^2} = 16\frac{\partial^2 y}{\partial x^2}$ if $y(x, 0) = 0,\ y(3, t) = 0.$
3. $\frac{\partial y}{\partial t} = \frac{\partial^2 y}{\partial x^2}$ if $y\left(\frac{\pi}{2}, t\right) = 0$

$$u = -x\,L^{-1}\left\{\frac{1}{p^4}\right\} = -\frac{xt^3}{3!} = -\frac{xt^3}{6}$$

$\therefore$ $$u = -\frac{xt^3}{6}.$$

Example 5. *Find the bounded solution of*

$$\frac{\partial y}{\partial t} = \frac{\partial^2 y}{\partial x^2},\ x > 0,\ t > 0$$

where $y(0, t) = 1,\ y(x, 0) = 0$

Solution. $y(0, t) = 1$ gives $\tilde{y}(0, p) = 1/p$

$y(x, 0) = 0$ means $\tilde{y}(x, 0) = 0.$

Taking Laplace transform of the given equation, we get

$$p\tilde{y}(x, p) - y(x, 0) = \frac{d^2\tilde{y}}{dx^2}.$$

Putting $y(x, 0) = 0$, we get

$$\frac{d^2\tilde{y}}{dx^2} = p\tilde{y}(x, p)$$

or $$(D^2 - p)\,\tilde{y}(x, p) = 0$$

The solution of this is

$$\tilde{y} = A\,e^{x\sqrt{p}} + B\,e^{-x\sqrt{p}} \qquad \ldots\text{(i)}$$

As y is bounded hence $L\{y\} = \tilde{y}$ will also be bounded.

$\therefore$ $\tilde{y}$ is finite as $x \to \infty$

i.e., $A = 0$, according to (i).

Now, (i) becomes

$$\tilde{y} = B\,e^{-x\sqrt{p}}.$$

Putting the condition, that $\tilde{y}(0, p) = \frac{1}{p}$, we get

$$B = \frac{1}{p}$$

$\therefore$ $$\tilde{y} = \frac{1}{p}\,e^{-x\sqrt{p}}$$

$$\therefore \qquad y = L^{-1}\left\{\frac{e^{-x\sqrt{p}}}{p}\right\} = L^{-1}\left\{\frac{1}{p\,e^{x\sqrt{p}}}\right\}$$

$$= erfc\left\{\frac{x}{2\sqrt{t}}\right\}$$

$$\therefore \qquad y = erfc\left(\frac{x}{2\sqrt{t}}\right).$$

Example 6. *Solve* $\dfrac{\partial y}{\partial t} = 3\dfrac{\partial^2 y}{\partial x^2}$, *if* $y\left(\dfrac{\pi}{2}, t\right) = 0$,

$$y\,(x, 0) = 30\cos 5x, \left(\frac{\partial y}{\partial x}\right)_{x=0} = 0.$$

Solution. Taking Laplace transform of the given equation, we get

$$p\tilde{y} - y\,(x, 0) = 3\frac{d^2\tilde{y}}{dx^2}$$

or
$$3\frac{d^2\tilde{y}}{dx^2} - p\tilde{y} = -30\cos 5x$$

or
$$\left(D^2 - \frac{p}{3}\right)\tilde{y} = -10\cos 5x$$

The solution of this equation is

$$\tilde{y} = A\,e^{x\sqrt{(p/3)}} + B\,e^{-x\sqrt{(p/3)}} + \frac{1}{D^2 - p/3}(-10\cos 5x)$$

$$= A\,e^{x\sqrt{(p/3)}} + B\,e^{-x\,(p/3)} - \frac{10\cos 5x}{(-5)^2 - (p/3)}$$

$$= A\,e^{x\sqrt{(p/3)}} + B\,e^{-x\sqrt{(p/3)}} + \frac{30\cos 5x}{75 + p} \qquad \ldots\text{(i)}$$

Now, by

$$\frac{\partial y}{\partial x} = 0 \text{ when } x = 0, \text{ we get}$$

$$L\left\{\frac{\partial y}{\partial x}\right\} = 0 \text{ at } x = 0, \quad \textit{i.e.,} \quad \frac{d\tilde{y}}{dx} = 0 \text{ at } x = 0.$$

Again $y\left(\dfrac{\pi}{2}, t\right) = 0$ means $L\left\{y\left(\dfrac{\pi}{2}, t\right)\right\} = 0.$

i.e., $\tilde{y}\left(\frac{\pi}{2}, p\right) = 0$

Now, from (i)

$$\frac{d\tilde{y}}{dx} = \sqrt{\left(\frac{p}{3}\right)}\left[A\, e^{x\sqrt{(p/3)}} - B\, e^{-x\sqrt{(p/3)}}\right] - \frac{150 \sin 5x}{75 + p}$$

By $\frac{d\tilde{y}}{dx} = 0$ at $x = 0$, we get

$$0 = \sqrt{(p/3)}\,[A - B] - 0$$

or $A = B.$

Now, (i) becomes

$$\tilde{y} = A\left[e^{x\sqrt{(p/3)}} + e^{-x\sqrt{p/3}}\right] + \frac{30 \cos 5x}{75 + p} \qquad \ldots\text{(ii)}$$

By the condition $\tilde{y}\left(\frac{\pi}{2}, p\right) = 0,$

$$0 = A\left[e^{\pi/2\sqrt{(p/3)}} + e^{-\pi/2\sqrt{(p/3)}}\right] + \frac{30 \cos (5\pi/2)}{75 + p}$$

or $$0 = 2A \cosh\left[\frac{\pi}{2}\sqrt{(p/3)}\right]$$

which gives $A = 0.$

Now, (ii) becomes

$$\tilde{y} = \frac{30 \cos 5x}{75 + p}$$

Taking inverse Laplace transform, we get

$$y = 30e^{-75t} \cos 5x.$$

EXERCISE 3(D)

Solve the following partial differential equations:

1. $\frac{\partial y}{\partial t} = \frac{\partial^2 y}{\partial x^2} - 4y$, if $y = (0, t) = 0$, $y(\pi, t) = 0$.
2. $\frac{\partial^2 y}{\partial t^2} = 16\frac{\partial^2 y}{\partial x^2}$ if $y(x, 0) = 0$, $y(3, t) = 0$.
3. $\frac{\partial y}{\partial t} = \frac{\partial^2 y}{\partial x^2}$ if $y\left(\frac{\pi}{2}, t\right) = 0$

$$\left(\frac{\partial y}{\partial x}\right)_0 = 0,\ y\,(x, 0) = \cos 5x.$$

4. $\dfrac{\partial y}{\partial t} = \dfrac{\partial^2 y}{\partial x^2}$, if $y\,(x, 0)$

$$= 3 \sin 2\pi\, x,\quad y\,(0, t) = 0,\quad y\,(1, t) = 0.$$

ANSWERS

1. $y = 6e^{-3t} \sin x - 4e^{-8t} \sin 2x.$
2. $y = 12 \cos \pi\, x \sin 4\pi\, t + 16 \cos 3\pi x \sin 12\, \pi\, t - 8 \cos \pi\, x \sin 20\pi\, t.$
3. $y = e^{-25t} \cos 5x.$
4. $y = 3e^{-4x^2 t} \sin 2\pi\, x.$

4

Application of Laplace Transforms to Solution of Integral Equations

4.1 DEFINITION

Integral Equation. An equation of the form

$$Y(t) = F(t) + \int_a^b K(u, t)\, Y(u)\, du$$

is called an *integral equation* where $F(t)$ and $K(u, t)$ are known, a and b are either given constants or functions of t. Here the function $Y(t)$ which appears under integral sign is to be determined.

Definition. An integral equation of the form

$$Y(t) + F(t) + \int_0^t K(t-u)\, Y(u)\, du$$

is called *integral equation of convolution type*. The above equation is also expressible as

$$Y(t) = F(t) + K(t) * Y(t).$$

Definition. An *integro-differential equation* is an integral equation in which various derivatives of the unknown function $Y(t)$ can also be present. For example

$$F'(t) = F(t) + \cos t + e^{-t} + \int_0^t \cos(t-u)\, F(u)\, du.$$

Definition. Abel's integral equation is an integral equation of the form

$$\int_0^t \frac{F(u)\, du}{(t-u)^n} = G(t)$$

where $F(u)$ is unknown and $G(t)$ is known and n is a constant such that $0 < n < 1$.

ILLUSTRATIVE EXAMPLES

Example 1. *Solve the integral equation*

$$F(t) = t + 2\int_0^t \cos(t-u)\, F(u)\, du.$$

Solution. The given equation is also expressible as

$$F(t) = t + 2 \cos t * F(t).$$

Taking Laplace transform

$$f(p) = \frac{1}{p^2} + \frac{2p}{p^2+1} \cdot f(p), \text{ where } L\{F(t)\} = f(p)$$

or
$$f(p)\left\{1 - \frac{2p}{p^2+1}\right\} = \frac{1}{p^2}$$

or
$$f(p) = \frac{(p^2+1)}{p^2(p-1)^2} = \frac{1}{(p-1)^2} + \frac{1}{p^2(p-1)^2}.$$

Taking inverse Laplace transform,

$$F(t) = L^{-1}\left\{\frac{1}{(p-1)^2}\right\} + L^{-1}\left\{\frac{1}{p^2(p-1)^2}\right\} \qquad \ldots \text{(i)}$$

$$L^{-1}\left\{\frac{1}{(p-1)^2}\right\} = e^t L^{-1}\left\{\frac{1}{p^2}\right\} = t\, e^t \qquad \ldots \text{(ii)}$$

$$\therefore \quad L^{-1}\left\{\frac{1}{p(p-1)^2}\right\} = \int_0^t u\, e^u\, du = \left[e^u \cdot u - \int e^u\, du\right]_0^t$$

$$= \left(u\, e^u - e^u\right)_0^t$$

$$= \left[(u-1)\, e^u\right]_0^t = e^t(t-1) + 1$$

$$L^{-1}\left\{\frac{1}{p^2(p-1)^2}\right\} = \int_0^t [e^u(u-1) + 1]\, du$$

$$= \int_0^t u e^u\, du - \int_0^t e^u\, du + \int_0^t du$$

$$= e^t (t-1) + 1 - (e^t - 1) + t$$

$$= e^t (t-2) + t + 2. \qquad \ldots\text{(iii)}$$

Writing (1) with the help of (2) and (3),

$$F(t) = t e^t + e^t (t-2) + t + 2$$

$$= 2e^t (t-1) + 2 + t.$$

Example 2. *Solve the integral equation*

$$F(t) = 1 + \int_0^t F(u) \sin (t-u)\, du$$

and verify your solution.

Solution. The given equation is expressible as

$$F(t) = 1 + F(t) * \sin t.$$

Taking Laplace transform,

$$f(p) = \frac{1}{p} + f(p) \frac{1}{p^2+1}, \text{ where } L\{F(t)\} = f(p)$$

or $$f(p) = \frac{(p^2+1)}{p^2 \cdot p} = \frac{1}{p} + \frac{1}{p^3}$$

or $$L^{-1}\{f(p)\} = L^{-1}\left\{\frac{1}{p}\right\} + L^{-1}\left\{\frac{1}{p^3}\right\}$$

or $$F(t) = 1 + \frac{t^2}{2}.$$

For $$L\{t^n\} = \frac{n!}{p^{n+1}}.$$

We verify this solution as follows:

$$\text{L.H.S.} = F(t) = 1 + \frac{t^2}{2}.$$

$$\text{R.H.S.} = 1 + \int_0^t F(u) \sin (t-u)\, du$$

$$= 1 - \int_0^t \left(1 + \frac{u^2}{2}\right) \sin (u-t)\, du$$

$$= 1 - \int_0^t \sin (u-t)\, du - \frac{1}{2} \int_0^t u^2 \sin (u-t)\, du$$

$$= 1 + [\cos(u-t)]_{u=0}^{t} - \frac{1}{2}\left[-\cos(u-t)\cdot u^2 + \int 2u\cos(u-t)\,du\right]_{u=0}^{t}$$

$$= 1 + (1 - \cos t) + \frac{t^2}{2} - \int_0^t u\cos(u-t)\,du$$

$$= 2 - \cos t + \frac{t^2}{2} - [u\sin(u-t) + \cos(u-t)]_{u=0}^{t}$$

$$= 2 - \cos t + \frac{t^2}{2} - [0 + (1 - \cos t)]$$

$$= 1 + \frac{t^2}{2} = \text{L.H.S.}$$

This completes the problem.

Example 3. *Solve* $\int_0^t \frac{F(u)\,du}{\sqrt{(t-u)}} = 1 + t + t^2.$

Solution. The given equation can be written as

$$F(t) * t^{-1/2} = 1 + t + t^2.$$

Taking Laplace transform,

$$f(p)\cdot\frac{\Gamma\left(\frac{1}{2}\right)}{p^{1/2}} = \frac{1}{p} + \frac{1}{p^2} + \frac{2!}{p^3}.$$

For $$L\{t^n\} = \frac{\Gamma(n+1)}{p^{n+1}}$$

or $$\sqrt{\pi}\cdot f(p) = \frac{1}{p^{1/2}} + \frac{1}{p^{3/2}} + \frac{2}{p^{5/2}}$$

or $$\sqrt{\pi}\cdot L^{-1}\{f(p)\} = L^{-1}\left\{\frac{1}{p^{1/2}} + \frac{1}{p^{3/2}} + \frac{2}{p^{5/2}}\right\}$$

$$\sqrt{\pi}\,\Gamma(t) = \frac{t^{-1/2}}{\Gamma\left(\frac{1}{2}\right)} + \frac{t^{1/2}}{\Gamma\left(\frac{3}{2}\right)} + \frac{2t^{3/2}}{\Gamma\left(\frac{5}{2}\right)}$$

or $$F(t) = \frac{1}{\pi}\left[t^{-1/2} + 2t^{1/2} + 2\cdot\frac{2}{3}\cdot\frac{2}{1} - t^{3/2}\right]$$

$$= \frac{1}{\pi}\left[t^{-1/2} + 2t^{1/2} + \frac{8}{3}t^{3/2}\right].$$

Example 4. *Solve the integral equation*

$$\int_0^t Y(u)\, Y(t-u)\, du = 16 \sin 4t.$$

Solution. The given equation is also expressible as

$$Y(t) * Y(t) = 16 \sin 4t.$$

Taking Laplace transform of both sides, we find, if

$$L\{Y(t)\} = y(p),$$

$$y \cdot y = 16 \frac{4}{p^2 + 16} = \frac{64}{p^2 + 16}$$

or $$y = \pm \frac{8}{\sqrt{(p^2 + 4^2)}}$$

or $$L^{-1}\{y\} = \pm 8\, L^{-1}\left\{\frac{1}{\sqrt{(p^2 + 4^2)}}\right\}$$

or $$Y(t) = \pm 8\, J_0(4t).$$

Example 5. *Solve* $F'(t) = t + \int_0^t F(t-u) \cos u\, du,\ F(0) = 4.$

Solution. The given equation is also expressible as

$$F'(t) = t + F(t) * \cos t.$$

Taking Laplace transform and noting that

$$L\{F'(t)\} = pf(p) - F(0) = pf(p) - 4$$

we obtain $$pf(p) - 4 = \frac{1}{p^2} + f(p) \cdot \frac{p}{p^2 + 1}$$

or $$f(p) \frac{p^3}{p^2 + 1} = \frac{1}{p^2} + 4$$

or $$f(p) = \frac{p^2 + 1}{p^5} + \frac{4(p^2 + 1)}{p^3} = \frac{1}{p^3} + \frac{1}{p^5} + \frac{4}{p} + \frac{4}{p^3}$$

$$= \frac{5}{p^3} + \frac{1}{p^5} + \frac{4}{p}$$

or $$L^{-1}\{f(s)\} = L^{-1}\left\{\frac{4}{p} + \frac{5}{p^3} + \frac{1}{p^5}\right\}$$

or $$F(t) = 4 + \frac{5t^2}{\Gamma(3)} + \frac{t^4}{\Gamma(5)}.$$

For $$L\{t^n\} = \frac{\Gamma(n+1)}{p^{n+1}}$$

$$= 4 + \frac{5t^2}{2} + \frac{t^4}{4!}$$

$$= 4 + \frac{5t^2}{2} + \frac{t^4}{24}.$$

Example 6. *Convert the differential equation*

$F''(t) + 2F'(t) - 8F(t) = 5t^2 - 3t$, $F(0) = -2$, $F'(0) = 3$ into integral equation.

Solution. We have

$$F''(t) + 2F'(t) - 8F(t) = 5t^2 - 3t \qquad \text{...(i)}$$

$$F(0) = -2, F'(0) = 3.$$

Method 1. Let $F''(t) = G(t)$. ...(ii)

Integration yields the result

$$F'(t) = \int_0^t G(u)\, du + C_1.$$

For $t = 0$, this gives

$$F'(0) = 0 + C_1 \quad \text{or} \quad 3 = C_1.$$

$$\therefore \qquad F'(t) = \int_0^t G(u)\, du + 3. \qquad \text{...(iii)}$$

Again integrating,

$$F(t) = \int_0^t (t-u)\, G(u)\, du + 3 = \int_0^t dt + C_2$$

or $$F(t) = \int_0^t (t-u)\, G(u)\, du + 3t + C_2.$$

Subjecting this to the condition

$$F(t) = -2 \text{ at } t - 0,$$

we get $\quad -2 = 0 + 0 + C_2 \quad$ or $\quad C_2 = -2.$

$$\therefore \quad F(t) = \int_0^t (t-u)\, G(u)\, du + 3t - 2 \qquad \ldots\text{(iv)}$$

Writing (i) with the help of (ii), (iii) and (iv),

$$G(t) + 2\int_0^t G(u)\, du + 6 - 8\int_0^t (t-u)\, G(u)\, du - 24 + 16 = 5t^2 - 3t$$

or
$$G(t) + \int_0^t [2 - 8t + 8u]\, G(u)\, du - 5t^2 - 21t + 22 = 0$$

where $\quad G(t) = F''(t).$

Method 2. Integrating (1) from 0 to t,

$$[F'(u)]_{u=0}^t + 2\,[F(u)]_{u=0}^t - 8\int_0^t F(u)\, du = \frac{5}{3}t^3 - \frac{3}{2}t^2$$

or
$$F'(t) - F'(0) + 2F(t) - 2F(0) - 8\int_0^t F(u)\, du = \frac{5t^3}{3} - \frac{3t^2}{2}.$$

But $\quad F'(0) = 3,\ F(0) = -2$ so that

$$-F'(t) - 2F(0) = 1.$$

$$\therefore \quad F'(t) + 2F(t) - 8\int_0^t F(u)\, du = \frac{5}{3}t^3 - \frac{3}{2}t^2 = 1.$$

Again integrating, we get

$$[F(u)]_{u=0}^t + 2\int_0^t F(u)\, du - 8\int_0^t (t-u)\, F(u)\, du = \frac{5t^4}{12} - \frac{t^3}{2} - t$$

or
$$F(t) - F(0) + \int_0^t (-8t + 8u + 2)\, F(u)\, du = \frac{5t^4}{12} - \frac{t^3}{2} - t$$

or
$$F(t) + \int_0^t (-8t + 8u + 2)\, F(u)\, du = \frac{5t^4}{12} - \frac{t^3}{2} - t - 2.$$

Note. In this problem, we have two answers for the same question, but they lead to the same conclusion.

Example 7. *Express the differential equation* $F''(t) + aF(t) = 0$, $F(0) = 0 = F(1)$ *as in integral equation.*

Solution. We have

$$F'(t) + aF(t) = 0 \qquad \ldots(\text{i})$$

$$F(0) = 0 = F(1) \qquad \ldots(\text{ii})$$

Method 1. Let $F'(t) = G(t)$.

Integrating, we get

$$F(t) = \int_0^t G(u)\,du + C_1 \qquad \ldots(\text{iii})$$

Again integrating,

$$F(t) = \int_0^t (t-u)\,G(u)\,du + C_1 t + C_2 \qquad \ldots(\text{iv})$$

For $t = 0$, this gives

$$0\,F(0) = 0 + C_2 \quad \text{or} \quad C_2 = 0.$$

Now (4) becomes

$$F(t) = \int_0^t (t-u)\,G(u)\,du + C_1 t, \qquad \ldots(\text{v})$$

For $t = 1$, this gives

$$0 = F(1) = \int_0^1 (1-u)\,G(u)\,du + C_1$$

or

$$C_1 = -\int_0^1 (1-u)\,G(u)\,du.$$

Now (5) becomes

$$F(t) = \int_0^t (t-u)\,G(u)\,du - \int_0^1 t(1-u)\,G(u)\,du$$

$$= \int_0^t (t-u)\,G(u)\,du + \int_0^1 (ut-t)\,G(u)\,du$$

$$= \int_0^t (t-u)\,G(u)\,du + \int_0^t (ut-t)\,G(u)\,du + \int_t^1 (ut-t)\,G(u)\,du$$

$$= \int_0^t (t-1)\,u\,G(u)\,du + \int_t^1 t(u-1)\,G(u)\,du$$

or

$$F(t) = \int_0^1 K(t,u)\,G(u)\,du$$

where $\quad K(t, u) = \begin{cases} (t-1)\,u & \text{if } u < t \\ t\,(u-1) & \text{if } u > t \end{cases}$

Using this in (i),

$$G(t) + a\int_0^1 K(t, u) = G(u)\,du = 0$$

where $\quad G(t) = F'(t),\ k(t, u) = \begin{cases} (t-1)\,u, & u < t \\ (u-1)\,t, & u > t \end{cases}$

Method 2. Integrating (1) from 0 to t,

$$\int_0^t F''(u)\,du + a\int_0^t F(u)\,du = 0$$

or $$[F'(u)]_0^t + a\int_0^t F(u)\,du = 0$$

or $$F(t) - F(0) + a\int_0^t F(u)\,du = 0.$$

Again integrating,

$$[F(u)]_0^t - F(0)\,[u]_0^t + a\int_0^t (t-u)\,F(u)\,du = 0$$

or $$F(t) - F(0) - t\,F(0) + a\int_0^t (t-u)\,F(u)\,du = 0$$

or $$F(t) - t\,F(0) + a\int_0^t (t-u)\,F(u)\,du = 0 \qquad \ldots\text{(i)}$$

For $t = 1$, this gives

$$F(1) - F(0) + a\int_0^2 (1-u)\,F(u)\,du = 0$$

or $$0 - F'(0) + a\int_0^1 (1-u)\,F(u)\,du = 0$$

or $$F'(0) = a\int_0^1 (1-u)\,F(u)\,du.$$

Using this in (1),

$$F(t) - ta\int_0^1 (1-u)\,F(u)\,du + a\int_0^t (t-u)\,F(u)\,du = 0$$

or $$F(t) + a\int_0^t t\,(u-1)\,F(u)\,du + a\int_0^t (t-u)\,F(u)\,du = 0$$

or $$F(t) + a\int_0^t t(u-1)F(u)\,du + a\int_t^1 t(u-1)F(u)\,du$$
$$+ a\int_0^t (t-u)F(u)\,du = 0$$

or $$F(t) + a\int_0^t u(t-1)F(u)\,du + a\int_t^1 t(u-1)F(u)\,du = 0.$$

Taking $K(u, t) = \begin{cases} u(t-1), & u < t \\ t(u-1), & u > t \end{cases}$

we get $$F(t) = a\int_0^1 K(u, t)F(u)\,du = 0.$$

Example 8. *Express* $2F''(t) - 3F'(t) - 2F(t) = 4e^{-t} + 2\cos t$, $F(0) = 4$, $F'(0) = -1$ *into integral equation.*

Solution. We have

$$2F''(t) - 3F'(t) - 2F(t) = 4e^{-t} + 2\cos t \quad \text{...(i)}$$

$$F(0) = 4, F'(0) = -1 \quad \text{...(ii)}$$

Method 1. Integrating (1) from 0 to t,

$$2[F'(u)]_0^t - 3[F(u)]_0^t - 2\int_0^t F(u)\,du = -4\left(e^{-u}\right)_0^t + 2(\sin u)_0^t$$

or $$2F'(t) - 2F'(0) - 3F(t) + 3F(0) - 2\int_0^t F(u)\,du = 4(1 - e^{-t}) + 2\sin t.$$

Using (ii), we get

$$2F'(t) - 3F(t) - 2\int_0^t F(u)\,du = -4e^{-t} + 2\sin t - 10.$$

Again integrating,

$$2[F(u)]_0^t - 3\int_0^t F(u)\,du - 2\int_0^t (t-u)F(u)\,du$$
$$= 4\left(e^{-u}\right)_0^t - 2(\cos u)_0^t - 10t$$

or

$$2[F(t) - F(0)] + \int_0^t (-2t + 2u - 3)F(u)\,du = 4(e^{-t} - 1) - 2(\cos t - 1) - 10t$$

or $$2F(t) + \int_0^t (-2t + 2u - 3)\, F(u)\, du = 4e^{-t} - 2\cos t - 10t + 6.$$

Method 2. Let $F'(t) = G(t)$.

Integrating, $F(t) = \int_0^t G(u)\, du + C_1$.

For $t = 0$, this gives $-1 = F(0) = 0 + C_1$ or $C_1 = -1$.

$$\therefore \quad F(t) = \int_0^t G(u)\, du - 1. \qquad \ldots\text{(ii)}$$

Again integrating,

$$F(t) = \int_0^t (t-u)\, G(u)\, du - t + C_2.$$

For $t = 0$, this gives $4 = F(0) = 0 - 0 + C_2$, $C_2 = 4$.

$$\therefore \quad F(t) = \int_0^t (t-u)\, G(u)\, du - t + 4 \qquad \ldots\text{(iii)}$$

Writing (1) with the help of (2) and (3),

$$2G(t) - 3\int_0^t G(u)\, du + 3 - 2\int_0^t (t-u)\, G(u)\, du + 2t - 8 = 4e^{-t} + 2\cos t$$

or $$2G(t) + \int_0^t (-2t + 2u - 3)\, G(u)\, du = 4e^{-t} + 2\cos t - 2t + 5.$$

Example 9. *Convert the integral equation*

$$F(t) = t^2 - 3t + 4 - 3\int_0^t (t-u)^2 F(u)\, du$$

into differential equation and associated conditions.

Solution. We have

$$F(t) = t^2 - 3t + 4 - 3\int_0^t (t-u)^2 F(u)\, du \qquad \ldots\text{(i)}$$

We know that

$$\frac{d}{dt}\int_{a(t)}^{b(t)} K(u,t)\, du = \int_{a(t)}^{b(t)} \frac{\partial K}{\partial t}\, du + K(b,t)\frac{db}{dt} - K(a,t)\frac{da}{dt} \qquad \ldots\text{(ii)}$$

Differentiating (i) and noting (ii), we get

$$F'(t) = 2t - 3 - 3\int_0^t 2(t-u)\,F(u)\,du \qquad \text{...(iii)}$$

Again differentiating,

$$F''(t) = 2 - 6\int_0^t F(u)\,du \qquad \text{...(iv)}$$

A final differentiation gives

$$F'''(t) = -6F(t)$$

or $$F'''(t) + 6F(t) = 0. \qquad \text{...(v)}$$

Putting $t = 0$ in (1), (3) and (4) respectively,

$$F(0) = 4,\ F(0) = -3, \quad F'(0) = 2$$

$$F'''(t) + 6F(t) = 0 \text{ with } F(0) = 4,\ F(0) = -3,\ F'(0) = 2.$$

EXERCISE 4(A)

Solve the following integral equations:

1. $F(t) = 1 + 2\int_0^t F(t-u)\,e^{-2u}\,du.$

2. $F(t) = 1 + 2\int_0^t F(t-u)\cos u\,du.$

3. $\int_0^t \frac{F(u)}{\sqrt{(t-u)}}\,du = 1 + t + t^2.$

4. $\int_0^t F(t-u)\,F(u)\,du = 2F(t) + t - 2.$

5. $F(t) = e^{-t} - 2\int_0^t F(u)\cdot\cos(t-u)\,du.$

6. Convert $F'(t) - tF(t) + t^2 F(t) = 1 + t,\ F(0) = 4,\ F(0) = 2$ into integral equation.

7. Solve $F(t) = t^2 + \int_0^t F(u)\cdot\sin(t-u)\,du.$

8. Convert the integral equation

$$F(t) = 3t - 4 - 2\sin t + \int_0^t \{(t-u)^2 - 3(t-u) + 2\}\,F(u)\,du$$

into a differential equation.

9. Convert the differential equation

$$F''(t) - 3F'(t) + 2F(t) = 4\sin t,\ F(0) = 1,\ F'(0) = -2$$

into an integral equation.

10. Solve $F(t) = a\sin t - 2\int_0^t F(u)\cos(t-u)\,du$.

ANSWERS

1. $F(t) = 1 + 2t$.
2. $F(t) = 1 + 2t\,e^t$.
3. $F(t) = \dfrac{t^{-1/2}}{3\pi}(3 + 6t + 8t^2)$.
4. $F(t) = 1$
5. $F(t) = e^{-t}(1-t)^2$
6. $G(t) + \int_0^t (t^3 - t - 4t^2)\,G(u)\,du = 1 + 3t - 4t^2 - 2t^2,\ G(t) = F''(t)$

   or

   $$F(t) - \int_0^t (t - 2u + tu^2 - u^3)\,F(u)\,du = t^2/2 + t^3/6 + 4.$$

7. $F(t) = t^2 + \dfrac{t^4}{12}$.
8. $F'''(t) - 2F''(t) + 3F'(t) - 2F(t) = 2\cos t$ with $F(0) = -4$, $F'(0) = -7$, $F''(0) = -2$.
9. $G(t) = 4\sin t + 4t - 8 + \int_0^t \{3 - 2(t-u)\}\,G(u)\,du,\ G(t) = F''(t)$

   or

   $$F(t) + \int_0^t \{2(t-u) - 3\}\,F(u)\,du = 1 - 4\sin t.$$

10. $F(t) = at\,e^{-t}$.

5

Application of Laplace Transforms to Boundary Value Problems

5.1 INTRODUCTION

In this chapter the following results are used frequently

$$L\{u(x, t)\} = u(x, p)$$

$$L\left\{\frac{\partial u}{\partial x}\right\} = \frac{d\bar{u}}{dx}, \quad L\left\{\frac{\partial^2 u}{\partial x^2}\right\} = \frac{d^2\bar{u}}{dx^2},$$

$$L\left\{\frac{\partial u}{\partial t}\right\} = p\bar{u} - u(x, 0),$$

$$L\left\{\frac{\partial^2 u}{\partial t^2}\right\} = p^2 u - p\bar{u}(x, 0) - u_t(x, 0).$$

5.2 APPLICATION TO ELECTRICAL CIRCUITS

A simple electrical circuit consists of the following in a series with a switch or key K,

(i) a generator or battery of power E volts,

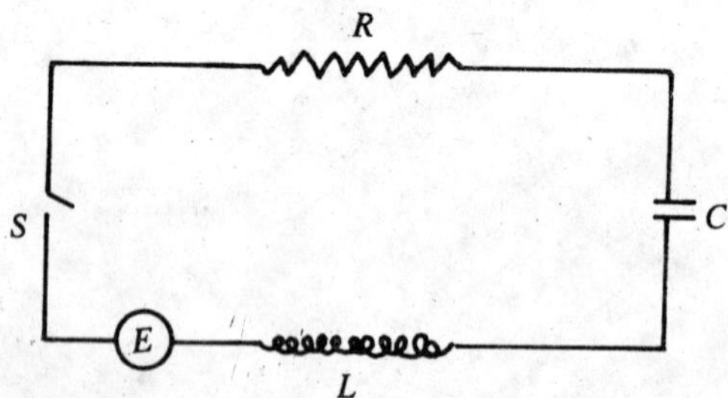

(ii) a resistance R (ohms)

(iii) an inductor having inductance L (henrys),

(iv) a condenser of capacity C (farads).

When the key K is closed, the circuit is closed, a charge Q (coulombs) will follow on the condenser at time t. The time rate of flow of charge, given by $dQ/dt = I$, is called the *current* and is measured in amperes when time t is measured in seconds.

The voltage developed across the resistance, inductance and condenser are respectively

$$RI, \quad L\frac{dI}{dt}, \quad \frac{Q}{C}.$$

The sum of these voltage is equal to the voltage E of the battery. Hence

$$L\frac{dI}{dt} + RI + \frac{Q}{C} = E$$

or
$$L\frac{d^2Q}{dt^2} + R\frac{dQ}{dt} + \frac{Q}{C} = E$$

This is the differential equation of the circuit.

ILLUSTRATIVE EXAMPLES

Example 1. *An inductor of 3 henrys is in series with a resistance of 30 ohms and an e.m.f. of 150 volts. Assuming that at $t = 0$, the current is zero, find the current at time $t > 0$.*

Solution. Given that

$$L = 3 \text{ henrys}, R = 30 \text{ ohms}, E = 150 \text{ volts}, I = 0 \text{ at } t = 0.$$

We have

$$L\frac{d^2Q}{dt^2} + R\frac{dQ}{dt} = E \qquad \text{(since condenser is not present)}$$

Putting the values,

$$3\frac{d^2Q}{dt^2} + 30\frac{dQ}{dt} = 150$$

or
$$3Q'' + 30Q' = 150$$

or
$$3L\{Q''\} + 30L\{Q'\} = 150L\{1\}$$

or
$$3\{p^2\overline{Q} - pQ(0) - Q'(0)\} + 30\{p\overline{Q} - Q(0)\} = \frac{150}{p} \qquad \ldots\text{(i)}$$

At $t = 0$, the current is zero, so that

$$\frac{dQ}{dt} = Q' = I = 0 \text{ at } t = 0,\ Q(0) = 0.$$

Now (i) becomes

$$3\{p^2\bar{Q}\} + 30p\bar{Q} = \frac{150}{p}$$

or
$$\bar{Q} = \frac{50}{p^2(p+10)}$$

$$\therefore \quad Q = 50L^{-1}\left\{\frac{1}{p^2(p+10)}\right\} \qquad \ldots\text{(ii)}$$

$$L^{-1}\left\{\frac{1}{(p+10)}\right\} = e^{-10t}$$

$$\therefore \quad L^{-1}\left\{\frac{1}{p(p+10)}\right\} = \int_0^t e^{-10u}\,du = \frac{1}{10}(1 - e^{-10t}).$$

Again
$$L^{-1}\left\{\frac{1}{p^2(p+10)}\right\} = \int_0^t \frac{1}{10}(1 - e^{-10u})\,du = \frac{1}{10}\left(t + \frac{e^{-10t} - 1}{10}\right)$$

Now (2) becomes

$$Q = 50\left(t + \frac{e^{-10t} - 1}{10}\right).$$

$$I = \frac{dQ}{dt} = 50\left[1 + \frac{-10e^{-10t} - 0}{10}\right] = 5(1 - e^{-10t}).$$

Example 2. *An inductor of 2 henrys, a resistance of 16 ohms and a capacitor of .02 farads are connected in series with an e.m.f. of 100 sin 3t volts. At t = 0 the charge on the capacitor and current in the circuit are zero. Find the charge and current at any time t > 0.*

Solution. Given $R = 16$ ohms, $C = \cdot 02$ farads, $L = 2$ henrys, $E = 100 \sin 3t$, $Q = \frac{dQ}{dt} = I = 0$ at $t = 0$.

We have

$$L\frac{d^2Q}{dt^2} + R\frac{dQ}{dt} + \frac{Q}{C} = E$$

or $\quad 2\dfrac{d^2Q}{dt^2} + 16\dfrac{dQ}{dt} + \dfrac{Q}{\cdot 02} = 100 \sin 3t$

or $\quad 2\dfrac{d^2Q}{dt^2} + 16\dfrac{dQ}{dt} + \dfrac{100}{2} Q = 100 \sin 3t$

or $\quad \dfrac{d^2Q}{dt^2} + 8\dfrac{dQ}{dt} + 25Q = 50 \sin 3t$

or $\quad Q'' + 8Q' + 25Q = 50 \sin 3t$

or $\quad L\{Q''\} + 8L\{Q'\} + 25L\{Q\} = 50L\{\sin 3t\}$

or $\quad \{p^2\overline{Q} - pQ(0) - Q'(0)\} + 8\{p\overline{Q} - Q(0)\} + 25\overline{Q} = \dfrac{50 \times 3}{p^2 + 9}$

Putting $Q(0) = t = Q'(0)$, we get

$$p^2\overline{Q} + 8p\overline{Q} + 25\overline{Q} = \frac{150}{p^2 + 9}$$

or $\quad \overline{Q} = \dfrac{150}{(p^2 + 9)(p^2 + 8p + 25)}$

$$= \frac{75}{52}\left[\frac{-p + 2}{p^2 + 9} + \frac{p + 6}{p^2 + 8p + 25}\right]$$

$$= \frac{75}{52}\left[\frac{-s}{p^2 + 9} + \frac{2}{p^2 + 9} + \frac{s + 4}{(p + 4)^2 + 9} + \frac{2}{(p + 4)^2 + 9}\right]$$

$$Q = L^{-1}\{\overline{Q}\} = \frac{75}{52}\left[-\cos 3t + \frac{2}{3}\sin 3t + e^{-4t}\cos 3t + \frac{2}{3}e^{-4t}\sin 3t\right]$$

$$= \frac{75}{52 \times 3}[(2 \sin 3t - 3 \cos 3t) + e^{-4t}(2 \sin 3t + 3 \cos 3t)]$$

$$\therefore \quad Q = \frac{25}{52}[(2 \sin 3t - 3 \cos 3t) + e^{-4t}(2 \sin 3t + 3 \cos 3t)]$$

$$I = \frac{dQ}{dt} = \frac{25}{52}[3(2 \cos 3t + 3 \sin 3t) + e^{-4t}\{-4(2 \sin 3t + 3 \cos 3t) + 3(2 \cos 3t - 3 \sin 3t)\}]$$

$$= \frac{25}{52}[3(2 \cos 3t + 3 \sin 3t) - e^{-4t}(17 \sin 3t + 6 \cos 3t)]$$

Example 3. *An electric circuit consists of an inductor of L henrys in series with a capacitor of C farads. At t = 0, an e.m.f. given by*

$$E(t) = \begin{cases} E_0 t/T_0, & 0 < t < T_0 \\ 0, & t > T_0 \end{cases}$$

is applied. Assuming that the current and charge on the capacitor are zero at $t = 0$, *find the charge at any time* $t > 0$.

Solution. For the sake of convenience, we suppose

$$T_0 = a \text{ and } \frac{E_0}{T_0} = b.$$

Given $E \begin{cases} bt, & 0 < t < a \\ 0, & t > a, \end{cases}$

$$Q = \frac{dQ}{dt} = 0 \text{ at } t = 0.$$

The differential equation for determination of Q is given by

$$L\frac{d^2Q}{dt^2} + \frac{Q}{C} = E$$

or
$$LQ'' + \frac{Q}{C} = E \qquad \left(\text{Since } R \text{ is absent and so } R\frac{dQ}{dt} = 0\right) \qquad \text{. . .(i)}$$

Taking Laplace Transform of (1),

$$L\{p^2\bar{Q} - pQ(0) - Q'(0)\} + \frac{\bar{Q}}{C} = \int_0^\infty E\, e^{-pt}\, dt$$

Subjecting this to $Q(0) = Q'(0) = 0$, we get

$$\left(p^2L + \frac{1}{C}\right)\bar{Q} = \int_0^a bte^{-pt}\, dt + \int_a^\infty 0\, e^{-pt}\, dt$$

$$= b\left[\frac{te^{-pt}}{-p} - \frac{e^{-pt}}{p^2}\right]_0^a = -b\left[\frac{ae^{-pa}}{p} + \frac{e^{-pa} - 1}{p^2}\right]$$

or
$$\bar{Q} = -\frac{b}{L\left(p^2 + \frac{1}{LC}\right)}\left(\frac{ae^{-pa}}{p} + \frac{e^{-pa} - 1}{p^2}\right).$$

Putting $\frac{1}{LC} = m^2$, we get

$$\bar{Q} = -\frac{bae^{-pa}}{L(p^2 + m^2)\,p} - \frac{be^{-pa}}{p^2L(p^2 + m^2)} + \frac{b}{Lp^2(p^2 + m^2)}.$$

Taking inverse Laplace transform, we get

$$Q = L^{-1}\left\{\frac{-abe^{-pa}}{Lp\,(s^2+m^2)} - \frac{be^{-pa}}{p^2L\,(p^2+m^2)} + \frac{b}{p^2L\,(p^2+m^2)}\right\} \qquad \ldots\text{(ii)}$$

Recall that if $L\,\{F(t)\} = f(p)$, then

$$L^{-1}\,\{e^{-ap}f(p)\} = \begin{cases} F(t-a), & t > a \\ 0, & t < a \end{cases}$$

$$= F(t-a)\,H(t-a)$$

where $H(t-a)$ is Heaviside unit step function,

$$L^{-1}\left\{\frac{1}{p^2+m^2}\right\} = \frac{1}{m}\sin mt,$$

$$L^{-1}\left\{\frac{1}{p\,(p^2+m^2)}\right\} = \int_0^t \frac{\sin mu}{m}\,du = \frac{(1-\cos mt)}{m^2},$$

$$L^{-1}\left\{\frac{1}{p^2\,(p^2+m^2)}\right\} = \int_0^t \left(\frac{1-\cos mu}{m^2}\right) du = \frac{1}{m^2}\left(t - \frac{\sin mt}{m}\right).$$

In view of this, we have

$$L^{-1}\left\{\frac{b}{p^2\,(p^2+m^2)\,L}\right\} = \frac{b}{Lm^2}\left(t - \frac{\sin mt}{m}\right),$$

$$L^{-1}\left\{\frac{-abe^{-pa}}{p\,(p^2+m^2)\,L}\right\} = \frac{-ab}{Lm^2}\,[1-\cos m\,(t-a)]\,H(t-a),$$

$$L^{-1}\left\{\frac{-be^{-pa}}{p^2\,(p^2+m^2)\,L}\right\} = \frac{-b}{Lm^2}\left[(t-a) - \frac{\sin m\,(t-a)}{m}\right] H(t-a).$$

Adding the last three equations and using (2),

$$Q = \frac{CE_0}{T_0}\left(t - \frac{\sin mt}{m}\right) - \frac{CE_0}{T_0}\,T_0\,[1-\cos m\,(t-a)]\,H(t-a)$$

$$- \frac{CE_0}{T_0}\left[(t-T_0) - \frac{\sin m\,(t-a)}{m}\right] H(t-a) \qquad \ldots\text{(iii)}$$

For $\dfrac{b}{Lm^2} = \dfrac{b}{L}\,CL = bC = \dfrac{CE_0}{T_0}.$

For $t < a$, *i.e.*, $t < T_0$ (iii) gives

$$Q = \frac{CE_0}{T_0}\,[t - \sqrt{(CL)} \cdot \sin(t/\sqrt{(CL)})]$$

For $\quad t > a$, *i.e.*, $t > T_0$ (iii) gives

$$Q = \frac{CE_0}{T_0}\left[t - (CL)^{1/2}\sin\frac{t}{(CL)^{1/2}}\right] - \frac{CE_0}{T_0}\,[T - T_0 \cos m\,(t - T_0)]$$

$$-\frac{CE_0}{T_0}\left[(t - T_0) - \frac{\sin m\,(t - T_0)}{m}\right]$$

$$= \frac{CE_0}{T_0}\left[T_0 \cos\left(\frac{t - T_0}{\sqrt{(CL)}}\right) + (CL)^{1/2}\sin\left(\frac{t - T_0}{(CL)^{1/2}}\right) - (CL)^{1/2} \cdot \sin\frac{t}{\sqrt{(LC)}}\right]$$

Hence $\quad Q = \dfrac{CE_0}{T_0}\left[t - \sqrt{(LC)} \cdot \sin\left(\dfrac{t}{\sqrt{(LC)}}\right)\right]$ if $t < T_0$

and

$$Q = \frac{CE_0}{T_0}\left[T_0 \cos\left(\frac{t - T_0}{\sqrt{(CL)}}\right) + (CL)^{1/2}\sin\left(\frac{t - T_0}{\sqrt{(CL)}}\right) - (CL)^{1/2} \cdot \sin\left(\frac{t}{\sqrt{(CL)}}\right)\right]$$

if $t > T_0$.

Example 4. *Constant voltage E is applied at t = 0 to a circuit with an inductance L, capacitance C and resistance R. Find the current I at time t, if the initial current and charge are zero.*

Solution. The differential equation for determination of Q is

$$L\frac{d^2Q}{dt^2} + R\frac{dQ}{dt} + \frac{Q}{C} = E$$

or $\quad LQ'' + RQ' + \dfrac{Q}{C} = E.$

But $\quad \dfrac{dQ}{dt} = I.$

$$LI' + RI + \frac{Q}{C} = E \text{ with } Q' = I,$$

Taking Laplace transform of both sides

$$\{p\bar{I} - I(0)\}\,L + \bar{I}R + \frac{\bar{Q}}{C} = \frac{E}{p} \text{ with } p\bar{Q} - Q(0) = \bar{I}.$$

Putting $Q(0) = I(0) = 0$, we get

$$p\bar{I}L + \bar{I}R + \frac{\bar{Q}}{C} = \frac{E}{p} \text{ with } p\bar{Q} = \bar{I}$$

or $$p\bar{I}L + \bar{I}R + \frac{\bar{I}}{pC} = \frac{E}{p}$$

or $$\bar{I}\left(p^2L + pR + \frac{1}{C}\right) = E$$

$$\bar{I} = \frac{E}{\left(p^2 + \frac{Rp}{L} + \frac{1}{LC}\right)L} = \frac{E}{\left[\left(p + \frac{R}{2L}\right)^2 - \frac{R^2}{4L^2} + \frac{1}{LC}\right]L}.$$

Putting $\frac{1}{LC} - \frac{R^2}{4L^2} = n^2$ and taking inverse Laplace transform, we get

$$I = L^{-1}\left\{\frac{E}{\left[\left(s + \frac{R}{2L}\right)^2 + n^2\right]L}\right\} \quad \text{...(i)}$$

Case I. When $n^2 > 0$, *i.e.*, $R^2 < \frac{4L}{C}$.

Now (i) gives

$$I = \frac{E}{L} \cdot e^{-Rt/2L} \cdot \frac{1}{n} \sin nt$$

Case II. When $n^2 < 0$, *i.e.*, $R^2 > \frac{4L}{C}$.

Now (i) gives

$$I = \frac{E}{L} L^{-1}\left[\frac{1}{\left(p + \frac{R}{2L}\right)^2 - k^2}\right],$$

where $$n^2 = -k^2, k^2 > 0.$$

$\therefore$ $$I = \frac{E}{Lk} e^{-Rt/2L} \sinh kt.$$

Case III. When $n^2 = 0$, *i.e.*, $R^2 = \frac{4L}{C}$.

Now (1) becomes

$$I = \frac{E}{L} \cdot L^{-1}\left\{\frac{1}{\left(p+\frac{R}{2L}\right)^2}\right\} = \frac{E}{L} \cdot e^{-Rt/2L} L^{-1}\left\{\frac{1}{p^2}\right\}$$

$$= \frac{Et}{L} e^{-Rt/2L}.$$

$$\text{Hence} \quad I = \begin{cases} \frac{Et}{L} e^{-Rt/2L} & \text{if } R^2 = \frac{4L}{C} \\ \frac{E}{L} e^{-Rt/2L} \cdot \frac{1}{n} \cdot \sin nt & \text{if } R^2 < \frac{4L}{C} \\ \frac{E}{Lk} e^{-Rt/2L} \cdot \sin kt & \text{if } R^2 > \frac{4L}{C} \end{cases}$$

Example 5. *An alternating E.M.F. $E \sin \omega t$ is applied to an inductance and a capacitance C in series. Show that the current in the circuit is $\frac{E\omega}{(n^2 - \omega^2) L}(\cos \omega t - \cos nt)$, where $n^2 = 1/LC$.*

Solution. The differential equation for the determination of the current I in the circuit is given by

$$L\frac{dI}{dt} + \frac{Q}{C} = E \sin \omega t \qquad \text{...(i)}$$

$$\text{where} \quad I = \frac{dQ}{dt} \qquad \text{...(ii)}$$

At time $t = 0$, $I = 0 = Q$.

Taking Laplace transform of both sides in (i),

$$L\,\{p\bar{I} - I(0)\} + \frac{1}{C}\bar{Q} = \frac{E\omega}{p^2 + \omega^2}$$

But $\quad I(0) = 0.$

$$\text{Hence} \quad Lp\bar{I} + \frac{1}{C}\bar{Q} = \frac{E\omega}{p^2 + \omega^2} \qquad \text{...(iii)}$$

But $\quad L\,\{I\} = L\left\{\frac{dQ}{dt}\right\}$

or, $\quad \bar{I} = p\bar{Q} - Q(0)$. But $Q(0) = 0$.

Hence $\bar{I} = p\bar{Q}$. Using this in (iii),

$$Lp\bar{I} + \frac{1}{Cp}\bar{I} = \frac{E\omega}{p^2 + \omega^2}$$

or

$$\bar{I} = \frac{E\omega}{(p^2 + \omega^2)\left(Lp + \frac{1}{Cp}\right)} \qquad \ldots\text{(iv)}$$

$$Lp + \frac{1}{Cp} = (LCp^2 + 1)\cdot\frac{1}{Cp} = \frac{1}{Cp}\left(\frac{p^2}{n^2} + 1\right) = \frac{(p^2 + n^2)}{n^2 pC}$$

$$= \frac{(p^2 + n^2)L}{p}$$

$$\therefore \quad \bar{I} = \frac{E\omega p}{(p^2 + \omega^2)(p^2 + n^2)L}$$

$$= \frac{E\omega}{(n^2 - \omega^2)L}\left\{\frac{p}{p^2 + \omega^2} - \frac{p}{p^2 + n^2}\right\}$$

Taking inverse Laplace transform,

$$I = \frac{E\omega}{L(n^2 - \omega^2)}\{\cos \omega t - \cos nt\}$$

5.3 APPLICATION TO DYNAMICS

ILLUSTRATIVE EXAMPLES

Example 1. *A mass m moves along the x-axis under the influence of a force which is proportional to its instantaneous speed and in a direction opposite to the direction of motion. Assuming that at t = 0, the particle is located at x = a and moving to the right with speed V_0, find the position where the mass comes to rest.*

Solution. The equation of motion of the particle is

$$m\frac{d^2x}{dt^2} = -\mu\frac{dx}{dt}$$

or

$$mx'' = -\mu x' \qquad \ldots\text{(i)}$$

with boundary conditions as

$$x(0) = a,\; x'(0) = V_0. \qquad \ldots\text{(ii)}$$

From (1), $mL\{x''\} + \mu L\{x'\} = 0$

or $$m\{p^2\bar{x} - px(0) - x'(0)\} + \mu\{(p\bar{x} - x(0)\} = 0.$$

In view of (2), this gives

$$m\{p^2\bar{x} - pa - V_0\} + \mu\{p\bar{x} - a\} = 0$$

or $$\bar{x} = \frac{mV_0 + \mu a + mpa}{mp^2 + \mu p} = \frac{mV_0 + \mu a + mpa}{mp\left(p + \frac{\mu}{m}\right)}$$

$$= \frac{mV_0 + \mu a}{mp\left(p + \frac{\mu}{m}\right)} + \frac{a}{p + \frac{\mu}{m}}$$

$$= \left(\frac{mV_0 + \mu a}{m}\right)\left\{\frac{m}{\mu p} - \frac{1}{p + \frac{\mu}{m}}\right\} + \frac{a}{p + \frac{\mu}{m}}$$

Taking inverse Laplace transform, we get

$$x = \left(\frac{mV_0 + \mu a}{m}\right)\left\{\frac{m}{\mu} - e^{-\mu t/m}\right\} + a\,e^{-\mu t/m} \qquad \text{...(iii)}$$

This $\Rightarrow$ $$\frac{dx}{dt} = \left[\frac{\mu(mV_0 + \mu a)}{m^2} - \frac{a\mu}{m}\right]e^{-\mu t/m}.$$

If $$\frac{dx}{dt} = 0, \text{ then } \left[\frac{\mu(mV_0 + \mu a)}{m^2} - \frac{a\mu}{m}\right]e^{-\mu t/m} = 0$$

or $$\frac{mV_0 + a\mu}{m} - a = 0 \qquad \text{...(iv)}$$

Now (3) becomes

$$x = a\left\{\frac{m}{\mu} - e^{-\mu t/m}\right\} + a\,e^{-\mu t/m} = \frac{am}{\mu} = \frac{mV_0 + a\mu}{\mu}, \text{ by (iv).}$$

Thus if $\frac{dx}{dt} = 0$, then $x = \frac{mV_0}{\mu} + a.$

Hence the mass comes to rest at a distance $\frac{mV_0}{\mu} + a$ from the centre O.

Example 2. *An iron ball of mass m falls from rest under gravity in a liquid which resists the motion with a force mk times the velocity. Determine the motion.*

5.4 APPLICATION TO BEAMS

Suppose a beam is kept along the x-axis and its ends are $x = 0, x = l$. Suppose the beam suffers a transverse deflection $y(x)$, which is produced by applying a vertical load $W(x)$ per unit length. The deflection is given by

$$\frac{d^4y}{dx^4} = \frac{W(x)}{El}, 0 < x < l,$$

where E is young's modulus of elasticity and I is moment of inertia of a cross section of the beam about the x-axis. The following are most common:

(i) *Free end.* $y'' = y''' = 0$.
(ii) *Clamped or fixed end.* $y = y' = 0$.
(iii) *Hinged or simply supported end.* $y = y'' = 0$.

ILLUSTRATIVE EXAMPLES

Example 1. *A beam which is clamped at its ends $x = 0, x = l$ carries a uniform load W_0 per unit length. Show that the deflection at any point is*

$$y(x) = \frac{W_0 x^2 (l - x)^2}{24EI}.$$

Solution. The deflection $y(x)$ is given by the differential equation

$$\frac{d^4y}{dx^4} = \frac{W_0}{EI}$$

Writing $\frac{W_0}{EI} = a$, we get

$$\frac{d^4y}{dx^4} = a \qquad \text{...(i)}$$

with boundary conditions

$$y(0) = 0 = y'(0) \qquad \text{...(ii)}$$

$$y(l) = 0 = y'(l). \qquad \text{...(iii)}$$

Taking Laplace transform of both sides in (1),

$$p^4 \bar{y} - p^3 y(0) - p^2 y'(0) - py''(0) - y'''(0) = a/p$$

In view of (2), this gives

$$p^4 \bar{y} - py''(0) - y'''(0) = a/p$$

Taking $b = y''(0)$, $c = y'''(0)$, we get

$$p^4 \bar{y} = bp + c + a/p$$

or $$\bar{y} = \frac{b}{p^3} + \frac{c}{p^4} + \frac{a}{p^5}$$

Taking inverse Laplace transform.

$$y = b\frac{x^2}{2!} + c\frac{x^3}{3!} + a\frac{x^4}{4!}$$

or $$y = \frac{bx^2}{2} + \frac{cx^3}{6} + \frac{ax^4}{24} \qquad \text{...(iv)}$$

Subjecting this to (3),

$$y(l) = 0 = \frac{bl^2}{2} + \frac{cl^3}{6} + \frac{al^4}{24}$$

$$y'(l) = 0 = bl + \frac{cl^2}{2} + \frac{al^3}{6}.$$

Solving this, $b = \frac{al^2}{12}, c = -\frac{al}{2}.$

Now (4) becomes

$$y = a\left[\frac{l^2x^2}{24} - \frac{lx^3}{12} + \frac{x^4}{24}\right] = \frac{ax^2}{24}(x^2 - 2lx + l^2)$$

$$= \frac{ax^2}{24}(l-x)^2 - \frac{W_0x^2(l-x)^3}{24EI}.$$

Example 2. *A beam which is hinged at its ends x = 0 and x = l carries a uniform load W_0 per unit length. Find the deflection at any point.*

Solution. The deflection $y(x)$ is given by the differential equation

$$\frac{d^4y}{dx^4} = \frac{W_0}{EI}, 0 < x < 1.$$

Writing a for W_n/EI, we obtain

$$\frac{d^4y}{dx^4} = a, \qquad \text{...(i)}$$

with boundary conditions.

$$y(0) = 0 = y''(0) \qquad \text{...(ii)}$$

$$y(l) = 0 = y''(l). \qquad \text{...(iii)}$$

Taking Laplace transform in (1),

$$p^4 \bar{y} - p^3 y(0) - p^2 y'(0) - p y''(0) - y'''(0) = a/p$$

In view of (2), this gives

$$p^4 \bar{y} - p^2 y'(0) - y'''(0) = a/p$$

Taking $b = y'(0)$, $c = y'''(0)$, we get

$$p^4 \bar{y} = p^2 b + c + a/p$$

or $$\bar{y} = \frac{b}{p^2} + \frac{c}{p^4} + \frac{a}{p^5}.$$

Taking inverse Laplace transform,

$$y = bx + \frac{cx^3}{3!} + \frac{ax^4}{4!}$$

or $$y = bx + \frac{cx^3}{6} + \frac{ax^4}{24} \qquad \text{...(iv)}$$

Subjecting this to (3),

$$y(l) = 0 = bl + \frac{cl^3}{6} + \frac{al^4}{24}$$

$$y''(l) = 0 + cl + \frac{al^2}{2}.$$

Solving, $c = -\frac{al}{2}$, $b = \frac{al^3}{24}$.

Now (iv) becomes

$$y = \frac{al^2 x}{24} - \frac{alx^3}{12} + \frac{ax^4}{24} = \frac{ax}{24}(l^3 - 2lx^2 + x^3)$$

$$= \frac{ax}{24}(l - x)(l^2 + lx - x^2)$$

$$= \frac{W_0 x}{24EI}(l - x)(l^2 + lx - x^2)$$

5.5 APPLICATION TO HEAT CONDUCTION EQUATION

One dimensional heat conduction equation is

$$\frac{\partial u}{\partial t} = k \frac{\partial^2 u}{\partial x^2}$$

where $u(x, t)$ is the temperature in a solid at position x and at time t, the constant k is called *diffusivity* and

$$k = \frac{K}{c\rho}$$

K = thermal conductivity, c = specific heat,

ρ = density.

The amount of heat per unit area per unit time conducted a cross plane is $K\frac{\partial u}{\partial x}$.

The temperature $u(r, t)$ in a cylinder is given by

$$\frac{\partial u}{\partial t} = k\left(\frac{\partial^2 u}{\partial r^2} + \frac{1}{r}\frac{\partial u}{\partial r}\right),$$

It is supposed that heat flow takes only along in radial direction.

ILLUSTRATIVE EXAMPLES

Example 1. *A semi-infinite solid $x > 0$ in initially at temperature zero. At time $t = 0$, a constant temperature $u_0 > 0$ is applied and maintained at the face $x = 0$. Find the temperature at any point of the solid at any time $t > 0$.*

Solution. The one dimensional heat conduction equation is

$$\frac{\partial u}{\partial t} = k\frac{\partial^2 u}{\partial x^2}. \qquad \ldots\text{(i)}$$

with the boundary conditions.

(i) $u(x, 0) = 0$, (ii) $u(0, t) = u_0$, (iii) u is finite.

Applying Laplace transform to (1),

$$L\left\{\frac{\partial u}{\partial t}\right\} = kL\left\{\frac{\partial^2 u}{\partial x^2}\right\}.$$

or $$p\bar{u} - u(x, 0) = k\frac{d^2\bar{u}}{dx^2}$$

or $$\frac{d^2 u}{dx^2} - \frac{p}{k}\bar{u} = 0. \text{ For } u(x, 0) = 0.$$

or $$\left(D^2 - \frac{p}{k}\right)\bar{u} = 0.$$

The solution of this is

$$\bar{u} = ae^{-x\sqrt{(p/k)}} + be^{x\sqrt{(p/k)}}.$$

Since $\bar{u}$ is finite, $b = 0$, otherwise u will be infinite when $x \to \infty$

$$\therefore \qquad u = ae^{-x\sqrt{(p/k)}} \qquad \ldots\text{(ii)}$$

$$u(0, t) = u_0 \;\&\; L\{u(0, t)\} = u_0 L\{1\} \Rightarrow \bar{u}(0, p) = u_0/p \qquad \ldots\text{(iii)}$$

Subjecting (2) to (3), $u_0/p = a$

Now (2) becomes

$$\bar{u} = \frac{u_0}{p} e^{-x\sqrt{(p/k)}}$$

$$u_0 = L^{-1}\{\bar{u}\} = u_0 L^{-1}\left\{\frac{e^{-x\sqrt{(p/k)}}}{p}\right\} = u_0 \, erfc\{x/2\sqrt{(kt)}\}$$

$$= u_0\left[1 - \frac{2}{\sqrt{\pi}}\int_0^{x/2\sqrt{(kt)}} e^{-u^2}\, du\right]$$

$$= u_0 \, erfc\{x/2\sqrt{(kt)}\}$$

$$= u_0\left[1 - erf\left\{\frac{x}{2\sqrt{(kt)}}\right\}\right]$$

Example 2. *A semi-infinite solid $x > 0$ has its initial temperature equal to zero. A constant h at flux A is applied at the face $x = 0$. Find the temperature at any point $x > 0$ of the solid given that*

$$= L^{-1}\left\{\frac{e^{-x\sqrt{p}}}{p^{3/2}}\right\} = e^{-x^2/4t^2}\left(\frac{t}{\pi}\right)^{1/2} - \frac{x}{2}\, erfc\left(\frac{x}{2\sqrt{t}}\right).$$

Solution. The temperature $u(x, t)$ is governed by the heat equation

$$\frac{\partial u}{\partial t} = k\frac{\partial^2 u}{\partial x^2}$$

with boundary conditions.

(i) $u(x, 0) = 0$, (ii) $K\dfrac{\partial u}{\partial x} = -A$ at $x = 0$, (iii) is finite when $x \to \infty$.

Taking Laplace transform in (i),

$$p\bar{u} - u(x, 0) = k\frac{d^2\bar{u}}{dx}$$

In view of (i), this gives

$$k\frac{d^2\bar{u}}{dx^2} - p\bar{u} = 0$$

or
$$\left(D^2 - \frac{p}{k}\right)\bar{u} = 0.$$

The solution of this is

$$\bar{u} = ae^{-x\sqrt{(p/k)}} + be^{x\sqrt{(p/k)}}.$$

Since $\bar{u}$ is finite, $b = 0$, otherwise u is infinite as $x \to \infty$.

Hence $\quad \bar{u} = ae^{-x\sqrt{(p/k)}}$ ...(ii)

$$\text{(ii)} \Rightarrow L\left\{k\frac{\partial u}{\partial x}\right\} = -AL\ \{1\} \Rightarrow K\frac{d\bar{u}}{dx} = -\frac{A}{p}.$$

$$(2) \Rightarrow \frac{d\bar{u}}{dx} = -a\sqrt{(p/k)} \cdot e^{-x\sqrt{(p/k)}}$$

$$\Rightarrow K\frac{d\bar{u}}{dx} = -ak\sqrt{(p/k)^{1/2}} \quad \text{at } x = 0$$

$$\Rightarrow -\frac{A}{p} = -aK\sqrt{(p/k)} \Rightarrow Ka = \frac{A}{p}\left(\frac{k}{p}\right)^{1/2} = \frac{A}{p^{3/2}}(k)^{1/2}$$

$$\therefore \quad a = \frac{Ak^{1/2}}{p^{3/2}K}$$

Now (ii) becomes $\bar{u} = \dfrac{Ak^{1/2}}{p^{3/2}K}e^{-x\sqrt{(p/k)}}$

$$\therefore \qquad u = \frac{Ak^{1/2}}{K}L^{-1}\left\{\frac{e^{-x\sqrt{(p/k)}}}{p^{3/2}}\right\} = \frac{Ak^{1/2}}{K}L^{-1}\left\{\frac{e^{-x\sqrt{p}/\sqrt{k}}}{p^{3/2}}\right\} \qquad \text{...(iii)}$$

But it is given that

$$L^{-1}\left\{\frac{e^{-x\sqrt{p}}}{p^{3/2}}\right\} = e^{-x^2/4t^2}(t/\pi)^{1/2} - \frac{x}{2}\,erfc\left(\frac{x}{2\sqrt{t}}\right).$$

This $\Rightarrow L^{-1}\left\{\dfrac{e^{-x\sqrt{p}/\sqrt{x}}}{p^{3/2}}\right\} = e^{-x^2/4kt^2}\cdot(t/\pi)^{1/2} - \dfrac{x}{2\sqrt{k}}\,erfc\left\{\dfrac{x}{2\sqrt{(kt)}}\right\},$

[on replacing by x by $x/\sqrt{k}$]

Using this in (iii), we get

$$u = \frac{Ak^{1/2}}{K}\left[e^{-x^2/4kt^2}(t/\pi)^{1/2} - \frac{x}{2\sqrt{k}}\,erfc\,\frac{x}{2\sqrt{(kt)}}\right].$$

Example 3. *A bar of length l is at constant temperature u_0. At $t = 0$ the end $x = l$ is suddenly given the constant temperature u_1 and the end $x = 0$ is insulated. Assuming that the surface of the bar is insulated, find the temperature at any point x of the bar at any time $t > 0$, given that*

$$L^{-1}\left\{\frac{\cosh(x\sqrt{p})}{s\cosh(a\sqrt{p})}\right\} = 1 + \frac{4}{k}\sum_{n=1}^{\infty}\frac{(-1)^n}{2n-1}e^{-(2n-1)^2\pi^2 t/4a^2} \times \cos\left(\frac{2n-1}{2a}\right)\pi x.$$

Solution. The temperature $u(x, t)$ is governed by the equation

$$\frac{\partial u}{\partial t} = k\frac{\partial^2 u}{\partial x^2} \qquad \ldots\text{(i)}$$

with the boundary conditions

(i) $u(x, 0) = u_0,\ 0 < x < l,$

(ii) $u(l, t) = u_1,$

(iii) $\dfrac{\partial u}{\partial x} = 0$ at $x = 0$.

(i) gives $L\left\{\dfrac{\partial u}{\partial t}\right\} = kL\left\{\dfrac{\partial^2 u}{\partial x^2}\right\}$

or $$p\bar{u} - u(x, 0) = k\frac{d^2\bar{u}}{dx^2}$$

or $$k\frac{d^2\bar{u}}{dx^2} - p\bar{u} = -u_0$$

or $$\left(D^2 - \frac{p}{k}\right)\bar{u} = \frac{-u_0}{k}.$$

The solution of this is

$$\bar{u} = a\cosh x\sqrt{\left(\frac{p}{k}\right)} + b\sinh x\sqrt{\left(\frac{p}{k}\right)} + \left(\frac{-u_0}{k}\right)\frac{1}{D^2 - \frac{p}{k}}e^{0p}$$

or $$\bar{u} = \frac{u_0}{p} + a\cosh x\sqrt{\left(\frac{p}{k}\right)} + b\sinh x\left(\frac{p}{k}\right) \qquad \ldots\text{(ii)}$$

$$\frac{d\bar{u}}{dx} = \sqrt{\left(\frac{p}{k}\right)}\left[a\sinh x\sqrt{\left(\frac{p}{k}\right)} + b\cosh x\sqrt{\left(\frac{p}{k}\right)}\right]$$

For $x = 0$, this gives $\frac{d\bar{u}}{dx} = b\sqrt{\left(\frac{p}{k}\right)}$. ...(iii)

(iii) $\Rightarrow L\left\{\frac{\partial u}{\partial x}\right\} = 0$ at $x = 0 \Rightarrow \frac{d\bar{u}}{dx} = 0$ at $x = 0 \Rightarrow b = 0$, according to (iii).

Now (ii) becomes, $\bar{u} = \frac{u_0}{p} + a \cosh x \left(\frac{p}{k}\right)^{1/2}$ ...(iv)

(ii) $\Rightarrow L\{u(l, t)\} = L\{u_2\} \Rightarrow \bar{u}(l, p) = \frac{u_1}{p}$

$\Rightarrow \frac{u_0}{p} + a \cosh l\sqrt{(p/k)} = \frac{u_1}{p}$, according to (iv)

$$\Rightarrow a = \frac{u_1 - u_0}{p \cosh l\sqrt{(p/k)}}$$

Using this in (iv),

$$\bar{u} = \frac{u_0}{p} + \frac{(u_1 - u_0)}{p} \frac{\cosh x\sqrt{(p/k)}}{\cosh l\sqrt{(p/k)}}.$$

$$u = L^{-1}\left\{\frac{u_0}{p}\right\} + (u_1 - u_0) L^{-1}\left\{\cosh x \frac{\sqrt{(p/k)}}{p \cosh l\sqrt{(p/k)}}\right\}$$

or $$u = u_0 + (u_1 - u_0)\left[1 + \frac{4}{\pi}\sum_{n=1}^{\infty} \frac{(-1)^n}{2n - 1} e^{-(2n-1)^2 \pi^2 kt/4l^2} \times \cos\frac{(2n-1)\pi x}{2l}\right].$$

Ans. $$u = u_1 + (u_1 - u_0)\frac{4}{\pi}\sum_{n=1}^{\infty} \frac{(-1)^n}{2n - 1} e^{-(2n-1)^2 \pi^2 kt/4l^2} \times \cos\frac{(2n-1)\pi x}{2l}.$$

This is obtained by putting $\frac{x}{\sqrt{k}}$ and $\frac{l}{\sqrt{k}}$ in place of x and a respectively in the given result.

Example 4. *The semi infinite solid $x < 0$ has thermal diffusivity k_1 and conductivity K_1. It is in contact along the plane $x = 0$ with semi infinite solid $x > 0$ in which these quantities are k_2, K_2. If the initial temperature of the first solid is constant V_0 and that of the second solid is zero, show that the temperature at time t in the second solid is*

$$\frac{V_0}{1+\sigma}\, erfc \left\{\frac{x}{2\sqrt{(k_2 t)}}\right\} \text{ where } \sigma = \frac{K_2\sqrt{k_1}}{K_1\sqrt{k_2}}.$$

Solution. The temperatures $U(x, t)$ and $V(x, t)$ at any points of the first and second solids at any time $t > 0$ are governed respectively by one dimensional heat equations:

$$\frac{\partial U}{\partial t} = k_1 \frac{\partial^2 U}{\partial x^2} \text{ for } -\infty < x \le 0 \quad \ldots(i)$$

and
$$\frac{\partial V}{\partial t} = k_2 \frac{\partial^2 V}{\partial x^2} \text{ for } 0 \le x < \infty \quad \ldots(ii)$$

With boundary conditions:

(a) $\lim_{x \to 0-} U(x, t) = \lim_{x \to 0+} V(x, t)$

i.e., $\lim_{h \to 0} U(0-h, t) = \lim_{h \to 0} V(0+h, t)$

(b) $U(x, 0) = V_0,\ V(x, 0) = 0$

(c) $\lim_{x \to 0-} [-K_1 U_x(x, t)] = \lim_{x \to 0+} [-K_2 V_x(x, t)]$

as amount of heat flowing into the element per second is

$$H_1 = -K_1 \frac{\partial U(x, t)}{\partial x}$$

(d) $\lim_{x \to -\infty} U(x, t)$ and $\lim_{x \to \infty} Y(x, t)$ are finite.

Taking Laplace transform of (1) and (2), we get

$$p\,\overline{U}(x, p) - U(x, 0) = k_1 \frac{d^2\overline{U}}{dx^2}$$

$$p\,\overline{V}(x, p) - V(x, 0) = k_2 \frac{d^2\overline{V}}{dx^2}$$

Putting the values of respective terms,

$$\frac{d^2\bar{u}}{dx^2} - \frac{p}{k_1}\bar{u}(x, p) = -\frac{V_0}{k_1}$$

and
$$\frac{d^2\overline{V}}{dx^2} - \frac{p}{k_2}\overline{V}(x, p) = 0$$

The solutions of these are

$$\overline{U}(x,p) = Ae^{ax} + Be^{-ax} + \frac{1}{D^2 - a^2}\left(-\frac{V_0}{k_1}\right) \qquad \text{...(iii)}$$

$$\overline{V}(x,p) = A_1 e^{bx} + B_1 e^{-bx} \qquad \text{...(iv)}$$

where $a^2 = \frac{p}{k_1},\ b^2 = \frac{p}{k_2}$.

But $$\frac{1}{D^2 - a^2}\left(-\frac{V_0}{k_1}\right) = -\frac{V_0}{k_1(-a^2)}\left[1 - \frac{D^2}{a^2}\right]^{-1}$$

$$= \frac{V_0}{p}\left(1 + \frac{D^2}{a^2}\right) = \frac{V_0}{p}$$

Now (iii) becomes

$$\overline{U}(x,p) = Ae^{ax} + Be^{-ax} + \frac{V_0}{p} \qquad \text{...(v)}$$

Taking Laplace transforms of the conditions (a), (c), (d), we get

(a_1) $\lim_{x \to 0-} 0(x,p) = \lim_{x \to 0+} \overline{V}(x,p)$

(c_1) $\lim_{x \to 0-} -K_1 \frac{\partial \overline{U}}{\partial x}(x,p) = \lim_{x \to 0+} -K_2 \frac{\partial \overline{V}}{\partial x}(x,p)$

(d_1) $\lim_{x \to -\infty} 0(x,p)$ and $\lim_{x \to \infty} \overline{V}(x,p)$ are finite.

The condition (d_1) declares that $B = 0, A_1 = 0$.

Now (4) and (5) $\Rightarrow \overline{V}(x,p) = B_1 e^{-px}$ ...(vi)

and $$\overline{U}(x,p) = 4e^{ax} + \frac{V_n}{p} \qquad \text{...(vii)}$$

Subjecting (6) and (7) to the conditions (a_1) and (c_1),

$$B_1 = A + \frac{V_0}{p} \text{ and}$$

$$-K_1\{Aae^{ax}\}_{x=0} = -K_2\{-B_1 be^{-bx}\}_{x=0}$$

This $\Rightarrow A + \frac{V_0}{p} = B_1,\ AK_1 a = -B_1 K_2 b$

$$\Rightarrow A + \frac{V_0}{p} = B_1, A = -B_1 \frac{K_2}{K_1} \cdot \frac{b}{a} = -B_1 \frac{K_2}{K_1} \left(\frac{k_1}{k_2} \right)^{1/2} = -B_1 \sigma$$

$$\Rightarrow -B_1 \sigma + \frac{V_0}{p} = B_1, A = -B_1 \sigma$$

$$\Rightarrow B_1 = \frac{V_0}{p(1+\sigma)}, A = -\frac{V_0 \sigma}{p(1+\sigma)}$$

Putting these values in (6) and (7), we get

$$\overline{V}(x, p) = \frac{V_0}{1+\sigma} \frac{1}{p} e^{-bx}$$

$$\overline{U}(x, p) = \frac{V_0 \sigma}{1+\sigma} \frac{1}{p} e^{ax} + \frac{V_0}{p}.$$

Taking inverse Laplace transform of $\overline{V}$, we get

$$V(x, t) = \frac{V_t}{1+\sigma} L^{-1} \left\{ \frac{1}{p} e^{-bx} \right\} = \frac{V_0}{1+\sigma} \, erfc \left\{ \frac{x}{2 (tk_2)^{1/2}} \right\}$$

as $$L^{-1} \left\{ \frac{e^{-\lambda \sqrt{p}}}{p} \right\} = erfc \left\{ \frac{\lambda}{2\sqrt{t}} \right\}.$$

Example 5. *The faces x = 0 and x = 1 of a slab of material for which k = 1 are kept at temperature 0 and 1 respectively until the temperature distribution becomes u = x. After time t = 0 both faces are held at temperature 0. Determine the temperature formula, given*

$$L^{-1} \left\{ \frac{\sinh x \sqrt{p}}{x \sinh a \sqrt{p}} \right\} = \frac{x}{a} + \frac{2}{\pi} \sum_{n=1}^{\infty} \frac{(-1)^n}{n} e^{-n^2 \pi^2 t/a^2} \sin \left(\frac{\pi n x}{a} \right).$$

Solution. The temperature $u(x, t)$ in the slab is governed by the differential equation

$$\frac{\partial u}{\partial t} = \frac{\partial^2 u}{\partial x^2} \qquad \ldots \text{(i)}$$

with boundary conditions

(i) $u(0, t) = 0$, (ii) $u(1, t) = 0$, (iii) $u(x, 0) = x$.

From (i), $L \left\{ \frac{\partial u}{\partial t} \right\} = L \left\{ \frac{\partial^3 u}{\partial x^2} \right\}$

or $$p\bar{u} - u(x, 0) = \frac{d^2\bar{u}}{dx^2}$$

But $u(x, 0) = x$.

Hence $$\frac{d^2\bar{u}}{dx^2} - p\bar{u} = -x$$

or $$(D^2 - p)\,\bar{u} = -x.$$

The solution of it is

$$\bar{u} = ae^{-x\sqrt{p}} + be^{x\sqrt{p}} + \frac{1}{D^2 - p}(-x)$$

$$= ae^{-x}\sqrt{p} + be^{x\sqrt{p}} + \frac{1}{p}\left(1 - \frac{L^x}{p}\right)^{-t} x$$

or $$\bar{u} = ae^{-x\sqrt{p}} + be^{x\sqrt{p}} + \frac{x}{p}$$

It is also expressed as

$$\bar{u} = a\cosh x\sqrt{p} + b\sinh x\sqrt{p} + \frac{x}{p} \quad \text{...(i)}$$

(i) $\Rightarrow L\{u(0, t)\} = 0 \Rightarrow \bar{u}(0, p) = 0$

$\Rightarrow 0 = a$ according to (1).

Now (1) becomes

$$\bar{u} = b\sinh x\sqrt{p} + \frac{x}{p} \quad \text{...(ii)}$$

(ii) $\Rightarrow L\{u(1, t)\} = 0 \Rightarrow \bar{u}(1, p) = 0$

$$\Rightarrow 0 = b\sinh\sqrt{p} + \frac{1}{p} \Rightarrow b = -\frac{1}{p\sinh\sqrt{p}}$$

Using this in (2), we get

$$\bar{u} = \frac{x}{p} - \frac{\sinh x\sqrt{p}}{p\sinh\sqrt{p}}$$

or $$u = L^{-1}\left\{\frac{x}{p}\right\} - L^{-1}\left\{\frac{\sinh x\sqrt{p}}{p\sinh\sqrt{p}}\right\}$$

or $$u = x - L^{-1}\left\{\frac{\sinh x\sqrt{p}}{p\sinh\sqrt{p}}\right\}$$

$$= x - \left[x + \frac{2}{\pi} \sum_{n=1}^{\infty} \frac{(-1)^n}{n} e^{-n^2\pi^2 t} \sin(n\pi x) \right]$$

$$= -\frac{2}{\pi} \sum_{n=1}^{\infty} \frac{(-1)^n}{n} e^{-n^2 n^2 t} \sin(n\pi x)$$

5.6 APPLICATIONS TO WAVE EQUATION

The transverse vibrations of an elastic string are governed by the equation

$$\frac{\partial^2 u}{\partial t^2} = a^2 \frac{\partial^2 u}{\partial x^2}, \text{ where } a^2 = T/\rho,$$

where u = deflection of the string,

T = constant tension in the string,

ρ = constant mass per unit length of string.

ILLUSTRATIVE EXAMPLES

Example 1. *An infinite long string having one end at x = 0 is initially at rest on the x-axis. The end x = 0 undergoes a periodic transverse displacement given by* $A_0 \sin nt$, $t > 0$. *Find the displacement of any point on the string at* $t > 0$.

Solution. The displacement of any point of the string is governed by the equation

$$\frac{\partial^2 u}{\partial t^2} = a^2 \frac{\partial^2 u}{\partial x^2}, \qquad \ldots(i)$$

with the boundary conditions

(i) $u(x, 0) = 0$,

(ii) $u(0, t) = A_0 \sin nt$,

(iii) $\dfrac{\partial u}{\partial t} = 0$ at $t = 0$.

(iv) u is finite for every x.

From (i), $L\left\{\dfrac{\partial^2 u}{\partial t^2}\right\} = a^2 L\left\{\dfrac{\partial^2 u}{\partial x^2}\right\}$

or $$p^2\bar{u} - pu(x, 0) - u(x, 0) = a^2 \frac{d^2 u}{dx^2}.$$

Subjecting this to boundary conditions,

$$p^2\bar{u} = a^2 \frac{d^2\bar{u}}{dx^2}$$

or $$\left(D^2 - \frac{p^2}{a^2}\right)\bar{u} = 0.$$

The solution of it is

$$\bar{u} = A\,e^{-xp/a} + Be^{xp/a}.$$

Since u is finite and so $\bar{u}$ is finite $\forall$ x.

This $\Rightarrow B = 0$.

$$\therefore \qquad \bar{u} = A\,e^{-xp/a}. \qquad \text{...(i)}$$

$$\text{(ii)} \Rightarrow \bar{u}(0, p) = A_0 \frac{n}{p^2 + n^2}$$

$$\Rightarrow A = nA_0/(p^2 + n^2), \text{ according to (i)}$$

Hence $$\bar{u} = \frac{nA_0\, e^{-xp/a}}{p^2 + n^2}$$

$$u = L^{-1}\left\{\frac{nA_0\, e^{-xp/a}}{p^2 + u^2}\right\} = A_0 L^{-1}\left\{\frac{n}{p^2 + n^2} \cdot e^{-(x/a)\,p}\right\}$$

$$= \begin{cases} A_0 \sin n\left(t - \dfrac{x}{a}\right) & \text{if } t > x/a \\ & \text{if } t < x/a \end{cases}$$

This follows from second shifting theorem

or $$u = A_0 \sin n\left(t - \frac{x}{a}\right) H\left(t - \frac{x}{a}\right)$$

where $H\left(t - \frac{x}{a}\right)$ is Heaviside's unit step function.

Example 2. *A tightly stretched flexible string has its ends fixed at $x = 0$ and $x = l$. At time $t = 0$, the string is given a shape defined by $y = \mu x(l - x)$, where μ is constant, and then released. Find the displacement of any point x of the string at any time $t > 0$, given that*

$$L^{-1}\left\{\frac{\cosh px}{s^2 \cosh pa}\right\} = \frac{1}{2}(t^2 + x^2 - a^2) - \frac{16a^2}{\pi^3} \sum_{n=1}^{\infty} \cdot \frac{(-1)^n}{(2n-1)^3}$$
$$\cos\frac{(2n-1)\,\pi x}{2a} \cos\frac{(2n-1)\,\pi t}{2a}.$$

Solution. The displacement $y(x, t)$ of any point of the string is governed by the equation

$$\frac{\partial^2 y}{\partial t^2} = a^2 \frac{\partial^2 y}{\partial x^2} \qquad \ldots(i)$$

with the conditions

(i) $y(x, 0) = \mu x(l - x)$,

(ii) $y_t(x, 0) = 0 \left[\frac{\partial y}{\partial t} = \text{at } t = 0\right]$

(iii) $y(0, t) = 0$,

(iv) $y(l, t) = 0$.

From (1), $L\left\{\frac{\partial^2 y}{\partial t^2}\right\} = a^2 L\left\{\frac{\partial^2 y}{\partial x^2}\right\}$

or $$p^2\bar{y} - py(x, 0) - y_t(x, 0) = a^2 \frac{d^2\bar{y}}{dx^2}.$$

Subjecting this to (i) and (ii), we get

$$p^2\bar{y} - p\mu x(l - x) - 0 = a^2 \frac{d^2\bar{y}}{dx^2}$$

or $$\left(D^2 - \frac{p^2}{a^2}\right)\bar{y} = \frac{p\mu x}{a^2}(l - x).$$

The solution of it is

$$\bar{y} = 4 \cosh\frac{px}{a} + B \sinh\frac{px}{a^2} - \frac{px}{a^2} \cdot \frac{1}{D^2 - \frac{p^2}{a}} x(l - x)$$

$$= A \cosh\frac{px}{a} + B \sinh\frac{px}{a} + \frac{\mu}{p}\left(1 - \frac{D^2}{p^2/a^2}\right)^{-1} (lx - x^2)$$

$$= A \cosh\frac{bx}{a} + B \sinh\frac{bx}{a} + \frac{\mu}{p}\left(lx - x^2 - \frac{2a^2}{p^2}\right)$$

or $$\bar{y} = A \cosh\frac{px}{a} + B \sinh\frac{px}{a} + \frac{\mu x(l - x)}{p} - \frac{2\mu a^2}{p^3} \qquad \ldots(i)$$

(iii) and (iv) $\Rightarrow \bar{y}(0, p) = 0, \bar{y}(l, p) = 0$.

From (i) $0 = \bar{y}(0, p) = A.1 + B.0 + \mu.0 - \frac{2\mu a^2}{p^3}$

or $$A = 2\mu a^2/p^3.$$

From (i) $0 = \bar{y}(l, p) = A \cosh \frac{pl}{a} + B \sinh \frac{pl}{a} - \frac{2\mu a^2}{p^2}$

or
$$\frac{2\mu a^2}{p^3} \cosh \frac{pl}{a} + B \sinh \frac{pl}{a} - \frac{2\mu a^2}{p^3} = 0$$

or
$$B = \frac{2\mu a^2}{p^3} \frac{\left(1 - \cosh \frac{pl}{a}\right)}{\sinh \frac{pl}{a}}$$

$$= -\frac{2\mu a^2}{p^3} \tanh \frac{pl}{2a}$$

Putting the values of A and B in (1),

$$\bar{y} = \frac{2\mu a^2}{p^3} \cosh \frac{px}{a} - \sinh \frac{px}{a} \tanh \frac{pl}{2a} + \frac{\mu x}{p}(l - x) - \frac{2\mu a^2}{p^3}$$

$$= \frac{\mu x}{p}(l - x) - \frac{2\mu a^2}{p^3} + \frac{2\mu a^2}{p^3} \frac{\cosh [p(2x - l) 2a]}{\cosh (pl/2a)}$$

Taking inverse Laplace transform

$$y = \mu x (l - x) - a^2 \mu t^2 + 2\mu a^2 L^{-1} \left\{ \frac{\cosh [p(2x - l)/2a]}{p^3 \cosh (pl/2a)} \right\} \quad \ldots \text{(ii)}$$

Writing $(2x - l)/2a$ in place of x, and $l/2a$ in place of a in the given result of inverse Laplace transform, we get

$$L^{-1} \left\{ \frac{\cosh [p(2x - l)/2a]}{p^3 \cosh (pl/2a)} \right\} = \frac{1}{2}\left[t^2 + \left(\frac{2x - l}{2a}\right)^2 - \left(\frac{l}{2a}\right)^2 \right]$$

$$+ \left(\frac{-4l^2}{a^2 \pi^3}\right) \sum_{n=1}^{\infty} \frac{(-1)^n}{(2n - 1)^3} \cos \left\{ \frac{(2n - 1)\pi(2x - l)}{2l} \right\} \cos \frac{(2n - 1)\pi t a}{l}.$$

$\therefore$
$$2\mu a^2 L^{-1} \left\{ \frac{\cosh \{p(2x - l)/2a\}}{p^3 \cosh (pl/2a)} \right\}$$

$$= \mu a^2 t^2 + \mu x^2 + \frac{l^2 \mu}{4} - \mu x l - \frac{\mu l^2}{4}$$

$$\frac{-8\mu l^2}{\pi^3} \sum_{n=1}^{\infty} \frac{(-1)^n}{(2n - 1)^3} \cos \frac{(2n - 1)\pi(2x - 1)}{2l} \cos \frac{(2n - 1)\pi t a}{l},$$

Using this in equation (2), we get

$$y = \frac{8\mu l^2}{\pi^2} \sum_{n=1}^{\infty} \frac{(-1)^n}{(2n-1)^3} \cos \frac{(2n-1)\,\pi\,(2x-1)}{2l} \cos \frac{(2n-1)\,\pi ta}{l}$$

Example 3. *A string is stretched between two fixed points (0, 0) and (c, 0). If it is displaced into the curve y = b sin (πx/c) and released from rest in that position at time t = 0. Find its displacement at any time t and at any point 0 < x < c.*

Solution. The displacement $y\,(x, t)$ of any point of the string is governed by the equation

$$\frac{\partial^2 y}{\partial t^2} - a^2 \frac{\partial^2 y}{\partial x^2} \qquad \ldots \text{(i)}$$

with the conditions.

(i) $y\,(0, t) = 0,$

(ii) $y\,(c, t) = 0,$

(iii) $y_t\,(x, 0) = 0,$

(iv) $y\,(x, 0) = b \sin (ax/c).$

From (i),

$$L\left\{\frac{\partial^2 y}{\partial t^2}\right\} = 0^2\, L\left\{\frac{\partial^2 y}{\partial x^2}\right\}$$

or
$$p^2 \bar{y} - py\,(x, 0) - y_t\,(x, 0) = a^2 \frac{d^2 \bar{y}}{dx^2}.$$

Subjecting this to boundary conditions,

$$p^2 \bar{y} - pb \sin \frac{\pi x}{c} - 0 = a^2 \frac{d^2 \bar{y}}{dx^2}$$

or
$$\left(D^2 - \frac{p^2}{a^2}\right) \bar{y} = -\frac{pb}{a^2} \sin \frac{\pi x}{c}.$$

The solution of this is

$$\bar{y} = Ae^{-px/a} + Be^{px/a} - \frac{pb}{a^2} \cdot \frac{1}{D^2 - \frac{p^2}{a^2}} \sin\left(\frac{\pi x}{c}\right)$$

$$-4e^{-px/a} + Be^{px/a} - \frac{pb}{a^2}\left[\frac{1}{\frac{-\pi^2}{c^2} - \frac{p}{a^2}}\right] \sin \frac{\pi x}{c}$$

or $$\bar{y} = Ae^{-px/a} + Be^{px/a} + pb\sin\left(\frac{\pi x}{c}\right)\frac{1}{p^2 + \left(\frac{\pi x}{c}\right)^2} \qquad \ldots(i)$$

(i) and (ii) $\Rightarrow \bar{y}(0, p) = 0 = \bar{y}(c, p)$.

From (i), $0 = \bar{y}(0, p) = A + B$

or $$A + B = 0. \qquad \ldots(ii)$$

Again from (1) $0 = \bar{y}(c, p) = Ae^{pc/a} + Be^{pc/a}$

or $$A + Be^{2pc/a} = 0, \qquad \ldots(iii)$$

(ii), (iii) gives $(1 - e^{2pc/a})B = 0$ or $B = 0$.

Now (ii) says that $A = 0$.

Using this in (i), we get

$$\bar{y} = b\sin\left(\frac{\pi x}{c}\right)\frac{p}{p^2 + \left(\frac{\pi a}{c}\right)^2}$$

This $\Rightarrow y = b\sin\frac{\pi x}{c}\cos\frac{\pi a}{c}t.$

Example 4. *Find the solution of the equation*

$$\frac{\partial u}{\partial t} = k\frac{\partial^2 u}{\partial x^2}.$$

which tends to zero as $x \to \infty$ and which satisfies the conditions

$$u = f(t), \text{ when } x = 0, t > 0$$

$$u = 0, \text{ when } x > 0, t = 0.$$

Solution. Taking Laplace transform of the given equation, we get

$$p\bar{u} - u(x, 0) = k\frac{d^2\bar{u}}{dx^2}$$

But $u(x, 0) = 0$

$$\therefore \quad \frac{d^2\bar{u}}{dx^2} - a^2\bar{u} = 0$$

or $$(D^2 - a^2)\bar{u} = 0,$$

where $a^2 = p/k$.

The solution of it is

$$\bar{u} = A\, e^{-ax} + B\, e^{ax}$$

But $u \to 0$ as $x \to \infty$. Hence $\bar{u} \to 0$ as $x \to \infty$.

This requires $B = 0$. Hence $\bar{u} = A\, e^{-ax}$ ...(i)

$$u = f(t),\ x = 0 \Rightarrow \bar{u} = \bar{f}(p),\ x = 0. \quad \text{...(ii)}$$

Subjecting (i) to the condition (ii), we get

$$\bar{f}(p) = A$$

$$\therefore \quad \bar{u} = \bar{f}(p)\, e^{-ax} = \bar{f}(p)\, e^{-x(p/k)^{1/2}}$$

Applying Laplace's inversion theorem, we get

$$u(x, t) = \frac{1}{2\pi i}\int_{y - i\infty}^{y + i\infty} e^{pt}\, \bar{f}(p)^{-x(p/k)^{1/2}}\, dp$$

Example. *Solve the boundary value problem*

$$\frac{\partial^2 u}{\partial t^2} = a^2 \frac{\partial^2 u}{\partial x^2},\ (x > 0,\ \ t > 0)$$

where $u(x, 0) = 0,\ u_t(x, 0),\ x > 0$

$$u(0, t) = F(t),\ \lim_{x \to \infty} u(x, t) = 0,\ t \geq 0.$$

Solution. Taking Laplace transform of the given equation,

$$p^2\bar{u}(x, p) - p\,u(x, 0) - u_t(x, 0) = a^2 \frac{d^2\bar{u}}{dx^2}$$

Putting the values of respective terms, we get

$$p^2\bar{u}(x, p) = a^2 \frac{d^2\bar{u}}{dx^2}$$

or
$$\left(D^2 - \frac{p^2}{a^2}\right)\bar{u} = 0$$

This $\Rightarrow \bar{u} = A\, e^{x(p/a)} + B\, e^{-x(p/a)}$ ...(i)

$$L\{u(0, t)\} = \bar{u}(0, p) = \int_0^\infty u(0, t)\, e^{-pt}\, dt$$

$$= \int_0^\infty F(t)\, e^{-pt}\, dt$$

or $\bar{u}(0,p) = \bar{F}(p)$ ...(ii)

$$\lim_{x \to \infty} u(x,t) = 0 \Rightarrow \lim_{x \to \infty} \bar{u}(x,p) = L\{0\} = 0$$

In view of (i), this suggests that $A = 0$.

Hence $\bar{u} = B\,e^{-x(p/a)}$ ...(iii)

Subjecting this to (2), $\bar{F}(p) = B\,e^{n} = B$

$\therefore$ $\bar{u} = e^{-x(p/a)}\,\bar{F}(p)$ or $u = L^{-1}\{\bar{F}(p)\,e^{-p(x/a)}\}$

By second shifting theorem,

$$u = F\left(t - \frac{x}{a}\right) H\left(t - \frac{x}{a}\right)$$

where $H\left(t - \frac{x}{a}\right)$ is Heavisides unit step function,

i.e.,
$$H\left(t - \frac{x}{a}\right) = \begin{cases} 1 & \text{if } t > \dfrac{x}{a} \\ 0 & \text{if } t > \dfrac{x}{a} \end{cases}.$$

Example 6. *Solve the boundary value problem*

$$\frac{\partial^2 u}{\partial t^2} = a^2 \frac{\partial^2 u}{\partial x^2}, \; (t > 0, \; x > 0)$$

where $u(x, 0) = 0,\ x \geq 0,\ u_t(x, 0) = 0,\ x > 0$

$$u(0, t) = t, \lim_{x \to \infty} u(x, t) = 0, t \geq 0.$$

Solution. Taking Laplace transform of the given equation,

$$L\left\{\frac{\partial^2 u}{\partial t^2}\right\} = a^2 L\left\{\frac{\partial^2 u}{\partial x^2}\right\}$$

or
$$p^2 \bar{u}(x,p) - pu(x,0) - u_t(x,0) = a^2 \frac{d^2 \bar{u}}{dx^2}$$

Putting the values of respective terms,

$$\frac{d^2 \bar{u}}{dx^2} - \frac{p^2}{a^2}\bar{u} = 0 \quad \text{or} \quad \left(D^2 - \frac{p^2}{a^2}\right)\bar{u} = 0$$

This $\Rightarrow \bar{u} = A\,e^{(p/a)x} + B\,e^{-x(p/a)}$ ...(i)

$$\lim_{x \to \infty} u(x, t) = 0 \Rightarrow \lim_{x \to \infty} L\{u(x, t)\} = L\{0\} \Rightarrow \lim_{x \to \infty} \bar{u}(x, p) = 0$$

This requires $A = 0$. Hence $\bar{u} = B\, e^{-p(x/a)}$ ...(ii)

$$u(0, t) = t \Rightarrow L\{u(0, t)\} = L\{\ \}$$

$$\Rightarrow \bar{u}(0, p) = \frac{1!}{p^{1+1}} \Rightarrow \bar{u}(0, p) = \frac{1}{p^2}$$

Subjecting (ii) to this condition,

$$\frac{1}{p^2} = B. \text{ Hence } \bar{u}(x, p) = \frac{1}{p^2} e^{-p(x/a)}$$

or
$$u = L^{-1}\left\{\frac{1}{p^2} e^{-p(x/a)}\right\} \qquad ...(iii)$$

But $L\{t^n\} = \dfrac{n!}{p^{n+1}}$. Hence $L\{t\} = \dfrac{1!}{p^2}$ or $L^{-1}\left\{\dfrac{1}{p^2}\right\} = t$

By second shifting theorem, (3) ⇒

$$u(x, t) = \left(t - \frac{x}{a}\right) H\left(t - \frac{x}{a}\right)$$

or
$$u(x, t) = \begin{cases} t - \dfrac{x}{a}, & t > \dfrac{x}{a} \\ 0, & t < \dfrac{x}{a} \end{cases}$$

Example 7. *Solve the boundary value problem,*

$$\frac{\partial^2 u}{\partial t^2} = a^2 \frac{\partial^2 u}{\partial x^2} - g, \quad (x > 0, \ t > 0)$$

with the boundary conditions:

$$u(x, 0) = 0 = u_t(x, 0), x \geq 0$$

$$u(0, t) = 0, \quad \lim_{x \to \infty} u_x(x, t) = 0, t \geq 0.$$

Solution. Taking Laplace transform of the given equation,

$$L\left\{\frac{\partial^2 u}{\partial t^2}\right\} = a^2 L\left\{\frac{\partial^2 u}{\partial x^2}\right\} - g\, L\{1\}$$

or
$$p^2 \bar{u}(x, p) - p u(x, 0) \ u_t(x, 0) = a^2 \frac{d^2 \bar{u}}{dx^2} - \frac{g}{p}$$

Putting the values of respective terms,

$$p^2\bar{u}(x,p) = a^2\frac{d^2\bar{u}}{dx^2} - \frac{g}{p}$$

or $$\left(D^2 - \frac{p^2}{a^2}\right)\bar{u}(x,p) = \frac{g}{pa^2}$$

This $$\Rightarrow \bar{u} = A\,e^{-px/a} + B\,e^{px/a} + \frac{1}{D^2 - \frac{p^2}{a^2}}\frac{g}{pa^2} \qquad \ldots(i)$$

But $$\frac{1}{D^2 - \frac{p^2}{a^2}}\cdot\frac{g}{pa^2} = \frac{g}{pa^2}\cdot\frac{1}{(-p^2/a^2)}\left[1 - \frac{a^2}{p^2}D^2\right]^{-1} 1$$

$$= \frac{g}{p^3}\left[1 + \frac{a^2}{p^2}D^2 \ldots\right], 1 = -\frac{g}{p^3}$$

Now (i) becomes $\bar{u}(x,p) = A\,e^{-p(x/a)} + B\,e^{(px/a)} - \dfrac{g}{p^2}$ ...(ii)

$$u(0,t) = 0 \Rightarrow L\{u(0,t)\} = L\{0\} \Rightarrow \bar{u}(0,p) = 0 \qquad \ldots(iii)$$

$$\lim_{x\to\infty} u_x(x,t) = 0 \Rightarrow \bar{u}_x(x,p) = 0 \quad \text{if} \quad x \to \infty \qquad \ldots(iv)$$

By (ii) and (iii), $0 = A + B - \dfrac{g}{p^2}$ ...(v)

(2) $\Rightarrow \bar{u}_x(x,p) = \dfrac{p}{a}[-A\,e^{-px/a} + B\,e^{px/a}]$

Subjecting this to (iv), $B = 0$. Hence $A = g/p^3$

Now (ii) is reduced to $\bar{u}(x,p) = \dfrac{g}{p^3}e^{-px/a} - \dfrac{g}{p^3}$

$$u = L^{-1}\left\{\frac{g}{p^3}e^{-px/a}\right\} - g\,L^{-1}\left\{\frac{1}{p^3}\right\}$$

$$= -g\,L^{-1}\left\{\frac{1}{p^2+1}\right\} + g\,L^{-1}\left\{\frac{e^{-p(x/a)}}{p^2+1}\right\}$$

$$= -g\frac{t^2}{2} + g\frac{1}{2}\left(t - \frac{x}{a}\right)^2 H\left(t - \frac{x}{a}\right)$$

where $$H\left(t-\frac{x}{a}\right)=\begin{cases}1 & \text{if } t>\frac{x}{a}\\ 0 & \text{if } t<\frac{x}{a}\end{cases}$$

Example 8. *Solve the boundary value problem*

$$\frac{\partial^2 u}{\partial t^2}=a^2\frac{\partial^2 u}{\partial x^2}+g,\ t>0,\ 0<x<l$$

with $$u=\frac{\partial u}{\partial t}=0 \text{ when } t=0,\ 0<x<l$$

$$u=0 \text{ when } x=0,\ t>0$$

$$\frac{\partial u}{\partial x}=0 \text{ when } x=l,\ t>0,$$

given that

$$L^{-1}\left\{\frac{\cosh px}{p^3\cosh pl}\right\}$$

$$=\frac{1}{2}(t^2+x^2-l^2)$$

$$-\frac{16l^2}{\pi^2}\sum_{n=1}^{\infty}\frac{(-1)^n}{(2n-1)^3}\cos\left\{\frac{(2n-1)\pi x}{2l}\right\}\cos\left\{\frac{(2n-1)\pi t}{2l}\right\}.$$

Solution. Taking Laplace transform of the given equation:

$$L\left\{\frac{d^2u}{dt^2}\right\}=a^2L\left\{\frac{\partial^2 u}{\partial x^2}\right\}+g\,L\{1\}$$

or $$p^2\bar{u}(x,p)-p\bar{u}(x,0)-u_t(x,0)=a^2\frac{d^2\bar{u}}{dx^2}+\frac{g}{p}$$

Putting the values of respective terms,

$$p^2\,\bar{u}(x,p)=a^2\frac{d^2\bar{u}}{dx^2}+\frac{g}{p}$$

or $$\left(D^2-\frac{p^2}{a^2}\right)\bar{u}=-\frac{g}{a^2p}$$

This $$\Rightarrow \bar{u}=Ae^{px/a}+Be^{-px/a}+\frac{1}{D^2-\frac{p^2}{a^2}}\left(-\frac{g}{a^2p}\right)$$

But $$\frac{1}{D^2 - \frac{p^2}{a^2}}\left(-\frac{g}{a^2 p}\right) = \left(-\frac{g}{a^2 p}\right)\frac{1}{(-p^2/a^2)}\left[1 - \frac{a^2 D^2}{p^2}\right]^{-1}$$

$$= \frac{g}{p^3}$$

$\therefore$ $$\bar{u} = A\, e^{px/a} + B\, e^{-px/a} + \frac{g}{p^3} \qquad \text{...(i)}$$

or $$\bar{u}(x, p) = A \cosh\left(\frac{px}{a}\right) + B \sinh\left(\frac{px}{a}\right) + \frac{g}{p^3} \qquad \text{...(ii)}$$

$$u(0, t) = 0 \Rightarrow L\{u(0, t)\} = L\{0\} \Rightarrow \bar{u}(0, p) = 0$$

$\therefore$ $$\bar{u}(x, p) = 0 \text{ if } x = 0 \qquad \text{...(iii)}$$

$$\frac{\partial u}{\partial x} = 0 \text{ when } x = l \Rightarrow L\left\{\frac{\partial u}{\partial x}\right\} = L\{0\} \Rightarrow \frac{d\bar{u}}{dx} = 0 \text{ if } x = l \qquad \text{...(iv)}$$

By (ii) and (iii), $0 = 1 \cdot A + (0) B + \frac{g}{p^3}$ or $A = -\frac{g}{p^3}$

$$(2) \Rightarrow \frac{d\bar{u}}{dx} = \frac{p}{a}\left[A \sinh\frac{pl}{a} + B \cosh\frac{pl}{a}\right] + 0$$

Subjecting this to the condition (iv)

$$0 = \frac{p}{a}\left[A \sinh\frac{pl}{a} + B \cosh\frac{pl}{a}\right]$$

or $$B = -A \tanh\left(\frac{pl}{a}\right) = \frac{g}{p^3} \tanh\left(\frac{pl}{a}\right).$$

Now (ii) becomes

$$\bar{u}(x, p) = \frac{g}{p^3}\left[-\cosh\frac{px}{a} + \tanh\left(\frac{pl}{a}\right)\sinh\left(\frac{px}{a}\right)\right] + \frac{g}{p^3} \qquad \text{...(v)}$$

But $$\cosh\frac{px}{a} - \tanh\left(\frac{pl}{a}\right)\sinh\left(\frac{px}{a}\right)$$

$$= \left[\cosh\frac{px}{a}\cosh\frac{pl}{a} - \sinh\left(\frac{pl}{a}\right)\sinh\frac{px}{a}\right]\frac{1}{\cosh\left(\frac{pl}{a}\right)}$$

$$= \cosh\left(\frac{pl}{a} - \frac{px}{a}\right)\frac{1}{\cosh(pl/a)} = \frac{\cosh\{p(l-x)/a\}}{\cosh\{pl/a\}}$$

$$\therefore \qquad \bar{u} = \frac{g}{p^3} - \frac{g}{p^3}\frac{\cosh\{(l-x)p/a\}}{\cosh\{pl/a\}}$$

Taking inverse Laplace transform,

$$u(x,t) = g\,L^{-1}\left\{\frac{1}{p^3}\right\} - g\,L^{-1}\left\{\frac{\cosh(l-x)(p/a)}{p^3\cosh(pl/a)}\right\}$$

Replacing x by $\frac{l-x}{a}$ and l by $\frac{l}{a}$ in the given result of inverse Laplace transform, we get

$$u = g\frac{t^2}{2} - g\left[\frac{1}{2}\left\{t^2 + \left(\frac{l-x}{a}\right)^2 - \frac{l^2}{a^2}\right\}\right]$$

$$+ \frac{16l^2 g}{\pi^3 a^2}\sum_{n=1}^{\infty}\frac{(-1)^n}{(2n-1)^3}\cos\left\{\frac{(2n-1)\pi(l-x)/a}{2(l/a)}\right\}\cos\frac{(2n-l)\pi t}{2(l/a)}$$

$$= \frac{g}{2}\left\{\frac{l^2}{a^2} - \frac{(l-x)^2}{a^2}\right\} + \frac{16l^2 g}{\pi^3 a^2}\sum_{n=1}^{\infty}\frac{(-1)^n}{(2n-1)^3}$$

$$\cos\left\{\frac{(2n-1)\pi(l-x)}{2l}\right\}\cdot\cos\left\{\frac{(2n-1)\pi ta}{2l}\right\}.$$

EXERCISE 5

1. Find the solution of $\frac{\partial u}{\partial t} = \frac{\partial^2 u}{\partial x^2}$, which tends to zero as $x \to \infty$ and which satisfies the conditions (i) $u = f(t)$ when $x = 0, t > 0$ (ii) $u = 0$ when $x > 0$, $t = 0$.
2. Solve the boundary value problem

$$\frac{\partial^2 y}{\partial t^2} = 4\frac{\partial^2 y}{\partial x^2},\ 0 < x < \pi,\ t > 0$$

$$y_x(0,t) = 0,\ y(\pi,t) = h,\ y(x,0) = 0,\ y_t(x,0) = 0$$

3. Solve $\frac{\partial^2 y}{\partial t^2} = a^2\frac{\partial^2 y}{\partial x^2}$, $x > 0, t > 0$

$$y_x(0,t) = A\sin\omega t,\ y(x,0) = 0,\ y_t(x,0) = 0.$$

4. A string is stretched between two fixed points (0, 0) and (c, 0). If it is

displaced into the curve $y = b \sin(\pi x/c)$ and released from rest in that position at time $t = 0$, set up and solve the boundary value problem for the displacements $y(x, t)$.

5. An infinite long string having one end $x = 0$ is initially at rest on the x-axis. The end $x = 0$ undergoes a periodic transverse displacement given by $A_0 \sin nt$, $t > 0$, find the displacement of any point on the string at $t > 0$.
6. An inductor of 2 henrys, a resistor of 16 ohms and a capacitor of .02 farads are connected in series with an e.m.f. of 300 volts. At $t = 0$, the charge on the capacitor and current in the circuit are zero. Find the charge and current at any time $t > 0$.
7. An inductor of 3 henrys is in series with a resistor of 30 ohms and an e.m.f. of 150 sin 20t volts. Assuming that at $t = 0$, the current is zero, find the current at any time $t > 0$.
8. A centilever beam, clamped at $x = 0$ and free at $x = l$, carries a uniform load W_0 per unit length. Show that the deflection is

$$y(x) = \frac{W_0 x^3}{24EI}(x^2 - 4lx + 6l^2).$$

9. Solve

$$\frac{\partial^2 u}{\partial x^2} - \frac{l}{a^2}\frac{\partial^2 u}{\partial t^2} = -\frac{g}{a^2},\; t > 0,\; 0 < x < t,$$

with $u = \dfrac{\partial u}{\partial t} = 0$ when $t = 0$,

$$u = 0 \text{ when } x = 0,\; t > 0,$$

$$\frac{\partial u}{\partial x} = 0 \text{ when } x = l,\; t > 0,$$

given that $L^{-1}\left\{\dfrac{\cosh px}{p^3 \cosh pl}\right\}$

$$= \frac{1}{2}(t^2 + x^2 - l^2) - \frac{16l^2}{\pi^3}\sum_{n=1}^{\infty}\left[\frac{(-1)^n}{(2n-1)^3}\cos\frac{(2n-1)\pi x}{2l} \times \cos\frac{(2n-l)\pi t}{2l}\right]$$

10. Solve $\dfrac{\partial^2 y}{\partial t^2} = a^2\dfrac{\partial^2 y}{\partial x^2}$,

with conditions

$$y = 0 \text{ when } t = 0 \text{ for } x \geq 0,$$

$$\frac{\partial y}{\partial t} = 0 \text{ when } t = 0 \text{ for } x > 0,$$

$y = t$ when $x = 0$ for $t \geq 0$.
$y(x, t) = 0$ when $x \to \infty$ for $t \geq 0$.

ANSWERS

1. $u = \dfrac{1}{2\pi i}\displaystyle\int_{y - i\infty}^{y + i\infty} e^{st}\,\bar{f}(s)\, e^{-x\sqrt{p}}\, dp.$

2. $y(x, t) = \dfrac{8h}{\pi}\displaystyle\sum_{n=1}^{\infty} \dfrac{(-1)^n}{2n-1} \sin\{(n - \tfrac{1}{2})x\} \sin(2n-1)t$

3. $y(x, t) = \dfrac{Aa}{\omega}\left\{\cos\omega\left(t - \dfrac{x}{a}\right) - 1\right\}$ if $t > \dfrac{x}{a}$ and 0 if it $\leq \dfrac{x}{a}$.

4. $y(x, t) = b\cos(\pi at/c)\sin(\pi x/c)$.

5. $u = \begin{cases} A_0 \sin n\left(t - \dfrac{x}{a}\right), & t > \dfrac{x}{a} \\ 0, & t < \dfrac{x}{a} \end{cases}$

6. $Q = 6 - e^{-4t}(6\cos 3t + 8\sin 3t)$, $I = 50e^{-4t}\sin 3t$.

7. $\sin 20t - 2\cos 20t + 2e^{-10t}$

9. $g\dfrac{x}{2a^2}(2l - x) - \dfrac{26l^2 g}{\pi^3 a^2}\displaystyle\sum_{n=1}^{\infty}\dfrac{(-1)^n}{(2n-1)^3}\cos\dfrac{(2n-1)\pi(l - x)}{2l}$

10. $\left(t - \dfrac{x}{a}\right) H\left(t - \dfrac{x}{a}\right).$

6

Fourier Transforms

6.1 DRITCHLET'S CONDITIONS

A function $f(x)$ is said to satisfy Dritchlet's conditions in the interval (a, b), if

(i) $f(x)$ is defined and single-valued except possibly at a finite number of points in the interval (a, b), and

(ii) $f(x)$ and $f'(x)$ are piece-wise continuous in the interval (a, b).

6.2 FOURIER SERIES

If $f(x)$ is a periodic function with period $2l$, *i.e.*, $f(x + 2l) = f(x)$ and satisfies Dritchlet's conditions in the interval $(-l, l)$, then at every point of continuity, we have

$$f(x) = \frac{1}{2} a_0 + \sum_{n=1}^{\infty} \left[a_n \cos \frac{n \pi x}{l} + b_n \cdot \sin \frac{n \pi x}{l} \right] \qquad \text{...(i)}$$

where $$a_n = \frac{1}{l} \int_{-l}^{l} f(x) \cos \frac{n \pi x}{l}\, dx \qquad \text{...(ii)}$$

and $$b_n = \frac{1}{l} \int_{-l}^{l} f(x) \sin \frac{n \pi x}{l}\, dl \qquad \text{...(iii)}$$

The series (i) is known as *Fourier series* of $f(x)$ and the coefficients a_n and b_n are called the *Fourier coefficients* corresponding to $f(x)$.

If the function $f(x)$ defined in the interval $(-l, l)$ be an odd function, *i.e.* if $f(-x) = -f(x)$, then

$$a_n = \frac{1}{l} \int_{-l}^{l} f(x) \cos \frac{n \pi x}{l}\, dx = 0$$

and $$b_n = \frac{1}{l} \int_{-l}^{l} f(x) \sin \frac{n \pi x}{l}\, dx$$

$$= \frac{2}{l}\int_0^l f(x) \sin \frac{n\pi x}{l}\, dx$$

Therefore in this case we get *Fourier's sine series.*

Again if $f(x)$ be an even function of x, *i.e.*, if $f(-x) = f(x)$, then

$$a_n = \frac{1}{l}\int_{-l}^{l} f(x) \cos \frac{n\pi x}{l}\, dx$$

$$= \frac{2}{l}\int_0^l f(x) \cos \frac{n\pi x}{l}\, dx$$

and $$b_n = \frac{1}{l}\int_{-l}^{l} f(x) \sin \frac{n\pi x}{l}\, dx = 0$$

and thus in this case we get *Fourier's cosine series.*

6.3 THE (INFINITE) FOURIER SINE TRANSFORM OF $F(X)$

The infinite Fourier sine transform of $F(x)$, $0 < x < \infty$ is defined by $f_s(p)$ or $F_s\{F(x)\}$ and is defined as

$$f_s(p) = F_s\{F(x)\} = \int_0^\infty F(x) \sin px\, dx.$$

Inversion Formula. The inverse formula for infinite Fourier sine transform is given by

$$F(x) = F_s^{-1}\{f_s(p)\} = \frac{2}{\pi}\int_0^\infty f_s(p) \sin px\, dp.$$

6.4 THE INFINITE FOURIER COSINE TRANSFORM OF $F(X)$

The infinite Fourier cosine transform of $F(x)$, $0 < x < \infty$ is denoted by $f_c(p)$ or $F_c\{F(x)\}$ and is defined as,

$$f_c(p) = F_c\{F(x)\} = \int_0^\infty F(x) \cos px\, dx.$$

Inversion Formula. The inverse formula for infinite Fourier cosine transform is given by

$$F(x) = F_c^{-1}\{f_c(p)\} = \frac{2}{\pi}\int_0^\infty F_c(p) \cdot \cos px\, dx$$

Remark. Some authors take $\sqrt{[(2/\pi)]}$ as the coefficient in the two equations instead of 1 and $\frac{2}{\pi}$ respectively.

6.5 THE INFINITE FOURIER TRANSFORM OF $F(x)$

The infinite Fourier transform of $F(x)$, $-\infty < x < \infty$ is denoted by $f(p)$ or $F\{F(x)\}$ and is defined as

$$f(p) = F\{F(x)\} = \int_{-\infty}^{\infty} F(x)\, e^{-ipx}\, dx \qquad \ldots \text{(i)}$$

Inversion Formula. The inverse formula for Fourier transform is given by

$$F(x) = F^{-1}\{f(p)\} = \frac{1}{2\pi}\int_{-\infty}^{\infty} f(p)\, e^{ipx}\, dp \qquad \ldots \text{(ii)}$$

Note. (i) Some authors define Fourier transform as follows:

$$f(p) = F\{F(x)\} = \int_{-\infty}^{\infty} F(x)\, e^{ipx}\, dx$$

and
$$F(x) = F^{-1}\{f(p)\} = \frac{1}{2\pi}\int_{-\infty}^{\infty} F(p)\, e^{-ipx}\, dp$$

But this definition and the definition given above lead to the same conclusion.

(ii) Some others take the coefficients in (i) and (ii) as $\sqrt{[(2/\pi)]}$ each, instead of 1 and $1/2\pi$.

6.6 RELATIONSHIP BETWEEN FOURIER TRANSFORM AND LAPLACE TRANSFORM

Let us define a function $F(t)$ as follows:

$$F(t) = \begin{cases} e^{-xt}\phi(t), & t > 0 \\ 0, & t < 0 \end{cases}$$

Then
$$\begin{aligned} F\{F(t)\} &= \int_{-\infty}^{\infty} e^{-iyt} F(t)\, dt \\ &= \int_{-\infty}^{0} e^{-iyt} F(t)\, dt + \int_{0}^{\infty} e^{-iyt} F(t)\, dt \\ &= \int_{-\infty}^{0} e^{-iyt}\, 0\, dt + \int_{0}^{\infty} e^{-iyt} . e^{-xt}\, \phi(t)\, dt \\ &= \int_{0}^{\infty} e^{-(x+iy)t}\, \phi(i)\, dt \\ &= \int_{0}^{\infty} e^{-pt}\, \phi(t)\, dt \cdot x + iy = p \\ &= L\{\phi(t)\} \end{aligned}$$

$\therefore \qquad F\{F(t)\} = L\{\phi(t)\}.$

This is the required relation between Fourier transform and Laplace transform.

ILLUSTRATIVE EXAMPLES

Example 1. *Find the Fourier transform of*

$$f(x) = \begin{cases} x, & |x| \le a \\ 0, & |x| > a \end{cases}.$$

Solution. We can write the given function as

$$f(t) = \begin{cases} t, & -a \le t \le a \\ 0, & |t| > a \end{cases}.$$

We have

$$F\{f(t)\} = \int_{-\infty}^{\infty} e^{-ipt} f(t)\, dt$$

$$= \int_{-\infty}^{-a} e^{-ipt} f(t)\, dt + \int_{-a}^{a} e^{-ipt} f(t)\, dt + \int_{a}^{\infty} e^{-ipt} f(t)\, dt$$

$$= \int_{\infty}^{a} e^{+ipy} f(y)\,(-dy) + \int_{-a}^{a} e^{-ipt} \cdot t\, dt + \int_{0}^{\infty} e^{-ipt} \cdot 0\, dt$$

$$= \int_{a}^{\infty} e^{ipy} f(-y)\, dy + \left[\frac{e^{-ipt}\,t}{-ip} + \frac{e^{-ipt}}{p^2}\right]_{-a}^{a} + 0$$

$$= \int_{a}^{\infty} e^{ipy} \cdot 0 \cdot dy - \frac{a}{ip}(e^{-ipa} + e^{ipa}) + \frac{1}{p^2}(e^{-ipa} - e^{ipa})$$

$$= 0 + \frac{ia}{p} \cdot 2\cos pa + \frac{1}{p^2} \cdot (-2i \sin pa)$$

$$= \frac{2i}{p^2}(ap \cos pa - \sin pa)$$

Example 2. *Find the Fourier transform of $f(x)$ defined by*

$$f(x) = \begin{cases} 1, & |x| < a \\ 0, & |x| > a \end{cases}$$

and hence evaluate

(i) $\int_{-\infty}^{\infty} \frac{\sin pa \cdot \cos px}{p} dp$,

(ii) $\int_{0}^{\infty} \frac{\sin p}{p} dp$.

Solution. Given that

$$f(x) = \begin{cases} 1, & \text{for } |x| < a; \text{ i.e., for } -a < x < a \\ 0, & \text{for } |x| > a \end{cases}$$

$$\therefore \quad F\{f(x)\} = \int_{-\infty}^{\infty} e^{-ipx} f(x)\, dx$$

$$= \int_{-\infty}^{-a} e^{-ipx} f(x)\, dx + \int_{-a}^{a} e^{-ipx} f(x)\, dx + \int_{a}^{\infty} e^{-ipx} f(x)\, dx$$

$$= \int_{\infty}^{a} -e^{ipy} f(-y)\, dy + \int_{-a}^{a} e^{-ipx} \cdot 1\, dx + \int_{a}^{\infty} e^{-ipx} \cdot 0 \cdot dx$$

$$= \int_{a}^{\infty} e^{ipy} f(-y)\, dy + \left[\frac{e^{-ipx}}{-ip}\right]_{-a}^{a} + 0$$

$$= \int_{a}^{\infty} e^{ipa} \cdot 0 \cdot dy + \frac{e^{ipa} - e^{-ipa}}{ip} + 0$$

$$= 0 + \frac{2}{p} \sin pa = \frac{2}{p} \sin pa.$$

Second Part. Let $F\{f(x)\} = f(p)$ we know that if

$$f(p) = F\{f(x)\} = \int_{-\infty}^{\infty} f(x)\, e^{-ipx}\, dx$$

then $$f(x) = F^{-1}\{f(p)\} = \frac{1}{2\pi} \int_{-\infty}^{\infty} f(p)\, e^{ipx}\, dp.$$

$$\therefore \quad \int_{-\infty}^{\infty} f(p)\, e^{ipx}\, dp = 2\pi f(x) = \begin{cases} 2\pi, & \text{if } |x| < a \\ 0, & \text{if } |x| > a \end{cases}$$

But $$f(p) = \frac{2 \sin pa}{p}, \text{ by first part}$$

$$\therefore \quad \int_{-\infty}^{\infty} \frac{2 \sin pa}{p} \cdot (\cos px + i \sin px)\, dp = \begin{cases} 2\pi & \text{if } |x| < a \\ 0, & \text{if } |x| > a \end{cases}$$

or $$\int_{-\infty}^{\infty} \frac{\sin pa \cos px}{p} dp + i\int_{-\infty}^{\infty} \frac{\sin pa \sin px}{p} dp = \begin{cases} \pi, & |x| < a \\ 0, & |x| > a \end{cases}$$

Equating real parts on both sides, we get

$$\int_{-\infty}^{\infty} \frac{\sin pa \cos px}{p} dp = \begin{cases} \pi & \text{if } |x| < a \\ 0, & \text{if } |x| > a \end{cases}$$

Third Part. If $x = 0$, $a = 1$, then the second part gives

$$\int_{-\infty}^{\infty} \frac{\sin p}{p} dp = \pi \text{ [for } |x| < a \Rightarrow 0 < 1 \text{ and } \cos 0 = 1]$$

or $$2\int_{0}^{\infty} \frac{\sin p}{p} dp = \pi$$

or $$\int_{0}^{\infty} \frac{\sin x}{x} dx = \frac{\pi}{2}.$$

Example 3. *Find the Fourier transforms of*

$$F(x) = \begin{cases} 1 - x^2, & \text{if } |x| \le 1 \\ 0, & \text{if } |x| > 1 \end{cases}$$

and hence evaluate

$$\int_{0}^{\infty} \left(\frac{x \cos x - \sin x}{x^3} \right) \cos \frac{x}{2} dx.$$

Solution. Given that

$$f(x) = \begin{cases} 1 - x^2, & -1 \le x \le 1 \\ 0, & |x| > 1 \end{cases}.$$

$\therefore$ $F\{f(x)\}$

$$= \int_{-\infty}^{\infty} e^{-ipx} f(x)\, dx$$

$$= \int_{-\infty}^{-1} e^{-ipx} f(x)\, dx + \int_{-1}^{1} e^{-ipx} f(x)\, dx + \int_{1}^{\infty} e^{-ipx} f(x)\, dx$$

$$= \int_{\infty}^{1} -e^{ipy} f(-y)\, dy + \int_{-1}^{1} e^{-ipx} (1 - x^2)\, dx + \int_{1}^{\infty} e^{-ipx} \cdot 0\, dx$$

$$= \int_{1}^{\infty} e^{ipy} f(-y)\, dy + \int_{-1}^{1} e^{-ipx} (1 - x^2)\, dx + 0$$

$$= \int_1^{\infty} e^{ipy} \cdot 0 \cdot dy + \int_{-1}^{1} e^{-ipx} (1 - x^2)\, dx$$

$$= \int_{-1}^{1} e^{-ipx} (1 - x^2)\, dx. \qquad \ldots \text{(i)}$$

Now, $$\int e^{-ipx} (1 - x^2)\, dx = \frac{e^{-ipx}}{-ip} - \left[\frac{x^2 e^{-ipx}}{-ip} - \int 2x \frac{e^{-ipx}}{-ip}\, dx\right]$$

$$= \frac{e^{-ipx}}{-ip}(1 - x^2) - \frac{2}{ip}\left[\frac{x e^{-ipx}}{-ip} + \int 1 \cdot \frac{e^{-ipx}}{ip}\, dx\right]$$

$$= \frac{e^{-ipx}}{-ip}(1 - x^2) + \frac{2x\, e^{-ipx}}{i^2 p^2} - \frac{2}{i^2 p^2}\left(\frac{e^{-ipx}}{-ip}\right)$$

$$= \frac{e^{-ipx}}{p^3}\left[(p^2 + 2)\, i - i p^2 x^2 - 2px\right].$$

Putting it in (i),

$$F\{f(x)\} = \left[\frac{e^{-ipx}}{p^3} \{(p^2 + 2)\, i - i p^2 x^2 - 2px\}\right]_{-1}^{1}$$

$$= \frac{1}{p^3}\left[(p^2 + 2)\, i\, (e^{-ip} - e^{ip}) - i p^2 (e^{-ip} - e^{ip}) - 2p\, (e^{-ip} + e^{ip})\right]$$

$$= \frac{1}{p^3}\left[- (p^2 + 2) \cdot 2i^2 \sin p + 2i^2 p^2 \sin p - 4p \cos p\right]$$

$$= \frac{1}{p^3} (4 \sin p - 4p \cos p).$$

Second Part. We know that if

$$f(p) = F\{f(x)\} = \int_{-\infty}^{\infty} f(p)\, e^{-ipx}\, dx$$

then $$F(x) = \frac{1}{2\pi} \int_{-\infty}^{\infty} f(p)\, e^{ipx}\, dp \qquad \ldots \text{(ii)}$$

But $f(p) = \dfrac{4}{p^3} (-p \cos p + \sin p)$, from part (i)

Hence from (ii)

$$\int_{-\infty}^{\infty} \frac{4}{p^3}(-p\cos p + \sin p)\, e^{ipx}\, dp = 2\pi\, F(x)$$

or

$$\int_{-\infty}^{\infty} \frac{(-p\cos p + \sin p)\cos px}{p^3} \cdot dp + i\int_{-\infty}^{\infty} \frac{(-p\cos p + \sin p)}{p^3} \cos px\, dp = \frac{\pi}{2} F(x)$$

Equating real parts, we get

$$\int_{-\infty}^{\infty} \frac{(-p\cos p + \sin p)}{p^3} \cos px\, dp = \frac{\pi}{2} F(x)$$

or
$$2\int_{0}^{\infty} \frac{(-p\cos p + \sin p)}{p^3} \cos px\, dp = \begin{cases} \frac{\pi}{2}(1 - x^2), & |x| < 1 \\ 0, & |x| > 1 \end{cases}.$$

Putting $x = \frac{1}{2}$, we get

$$2\int_{0}^{\infty} \frac{(-p\cos p + \sin p)}{p^3} \cos\left(\frac{p}{2}\right) dp = \frac{\pi}{2}\left(1 - \frac{1}{4}\right) = \frac{3\pi}{8}$$

or
$$\int_{0}^{\infty} \frac{(-p\cos p + \sin p)}{p^3} \cos\left(\frac{p}{2}\right) dp = \frac{3\pi}{16}$$

or
$$\int_{0}^{\infty} \frac{(-x\cos x + \sin x)}{x^3} \cos\left(\frac{x}{2}\right) dx = \frac{3\pi}{16}$$

or
$$\int_{0}^{\infty} \frac{x\cos x - \sin x}{x^3} \cos\left(\frac{x}{2}\right) dx = -\frac{3\pi}{16}$$

Example 4. *Find the Fourier sine transform of*

$$f(x) = \begin{cases} x & \text{for } 0 < x < 1 \\ 2 - x & \text{for } 1 < x < 2 \\ 0 & \text{for } x > 2 \end{cases}.$$

Solution. $F_s\{f(x)\} = \int_{0}^{\infty} f(x)\sin px\, dx$

$$= \int_{0}^{1} f(x)\sin px\, dx + \int_{1}^{2} f(x)\cdot \sin px\, dx + \int_{2}^{\infty} f(x)\sin px\, dx$$

$$= \int_{0}^{1} x\sin px\, dx + \int_{1}^{2} (2 - x)\sin px\, dx + \int_{2}^{\infty} 0\cdot \sin px\, dx$$

$$= \left[-\frac{x\cos px}{p} + \frac{\sin px}{p^2}\right]_0^1 + \left[\frac{2\cos px}{p}\right]_1^2 - \left[-\frac{x\cos px}{p} + \frac{\sin px}{p}\right]_1^2$$

$$= \left[-\frac{\cos p}{p} + \frac{\sin p}{p^2}\right] - \frac{2}{p}\cos 2p + \frac{2}{p}\cos p + \frac{2\cos 2p - \cos p}{p} - \left[\frac{\sin 2p - \sin p}{p^2}\right]$$

$$= \frac{2\sin p - 2\sin p\cos p}{p^2} = \frac{2(1-\cos p)\sin p}{p^2}.$$

Example 5. *Find sine and cosine transform of* $x^n e^{-ax}$.

Solution. We know that

$$\int_0^\infty e^{-ax}\cos px\,dx = \frac{a}{a^2+p^2} \quad \text{...(i)}$$

and
$$\int_0^\infty e^{-ax}\sin px\,dx = \frac{p}{p^2+a^2} \quad \text{...(ii)}$$

Differentiating (i) n times w.r.t. a, we get

$$\int_0^\infty e^{-ax}(-x)^n\cos px\,dx = \frac{d^n}{da^n}\left\{\frac{a}{a^2+p^2}\right\}$$

or
$$(-1)^n\int_0^\infty e^{-ax}x^n\cos px\,dx = (-1)^n\frac{n!}{p^{n+1}}\{\cos(n+1)\theta\}(\sin\theta)^{n+1}$$

where $\tan\theta = p/a$

or
$$\int_0^\infty e^{-ax}x^n\cos px\,dx = \frac{n!}{p^{n+1}}\{\cos(n+1)\theta\}(\sin\theta)^{n+1}.$$

$$\therefore \quad f_c(p) = \frac{n!\{\cos(n+1)\theta\}}{(a^2+p^2)^{(n+1)/2}} \quad \text{...(iii)}$$

Differentiating (ii) w.r.t. a, n times we get

$$\int_0^\infty e^{-ax}\{\sin px\}(-x)^n\,dx = p\cdot\frac{d^n}{da^n}\cdot\left(\frac{1}{a^2+p^2}\right)$$

or
$$(-1)^n\int_0^\infty e^{-ax}x^n\sin px\,dx = p(-1)^n\frac{n!}{p^{n+2}}\{\sin(n+1)\theta\}(\sin\theta)^{n+1}$$

or
$$f_s(p) = n!\{\sin(n+1)\theta\}/(a^2+p^2)^{(n+1)/2} \quad \text{...(iv)}$$

From (iii) and (iv), the required result follows.

EXERCISE 6(A)

1. Find the Fourier complex transform of $F(x)$, if

$$F(x) = \begin{cases} e^{-i\omega x}, & a < x < b \\ 0, & x < a, x > b \end{cases}$$

2. Find the Fourier transform of $F(x)$, if

$$f(x) = \begin{cases} 1/2\varepsilon, & |x| \le \varepsilon \\ 0, & |x| > \varepsilon \end{cases}$$

3. Find the Fourier sine and cosine transform of $f(x)$, if

$$f(x) = \begin{cases} 1, & 0 \le x < 1 \\ 0, & x > 1 \end{cases}.$$

ANSWERS

1. $i\left[\dfrac{e^{-i(p+\omega)b} - e^{-i(p+\omega)a}}{p+\omega}\right]$.

2. $\dfrac{\sin p\varepsilon}{p\varepsilon}$.

3. $\dfrac{1-\cos p}{p}, \dfrac{\sin p}{p}$.

6.7 LINEARITY PROPERTY

Theorem. *If c_1 and c_2 are arbitrary constants, then*

$$F\{c_1 F(x) \pm c_2 G(x)\} = c_1 F\{F(x)\} \pm c_2 F\{G(x)\}.$$

Proof. We have

$$F\{c_1 F(x) \pm c_2 G(x)\}$$

$$= \int_{-\infty}^{\infty} e^{-ipx} [c_1 F(x) \pm c_2 G(x)]\, dx$$

$$= \int_{-\infty}^{\infty} [c_1 e^{-ipx} F(x) \pm c_2 e^{-ipx} G(x)]\, dx$$

$$= \int_{-\infty}^{\infty} c_1 e^{-ipx} F(x)\, dx \pm \int_{-\infty}^{\infty} c_2 e^{-ipx} G(x)\, dx$$

$$= c_1 F\{F(x)\} \pm c_2 F\{G(x)\}$$

6.8 CHANGE OF SCALE PROPERTY

Theorem 1. *If $f(p)$ is the Fourier transform of $F(x)$, then $\frac{1}{a} f\left(\frac{p}{a}\right)$ is the Fourier transform of $F(ax)$.*

Proof. We have

$$F\{F(x)\} = \int_{-\infty}^{\infty} e^{-ipx} F(x)\, dx = f(p)$$

$$\therefore \quad F\{F(ax)\} = \int_{-\infty}^{\infty} e^{-ipx} F(ax)\, dx$$

$$= \int_{-\infty}^{\infty} e^{-ipt/a} F(t) \frac{dt}{a}, \quad ax = t$$

$$= \frac{1}{a} \int_{-\infty}^{\infty} e^{-(ip/a)t} F(t)\, dt.$$

$$= \frac{1}{a} f(p/a) \text{ by definition.}$$

Theorem 2. *If $f_s(p)$ is the Fourier sine transform of $F(x)$, then Fourier sine transform of $F\left(\frac{x}{a}\right)$ is $a f_s(ap)$.*

Proof. $$F_s\left\{F\left(\frac{x}{a}\right)\right\} = \int_0^{\infty} F\left(\frac{x}{a}\right) \sin px\, dx$$

$$= \int_0^{\infty} F(t) \sin(p\, at)\, a\, dt, \quad \frac{x}{a} = t$$

$$= \int_0^{\infty} a F(t) \cos(p\, at)\, dt$$

$$= a f_s(ap).$$

Theorem 3. $F_c\left\{F\left(\frac{x}{a}\right)\right\} = a f_c(ap)$.

It can easily be proved as Theorem 2.

6.9 SHIFTING PROPERTY

Theorem. *If $f(p)$ is the Fourier transform of $F(x)$, then $e^{-iap} f(p)$ is the Fourier transform of $F(x-a)$.*

Proof. $F\{F(x-a)\} = \int_{-\infty}^{\infty} e^{-ipx} F(x-a)\, dx,$

$$= \int_{-\infty}^{\infty} e^{-ip(a+t)} F(t)\, dt, \quad x - a = t$$

$$= \int_{-\infty}^{\infty} e^{-ipa} . e^{-ipt} F(t)\, dt$$

$$= e^{-ipa} \int_{-\infty}^{\infty} e^{-ipt} F(t)\, dt$$

$$= e^{-ipa} f(p).$$

6.10 MODULATION THEOREM

Theorem. *If $F(x)$ has the Fourier transform of $f(p)$, then $F(x)$ cos ax has the Fouriertransform*

$$\frac{1}{2} f(p-a) + \frac{1}{2} f(p+a).$$

Proof. We know that

$$\cos\theta = \frac{e^{i\theta} + e^{-i\theta}}{2}$$

$$\therefore \quad F\{F(x)\cos ax\} = \int_{-\infty}^{\infty} e^{-ipx} F(x) \cos ax\, dx$$

$$= \int_{-\infty}^{\infty} e^{-ipx} F(x) \frac{e^{iax} + e^{-iax}}{2}\, dx$$

$$= \frac{1}{2}\int_{-\infty}^{\infty} [e^{-i(p-a)x} F(x) + e^{-i(p+a)x} F(x)]\, dx$$

$$= \frac{1}{2}\left[\int_{-\infty}^{\infty} e^{-i(p-a)x} F(x)\, dx + \int_{-\infty}^{\infty} e^{-i(p+a)x} F(x)\right] dx$$

$$= \frac{1}{2} [f(p-a) + f(p+a)]$$

6.11 DERIVATIVE THEOREM

Theorem 1. *The Fourier transform of $F'(x)$ the derivative of $F(x)$ is $ipf(p)$, where $f(p)$ is the Fourier transform of $F(x)$.*

Proof. By definition

$$F\{F'(x)\} = \int_{-\infty}^{\infty} e^{-ipx} F'(x)\, dx$$

Integrating by parts

$$F\{F'(x)\} = \left[F(x)\, e^{-ipx}\right]_{-\infty}^{\infty} - \int_{-\infty}^{\infty} F(x)\, e^{-ipx}(-ip)\, dx$$

$$= 0 + ip\int_{-\infty}^{\infty} F(x)\, e^{-ipx}\, dx$$

If $F(x) \to 0$ as $x \to \pm\infty$

$$= ip\, f(p).$$

Theorem 2. $F\left\{\dfrac{d^n F}{dx^n}\right\} = (ip)^n f(p)$, *where* $F\{F(x)\} = f(p)$, *if the first* $(n-1)$ *derivatives of* $F(x)$ *vanish identically as* $x \to \pm\infty$.

Proof. Suppose the first $(n-1)$ derivatives of $F(x)$ vanish as $x \to \pm\infty$.

$$\therefore \quad F\left\{\frac{d^n F}{dx^n}\right\} = \int_{-\infty}^{\infty} \frac{d^n F}{dx^n} e^{-ipx}\, dx$$

Integrating by parts

$$= \left[\frac{d^{n-1} F}{dx^{n-1}} e^{-ipx}\right]_{-\infty}^{\infty} - \int_{-\infty}^{\infty} \frac{d^{n-1}}{dx^{n-1}} e^{-ipx}(-ip)\, dx$$

$$= 0 + ip\int_{-\infty}^{\infty} \frac{d^{n-1} F}{dx^{n-1}} e^{-ipx}\, dx$$

$$= (ip)^1 F\left\{\frac{d^{n-1} F}{dx^{n-1}}\right\}$$

Similarly, we can show that

$$F\left\{\frac{d^n F}{dx^n}\right\} = (ip)^n F\{f(x)\}$$

$$= (ip)^n f(p)$$

6.12 CONVOLUTION

$$F * G = \frac{1}{\sqrt{(2\pi)}}\int_{-\infty}^{\infty} F(u)\, G(x-u)\, du.$$

Convolution Theorem. *If F {f (x)} and F {g (x)} are the Fourier transform of functions f (x) and g (x) respectively, then Fourier transform of the convolution of f (x) and g (x) is the product of their Fourier transforms, i.e.,*

$$F\{f(x) * g(x)\} = F\{f(x)\} \cdot F\{g(x)\}.$$

Proof. We have

$$F\{f(x) * g(x)\} \int_{-\infty}^{\infty} \{f(x) * g(x)\}\, e^{-ipx}\, dx$$

$$= \int_{x=-\infty}^{\infty} \left[\frac{1}{2\pi} \int_{u=-\infty}^{\infty} f(u)\, g(x-u)\, du\right] e^{-ipx}\, dx$$

(on changing the order of integration)

$$F\{f(x) * g(x)\} = \int_{u=-\infty}^{\infty} \left[\frac{f(u)}{2\pi} \int_{x=-\infty}^{\infty} g(x-u)\, e^{-ipx}\, dx\right] du$$

$$= \int_{u=-\infty}^{\infty} \frac{f(u)}{\sqrt{(2\pi)}}$$

$$\left[\frac{1}{\sqrt{(2\pi)}} \int_{x=-\infty}^{\infty} g(x-u)\, e^{-ip(x-u)}\, d(x-u)\right] e^{-ipu}\, du$$

$$= \int_{u=-\infty}^{\infty} \frac{f(u)}{\sqrt{(2\pi)}}\, e^{-ipu}\, du \cdot F\{g(x)\}$$

$$= F\{f(x)\} \cdot F\{g(x)\}$$

Note. Following integrals must be remembered before attempting the problems.

(1) $\displaystyle\int_0^{\infty} \frac{\sin ax}{x}\, dx = \frac{\pi}{2},\ a > 0.$

(2) $\displaystyle\int_0^{\infty} e^{-ax} \sin bx\, dx = \frac{b}{a^2 + b^2}$

$\displaystyle\int_0^{\infty} e^{-ax} \cos bx\, dx = \frac{a}{a^2 + b^2}$

(3) $\displaystyle\Gamma n = a^n \int_0^{\infty} e^{-ax}\, x^{n-1}\, dx$

(4) $\displaystyle\int_0^{\infty} e^{-x^2}\, dx = \frac{\sqrt{\pi}}{2}.$

ILLUSTRATIVE EXAMPLES

Example 1. *Find the Fourier cosine transform of* e^{-x^2}.

Solution. By definition

$$F_c\left\{e^{-x^2}\right\} = \int_0^\infty e^{-x^2} \cos px \, dx = I \quad \text{(say)}$$

Then $$\frac{dI}{dp} = \frac{1}{2}\int_0^\infty \left(-2xe^{-x^2}\right) \sin px \, dx$$

Integrating by parts, we get

$$= \frac{1}{2}\left[e^{-x^2} \sin px - \int p\, e^{-x^2} \cos px \, dx\right]_0^\infty$$

$$= -\frac{p}{2}\int_0^\infty e^{-x^2} \cos px \, dx = -\frac{p}{2} I$$

$\therefore$ $$\frac{dI}{dp} = \frac{p}{2} I$$

or $$\frac{dI}{I} = -\frac{1}{2} p \, dp$$

Integrating,

$$\log I = -\frac{p^2}{4} + \log A$$

or $$I = A\, e^{(-p^2/4)} \qquad \ldots\text{(i)}$$

when $$p = 0,\ I = \int_0^\infty e^{-x^2} (\cos 0)\, dx$$

$$I = \int_0^\infty e^{-x^2} dx = \frac{\sqrt{\pi}}{2}.$$

Putting this value in (i), we get

$$\frac{\sqrt{\pi}}{2} = A$$

$\therefore$ $$I = \frac{\sqrt{\pi}}{2} \cdot e^{-p^2/4}.$$

Example 2. *Find the sine transform of* $\frac{x}{1+x^2}$.

Solution. First we shall determine cosine transform of $\frac{1}{1+x^2}$.

$$\therefore \quad F_c\left\{\frac{1}{1+x^2}\right\} = \int_0^\infty \frac{\cos px}{1+x^2}\,dx = I \quad \text{(say)}$$

Then $$I = \int_0^\infty \frac{\cos px}{1+x^2}\,dx \qquad \text{...(i)}$$

Differentiating w.r.t. p, we get

$$\frac{dI}{dp} = \int_0^\infty -\frac{x\sin px}{1+x^2}\,dx = F_s\left\{\frac{-x}{1+x^2}\right\} \qquad \text{...(ii)}$$

$$= -\int_0^\infty \frac{x^2 \sin px \cdot dx}{x(1+x^2)}$$

$$= -\int_0^\infty \frac{\sin px\,(1+x^2-1)\,dx}{x(1+x^2)}$$

$$= -\int_0^\infty \frac{\sin px}{x}\,dx + \int_0^\infty \frac{\sin px \cdot dx}{x(1+x^2)}$$

$$= -\frac{\pi}{2} + \int_0^\infty \frac{\sin px\,dx}{x(1+x^2)} \qquad \text{...(iii)}$$

Differentiating again w.r.t. p,

$$\frac{d^2I}{dp^2} = \int_0^\infty \frac{x\cos px\,dx}{x(1+x^2)}$$

$$= \int_0^\infty \frac{\cos px\,dx}{(1+x^2)} = I$$

$$\therefore \quad \frac{d^2I}{dp^2} - I = 0$$

Solution of this equation will be

$$I = A\,e^{-p} + B\,e^{p} \qquad \text{...(iv)}$$

Putting $p = 0$ in (i), we get

$$I = \int_0^\infty \frac{1}{1+x^2}\,dx = \left[\tan^{-1}\right]_0^\infty$$

$$= \left[\tan^{-1}\infty - \tan^{-1}0\right] = \frac{\pi}{2}$$

$\therefore \qquad I = \frac{\pi}{2}$ when $p = 0$.

Using this condition in (iv), we get

$$\frac{\pi}{2} = A + B \qquad \ldots(v)$$

Putting $p = 0$, in (iii), we get

$$\frac{dI}{dp} = -\frac{\pi}{2}.$$

From (iv),

$$\frac{dI}{dp} = -A\,e^{-p} + B\,e^{p}$$

we have for $p = 0\,\frac{dI}{dp} = -\pi/2$. Using it, we get

$$-\frac{\pi}{2} = -A + B \qquad \ldots(vi)$$

From (v) and (vi), we have $B = 0$, $A = \frac{\pi}{2}$.

$$\therefore \qquad I = A\,e^{-p} + B\,e^{p} = \frac{\pi}{2}e^{-p} + 0 \qquad \ldots(vii)$$

Thus $\qquad F_c\left\{\frac{1}{1+x^2}\right\} = \frac{\pi}{2}e^{-p}$

$$\therefore \qquad \frac{dI}{dp} = -\frac{\pi}{2}e^{-p}$$

Using this in (ii),

$$-\frac{\pi}{2}e^{-p} = F_s\left\{\frac{-x}{1+x^2}\right\}$$

or $\qquad F_s\left\{\frac{x}{1+x^2}\right\} = \frac{\pi}{2}e^{-p}.$

Example 3. *Show that the Fourier transform of*

$$f(x) = e^{-x^2/2} \text{ is } \sqrt{[(2\pi)]}\; e^{-p^2/2}.$$

Solution. We have

$$F\{f(x)\} = \int_{-\infty}^{\infty} e^{-ipx} f(x)\, dx$$

$$= \int_{-\infty}^{\infty} e^{-x^2/2}\, e^{-ipx}\, x$$

$$= \int_{-\infty}^{\infty} e^{-(x+ip)^2/2} \cdot e^{-p^2/2}\, dx$$

$$= \int_{-\infty}^{\infty} e^{-p/2} \cdot e^{-y^2} \sqrt{2} \cdot dy, \text{ where } \frac{x+ip}{\sqrt{2}} = y$$

$$= \sqrt{2} \cdot e^{-p^2/2} \int_{-\infty}^{\infty} e^{-y^2}\, dy = 2\sqrt{2e^{-p^2/2}} \int_{0}^{\infty} e^{-y^2}\, dy$$

$$= 2\sqrt{2}\, e^{-p^2/2} \cdot \frac{\sqrt{\pi}}{2} = e^{-p^2/2} \sqrt{(2\pi)}.$$

Example 4. *Find* $F_s^{-1}\{e^{-\pi p}\}$.

Solution. $$F_s^{-1}\{e^{-\pi p}\} = \frac{2}{\pi} \int_0^{\infty} e^{-\pi p} \sin px\, dp$$

$$= \frac{2}{\pi} \cdot \frac{x}{\pi^2 + x^2} \qquad \left[\because \int_0^{\infty} e^{-ax} \sin bx\, dx = \frac{b}{a^2 + b^2}\right]$$

$$= \frac{2x}{\pi(\pi^2 + x^2)}.$$

Example 5. *Find $f(x)$, if its Fourier cosine transform is*

$$\frac{1}{1+p^2}.$$

Solution. $$F_c^{-1}\{f(p)\} = F_c^{-1}\left\{\frac{1}{1+p^2}\right\}$$

$$= \frac{2}{\pi} \int_0^{\infty} \frac{1}{1+p^2} \cdot \cos px\, dp = f(x) \quad \text{(say)} \qquad \ldots(\text{i})$$

Then $$\frac{df}{dx} = \frac{2}{\pi} \int_0^{\infty} \frac{-p \sin px}{1+p^2} \cdot dp \qquad \ldots(\text{ii})$$

$$= -\frac{2}{\pi}\int_0^\infty \frac{p^2 \cdot \sin px}{p(1+p^2)}\, dp$$

$$= -\frac{2}{\pi}\int_0^\infty \frac{(1+p^2-1)\sin px}{(1+p^2)\,p}\, dp$$

$$= -\frac{2}{\pi}\int_0^\infty \frac{\sin px\, dp}{p} + \frac{2}{\pi}\int_0^\infty \frac{\sin px\, dp}{p(1+p^2)}$$

$$= -\frac{2}{\pi}\cdot\frac{\pi}{2} + \frac{2}{\pi}\int_0^\infty \frac{\sin px \cdot dp}{p(1+p^2)} \qquad \text{...(iii)}$$

Differentiating w.r.t. x, again

$$\frac{d^2f}{dx^2} = \frac{2}{\pi}\int_0^\infty \frac{\cos px \cdot dx}{1+p^2} = f(x)$$

or

$$\frac{d^2f}{dx^2} - f = 0$$

Its solution is

$$f = A\, e^{-x} + B\, e^{x} \qquad \text{...(iv)}$$

Putting $x = 0$ in (i) and (iii) respectively,

$$f = \frac{2}{\pi}\int_0^\infty \frac{dp}{1+p^2} = \frac{2}{\pi}\left[\tan^{-1} p\right]_0^\infty$$

$$= \frac{2}{\pi}\cdot\frac{\pi}{2} = 1$$

and

$$\frac{df}{dx} = -1.$$

$\therefore$

$$f = 1 \text{ when } x = 0 \qquad \text{...(v)}$$

and

$$\frac{df}{dx} = -1 \text{ when } x = 0 \qquad \text{...(vi)}$$

Using condition (v) in (iv)

$$A + B = 1 \qquad \text{...(vii)}$$

From (iv), we get

$$\frac{df}{dx} = -A\, e^{-x} + B\, e^{x}$$

Using the condition (vi), we get

$$-A + B = -1 \qquad \text{...(viii)}$$

From (vii) and (viii),

$$B = 0, A = 1.$$

Hence, by (iv) $f = e^{-x}$.

Example 6. *Find the complex Fourier transform of $e^{-|x|}$.*

Solution. We have

$$F\{e^{-|x|}\} = \int_{-\infty}^{\infty} e^{-|x|}\, e^{-ipx}\, dx$$

$$= \int_{-\infty}^{0} e^{-|x|}\, e^{-ipx}\, dx + \int_{0}^{\infty} e^{-|x|}\, e^{-ipx}\, dx$$

$$= \int_{-\infty}^{0} e^{x} \cdot e^{-ipx}\, dx + \int_{0}^{\infty} e^{-x} \cdot e^{-ipx}\, dx$$

$$= -\int_{\infty}^{0} e^{x(1-ip)}\, dx + \int_{0}^{\infty} e^{-x(1+ip)}\, dx$$

$$= \left[\frac{e^{x}(1-ip)}{1-ip}\right]_{-\infty}^{0} + \left[\frac{e^{-x(1+ip)}}{-(1+ip)}\right]_{0}^{\infty}$$

$$= \frac{1}{1-ip} + \frac{1}{1+ip} = \frac{2}{1+p^2}$$

Example 7. *Find sine transform of $\dfrac{e^{-ax}}{x}$.*

Solution. We have

$$F_s\left\{\frac{e^{-ax}}{x}\right\} = \int_0^{\infty} \frac{e^{-ax}}{x} \sin px \cdot dx = I \quad \text{(say)}$$

Then $$I = \int_0^{\infty} \frac{e^{-ax}}{x} \sin px \cdot dx \qquad \ldots\text{(i)}$$

Differentiating w.r.t. p, we get

$$\frac{dI}{dp} = \int_0^{\infty} \frac{e^{-ax}}{x} \cdot x \cos px \cdot dx$$

$$= \int_0^{\infty} e^{-ax} \cos px \cdot dx$$

$$= \frac{a}{a^2 + p^2}$$

$$\therefore \quad \frac{dI}{dp} = \frac{a}{a^2 + p^2}$$

Integrating, we get

$$I = \tan^{-1}\left(\frac{p}{a}\right) + A$$

For $\quad p = 0, I = A$

But $\quad I = 0$, for $p = 0$, by (i)

$\therefore \quad A = 0$

$\therefore \quad I = \tan^{-1}(p/a)$.

Example 8. *Find the sine transform of the function*

$$F(x) = \begin{cases} \sin x, & \text{when } 0 < x < a \\ 0, & \text{when } x > a \end{cases}.$$

Solution. We have

$$F_s\{F(x)\} = \int_0^\infty F(x) \sin px \, dx$$

$$= \int_0^a F(x) \sin px \, dx + \int_a^\infty F(x) \sin px \, dx$$

$$= \int_0^a \sin x \sin px \, dx + 0$$

$$= \frac{1}{2}\int_0^a [\cos(1-p)x - \cos(1+p)x] \, dx$$

$$= \frac{1}{2}\left[\frac{\sin(1-p)x}{1-p} - \frac{\sin(1+p)x}{1+p}\right]_0^a$$

$$= \frac{1}{2}\left[\frac{\sin(1-p)a}{1-p} - \frac{\sin(1+p)a}{1+p}\right]$$

Example 9. *Find $f(x)$ if its sine transform is $\dfrac{e^{-ap}}{p}$.*

Hence deduce $F_s^{-1}\{1/p\}$.

Solution. We have

$$F_s^{-1}\{f_s(p)\} = f(x) = \frac{2}{\pi}\int_0^\infty f_s(p)\sin px\, dp$$

or $$f(x) = \frac{2}{\pi}\int_0^\infty \frac{e^{-ap}}{p}\sin px\, dp \qquad \ldots(\text{i})$$

$\therefore$ $$\frac{df}{dx} = \frac{2}{\pi}\int_0^\infty \cos px \cdot dp$$

$$= \frac{2}{\pi}\cdot\frac{a}{x^2+a^2}$$

$\therefore$ $$f = \frac{2}{\pi}\int \frac{a\,dx}{x^2+a^2} = \frac{2}{\pi}\tan^{-1}\left(\frac{x}{a}\right) + A$$

or $$f = \frac{2}{\pi}\tan^{-1}\left(\frac{x}{a}\right) + A \qquad \ldots(\text{ii})$$

when $x = 0, f = 0$, by (i).

Using this condition in (ii), we get

$$A = 0.$$

$\therefore$ $$f(x) = \frac{2}{\pi}\tan^{-1}\left(\frac{x}{a}\right) \qquad \ldots(\text{iii})$$

Deduction.

$$F_s^{-1}\left\{\frac{1}{p}\right\} = F_s^{-1}\left\{\frac{e^{-ap}}{p}\right\}_{a=0}$$

Hence, by putting $a = 0$ in (iii), we get

$$F_s^{-1}\left\{\frac{1}{p}\right\} = \frac{2}{\pi}\tan^{-1}\infty = 1.$$

Example 10. *Find the Fourier sine and cosine transform of the function* x^{m-1}.

Solution. We have

$$f_c(p) = \int_0^\infty f(x)\cos px\, dx$$

$$= \int_0^\infty x^{m-1}\cos px\, dx \qquad \ldots(\text{i})$$

and $$f_s(p) = \int_0^\infty f(x) \sin px \, dx$$

$$= \int_0^\infty x^{m-1} \sin px \, dx \qquad \ldots \text{(ii)}$$

Now, by definition of Gamma function, we have

$$\Gamma(n) = \int_0^\infty e^{-x} x^{n-1} \, dx$$

Putting $x = ipy$ and using the fact that $i = e^{i\pi/2}$, we get

$$\Gamma(n) = \int_0^\infty e^{-ipy} (ipy)^{n-1} (ip \, dy)$$

or $$\frac{\Gamma(n)}{p^n} = \int_0^\infty e^{-ipy} y^{n-1} i^n \, dy$$

$$= e^{(i\pi/2)n} \int_0^\infty e^{-ipy} y^{n-1} \, dy$$

or $$\int_0^\infty e^{-ipy} y^{n-1} \, dy = \frac{\Gamma(n)}{p^n} e^{-in\pi/2}$$

or $$\int_0^\infty (\cos py + i \sin py) \, y^{n-1} \, dy = \frac{\Gamma(n)}{p^n} \left[\cos \frac{n\pi}{2} - i \sin \frac{n\pi}{2} \right]$$

Equating real and imaginary parts we get

$$\int_0^\infty y^{n-1} \cos(py) \, dy = \frac{\Gamma(n)}{p^n} \cos\left(\frac{n\pi}{2}\right)$$

and $$\int_0^\infty y^{n-1} \sin(py) \, dy = -\frac{\Gamma(n)}{p^n} \sin\left(\frac{n\pi}{2}\right)$$

Replacing n by m and using the property of definite integral

$$\int_a^b f(y) \, dy = \int_a^b f(x) \, dx, \text{ we get}$$

$$\int_0^\infty x^{m-1} \cos(px) \, dx = f_c(p) = \frac{\Gamma(m)}{p^m} \cos \frac{m\pi}{2}$$

and $$\int_0^\infty x^{m-1} \sin(px) \, dx = f_s(p) = \frac{\Gamma(m)}{p^m} \sin \frac{m\pi}{2}.$$

Example 11. *Find the cosine transform of a function of x which is unity for $0 < x < a$ and zero for $x \geq a$. What is the function whose cosine transform is $\left(\frac{\sin ap}{p}\right)$.*

Solution. The given function may be written as

$$f(x) = \begin{cases} 1, & 0 < x < a \\ 0, & x \geq a \end{cases}$$

(i)
$$F_c\{f(x)\} = \int_0^\infty f(x) \cos px \, dx$$

$$= \int_0^a f(x) \cos px \, dx + \int_a^\infty f(x) \cos px \, dx$$

$$= \int_0^a 1 \cdot \cos px \, dx + \int_0^\infty 0 \cdot \cos px \, dx$$

$$= \frac{\sin ap}{p}$$

(ii) Given $F_c\{g(x)\} = \frac{\sin ap}{p}$

$$\therefore \quad g(x) = \frac{2}{\pi}\int_0^\infty \frac{\sin ap}{p} \cos px \, dx$$

$$= \frac{1}{\pi}\int_0^\infty \frac{\sin (a+x)p + \sin (a-x)p}{p} dp$$

$$= \frac{1}{\pi}\int_0^\infty \frac{\sin (a+x)p}{p} dp + \frac{1}{\pi}\int_0^\infty \frac{\sin (a-x)}{p} dp$$

$$= \begin{cases} 1/\pi\,(\pi/2 + \pi/2) & \text{if } x < a \\ 1/\pi\,(\pi/2 - \pi/2) & \text{if } x > a \end{cases}$$

$$\therefore \quad g(x) = \begin{cases} 1 & \text{if } x < a \\ 0 & \text{if } x > a \end{cases}$$

Example 12. *Find Fourier sine and cosine transform of $f(x) = x$.*

Solution. $f_c(p) = \int_0^\infty x \cos px \, dx$

and $f_s(p) = \int_0^\infty x \sin px \, dx.$

Let $\quad f(p) = \int_0^\infty x\, e^{-ipx}\, dx$

Let $\quad ipx = y$ then $ip\, dx = dy$

$$\therefore \quad f(p) = \int_0^\infty \frac{y}{ip} e^{-y} \frac{dy}{ip}$$

$$= -\frac{1}{p^2}\int_0^\infty y^{2-1} e^{-y}\, dy$$

$$= -\frac{\Gamma(2)}{p^2} = -\frac{1}{p^2}$$

$$\therefore \quad \int_0^\infty x\, e^{-ipx}\, dx = -\frac{1}{p^2}$$

or $$\int_0^\infty x(\cos px - i \sin px)\, dx = -\frac{1}{p^2}$$

Equating real and imaginary parts, we get

$$\int_0^\infty x \cos px\, dx = f_c(p) = -\frac{1}{p^2}$$

$$\int_0^\infty x \sin px\, dx = f_s(p) = 0.$$

Example 13. *Find $f(x)$ if its cosine transform is*

$$f_c(\mathrm{p}) = \begin{cases} \frac{1}{2\pi}\left(a - \frac{p}{2}\right) & \text{if } p < 2a \\ 0 & \text{if } p \geq 2a \end{cases}$$

Solution. We have

$$f(x) = \frac{2}{\pi}\int_0^\infty f_c(p) \cos px\, dp$$

$$= \frac{2}{p}\int_0^{2a} f_c(p) \cos px\, dp + \frac{2}{\pi}\int_{2a}^\infty f_c(p) \cos px\, dx$$

$$= \frac{2}{\pi}\int_0^{2a} \frac{1}{2\pi}\left(a - \frac{p}{2}\right) \cos px\, dp + 0$$

$$= \frac{1}{\pi^2}\left[\left(\frac{a \sin px}{x}\right)_0^{2a} - \frac{1}{2}\left\{\left(\frac{p \sin px}{x}\right)_0^{2a} - \int_0^{2a} \frac{\sin px}{x}\, dp\right\}\right]$$

$$= \frac{1}{\pi^2}\left[\frac{a}{x} \sin 2ax - \frac{a}{x} \sin 2ax + \frac{1}{2}\left(\frac{-\cos px}{x^2}\right)_0^{2a}\right]$$

$$= \frac{1}{2\pi^2 x^2}(1 - \cos 2ax) = \frac{\sin^2 ax}{\pi^2 x^2}$$

Example 14. *Find the inverse Fourier transforms of* $f(p) = e^{-|p|y}$ *where* y *belongs to* $(-\infty, \infty)$.

Solution. We have

$$|p| = \begin{cases} -p, & p \le 0 \\ p, & p \ge 0 \end{cases}$$

$$\therefore \quad F^{-1}\{f(p)\} = \frac{1}{2\pi}\int_{-\infty}^{\infty} f(p)\, e^{ipx}\, dp$$

$$= \frac{1}{2\pi}\left[\int_{-\infty}^{0} f(p)\, e^{ipx}\, dp + \int_0^{\infty} f(p)\, e^{-px}\, dp\right].$$

$$= \frac{1}{2\pi}\left[\int_{-\infty}^{0} e^{-|p|y} \cdot e^{ipx}\, dp + \int_0^{\infty} e^{-|p|y}\, e^{ipx}\, dp\right]$$

$$= \frac{1}{2\pi}\left[\int_{-\infty}^{0} e^{(y+ix)p}\, dp + \int_0^{\infty} e^{-p(y-ix)}\, dp\right]$$

$$= \frac{1}{2\pi}\left[\frac{1}{y+ix}\left\{e^{(y+ix)p}\right\}_{-\infty}^{0} + \frac{1}{ix-y}\left\{e^{-(y-ix)p}\right\}_0^{\infty}\right]$$

$$= \frac{1}{2\pi}\left[\frac{1}{y+ix}(1-0) + \frac{1}{ix-y}(0-1)\right]$$

$$= \frac{y}{\pi(y^2 - x^2)}.$$

EXERCISE 6(B)

1. Find the sine and cosine transforms of $2e^{-5x} + 5e^{-2x}$.
2. Find cosine transform of $\frac{1}{1+x^2}$.
3. Find Fourier sine and cosine transform of e^{-x} and using the inversion formulae recover the original functions in both the cases.
4. Find $F_c\{x^{-n}\}$ and $F_s\{x^{-n}\}$.
5. Find cosine transform of function $f(x)$ such that

$$f(x) = \begin{cases} \cos x & \text{when } 0 < x < a \\ 0 & \text{when } \quad x > a \end{cases}$$

6. Find sine transform of $f(x) = \frac{1}{x}$.
7. Find $F_s^{-1}\left\{\frac{e^{-ap}}{p}\right\}$ and hence deduce $F_s^{-1}\left\{\frac{1}{p}\right\}$.
8. Find the Fourier sine transform of $f(x)$, if

$$f(x) = \begin{cases} 0, & 0 < x < a \\ x, & a \le x \le b. \\ 0, & x > b \end{cases}$$

9. Find Fourier sine and cosine transforms of $f(x)$ given by

$$f(x) = \begin{cases} 1 & 0 \le x < 1 \\ 0 & x > 1 \end{cases}.$$

10. Find the sine transform of $\frac{1}{e^{\pi x} - e^{-\pi x}}$ and deduce that Fourier transform of cosech πx is $\frac{1}{(2\pi)^{1/2}}$ tan $h\,(p/2)$.
11. Prove $F_s\left\{\frac{1}{x}\right\} = \frac{\pi}{2}$.
12. Find $f(x)$ if $f_s(p) = p^n e^{-}ap$.

ANSWERS

1. $f_c(p) = 10\left(\frac{1}{p^2+4} + \frac{1}{p^2+25}\right), f_s(p) = p\left[\frac{2}{p^2+25} + \frac{5}{p^2+4}\right]$.

2. $\dfrac{\pi}{2}e^{-p}$.

3. $\dfrac{p}{1+p^2}, \dfrac{1}{1+p^2}$.

4. $\dfrac{p^{n-1}}{\Gamma(n)}\dfrac{\pi}{2}\sec\dfrac{n\pi}{2}, \dfrac{p^{n-1}}{\Gamma(n)}\cdot\dfrac{\pi}{2}\cdot\text{cosec}\,\dfrac{n\pi}{2}$.

5. $\dfrac{1}{2}\left[\dfrac{\sin(1+p)a}{1+p}+\dfrac{\sin(1-p)a}{1-p}\right]$.

6. $\dfrac{\pi}{2}$.

7. $\dfrac{2}{\pi}\tan^{-1}\left(\dfrac{x}{a}\right), \dfrac{\pi}{2}$.

8. $\dfrac{1}{p}(-b\cos pb + a\cos pa) + \dfrac{1}{p^2}(\sin pb - \sin pa)$.

9. $\dfrac{1-\cos p}{p}, \dfrac{\sin p}{p}$.

10. $\dfrac{1}{4}\tan h\left(\dfrac{p}{2}\right), \dfrac{1}{\sqrt{\{(2\pi)\}}}\tan h\,(p/2)$.

12. $\dfrac{2}{\pi}n!\dfrac{\sin(n+1)\theta}{(x^2+a^2)^{(n+1)/2}}$ where $\tan\theta = \dfrac{x}{a}$.

MISCELLANEOUS ILLUSTRATIVE EXAMPLES

Example 1. *Solve by Fourier transform method*

$$\int_0^\infty f(\text{x})\cos\lambda x\,dx = e^{-\lambda}.$$

Solution. Given equation can be written as

$$\int_0^\infty f(x)\cos px\,dx = e^{-p} \qquad \text{...(i)}$$

By definition of cosine transform and its inverse, we have

$$F_c\{f(x)\} = \int_0^\infty f(x)\cos px\,dx = f_c(p) \qquad \text{...(ii)}$$

and

$$F_c^{-1}\{f_c(p)\} = f(x) = \frac{2}{\pi}\int_0^\infty f_c(p)\cos px\,dp \qquad \text{...(iii)}$$

Equating (i) to (ii), we obtain

$$f_c(p) = e^{-p}.$$

Using this in equation (iii), we obtain

$$f(x) = \frac{2}{\pi}\int_0^\infty e^{-p} \cos px \, dp$$

$$= \int_0^\infty e^{-1 \cdot p} \cos xp \, dp = \frac{2}{\pi} \cdot \frac{1}{1 + x^2}$$

$$\left[\because \int_0^\infty e^{-ax} \cos bx \, dx = \frac{a}{a^2 + b^2}\right],$$

$$\therefore \quad f(x) = \frac{2}{\pi(1 + x^2)}.$$

Example 2. *Solve the equation*

$$\int_0^\infty F(x) \cos \lambda x \, dx = \begin{cases} 1 - \lambda & \text{for } 0 \le \lambda \le 1 \\ 0 & \text{for } \lambda > 1 \end{cases}.$$

Solution. By definition

$$F_c\{F(x)\} = \int_0^\infty F(x) \cos \lambda x \, dx = f_c(\lambda) \qquad \ldots\text{(i)}$$

Then $f_c(\lambda) = \begin{cases} 1 - \lambda & \text{for } 0 \le \lambda \le 1 \\ 0 & \text{for } \lambda > 1 \end{cases}$

The inverse formula relative to (i) is

$$F_c^{-1}\{f_c(\lambda)\} = F(x) = \frac{2}{\pi}\int_0^\infty f_c(\lambda) \cdot \cos \lambda x \, d\lambda$$

From which,

$$\frac{\pi}{2} F(x) = \int_0^\infty f_c(\lambda) \cos \lambda x \, d\lambda$$

$$= \int_0^1 f_c(\lambda) \cos \lambda x \, d\lambda + \int_1^\infty f_c(\lambda) \cos \lambda x \, d\lambda$$

$$= \int_0^1 (1 - \lambda) \cos \lambda x \, d\lambda + \int_1^\infty 0 \cdot \cos \lambda x \, d\lambda$$

$$= \int_0^1 (1 - \lambda) \cos \lambda x \, d\lambda$$

$$= \int_0^1 (1-\lambda)\cos\lambda x\, d\lambda$$

$$= \left[(1-\lambda)\frac{\sin\lambda x}{x} + \int \frac{\sin\lambda x}{x}\, d\lambda\right]_0^1$$

$$= 0 - \frac{1}{x^2}(\cos x - 1)$$

$$= \frac{1-\cos x}{x^2}$$

$$\therefore \qquad F(x) = \frac{2}{\pi x^2}(1-\cos x).$$

Example 3. *Show that*

$$\int_0^\infty \frac{\cos\lambda x}{\lambda^2+1}\, d\lambda = \frac{\pi}{2} e^{-x},\ x \geq 0.$$

Solution. We know that

$$\int_0^\infty e^{-ax}\cos bx\, dx = \frac{a}{a^2+b^2}$$

From which,

$$\int_0^\infty e^{-x}\cos\lambda x\, dx = \frac{1}{1+\lambda^2}.$$

Comparing this with equation,

$$F_c\{f(x)\} = f_c(\lambda) = \int_0^\infty f(x)\cos\lambda x\, dx \qquad \text{...(i)}$$

We get

$$f_c(\lambda) = \frac{1}{1+\lambda^2}, f(x) = e^{-x}.$$

The inverse formula corresponding to (i) is

$$F_c^{-1}\{f_c(\lambda)\} = f(x) = \frac{2}{\pi}\int_0^\infty f_c(\lambda)\cos\lambda x\, d\lambda.$$

Putting the values

$$e^{-x} = \frac{2}{\pi}\int_0^\infty \frac{1}{1+\lambda^2}\cos\lambda x\, d\lambda$$

or $$\frac{\pi}{2} e^{-x} = \int_0^\infty \frac{\cos \lambda x}{1+\lambda^2}\, d\lambda.$$

Example 4. *Solve for F (x) the equation*

$$\int_0^\infty F(x) \sin(xt)\, dx = \begin{cases} 1, & 0 \le t < 1 \\ 2, & 1 \le t < 2. \\ 0, & t \ge 2 \end{cases}$$

Solution. By definition

$$F_s\{F(x)\} = \int_0^\infty F(x) \sin px\, dx = f_s(p) \qquad \ldots\text{(i)}$$

Then $$f_s(p) = \begin{cases} 1, & 0 \le t < 1 \\ 2, & 1 \le t < 2. \\ 0, & t \ge 2 \end{cases}$$

The sine inversion formula relative to (i) is

$$F_s^{-1}\{f_s(p)\} = F(x) = \frac{2}{\pi} \int_0^\infty f_s(p) \sin px\, dp$$

From which $$\frac{\pi}{2} F(x) = \int_0^\infty f_s(p) \sin px\, dp$$

$$= \int_0^1 f_s(p) \sin px\, dp + \int_1^2 f_s(p) \sin px\, dp + \int_2^\infty f_s(p) \sin px\, dp$$

$$= \int_0^1 1 \cdot \sin px\, dp + \int_1^2 2 \sin px\, dp + \int_0^\infty 0 \cdot \sin px\, dp$$

$$= \left[\frac{-\cos px}{x}\right]_0^1 + 2\left[\frac{-\cos px}{p}\right]_1^2 + 0$$

$$= \left[\frac{1}{x}[1 - \cos x + 2(\cos x - \cos 2x)]\right]$$

$$= \frac{1 + \cos x - 2\cos 2x}{x}$$

or $$\frac{\pi}{2} F(x) = \frac{1 + \cos x - 2\cos 2x}{x}$$

or $$F(x) = \frac{2}{\pi x}(1 + \cos x - 2\cos 2x).$$

7

The Finite Fourier Transform and Fourier Integral

7.1 THE FINITE FOURIER COSINE TRANSFORM OF $F(x)$, $0 < x < l$ is defined by

$$F_c\{F(x)\} = f_c(p) = \int_0^l F(x)\cos\frac{p\pi x}{l}\,dx$$

where p is a positive integer. The function $F(x)$ is then called the *inverse finite cosine transform* of $f_c(p)$ and is given by

$$F_c^{-1}\{f_c(p)\} = F(x) = \frac{1}{l}f_c(0) + \frac{2}{l}\sum_{n=1}^{\infty} f_c(p)\cos\frac{p\pi x}{l}.$$

This formula is obtained from Fourier cosine series for $F(x)$, *i.e.*,

$$F(x) = \frac{a_0}{2} + \sum_{n=1}^{\infty} a_n\cos\frac{n\pi x}{l}.$$

7.2 THE FINITE FOURIER SINE TRANSFORM OF $F(x)$, $0 < x < l$ is defined by

$$F_s\{F(x)\} = f_s(p) = \int_0^l F(x)\sin\frac{p\pi x}{l}\,dx$$

where p is a positive integer. The function $F(x)$ is then called the *inverse finite Fourier sine transform* of $f_s(p)$ and is given by

$$F_s^{-1}\{f_s(p)\} = F(x) = \frac{2}{l}\sum_{n=1}^{\infty} f_s(p)\sin\frac{p\pi x}{l}.$$

This formula is obtained from fourier sine series

$$f(x) = \sum_{n=1}^{\infty} b_n \sin \frac{n\pi x}{l}.$$

7.3 FOURIER INTEGRAL

Theorem. *If $f(x)$ satisfies the following conditions:*

(*i*) *$f(x)$ satisfies the Dritchlet conditions in every interval*

$$-l \leq x \leq l.$$

(*ii*) $\int_{-\infty}^{\infty} |f(x)|\, dx$ *converges, i.e., $f(x)$ is absolutely integrable in the interval* $-\infty < x < \infty$, *then*

$$f(x) = \frac{1}{2\pi} \int_{p=-\infty}^{\infty} \int_{t=-\infty}^{\infty} f(t) \cos p\,(x - t)\, dp\, dt.$$

The integral on R.H.S. is called Fourier integral or Fourier integral expansion of $f(x)$.

Proof. Let us consider a function satisfying Dritchlet's condition in every interval $(-c, c)$, however large. Also suppose that

$$\int_{-\infty}^{\infty} |f(x)|\, dx \qquad \ldots\text{(i)}$$

is convergent. Then in the interval $(-c, c)$,

$$f(x) = \frac{a_0}{2} + \sum_{n=1}^{\infty} \left(a_n \cos \frac{n\pi x}{c} + b_n \sin \frac{n\pi x}{c} \right) \qquad \ldots\text{(ii)}$$

where $a_n = \frac{1}{c} \int_{-c}^{c} f(t) \cos \frac{n\pi t}{c}\, dt,\ n = 0, 1, 2,$

and $b_n = \frac{1}{c} \int_{-c}^{c} f(t) \sin \frac{n\pi t}{c}\, dt,\ n = 0, 1, 2, \ldots$

Putting the values of a_n and b_n in (ii),

$$f(x) = \frac{1}{2c} \int_{-c}^{c} f(t)\, dt$$

$$+ \frac{1}{c} \sum_{n=1}^{\infty} \int_{-c}^{c} f(t) \left\{ \cos \frac{n\pi t}{c} \cos \frac{n\pi x}{c} + \sin \frac{n\pi t}{c} \sin \frac{n\pi x}{c} \right\}$$

$$= \frac{1}{2c}\int_{-c}^{c} f(t)\,dt + \frac{1}{c}\sum_{n=1}^{\infty}\int_{-c}^{c} f(t)\cos\frac{n\pi}{c}(t-x)\,dt$$

Making use of the fact that $f(x)$ is uniformly convergent in the closed interval $-c \le x \le c$, we get

$$f(x) = \frac{1}{2c}\int_{-c}^{c} f(t)\,dt + \frac{1}{c}\int_{-c}^{c} f(t)\left[\sum_{n=1}^{\infty}\cos\frac{n\pi(t-x)}{c}\right]$$

$$= \frac{1}{2c}\int_{-c}^{c} f(t)\left[1 + \lim_{n\to\infty}\sum_{r=1}^{n} 2\cos\frac{r\pi(t-x)}{c}\right]dt$$

$$= \frac{1}{2c}\int_{-c}^{c} f(t)\left[1 + \lim_{n\to\infty}\sum_{r=1}^{n}\left\{\cos\frac{r\pi(t-x)}{c} + \cos\frac{-r\pi(t-x)}{c}\right\}\right]dt$$

$$= \frac{1}{2c}\int_{-c}^{c} f(t)\left[1 + \lim_{n\to\infty}\sum_{r=-n}^{n}\cos\frac{r\pi(t-x)}{c}\right]dt$$

$$= \frac{1}{2c}\int_{-c}^{c} f(t)\,dt + \frac{1}{2\pi}\int_{-c}^{c} f(t)\left[\lim_{n\to\infty}\sum_{r=-n}^{n}\frac{1}{c/\pi}\cdot\cos\left(\frac{r}{c/\pi}\right)(t-x)\right]dt$$

Making use of definition of integral as a limit of sum, we get

$$f(x) = \frac{1}{2c}\int_{-c}^{c} f(t)\,dt + \frac{1}{2\pi}\int_{-c}^{c} f(t)\left[\int_{-\infty}^{\infty}\cos u(t-x)\,du\right]dt$$

or

$$f(x) = \frac{1}{2c}\int_{-c}^{c} f(t)\,dt + \frac{1}{2\pi}\int_{-c}^{c} f(t)\,dt\int_{-\infty}^{\infty}\cos u(t-x)\,du$$

Making $c \to \infty$ and using the fact (i), we get

$$f(x) = 0 + \frac{1}{2\pi}\int_{-\infty}^{\infty} f(t)\,dt\int_{-\infty}^{\infty}\cos u(t-x)\,du$$

or

$$f(x) = \frac{1}{2\pi}\int_{-\infty}^{\infty}\int_{-\infty}^{\infty} f(t)\cos u(t-x)\,dt\,du$$

Finally, if $-\infty < x < \infty$, then

$$f(x) = \frac{1}{2\pi}\int_{p=-\infty}^{\infty}\int_{t=-\infty}^{\infty} f(t)\cos p(t-x)\,dp\,dt.$$

7.4 DIFFERENT FORMS OF FOURIER INTEGRAL FORMULA

(i) $f(x) = \frac{1}{\pi}\int_{p=0}^{\infty}\int_{t=-\infty}^{\infty} f(t)\cos p(t-x)\,dp\,dt.$

Proof. By Fourier's integral formula

$$f(x) = \frac{1}{2\pi}\int_{p=-\infty}^{\infty}\cos p(t-x)\,dp\int_{-\infty}^{\infty} f(t)\,dt$$

$$= \frac{2}{2\pi}\int_{0}^{\infty}\cos p(t-x)\,dp\int_{-\infty}^{\infty} f(t)\,dt$$

$$\left[\because \int_{-a}^{a} f(p)\,dp = 2\int_{0}^{a} f(p)\,dp \text{ if } f(p) = f(-p)\right]$$

$$= \frac{1}{\pi}\int_{0}^{\infty}\int_{-\infty}^{\infty} f(t)\cos p(t-x)\,dp\,dt.$$

(ii) Cosine Form:

$$f(x) = \frac{2}{\pi}\int_{0}^{\infty}\int_{0}^{\infty} f(t)\cos pt\cos px\,dp\,dt.$$

Proof. By Fourier integral formula

$$f(x) = \frac{1}{\pi}\int_{0}^{\infty}\int_{-\infty}^{\infty} f(t)\cos p(t-x)\,dp\,dt \qquad \text{[By case (i)]}$$

Taking $A(p) = \int_{-\infty}^{\infty} f(t)\cos pt\,dt$

and $B(p) = \int_{-\infty}^{\infty} f(t)\sin pt\,dt$

we obtain

$$f(x) = \frac{1}{\pi}\int_{0}^{\infty}[A(p)\cdot\cos px + B(p)\sin px]\,dp \qquad \text{...(i)}$$

Let $f(t)$ be an even function of t so that $f(-t) = f(t)$. Then $f(t)\cos pt$ is even and $f(t)\sin pt$ is odd function of t.

Consequently,

$$A(p) = 2\int_{0}^{\infty} f(t)\cos pt\,dt,\ B(p) = 0.$$

Putting these values in (i), we get

$$f(x) = \frac{1}{\pi}\int_0^\infty [A(p) \cos px + 0 \cdot \sin px]\, dp$$

$$= \frac{2}{\pi}\int_0^\infty \int_0^\infty f(t) \cos pt \cos px \, dp\, dt$$

This is the required form.

(iii) Sine Form:

$$f(x) = \frac{2}{\pi}\int_0^\infty \int_0^\infty f(t) \sin pt \sin px \, dp\, dt$$

Proof. As in case (ii), we have

$$f(x) = \frac{1}{\pi}\int_0^\infty [A(p) \cos px + B(p) \sin px]\, dp \qquad \ldots\text{(i)}$$

Let $f(t)$ be an odd function of t so that $f(-t) = -f(t)$. Then $f(t) \cos pt$ and $f(t) \sin pt$ are odd and even functions of t respectively. Obviously

$$A(p) = 0,\ B(p) = 2\int_0^\infty f(t) \sin pt \, dt$$

Putting these values in (i), we get

$$f(x) = \frac{2}{\pi}\int_0^\infty \int_0^\infty f(t) \sin pt \sin px \, dp \cdot dt.$$

(iv) Exponential Form:

$$f(x) = \frac{1}{2\pi}\int_{-\infty}^\infty \int_{-\infty}^\infty f(t)\, e^{-ipt} \cdot e^{ipx}\, dp \cdot dt$$

Proof. By Fourier integral formula

$$f(x) = \frac{1}{\pi}\int_{p=0}^\infty \int_{t=-\infty}^\infty f(t) \cos p(t-x)\, dp\, dt$$

$$= \frac{1}{2\pi}\int_{p=0}^\infty \int_{t=-\infty}^\infty f(t)\, [e^{-ip(t-x)} + e^{ip(t-x)}]\, dp \cdot dt$$

$$= \frac{1}{2\pi}\int_0^\infty \int_{-\infty}^\infty f(t),\ [e^{-ipt} \cdot e^{ipx} + e^{ipt} \cdot e^{-ipx}]\, dp \cdot dt$$

$$= \frac{1}{2\pi}\int_0^\infty \int_{-\infty}^\infty f(t)\, e^{-ipt} \cdot e^{-ipx}\, dp \cdot dt + \frac{1}{2\pi}\int_0^\infty \int_{-\infty}^\infty f(t)\, e^{ipt} e^{-ipx}\, dp \cdot dt$$

Putting $p = -p'$ in the second integral

$$f(x) = \frac{1}{2\pi}\int_0^{\infty}\int_{-\infty}^{\infty} f(t)\, e^{-ipt} \cdot e^{ipx}\, dp \cdot dt + \frac{1}{2\pi}\int_0^{-\infty}\int_{-\infty}^{\infty} f(t)\, e^{-ip't}\, e^{ip'x}\, (-dp') \cdot dt$$

or

$$f(x) = \frac{1}{2\pi}\int_0^{\infty}\int_{-\infty}^{\infty} f(t)\, e^{-ipt} \cdot e^{ipx}\, dx\, dt + \frac{1}{2\pi}\int_{-\infty}^{0}\int_{-\infty}^{\infty} f(t) \cdot e^{-ipt} \cdot e^{ipx}\, dp\, dt$$

(on dropping primes)

or $$f(x) = \frac{1}{2\pi}\int_{-\infty}^{\infty}\int_{-\infty}^{\infty} f(t)\, e^{-ipt} \cdot e^{ipx}\, dp\, dt \qquad \ldots\text{(ii)}$$

Note. Putting $p = -p'$ in the last integral, we get

$$f(x) = \frac{1}{2\pi}\int_{\infty}^{-\infty}\int_{-\infty}^{\infty} f(t)\, e^{ip't} \cdot e^{-ip'x}\, (-dp') \cdot dt$$

$$= \frac{1}{2\pi}\int_{-\infty}^{\infty} f(t)\, e^{ipt} \cdot e^{-ipx}\, dp\, dt \qquad \ldots\text{(iii)}$$

From (ii) and (iii), it is clear that *the negative sign in the exponent-ipt can be shifted to ipx without effecting the value of integral.* Thus (iii) is an alternate form of (ii).

7.5 PARSEVAL'S IDENTITY FOR FOURIER SERIES

Let the Fourier series corresponding to $f(x)$ converges uniformly to $f(x)$ in the interval $-l < x < l$, then

$$\frac{1}{l}\int_{-l}^{l} [f(x)]^2\, dx = \frac{a_0^2}{2} + \sum_{n=1}^{\infty} (a_n^2 + b_n^2)$$

where the integral on L.H.S. is supposed to exist.

Proof. Let the Fourier series of $f(x)$ converges uniformly to $f(x)$ at every point of the interval $-l < x < l$, so that

$$f(x) = \frac{a_0}{2} + \sum_{n=1}^{\infty}\left(a_n \cos\frac{n\pi x}{l} + b_n \sin\frac{n\pi x}{l}\right) \qquad \ldots\text{(i)}$$

and that term by term integration of this series is possible. Here

$$a_n = \frac{1}{l}\int_{-l}^{l} f(x) \cos\frac{n\pi x}{l}\, dx$$

$(n = 0, 1, 2, \ldots)$

and $$b_n = \frac{1}{l}\int_{-l}^{l} f(x) \sin \frac{n\pi x}{l}\, dx$$

$(n = 1, 2, 3, \ldots)$

Multiplying (i) by $f(x)$ and integrating term by term from $-l$ to $+l$, we get

$$\int_{-l}^{l} [f(x)]^2\, dx = \frac{a_0}{2}\int_{-l}^{l} f(x)\, dx + \sum_{n=1}^{\infty} a_n \int_{-l}^{l} f(x) \cos \frac{n\pi x}{l}\, dx$$

$$+ \sum_{n=1}^{\infty} b_n \int_{-l}^{l} f(x) \sin \frac{n\pi x}{l}\, dx$$

$$= \frac{a_0}{2} \cdot la_0 + \sum l(a_n^2 + b_n^2)$$

or $$\frac{1}{l}\int_{-l}^{l} [f(x)]^2\, dx = \frac{a_0^2}{2} + \sum (a_n^2 + b_n^2)$$

7.6 PARSEVAL'S IDENTITY FOR FOURIER TRANSFORM. RAYLEIGH'S THEOREM

Theorem. *If $f(p)$ and $g(p)$ are complex Fourier transforms of $F(x)$ and $G(x)$ respectively, then*

(*i*) $$\frac{1}{2\pi}\int_{-\infty}^{\infty} f(p)\, \{\overline{g(p)}\}\, dp = \int_{-\infty}^{\infty} F(x)\, \{\overline{G(x)}\}\, dx$$

(*ii*) $$\frac{1}{2\pi}\int_{-\infty}^{\infty} |f(p)|^2\, dp = \int_{-\infty}^{\infty} |F(x)|^2\, dx$$

where bar represents the complex conjugate.

Proof. Using the inversion formula for Fourier transform, we get

$$G(x) = \frac{1}{2\pi}\int_{-\infty}^{\infty} g(p)\, e^{ipx}\, dp \qquad \ldots\text{(i)}$$

Taking complex conjugate of both sides of (i), we get

$$\overline{G(x)} = \frac{1}{2\pi}\int_{-\infty}^{\infty} \overline{g(p)}\, e^{-ipx}\, dx \qquad \ldots\text{(ii)}$$

$\therefore$ $$\int_{-\infty}^{\infty} F(x)\, \overline{G(x)}\, dx$$

$$= \int_{-\infty}^{\infty} F(x)\, dx \left\{ \frac{1}{2\pi} \int_{-\infty}^{\infty} \overline{g(p)}\, e^{-ipx}\, dp \right\}, \qquad \text{[by (ii)]}$$

$$= \frac{1}{2\pi} \int_{-\infty}^{\infty} \int_{-\infty}^{\infty} F(p)\, \overline{\overline{g(p)}}\, e^{-ipx}\, dx\, dp$$

(on changing order of integration)

$$= \frac{1}{2\pi} \int_{-\infty}^{\infty} \int_{-\infty}^{\infty} f(x)\, \overline{\overline{g(p)}}\, e^{-ipx}\, dp\, dx$$

$$= \frac{1}{2\pi} \int_{-\infty}^{\infty} \overline{g(p)}\, dp \left[\int_{-\infty}^{\infty} F(x)\, e^{-ipx}\, dx \right]$$

$$= \frac{1}{2\pi} \int_{-\infty}^{\infty} \overline{g(p)}\, dp\, \{f(p)\} \qquad \text{[by Definition of Fourier transform]}$$

$$= \frac{1}{2\pi} \int_{-\infty}^{\infty} f(p)\, \overline{g(p)}\, dp$$

Thus we have proved that

$$\int_{-\infty}^{\infty} F(x)\, \overline{G(x)}\, dx = \frac{1}{2\pi} \int_{-\infty}^{\infty} f(p)\, \overline{\overline{g(p)}}\, dp \qquad \text{. . .(ii)}$$

This proves the first part.
Putting $G(x) = F(x)$ in (iii), we get

$$\int_{-\infty}^{\infty} F(x)\, \overline{F(x)}\, dx = \frac{1}{2\pi} \int_{-\infty}^{\infty} f(p)\, \overline{f(p)}\, dp$$

or

$$\int_{-\infty}^{\infty} |F(x)|^2\, dx = \frac{1}{2\pi} |f(p)|^2\, dp.$$

Note. Exactly by the same method we can prove the following results:

(i) $\frac{2}{\pi} \int_0^{\infty} f_s(p)\, g_s(p)\, dp = \int_0^{\infty} F(x)\, G(x)\, dx$

(ii) $\frac{2}{\pi} \int_0^{\infty} |f_s(p)|^2\, dp + \int_0^{\infty} |F(x)|^2\, dx$

(iii) $\frac{2}{\pi} \int_0^{\infty} f_c(p) \cdot g_c(p)\, dp = \int_0^{\infty} F(x)\, G(x)\, dx$

(iv) $\frac{2}{\pi} \int_0^{\infty} |f_c(p)|^2\, dp = \int_0^{\infty} |F(x)|^2\, dx.$

7.7 REIMANN-LEBESGUE THEOREM

If $f(x)$ converges uniformly at every point of the interval $-l < x < l$ and if the Fourier series corresponding to $f(x)$ converges to $f(x)$, then

$$\lim_{n \to \infty} a_n = 0, \quad \lim_{n \to \infty} b_n = 0,$$

where $\langle a_n \rangle$ and $\langle b_n \rangle$ are Fourier coefficients of the function f.

Proof. As we have proved in § 5.5, that

$$\frac{1}{l}\int_{-l}^{l} |f(x)|^2\, dx = \frac{a_0^2}{2} + \sum_{n=1}^{\infty} (a_n^2 + b_n^2) \qquad \ldots(i)$$

Since $f(x)$ is uniformly convergent and hence $\frac{1}{l}\int_{-l}^{l} [f(x)]^2\, dx$ is finite so that R.H.S. series of (i) is convergent. Consequently $\Sigma\, a_n$ and $\Sigma\, b_n$ both are convergent. The condition for this is

$$\lim_{n \to \infty} a_n = 0 = \lim_{n \to \infty} b_n$$

For $\quad \Sigma\, u_n$ is convergent, we have

$$\lim_{n \geq \infty} u_n = 0.$$

ILLUSTRATIVE EXAMPLES

Example 1. *Find finite Fourier sine and consine transform of $f(x) = x^2$, $0 < x < 4$.*

Solution. (i) $F_s\{f(x)\}$

$$= \int_0^t f(x) \sin \frac{n\pi x}{l}\, dx$$

$$= \int_0^4 x^2 \sin \frac{n\pi x}{4}\, dx$$

$$\left[-\frac{4}{n\pi} x^2 \cos \frac{n\pi x}{4}\right]_0^4 + \int_0^4 2x \frac{4}{n\pi} \cos \frac{n\pi x}{4}\, dx$$

$$= -\frac{4^3}{n\pi} \cos n\pi + \frac{8}{n\pi}\left[\frac{4x}{n\pi} \sin \frac{n\pi x}{4} + \frac{4^2}{n^2\pi^2} \cos \frac{n\pi x}{4}\right]_0^4$$

$$= -\frac{64}{n\pi}\cos n\pi + \frac{8\cdot 4^2}{n\pi\cdot n^2\pi^2}(\cos n\pi - 1)$$

$$= -\frac{64}{n\pi}\cos n\pi + \frac{128}{n^3\pi^3}(\cos n\pi - 1)$$

(ii) $F_c\{f(x)\}$

$$= \int_0^4 f(x)\cos\frac{n\pi x}{4}\,dx$$

$$= \int_0^4 x^2\cos\frac{n\pi x}{4}\,dx$$

$$= \left[\frac{4x^2}{n\pi}\sin\frac{n\pi x}{4}\right]_0^4 - \int_0^4 \frac{4}{n\pi}\cdot 2x\sin\frac{n\pi x}{4}\,dx$$

$$= 0 - \frac{8}{n\pi}\left[-\frac{4x}{n\pi}\cos\frac{n\pi x}{4} + \frac{4^2}{n^2\pi^2}\sin\frac{n\pi x}{4}\right]_0^4$$

$$= \frac{128}{n^2\pi^2}\cos n\pi.$$

Example 2. *Find the finite cosine transform of* $(1 - x/\pi)^2$.

Solution. $$f_c(p) = \int_0^\pi f(x)\cos\left(\frac{p\pi x}{\pi}\right)dx$$

$$= \int_0^\pi \left(1 - \frac{x}{\pi}\right)^2 \cos px\,dx$$

$$= \left[\frac{\sin px}{p}\left(1 - \frac{x}{\pi}\right)^2\right]_0^p - \int_0^\pi -2\left(1 - \frac{x}{\pi}\right)\cdot\frac{1}{\pi}\frac{\sin px}{p}\,dx$$

$$= 0 + \frac{2}{p\pi}\left[\left\{\frac{-\cos px}{p}\left(1 - \frac{x}{\pi}\right)\right\}_0^\pi - \int_0^\pi \frac{\cos px}{p}\frac{1}{\pi}\,dx\right]$$

$$= \frac{2}{p^2\pi}\left[1 - \frac{1}{\pi}\left(\frac{\sin px}{p}\right)\right]_0^\pi$$

$$= \frac{2}{p^2\pi}(1 - 0) = \frac{2}{\pi p^2} \text{ if } p > 0$$

If $p = 0$, then

$$f_c(0) = \int_0^\pi \left(1 - \frac{x}{\pi}\right)^2 (\cos 0x)\, dx$$

$$= \left[\frac{1}{3}\left(1 - \frac{x}{\pi}\right)^3 \left(\frac{1}{-1/\pi}\right)\right]_0^\pi$$

$$= -\frac{\pi}{3}\left[\left(1 - \frac{x}{\pi}\right)^3\right]_0^\pi = \frac{\pi}{3}$$

$$\therefore \qquad f_c(p) = \begin{cases} \dfrac{\pi}{3}, & \text{if } p = 0 \\ \dfrac{2}{\pi p^2}, & \text{if } p = 1, 2, 3, \ldots \end{cases}$$

Example 3. *Find the finite sine transform of*

(i) e^{ax}

(ii) $\cos ax$

(iii) $\sin ax$

(iv) x^3.

Solution. (i) $F_s\{e^{ax}\}$

$$= \int_0^\pi e^{ax} \sin px\, dx = \frac{1}{a^2 + p^2}\left[e^{ax}(a \sin px - p \cos px)\right]_0^\pi$$

$$= \frac{1}{a^2 + p^2}\left[p\,(1 - e^{a\pi} \cos p\pi)\right]$$

$$= \frac{p}{a^2 + p^2}\left[1 - (-1)^p e^{a\pi}\right]$$

(ii) $F_s\{\cos ax\}$

$$= \int_0^\pi \cos ax \sin px\, dx$$

$$= \frac{1}{2}\int_0^\pi [\sin (a + p)\, x + \sin (p - a)\, x]\, dx$$

$$= \frac{1}{2}\left[\frac{-\cos (a + p)\, x}{a + p} - \frac{\cos (p - a)\, x}{p - a}\right]_0^\pi$$

$$= \frac{1}{2}\left[\frac{1}{a+p} - \frac{\cos(a+p)\pi}{a+p} + \frac{1}{p-a} - \frac{\cos(p-a)\pi}{p-a}\right]$$

$$= \frac{1}{2(p^2 - a^2)}$$

$$[p - a + a + p - (p-a)\cos(a+p)\pi - (p+a)\cos(p-a)\pi]$$

$$= \frac{1}{2(p^2 - a^2)}$$

$$[2p - p\{\cos(a+p)\pi + \cos(p-a)\pi\} + a\{\cos(p+a)\pi - \cos(p-a)\pi\}]$$

$$= \frac{1}{2(p^2 - a^2)}[2p - 2p\cos p\pi \cdot \cos a\pi + 2a\sin p\pi \cdot \sin(-a\pi)]$$

$$= \frac{1}{(p^2 - a^2)}[p - p(-1)^p \cos a\pi + a \cdot 0 \sin(-a\pi)]$$

$$= \frac{p}{p^2 - a^2}[1 - (-1)^p \cos a\pi]$$

where p is a positive integer.

(iii) $F_s\{\sin ax\}$

$$= \int_0^\pi \sin ax \sin px \, dx = \frac{1}{2}\int_0^\pi [\cos(a-p)x - \cos(a+p)x] \, dx$$

$$= \frac{1}{2}\left[\frac{\sin(a-p)x}{a-p} - \frac{\sin(a+p)x}{a+p}\right]_0^\pi$$

$$= \frac{1}{2}[0 - 0] = 0, \text{ if } a \neq p \text{ and } a, p \text{ are integers.}$$

Also, if $p = a$, then

$$F_s\{\sin ax\} = \frac{1}{2}\int_0^\pi (1 - \cos 2px) \, dx$$

$$= \frac{1}{2}\left[x - \frac{\sin 2px}{2p}\right]_0^\pi = \pi/2$$

$$\therefore \quad F_s\{\sin ax\} = \begin{cases} 0, & \text{if } a \neq p \text{ and } a, p \text{ are integers} \\ \pi/2, & \text{if } a = p \end{cases}$$

(iv) $F_s\{x^3\}$

$$= \frac{1}{2}\int_0^{\pi} x^3 \sin px\, dx = \left[\frac{-x^3 \cos px}{p}\right]_0^{\pi} + \frac{3}{p^2}\int_0^{\pi} x^2 \cos px\, dx$$

$$= -\frac{\pi^3}{p}\cos \pi p + \frac{3}{p}\left[\left(\frac{x^2 \sin px}{p}\right)_0^{\pi} - \frac{2}{p}\int_0^{\pi} x \sin px\, dx\right]$$

$$= -\frac{\pi^3}{p}\cos \pi p + \frac{6\pi}{p^3}\cos \pi p - \frac{6}{p^4}[\sin px]_0^{\pi}$$

$$= -\frac{\pi^3}{p}\cos \pi p + \frac{6\pi}{p}\cos \pi p$$

$$= \frac{\pi}{p}(-1)^p\left[\frac{6}{p^2} - \pi^2\right], \text{ if } p = 1, 2, 3, \ldots$$

Example 4. *If* $f(n) = \dfrac{\cos(2n\pi/3)}{(2n+1)^2}$, *then find* $F_c^{-1}\{f(n)\}$ *and* $F_s^{-1}\{f(n)\}$, *if* $0 < x < 1$.

Solution. (i) $F_c^{-1}\{f(n)\} = \dfrac{1}{l}f_c(0) + \dfrac{2}{l}\sum_{n=1}^{\infty} \cos\left(\dfrac{n\pi x}{l}\right) f_c(n)$

$$= \frac{1}{l}f(0) + \frac{2}{1}\sum_{n=1}^{\infty} \cos n\pi x \cdot f(n)$$

$$= 1 + 2\sum_{n=1}^{\infty} \frac{\cos n\pi x \cdot \cos(2n\pi/3)}{(2n+1)^2}$$

(ii) $F_s^{-1}\{f_s(n)\} = \dfrac{2}{l}\sum_{n=1}^{\infty} \sin\left(\dfrac{n\pi x}{l}\right) f_s(n)$

$$= 2\sum_{n=1}^{\infty} \sin n\pi x \cdot \frac{\cos 2n\pi/3}{(2n+1)^2}$$

Example 5. *Find* $f(x)$ *if its finite sine transform is given by*

$$f_s(p) = \frac{1 - \cos p\pi}{p^2\pi^2}, \text{ where } 0 < x < \pi,\ p = 1, 2, 3, \ldots$$

Solution. We know that

$$f(x) = \frac{2}{l} \sum_{n=1}^{\infty} f_s(n) \sin \frac{n\pi x}{l}$$

In this case

$$f(x) = \frac{2}{\pi} \sum_{p=1}^{\infty} f_s(p) \sin\left(\frac{p\pi x}{\pi}\right)$$

$$= \frac{2}{\pi} \sum_{p=1}^{\infty} \frac{(1-\cos p\pi)}{p^2\pi^2} \sin px$$

or

$$f(x) = \frac{2}{\pi^2} \sum_{p=1}^{\infty} \left(\frac{1-\cos \pi p}{p^2}\right) \sin px.$$

Example 6. *Find finite cosine transform of $f(x)$ if*

$f(x) = \sin nx.$

Solution. $F_c\{\sin nx\}$

$$\int_0^{\pi} \sin nx \cos px \, dx = \frac{1}{2}\int_0^{\pi} [\sin(n+p)x] + \sin(n-p)x]\, dx$$

$$= -\frac{1}{2}\left[\frac{\cos(n+p)x}{n+p} + \frac{\cos(n-p)x}{n-p}\right]_0^x$$

$$= -\frac{1}{2}\left[\frac{\cos(n+p)\pi}{n+p} - \frac{1}{n+p} + \frac{\cos(n-p)\pi}{n-p} - \frac{1}{n-p}\right]$$

$$= -\frac{1}{2}\left[\frac{(-1)^{n+p}}{n+p} + \frac{(-1)^{n-p}}{n-p} - \frac{1}{n+p} - \frac{1}{n-p}\right]$$

$$= \begin{cases} 0, & \text{if } n+p \text{ is even} \\ \dfrac{2n}{n^2-p^2}, & \text{if } n+p \text{ is odd.} \end{cases}$$

Example 7. *Show that*

$$F_c\{3x^2\} = \begin{cases} \pi^2, & \textit{when } n = 0 \\ \dfrac{6\pi(-1)^n}{n^2}, & \textit{when } n = 1, 2, 3, \ldots \end{cases}$$

Solution. $F_c\{3x^2\} = \int_0^{\pi} 3x^2 \cos \frac{n\pi x}{\pi} dx$

$$\int_0^{\pi} 3x^2 \cos nx\, dx$$

Now, if $n = 0$, then

$$F_c\{3x^2\} = \int_0^{\pi} 3x^2\, dx = \pi^3$$

If $n = 1, 2, 3, \ldots$, then

$$\begin{aligned} F_c\{3x^2\} &= \int_0^{\pi} 3x^2 \cos nx\, dx \\ &= 3\left\{\left[\frac{x^2 \sin nx}{n}\right]_0^{\pi} - \int_0^{\pi} \frac{2x}{n} \sin nx\, dx\right\} \\ &= -\frac{6}{\pi}\int_0^{\pi} x \sin nx\, dx \\ &= -\frac{6}{n}\left[\frac{-x}{n}\cos nx + \frac{\sin nx}{n^2}\right]_0^{\pi} \\ &= \frac{6\pi}{n^2}\cos n\pi = \frac{6\pi}{n^2}(-1)^n. \end{aligned}$$

Example 8. *Find $f(x)$ if*

$$f_c(p) = \left(6 \sin \frac{p\pi}{2} - \cos p\pi\right) \quad (2p + 1)\,\pi$$

for $p = 1, 2, 3, \ldots$

and $f_c(p) = \frac{2}{\pi}$ *for* $p = 0$

where $0 < x < 4.$

Solution. We know that

$$f(x) = F_c^{-1}\{f_c(p)\} = \frac{1}{l} f_c(0) + \frac{2}{l} \sum_{p=1}^{\infty} f_c(p) \cos \frac{p\pi x}{l}$$

$$= \frac{1}{4} \cdot \frac{2}{\pi} + \frac{2}{4} \sum_{p=1}^{\infty} \frac{\left(6 \sin \frac{p\pi}{2} - \cos p\pi\right)}{(2p+1)\pi} \cdot \cos\left(\frac{p\pi x}{4}\right)$$

$$= \frac{1}{2\pi} + \frac{1}{2\pi} \sum_{p=1}^{\infty} \frac{\left(6 \sin \frac{p\pi}{2} - \cos p\pi\right)}{(2p+1)} \cdot \cos\left(\frac{px\pi}{4}\right)$$

Example 9. *Find $f(x)$ if its finite sine transform is given by*

$$f_s(p) = \frac{2\pi(-1)^{p-1}}{p^3}$$

where $p = 1, 2, 3, \ldots$ and $2 < x < \pi$.

Solution. $f(x) = F_s^{-1}\{f_s(p)\}$

$$= \frac{2}{l} \sum_{p=1}^{\infty} f_s(p) \sin \frac{p\pi x}{l}$$

$$= \frac{2}{\pi} \sum_{p=1}^{\infty} \frac{2\pi(-1)^{p-1}}{p^3} \sin px$$

$$= 4 \sum_{p=1}^{\infty} \frac{(-1)^{p-1}}{p^3} \sin px.$$

EXERCISE 7(A)

1. Find the finite sine transform of

   $f(x) = 2x$, where $0 < x < 4$.

2. Find the finite Fourier cosine transform of x where

   $0 < x < \pi$.

3. Find finite cosine transform of $f(x)$ if

$$f(x) = \begin{cases} 1, & 0 < x < \pi/2 \\ -1, & \pi/2 < x < \pi \end{cases}.$$

4. Show that

$$F_c\left\{\frac{x^2}{2\pi}-\frac{\pi}{6}\right\} \begin{aligned} &= 0, && \text{if } n = 0 \\ &= (-1)^n/n^2 && \text{if } n = 1, 2, \ldots \end{aligned}$$

5. Find $F(x)$ if $F_c\{F(x)\} = \dfrac{\sin(n\pi/2)}{2n}$, $n = 1, 2, 3, \ldots$ and $\dfrac{\pi}{4}$ if $n = 0$, where $0 < x < 2\pi$.

6. Find $F(x)$ if $F_s\{F(x)\} = \dfrac{16(-1)^{n-1}}{n^3}$, if $0 < x < 8$, where $n = 1, 2, 3, \ldots$.

7. If $f_s(n) = 2\pi \dfrac{(-1)^{n-1}}{n^2}$, $n = 1, 2, 3, \ldots$, where $0 < x < \pi$, then find $f(x)$.

ANSWERS

1. $\dfrac{-32}{n\pi}(-1)^n$.

2. $\dfrac{1}{p^2}[(-1)^p - 1]$

3. 0 if $n = 0$, $\dfrac{2}{n}\sin\left(\dfrac{n\pi}{2}\right)$ if $n = 1, 2, 3, \ldots$

4. $\dfrac{6\pi}{n^3}(-1)^{n+1} \cdot \dfrac{2}{n^3}[1-(-1)^n]$.

5. $\dfrac{1}{4}+\dfrac{1}{2}\pi\displaystyle\sum_{n=1}^{\infty}\dfrac{\sin(n\pi/2)}{n}\cos nx$.

6. $4\displaystyle\sum_{n=1}^{\infty}\dfrac{(-1)^{n-1}}{n^3}\sin\dfrac{n\pi x}{8}$.

7. $\dfrac{2}{p}\sin\dfrac{p\pi}{2}$, $p > 0$.

ILLUSTRATIVE EXAMPLES

Example 1. *Use Parseval's identities to prove that*

(*i*) $$\int_0^{\infty}\frac{dt}{(a^2+t^2)(b^2+t^2)} = \frac{\pi}{2ab(a+b)}$$

(*ii*) $$\int_0^{\infty}\frac{\sin at\,dt}{t(a^2+t^2)} = \frac{\pi}{2}\left(\frac{1-e^{-a^2}}{a^2}\right).$$

Solution. (i) Let $F(x) = e^{-ax}$, $G(x) = e^{-bx}$

then $$f_c(p) = \int_0^\infty F(x) \cos px \, dx$$

$$= \int_0^\infty e^{-ax} \cos px \, dx = \frac{a}{a^2 + p^2}$$

or $$f_c(p) = \frac{a}{a^2 + p^2} \qquad \ldots \text{(i)}$$

Similarly, $$g_c(p) = \frac{b}{b^2 + p^2} \qquad \ldots \text{(ii)}$$

By Parseval's identity for Fourier transform, we get

$$\frac{2}{\pi} \int_0^\infty f_c(p)\, g_c(p)\, dp = \int_0^\infty F(x)\, G(x)\, dx$$

Putting values, we get

$$\frac{2}{\pi} \int_0^\infty \frac{a}{a^2 + p^2} \cdot \frac{b}{(b^2 + p^2)} dp = \int_0^\infty e^{-ax} \cdot e^{-bx} dx$$

or $$\int_0^\infty \frac{dp}{(a^2 + p^2)(b^2 + p^2)} = \frac{\pi}{2ab} \left[\frac{e^{-(a+b)x}}{-(a+b)} \right]_0^\infty$$

$$= \frac{\pi}{2ab(a+b)} [1 - 0]$$

or $$\int_0^\infty \frac{dt}{(a^2 + t^2)(b^2 + t^2)} = \frac{\pi}{2ab(a+b)}.$$

(ii) Let $F(x) = e^{-ax}$, then

$$f_c(p) = \frac{a}{a^2 + p^2}.$$

Let $$G(x) = \begin{cases} 1, & 0 < x < a \\ 0, & x > a \end{cases}.$$

Then $$g_c(p) = \int_0^\infty G(x) \cos px \, dx$$

$$= \int_0^a G(x) \cos px \, dx + \int_0^\infty G(x) \cos px \, dx$$

$$= \int_0^a \cos px \, dx + \int_a^\infty 0 \cdot \cos px \, dx$$

$$= \left[\frac{\sin px}{p}\right]_0^a = \frac{\sin ap}{p}$$

or $$g_c(p) = \frac{\sin ap}{p}$$

Now, by Parseval's identity, we have

$$\frac{2}{\pi}\int_0^\infty f_c(p)\, g_c(p)\, dp = \int_0^\infty F(x)\, G(x)\, dx$$

Putting the values, we get

$$\frac{2}{\pi}\int_0^\infty \frac{a}{a^2+p^2}\frac{\sin ap}{p}\, dp = \int_0^\infty e^{-ax}\, G(x)\, dx$$

or $$\frac{2a}{\pi}\int_0^\infty \frac{\sin ap}{p(a^2+p^2)}\, dp$$

$$= \int_0^a e^{-ax}\, G(x)\, dx + \int_a^\infty e^{-ax}\, G(x)\, dx$$

$$= \int_0^a e^{-ax}\cdot 1\, dx + \int_a^\infty e^{-ax}\cdot 0\, dx$$

$$= \left[\frac{e^{-ax}}{-a}\right]_0^a = \frac{1}{a}(1 - e^{-a^2})$$

or $$\frac{2a}{\pi}\int_0^\infty \frac{\sin ap}{p(p^2+a^2)}\, dp = \frac{1}{a}(1 - e^{-a^2})$$

$\therefore$ $$\int_0^\infty \frac{\sin at}{t(t^2+a^2)}\cdot dt = \frac{\pi}{2a^2}(1 - e^{-a^2}).$$

Example 2. *Express the function*

$$f(x) = \begin{cases} 1, & \text{for } |x| \le 1 \\ 0, & \text{for } |x| > 1 \end{cases}$$

as a Fourier integral. Hence evaluate

$$\int_0^\infty \frac{\sin\lambda \cos\lambda x}{\lambda}\, d\lambda.$$

Solution. By Fourier integral formula,

$$f(x) = \frac{1}{\pi}\int_{p=0}^\infty \int_{t=-\infty}^\infty f(t)\cos p(t-x)\, dp\, dt$$

$$= \frac{1}{\pi} \int_{p=0}^{\infty} \int_{t=-1}^{1} \cos p\,(t - x)\, dp\, dt \qquad \text{[by definition of } f(x)]$$

$$= \frac{1}{\pi} \int_{p=0}^{\infty} \left[\frac{\sin p\,(t-x)}{p} \right]_{-1}^{1} dp$$

$$= \frac{1}{\pi} \int_{p=0}^{\infty} \left[\frac{\sin p\,(1-x) - \sin p\,(-1-x)}{p} \right] dp$$

$$= \frac{1}{\pi} \int_{0}^{\infty} \left[\frac{\sin p\,(1-x) + \sin p\,(1+x)}{p} \right] dp$$

$$= \frac{2}{\pi} \int_{0}^{\infty} \frac{\sin p \cos px}{p}\, dp = \frac{2}{\pi} \int_{0}^{\infty} \frac{\sin \lambda \cos \lambda x}{\lambda}\, d\lambda$$

or
$$f(x) = \frac{2}{\pi} \int_{0}^{\infty} \frac{\sin \lambda \cos \lambda x}{\lambda}\, d\lambda \qquad \ldots \text{(i)}$$

This is the representation of $f(x)$ as Fourier integral.

Second Part. From (i)

$$\int_{0}^{\infty} \frac{\sin \lambda \cos \lambda x}{\lambda}\, d\lambda = \frac{\pi}{2} f(x) = \begin{cases} \pi/2, & |x| \le 1 \\ 0, & |x| > 1 \end{cases}.$$

Example 3. *Using Fourier integral, show that*

$$e^{-ax} = \frac{2a}{\pi} \int_{0}^{\infty} \frac{\cos \lambda x}{\lambda^2 + a^2}\, d\lambda,\ a > 0,\ x \ge 0.$$

Solution. By Fourier cosine integral formula

$$f(x) = \frac{2}{\pi} \int_{0}^{\infty} \int_{0}^{\infty} f(t) \cos pt \cos px\, dp\, dt$$

Taking $f(t) = e^{-at}$, we get

$$e^{-ax} = \frac{2}{\pi} \int_{0}^{\infty} \cos px\, dp \int_{0}^{\infty} e^{-at} \cos pt\, dt$$

or
$$e^{-ax} = \frac{2}{\pi} \int_{0}^{\infty} \cos px\, dp \frac{a}{p^2 + a^2}$$

$$= \frac{2a}{\pi} \int_{0}^{\infty} \frac{\cos px\, dp}{p^2 + a^2}$$

$$= \frac{2a}{\pi} \int_0^{\infty} \frac{\cos \lambda x \, d\lambda}{\lambda^2 + a^2}$$

or $$e^{-ax} = \frac{2a}{\pi} \int_0^{\infty} \frac{\cos \lambda x \, d\lambda}{\lambda^2 + a^2}$$

Example 4. *Using Fourier integral formula, show that*

$$e^{-x} \cos x = \frac{2}{\pi} \int \frac{(u^2 + 2) \cos ux}{u^4 + 4} \, du.$$

Solution. Since we have cosine terms in the integrand, hence we shall use Fourier cosine integral formula, *i.e.*,

$$f(x) = \frac{2}{\pi} \int_0^{\infty} \int_0^{\infty} f(t) \cos ut \cos ux \, dt$$

Taking $f(t) = e^{-t} \cos t$, we get

$$e^{-x} \cos x = \frac{2}{\pi} \int_0^{\infty} \cos ux \, du \int_0^{\infty} e^{-t} \cos t \cos ut \, dt$$

$$= \frac{1}{\pi} \int_0^{\infty} \cos ux \, dx \int_0^{\infty} e^{-t} [\cos (u + 1) t + \cos (u - 1) t] \, dt$$

$$= \frac{1}{\pi} \int_0^{\infty} \cos ux \cdot du \left[\frac{1}{(u + 1)^2 + 1} + \frac{1}{(u - 1)^2 + 1} \right]$$

$$= \frac{1}{\pi} \int_0^{\infty} \frac{2 (u^2 + 2) \cos ux \, du}{(u^2 + 2u + 2)(u^2 - 2u + 2)}$$

$$= \frac{1}{\pi} \int_0^{\infty} \frac{2 (u^2 + 2) \cos ux \, du}{[(u^2 + 2)^2 - (2u)^2]}$$

$$= \frac{2}{\pi} \int_0^{\infty} \frac{(u^2 + 2) \cos ux \, du}{u^2 + 4}.$$

Example 5. *Using Fourier integral method, prove that*

$$e^{-ax} - e^{-bx} = \frac{3 (b^2 - a^2)}{\pi} \int_0^{\infty} \frac{u \sin ux \, du}{(u^2 + a^2)(u^2 + b^2)}$$

where $a > 0, \; b > 0.$

Solution. As the integrand contains sine term hence it suggests that we should use Fourier sine integral formula in order to solve this problem.

$$\therefore \qquad f(x) = \frac{2}{\pi}\int_0^\infty \int_0^\infty f(t)\sin ut \sin ux \, du\, dt \qquad \ldots(i)$$

We know that

$$\int_0^\infty e^{-at}\sin bt\, dt = \frac{b}{a^2+b^2}$$

Hence, $\displaystyle\int_0^\infty (e^{-at} - e^{-bt})\sin ut\, dt = \frac{u}{a^2+u^2} - \frac{u}{b^2+u^2}$

or
$$\int_0^\infty (e^{-at} - e^{-bt})\sin ut\, dt = \frac{(b^2-a^2)\,u}{(a^2+u^2)(b^2+u^2)} \qquad \ldots(ii)$$

Taking $f(x) = e^{-ax} - e^{-bx}$ in (i), we get

$$e^{-ax} - e^{-bx} = \frac{2}{\pi}\int_0^\infty\int_0^\infty (e^{-at} - e^{-bt})\sin ut \sin ux\, du\, dt$$

$$= \frac{2}{\pi}\int_0^\infty \sin ux\cdot du\int_0^\infty (e^{-at} - e^{-bt})\sin ut\cdot dt$$

$$= \frac{2}{\pi}\int_0^\infty \frac{(b^2-a^2)\,u\sin ux\cdot du}{(a^2+u^2)(b^2+u^2)} \qquad \text{[by (ii)]}$$

or
$$e^{-ax} - e^{-bx} = \frac{2(b^2-a^2)}{\pi}\int_0^\infty \frac{u\sin ux\cdot du}{(a^2+u^2)(b^2+u^2)}$$

EXERCISE 7(B)

1. Find Fourier transform of $f(x)$ defined by

$$f(x) = \begin{vmatrix} 1, & |x| < a \\ 0, & |x| > a \end{vmatrix}$$

and hence prove that $\displaystyle\int_0^\infty \frac{\sin^2 ax}{x^2}\, dx = \frac{\pi a}{2}$.

2. Using Fourier integral formula, show that

$$\frac{\pi}{2}e^{-x} = \int_0^\infty \frac{\cos\lambda x}{\lambda^2+1}\, d\lambda.$$

3. If $f(x) = \begin{cases} 1, & |x| < a \\ 0, & |x| > a \end{cases}$ and $f(p) = \dfrac{2\sin pa}{a}, p \neq 0.$

4. Find the Fourier integral of the function

$$f(x) = \begin{bmatrix} 0, & x < 0 \\ \frac{1}{2}, & x = 0 \\ a^{-x}, & x > 0 \end{bmatrix}$$

Verify the representation directly at the point $x = 0$. And show that f satisfies all the conditions in Fourier integral theorem.

ANSWERS

1. $\frac{2}{p}\sin pa, \frac{\pi}{2}a.$ 2. $e^{-x}.$ 4. $\frac{1}{\pi}\int_0^\infty \left[\frac{\cos px + p\sin px}{1+p^2}\right] dp.$

8

Applications of Fourier Transform to Boundary Value Problems

8.1 INTRODUCTION

(i) Infinite Fourier transform

$$F\{f(x)\} = \int_{-\infty}^{\infty} f(x)\, e^{-ipx}\, dx = \bar{f}(p),$$

$$F_0\{f(x)\} = \int_0^{\infty} f(x) \cos px\, dx = \bar{f}_c(p),$$

$$F_s\{f(x)\} = \int_0^{\infty} f(x) \sin px\, dx = \bar{f}_s(x),$$

$$F_s^{-1}\{\bar{f}_s(s)\} = \frac{2}{\pi} \int_0^{\infty} \bar{f}(p) \sin px\, ds = f(x),$$

$$F_c^{-1}\{\bar{f}_c(s)\} = \frac{2}{\pi} \int_0^{\infty} \bar{f}_c(p) \cos px\, ds = f(x).$$

(ii) Finite Fourier transform

Suppose $0 < x < l$.

$$F_s\{f(x)\} = \int_0^{l} f(x) \sin \frac{p\pi x}{l}\, dx = \bar{f}_s(p),$$

$$F_s^{-1}\{\bar{f}_s(p)\} = f(x) = \frac{2}{l} \sum_{s=1}^{\infty} \bar{f}_s(p) \sin \frac{p\pi x}{l},$$

$$F_c\{f(x)\} = \bar{f}_c(p) = \int_0^{l} f(x) \cos \frac{p\pi x}{l}\, dx,$$

$$F_c^{-1}\{\bar{f}_c(p)\} = f(x) = \frac{1}{l}\bar{f}_c(0) + \frac{2}{l}\sum_{s=1}^{\infty} \bar{f}_c(p)\cos\frac{p\pi x}{l}.$$

The above results should be committed to memory for further study.

8.2 CHOICE OF INFINITE SINE OR COSINE TRANSFORMS

The choice of sine or cosine transform is decided by the form of boundary conditions.

$$F_c\left\{\frac{\partial^2 u}{\partial x^2}\right\} = \int_0^\infty \frac{\partial^2 u}{\partial x^2}\cos px\,dx = \left[\frac{\partial u}{\partial x}\cos px\right]_0^\infty + p\int_0^\infty \frac{\partial u}{\partial x}\sin x\,dx$$

$$= \left(-\frac{\partial u}{\partial x}\right)_{x=0} + p\,[u\sin px]_0^\infty - p^2\int_0^\infty u\cos px\,dx \text{ if } \lim_{x\to\infty}\frac{\partial u}{\partial x} = 0$$

$$= -\left(\frac{\partial u}{\partial x}\right)_{x=0} - p\,\bar{u}_c \text{ if } \lim_{x\to\infty} u = 0$$

$$\therefore \quad F_c\left\{\frac{\partial^2 u}{\partial x^2}\right\} = -\left(\frac{\partial u}{\partial x}\right)_{x=0} - \bar{u}_c \text{ where } F_c\{u\} = \bar{u}_c \qquad \ldots\text{(i)}$$

$$F_s\left\{\frac{\partial^2 u}{\partial x^2}\right\} = \int_0^\infty \frac{\partial^2 u}{\partial x^2}\sin px\,dx = \left[\frac{\partial u}{\partial x}\sin x\right]_0^\infty - p\int_0^\infty \frac{\partial u}{\partial x}\cos px\,dx$$

$$= -p\left[(u\cos px)_{x=0}^{\infty} + p\int_0^\infty u\sin px\,dx\right] \text{ if } \lim_{x\to\infty}\frac{\partial u}{\partial x} = 0$$

$$= p\,(u)_{x=0} - p^2\bar{u}_e \text{ if } \lim_{x\to\infty} u = 0$$

$$\therefore \quad F_s\left\{\frac{\partial^2 u}{\partial x^2}\right\} = p\,(u)_{r=0} - p^2\bar{u}_e \qquad \ldots\text{(ii)}$$

From (1) and (2), it follows that if we want to remove the term $\frac{\partial^2 u}{\partial x^2}$ from a differential equation then we require

(i) $\left(\frac{\partial u}{\partial x}\right)_{x=0}$ in cosine transform

(ii) $(u)_{x=0}$ in sine transform.

Similarly we can show that in case of finite transform, exclusion of $\frac{\partial^2 u}{\partial x^2}$ from a differential equation requires

(i) $u(0, t)$ and $u(l, t)$ in finite sine transform

(ii) $\left(\frac{\partial u}{\partial x}\right)_{x=0}$ and $\left(\frac{\partial u}{\partial x}\right)_{x=l}$ in finite cosine transform.

8.3 APPLICATIONS OF INFINITE FOURIER TRANSFORM

ILLUSTRATIVE EXAMPLES

Example 1. *Solve* $\frac{\partial u}{\partial t} = \frac{\partial^2 u}{\partial x^2}$, *with the conditions (i)* $u(0, t) = 0$,

(ii) $u = \begin{cases} 1, & 0 < x < 1 \\ 0, & x \geq 1 \end{cases}$ *when* $t = 0$

(iii) $u(x, t)$ *is bounded.*

Solution. $(u)_{x=0}$ is given and so we shall apply sine transform to the given equation so that

$$\int_0^\infty \frac{\partial u}{\partial t} \sin px \, dx = \int_0^\infty \frac{\partial^2 u}{\partial x^2} \sin px \, dx$$

or
$$\frac{\partial}{\partial t}\int_0^\infty n \sin px \, dx = \left[\frac{\partial u}{\partial x} \sin px\right]_0^\infty - p\int_0^\infty \frac{\partial u}{\partial x} \cos px \, dx$$

or
$$\frac{d\bar{u}_s}{dt} = -p\int_0^\infty \frac{\partial u}{\partial x} \cos px \, dx. \text{ For } \frac{\partial u}{\partial x} \to 0 \text{ as } x \to \infty$$

$$= -p\left[(u \cos px)_0^\infty + p\int_0^\infty u \sin px \, dx\right]$$

$$= pu(0, t) - p^2\bar{u}_s. \text{ For } u \to 0 \text{ as } x \to \infty$$

$$= -p^2\bar{u}_s, \qquad \text{[by boundary condition (i)]}$$

or
$$\frac{d\bar{u}_s}{dt} + p\bar{u}_s^2 = 0.$$

The solution of this is $\bar{u}_s = A\, e^{-p^2 t}$. . . .(i)

This $\Rightarrow \bar{u}_s(p, 0) = A \Rightarrow A = \int_0^\infty u(x, 0) \sin px \, dx$

$$\Rightarrow A = \int_0^1 1 \sin px \, dx + \int_1^\infty 0 \sin px \, dx = -\left[\frac{\cos px}{p}\right]_{x=0}^1 + 0$$

$$\Rightarrow A = \frac{1 - \cos p}{p}.$$

Now (1) becomes

$$\bar{u}_s = \left(\frac{1 - \cos p}{p}\right) e^{-p^2 t}$$

Applying inverse Fourier sine transform,

$$u(x, t) = \frac{2}{\pi} \int_0^\infty \left(\frac{1 - \cos p}{p}\right) e^{-p^2 t} \sin px \, dp.$$

Example 2. *Use finite cosine transform to solve*

$$\frac{\partial V}{\partial t} = k \frac{\partial^2 V}{\partial x^2}, \; 0 < x < \pi, \; t > 0$$

with the boundary conditions $\frac{\partial V}{\partial x} = 0$ *when* $x = 0$ *and* $x = \pi$, $t > 0$ *and the initial condition* $V = f(x)$ *when* $t = 0$, $0 < x < \pi$.

Solution. Taking finite Fourier cosine transform of the given equation,

$$\frac{1}{k} \int_0^\pi \frac{\partial V}{\partial t} \cos px \, dx = \int_0^\pi \frac{\partial^2 V}{dx^2} \cos px \, dx$$

or $$\frac{1}{k} \frac{d\bar{V}_0}{dt} = \left\{\frac{\partial V}{\partial x} \cos px\right\}_{x=0}^\pi + p \int_0^\pi \frac{\partial V}{\partial x} \sin px \, dx$$

$$= 0 + p\left[\{V(x, t) \sin px\}_{x=0}^\pi - p \int_0^\pi V \cos px \, dx\right]$$

$$= -p^2 \bar{V}_c$$

or $\frac{d\bar{V}_c}{dt} = -kp^2 \bar{V}_c$. Its solution is ...(i)

$$\bar{V}_c(p, t) = A \, e^{-p^2 kt}$$

$$V = f(x) \Rightarrow \bar{V}_0(p, 0) = \int_0^{\pi} f(x) \cos px \, dx$$

Using (1), $A = \int_0^{\pi} f(x) \cos px \, dx = A\,(p)$ ...(ii)

By def. of inverse finite Fourier transform,

$$V(x, t) = \frac{1}{\pi} \bar{V}_0(0, t) + \frac{2}{\pi} \sum_{p=1}^{\infty} \bar{V}_0 \cos px$$

or
$$V(x, t) = \frac{A}{\pi} + \frac{2}{\pi} \sum_{p=1}^{\infty} A\,(p)\, e^{-p^2 kt} \cos px.$$

Example 3. *Solve* $\frac{\partial u}{\partial t} = 2\frac{\partial^2 u}{\partial x^2}$ *if* $u\,(0, t) = 0$, $u\,(x, 0) = e^{-x}$, $u\,(x, t)$ *is bounded.*

Solution. Since $(u)_{x=0}$ is given and so we shall apply Fourier sine transform to the given differential equation, so that

$$\int_0^{\infty} \frac{\partial u}{\partial t} \sin px \, dx = 2\int_0^{\infty} \frac{\partial^2 u}{\partial x^2} \sin px \, dx$$

or
$$\frac{\partial}{\partial t}\int_0^{\infty} u \sin px \, dx = 2\left[\left(\frac{\partial u}{\partial x} \sin px\right)_0^{\infty} - p\int_0^{\infty} \frac{\partial u}{\partial x} \cos px \, dx\right]$$

or
$$\frac{d\bar{u}_s}{dt} = -2p\left[(u \cos px)_0^{\infty} + p\int_0^{\infty} u \sin px \, dx\right]$$

For $\lim_{x \to \infty} \frac{\partial u}{\partial x} = \text{finite}$

$$= 2pu\,(0, t) - 2p^2\bar{u}_s. \text{ For } \lim_{x \to \infty} \frac{24}{2x} u = \text{finite}$$

$$= -2p^2\bar{u}_s. \text{ For } u\,(0, t) = 0$$

or
$$\frac{d\bar{u}_s}{dt} + 2p^2\bar{u}_s = 0.$$

The solution of this is $\bar{u}_s = A\, e^{-2p^2 t}$. ...(i)

This $\Rightarrow \bar{u}_s(p, 0) = A \Rightarrow A = \int_0^\infty u(x, 0) \sin px\, dx$

$$\Rightarrow A = \int_0^\infty e^{-x} \sin px\, dx$$

$$\Rightarrow A = \frac{p}{p^2+1} \text{ For } \int_0^\infty e^{-ax} \sin bx\, dx = \frac{b}{a^2+b^2}$$

Now (1) is reduced to $\bar{u}_s = \left(\frac{p}{p^2+1}\right) e^{-2p^2 t}$.

Applying inverse Fourier sine transform,

$$u(x, t) = \frac{2}{\pi} \int_0^\infty \left(\frac{p}{p^2+1}\right) e^{-p^2 t} \sin px\, dp.$$

Example 4. *The temperature u in a semi-infinite rod* $0 \le x < \infty$ *is determined by*

$$\frac{\partial u}{\partial t} = k \frac{\partial^2 u}{\partial x^2}$$

with the conditions

(*i*) $u = 0$ when $t = 0, x > 0$,

(*ii*) $\frac{\partial u}{\partial x} = -\mu$ *when* $x = 0$

(*iii*) *partial derivatives of u tend to zero as* $x \to \infty$.

Determine the temperature formula.

Solution. Since $\left(\frac{\partial u}{\partial x}\right)_{x=0}$ is given and so we shall apply Fourier cosine transform to the given equation so that

$$\int_0^\infty \frac{\partial u}{\partial t} \cos px\, dx = k \int_0^\infty \frac{\partial^2 u}{\partial x^2} \cos px\, dx$$

or
$$\frac{\partial}{\partial t} \int_0^\infty u \cos px\, dx = k \left[\left(\frac{\partial u}{\partial x} \cos px\right)_0^\infty + p \int_0^\infty \frac{\partial u}{\partial x} \sin px\, dx \right]$$

or
$$\frac{d\bar{u}_c}{dt} = -k \left(\frac{\partial u}{\partial x}\right)_{x=0} + pk \left[(u \sin px)_0^\infty - p \int_0^\infty u \cos px\, dx \right]$$

$$= k\mu - p^2 k\bar{u}_c. \text{ For } \lim_{x \to \infty} u = 0$$

or $$\frac{d\bar{u}_c}{dt} + p^2 k\bar{u}_c = k\mu. \qquad \text{...(i)}$$

This is the linear differential equation of first order.

I.F. $= e^{\int k p^2 dt} = e^{p^2 kt}$.

The solution of (i) is

$$a^{p^2 tk}\,\bar{u}_c = \int k\mu\, e^{p^2 tk}\, dt + A = A + \frac{\mu}{p^2} - e^{k\,p^2 t}$$

or $$\bar{u}_c = A\, e^{-p^2 tk} + \frac{\mu}{p^2} \qquad \text{...(ii)}$$

$$u = 0 \text{ at } t \to \infty \Rightarrow \bar{u}_0 = 0 \text{ at } t = 0$$

$$\Rightarrow 0 = A + \frac{\mu}{p^2}, \qquad \text{[by (ii)]}$$

$$\Rightarrow A = -\frac{\mu}{p^2}.$$

Now (ii) becomes $\bar{u}_c = \frac{\mu}{p^2}(1 - e^{-p^2 tk})$.

Applying inverse cosine Fourier transform,

$$u\,(x, t) = \frac{2}{\pi}\int_0^\infty \frac{u}{p^2}(1 - e^{-p^2 tk}) \cos px\, dp.$$

Example 5. *Use the complex form of the Fourier transform to show that*

$$u = \frac{1}{2\sqrt{(\pi t)}} \int_{-\infty}^{\infty} f(u)\, exp\left\{-\frac{(x-u)^2}{4t}\right\} du$$

is the solution of the boundary value problem

$$\frac{\partial u}{\partial t} = \frac{\partial^2 u}{\partial x^2}, \; -\infty < x < \infty, t > 0$$

$$u = f(x), \text{ when } t = 0.$$

Solution. Taking Fourier transform of the given differential equation,

$$\int_{-\infty}^{\infty} \frac{\partial u}{\partial t} e^{-tpx}\, dx = \int_{-\infty}^{\infty} \frac{\partial^2 u}{\partial x^2} e^{-tpx}\, dx$$

or $$\frac{\partial}{\partial t}\int_{-\infty}^{\infty} ue^{-ipx}\,dx = (ip)^2 F\{u\},$$

or $$\frac{d\bar{u}}{dt} = -p^2\,\bar{u}$$

or $$\frac{d\bar{u}}{dt} + p^2\,\bar{u} = 0.$$

This solution of this is

$$\bar{u} = A\,e^{-p^2 t}. \qquad \ldots(i)$$

This $\Rightarrow \bar{u}(p, t) = A\,e^{-p^2 t} \Rightarrow \bar{u}(p, 0) = A$

$$\Rightarrow A = \int_{-\infty}^{\infty} u(x, 0)\,e^{-ipx}\,dx$$

or $$A = \int_{-\infty}^{\infty} f(x)\,e^{-ipx}\,dx.$$

For $u(x, 0) = f(x)$.

Using this in (1),

$$\bar{u} = e^{-p^2 t}\int_{-\infty}^{\infty} f(x)\,e^{-ipx}\,dx$$

or $$\bar{u} = e^{-p^2 t}\int_{-\infty}^{\infty} f(u)\,e^{-ipu}\,du$$

Taking inverse Fourier transform

$$u(x, t) = \frac{1}{2\pi}\int_{-\infty}^{\infty} e^{-p^2 t}\left[\int_{-\infty}^{\infty} f(u)\,e^{-pu}\,du\right] e^{ipx}\,dp$$

$$= \frac{1}{2\pi}\int_{-\infty}^{\infty} f(u)\left[\int_{-\infty}^{\infty} e^{-p^2 t + ip(x-u)}\,dp\right] du$$

$$= \frac{1}{2\pi}\int_{-\infty}^{\infty} f(u)\left[\int_{-\infty}^{\infty} \exp\left\{-t\left(p^2 - ip\left(\frac{x-u}{t}\right)\right)\right\} dp\right] du$$

$$= \frac{1}{2\pi}\int_{-\infty}^{\infty} f(u)\left[\int_{-\infty}^{\infty} \exp\left\{-t\left[\left(p - i\left(\frac{x-u}{2t}\right)\right)^2 + \left(\frac{x-u}{2t}\right)^2\right]\right\} dp\right] du$$

$$= \frac{1}{2\pi}\int_{-\infty}^{\infty} f(u)\left[\int_{-\infty}^{\infty} \exp\left\{-t\left(p - i\left(\frac{x-u}{2t}\right)\right)^2\right\} \times \exp\left\{-\frac{(x-u)^2}{4t}\right\} dp\right] du.$$

Putting $\sqrt{t}\left\{p - i\left(\frac{x-u}{2t}\right)\right\} = y$, so that $dp\sqrt{t} = dy$, we get

$$u(x, t) = \frac{1}{2\pi}\int_{-\infty}^{\infty} f(u)\left[\int_{-\infty}^{\infty} e^{-y^2} e^{-(x-u)^2/4t}\frac{dy}{\sqrt{t}}\right] du$$

$$= \frac{1}{2\pi\sqrt{t}}\int_{-\infty}^{\infty} f(u)\, e^{-(x-u)^2/4t}\left[\int_{-\infty}^{\infty} e^{-y^2}\right] du$$

$$= \frac{1}{2\pi\sqrt{t}}\int_{-\infty}^{\infty} f(u)\sqrt{\pi}\exp\left\{-\frac{(x-u)^2}{4t}\right\} du$$

$$= \frac{1}{2\sqrt{(\pi t)}}\int_{-\infty}^{\infty} f(u)\exp\left\{-\frac{(x-u)^2}{4t}\right\} du.$$

Example 6. *Use the method of Fourier transform to determine the displacement $y(x, t)$ of an infinite string, given that the string is initially at rest and the initial displacement is $f(x)$, $-\infty < x < \infty$. Show that the solution can also be put in the form*

$$y(x, t) = \frac{1}{2}[f(x + ct) + f(x - ct)].$$

Solution. Displacement $y(x, t)$ of any point of an infinite string is governed by the equation

$$\frac{\partial^2 y}{\partial t^2} = c^2\frac{\partial^2 y}{\partial x^2}, \qquad \ldots(i)$$

where $-\infty < x < \infty$, $t > 0$ with conditions (i) $y(x, 0) = f(x)$.

(ii) $\frac{\partial y}{\partial t} = 0$ at $t = 0$ (since the string is initially at rest).

From (1), $F\left\{\frac{\partial^2 y}{\partial t^2}\right\} = c^2 F\left\{\frac{\partial^2 y}{\partial x^2}\right\}$

or
$$\int_{-\infty}^{\infty}\frac{\partial^2 y}{\partial t^2} e^{-ipx}\, dx = c^2\int_{-\infty}^{\infty}\frac{\partial^2 y}{\partial x^2} e^{-ipx}\, dx$$

or
$$\frac{\partial^2}{\partial t^2}\int_{-\infty}^{\infty} y e^{-ipx}\, dx = c^2 (ip)^2\, \bar{y}(p, t)$$

or
$$\frac{d^2\bar{y}}{dt^2} + c^2p^2\,\bar{y} = 0.$$

Its solution is

$$\bar{y} = A \cos cpt + B \sin cpt, \qquad \ldots\text{(i)}$$

But $\dfrac{\partial y}{\partial t} = 0$ at $t = 0$ and so $\dfrac{d\bar{y}}{dt} = 0$ at $t = 0$.

From (1), $0 = \dfrac{d\bar{y}}{dt} = cp\,[-A \sin cpt + B \cos cpt]_{t=0}$

$$0 = cp\,[A \cdot 0 + B] \text{ or } B = 0.$$

$\therefore$ From (1), $\bar{y} = A \cos cpt \qquad \ldots$(ii)

(i) $\Rightarrow F\{y(x, 0)\} = F\{f(x)\}$

$$\Rightarrow \bar{y}(p, 0) = \int_{-\infty}^{\infty} f(x)\, e^{-ipx}\, dx = \bar{f}(p)$$

$$\Rightarrow \bar{y}(p, 0) = \bar{f}(p)$$

$$\Rightarrow A = \bar{f}(p), \text{ according (ii).}$$

Now (ii) becomes

$$y = \bar{f}(p) \cos cpt.$$

Taking inverse Fourier transform, we get

$$y(x, t) = \frac{1}{2\pi}\int_{-\infty}^{\infty} \bar{f}(p) \cos cpt \cdot e^{tpx}\, dp$$

$$= \frac{1}{2\pi}\int_{-\infty}^{\infty} \bar{f}(p) \left(\frac{e^{icpt} + e^{-ipt}}{2}\right) c^{-ipx}\, ds$$

$$= \frac{1}{2\pi}\int_{-\infty}^{\infty} \bar{f}(p) \left[\frac{e^{-ip(x+ct)} + e^{ip(x-ct)}}{2}\right] dp$$

$$= \frac{1}{2}\left[\frac{1}{2\pi}\int_{-\infty}^{\infty} \bar{f}(p)\, e^{ip(x+ct)}\, ds + \frac{1}{2\pi}\int_{-\infty}^{\infty} \bar{f}(p)\, e^{ip(x-ct)}\, dp\right]$$

Using the fact that $g(x) = \dfrac{1}{2\pi}\displaystyle\int_{-\infty}^{\infty} \bar{g}(p)\, e^{ipx}\, dp$, we get

$$y(x, t) = \frac{1}{2}\,[f(x + ct) + f(x - ct)].$$

Example 7. *Using a cosine transform to show that the steady temperature in the semi infinite solid y > 0 when the temperature on the surface y = 0 is kept at unity over the strip |x| < a and at zero outside the strip is*

$$\frac{1}{\pi}\left[\tan^{-1}\left(\frac{a+x}{y}\right)+\tan^{-1}\left(\frac{a-x}{y}\right)\right].$$

It is given that

$$\int_0^\infty e^{-cx}\cdot x^{-1}\sin bx\,dx=\tan^{-1}\frac{b}{c},\ c>0,\ b>0.$$

Solution. The steady temperature in the semi-infinite solid is governed by the equation

$$\frac{\partial^2 u}{\partial x^2}+\frac{\partial^2 u}{\partial y^2}=0, \qquad \text{...(i)}$$

where $0<y<\infty,\ -\infty<x<\infty.$

with the conditions

(i) $u = 1$, when $y = 0,\ -a < x < a,$

(ii) $u = 0$, when $y = 0,\ |x| < a,$ *i.e.*, $|x| \geq a.$

Taking Fourier cosine transform of (1),

$$\int_0^\infty \frac{\partial^2 u}{\partial x^2}\cos px\,dx+\int_0^\infty \frac{\partial^2 u}{\partial y^2}\cos px\,dx=0$$

or
$$\left(\frac{\partial u}{\partial x}\cos px\right)_0^\infty+\int_0^\infty \frac{\partial u}{\partial x}p\sin px\,dx+\frac{d^2\bar{u}_c}{dy^2}=0$$

$$\left(\text{if } \frac{\partial u}{\partial x}\to 0 \text{ as } x\to\infty,\ \frac{\partial u}{\partial x}\to 0 \text{ as } x\to 0\right)$$

or
$$\frac{d^2\bar{u}_c}{dy^2}+p\left[(u\sin px)_0^\infty-p\int_0^\infty u\cos px\,dx\right]=0$$

or
$$\frac{d^2\bar{u}_c}{dy^2}-p^2\bar{u}_c=0 \text{ if } \lim_{x\to\infty} u=0.$$

The solution of this is

$$\bar{u}_c=Ae^{-py}+Be^{py}.$$

But $\bar{u}_c$ is finite and so $B = 0$, otherwise $\bar{u}_c$ becomes infinite as $y\to\infty$.

$$\therefore \qquad \bar{u}_y=Ae^{-py}. \qquad \text{...(i)}$$

This $\Rightarrow A = (\bar{u}_c)_{y=0} = \int_0^\infty (u)_{y=0} \cos px \, dx$

$$= \int_0^a 1 \cos px \, dx + \int_a^\infty 0 \cos px \, dx = \left(\frac{\sin px}{p}\right)_0^a$$

$$= \frac{\sin pa}{p}.$$

Now (1) becomes

$$\bar{u}_0 = \frac{e^{-py}}{p} \sin pa.$$

Applying inverse Fourier cosine transform,

$$u = \frac{2}{\pi} \int_0^\infty e^{-py} p^{-1} \cdot \sin pa \cos px \, ds$$

$$= \frac{1}{\pi} \int_0^\infty e^{-py} \cdot p^{-1} [\sin (a + x) p + \sin (a - x) p] \, dp$$

$$= \frac{1}{\pi} \left[\tan^{-1}\left(\frac{a+x}{y}\right) + \tan^{-1}\left(\frac{a-x}{y}\right)\right]$$

according to the given result.

8.4 APPLICATIONS OF FINITE FOURIER TRANSFORM

ILLUSTRATIVE EXAMPLES

Example 1. *Determine a function $V(x, y)$ which is harmonic in the open square $0 < x < \pi$, $0 < y < \pi$, takes a constant value V_0 on the edge $y = \pi$ and vanishes on the other edges of the square.*

or

Find the steady temperature $V(x, y)$ in a long square bar of side π when one face is kept at constant temperature V_0 and the other faces at zero temperature. Also $V(x, y)$ is bounded.

Solution. The steady temperature $V(x, y)$ is governed by the equation

$$\frac{\partial^2 V}{\partial x^2} + \frac{\partial^2 V}{\partial y^2} = 0. \qquad \ldots(i)$$

(V is harmonic $\Rightarrow$ V satisfies Laplace's equation) with the conditions

(i) $V(x, \pi) = V_0$,

(ii) $V(0, y) = 0 = V(\pi, y)$ for every y

(iii) $V(x, y)$ is bounded.

Taking finite Fourier sine transform of (i),

$$\int_0^\pi \frac{\partial^2 V}{\partial x^2} \sin px\, dx + \int_0^\pi \frac{\partial^2 V}{\partial y^2} \sin px\, dx = 0$$

or
$$\left(\frac{\partial V}{\partial x} \sin px\right)_0^\pi - p\int_0^\pi \frac{\partial V}{\partial x} \cos px\, dx + \frac{\partial^2}{\partial y^2}\int_0^\pi V \sin px\, dx = 0$$

or
$$\frac{d^2\overline{V}_s}{dy^2} + 0 - p\left[(V\cos px)_0^\pi + p\int_0^\pi V \sin px\, dx\right] = 0$$

or
$$\frac{d^2\overline{V}_s}{dy^2} p^2\overline{V}_s - p\,[V(\pi, y) \cos p\pi - V(0, y) \cos 0] = 0$$

or
$$\frac{d^2\overline{V}_s}{dy^2} - p^2\overline{V}_0 = 0, \text{ according to (ii)}$$

The solution of this is

$$\overline{V}_s = A \cosh py + B \sinh py, \quad \ldots\text{(ii)}$$

$$V(x, \pi) = V_0 \Rightarrow F_s\{V(x, \pi)\} = F_s\{V_0\}$$

$$\Rightarrow \quad \int_0^\pi V(x, \pi) \sin px\, dx = \int_0^\pi V_0 \sin px\, dx$$

$$\Rightarrow \quad \overline{V}_s(p, \pi) = \frac{V_0}{p}(-\cos px)_0^\pi = V_0\left(\frac{1 - \cos p\pi}{p}\right).$$

$$\therefore \quad \overline{V}_s(p, \pi) = V_0 \frac{(1 - \cos p\pi)}{p} \quad \ldots\text{(iii)}$$

Again $V(x, 0) = 0 \Rightarrow \overline{V}_s(p, 0) = 0$

$\Rightarrow$ $A.1 + B.0 = 0$, according to (ii)

$\Rightarrow$ $A = 0$.

$\therefore$ From (ii), $\overline{V}_s = B \sinh py$, ...(iv)

This $\Rightarrow \bar{V}_s(p, \pi) = B \sinh p\pi$

$$\Rightarrow V_0\left(\frac{1-\cos p\pi}{p}\right) = B \sinh p\pi$$

$$\Rightarrow B = \frac{V_0(1-\cos p\pi)}{p \sinh p\pi}$$

Now (iv) takes the form

$$\bar{V}_s = \frac{V_0(1-\cos p\pi)\sinh py}{p \sinh p\pi}$$

Taking inverse finite sine transform,

$$V(x, y) - \frac{2}{\pi}\sum_{p=1}^{\infty} \frac{V_0(1-\cos p\pi)\sinh py \sin px}{p \sinh p\pi}$$

$$= \frac{2V_0}{\pi}\sum_{p=1}^{\infty} \frac{[1-(-1)p]\sinh py \cdot \sin px}{p \sinh p\pi}$$

$$= \frac{4V_0}{\pi}\sum_{n=0}^{\infty} \frac{\sinh(2n+1)y \cdot \sin(2n+1)x}{(2n+1)\sinh(2n+1)\pi}.$$

(since other terms for which s is even are zero).

Example 2. *A string of density* ρ *and length* π *is stretched to a tension* ρc^2. *At time* $t = 0$, *one end* ($x = 0$) *is given a small oscillation* $a \sin \omega t$. *If the other end remains fixed, use a finite sine transform to show that the displacement of the point x at time t is*

$$a \sin \omega t \cdot \sin \frac{\omega(\pi - x)}{c} \operatorname{cosec} \frac{\pi\omega}{c} + \left(\frac{2a\omega c}{\pi}\right) \sum_{p=1}^{\infty} (\omega^2 - p^2c^2)^{-1} \sin px \sin pct.$$

Solution. The displacement $V(x, t)$ is governed by the equation

$$\frac{\partial^2 V}{\partial t^2} = c^2 \frac{\partial^2 V}{\partial x^2},$$

where $\rho c^2 = T = \text{tension}, 0 < x < \pi.$

Boundary conditions are

(i) $V(0, t) = a \sin \omega t,$

(ii) $V(\pi, t) = 0,$

(iii) $\left(\frac{\partial V}{\partial t}\right) = 0$ at $t = 0$,

(iv) $V(x, 0) = 0$.

Taking finite Fourier sine transform,

$$\int_0^\pi \frac{\partial^2 V}{\partial t^2} \sin px \, dx = c^2 \int_0^\pi \frac{\partial^2 V}{\partial x^2} \sin px \, dx$$

or $$\frac{\partial^2}{\partial t^2} \int_0^\pi V \sin px \, dx = c^2 \left[\left(\frac{\partial V}{\partial x} \sin px \right)_0^\pi - p \int_0^\pi \frac{\partial V}{\partial x} \cos px \, dx \right]$$

or $$\frac{d^2 \overline{V}_s}{dt^2} = -c^2 p \left[(V \cos px)_0^\pi + p \int_0^\pi V \sin px \, dx \right]$$

$$= -c^2 p \, [V(\pi, t) \cos p\pi - V(0, t) \pm p\overline{V}_s]$$

$$= -c^2 p \, [0 - a \sin \omega t + p\overline{V}_s],$$

by (i) and (ii)

$$\frac{d^2 \overline{V}_s}{dt^2} + c^2 p^2 \overline{V}_s = ac^2 p \sin \omega t.$$

The solution of this is

$$\overline{V}_s = A \cos cpt + B \sin cpt + ac^2 p \frac{1}{D^2 + c^2 p^2} \sin \omega t$$

or $$\overline{V}_s(p, t) = A \cos cpt + B \sin cpt + \frac{ac^2 p \sin \omega t}{c^2 p^2 - \omega^2}. \qquad \text{...(ii)}$$

This $\Rightarrow \overline{V}_s(p, 0) = A$ ...(iii)

and $$\frac{d\overline{V}_s}{dt} = cp\,[-A \sin cpt + B \cos cpt] + \frac{ac^2 p\omega \cos \omega t}{c^2 p^2 - \omega^2},$$

$\therefore$ $$\left(\frac{d\overline{V}_s}{dt}\right)_{t=0} = cpB + \frac{ac^2 p\omega}{c^2 p^2 - \omega^2}. \qquad \text{...(iv)}$$

(iii) $\Rightarrow F_s \left\{ \frac{\partial V}{\partial t} \right\} = 0$ at $t = 0$

$$\Rightarrow \frac{d\overline{V}_s}{dt} = 0 \text{ at } t = 0$$

$$\Rightarrow 0 = cp\,B + \frac{ac^2 p\omega}{c^2p^2 - \omega^2}, \text{ according to (iv)}$$

$$\Rightarrow B = \frac{-ac\omega}{c^2p^2 - \omega^2}.$$

(iv) $\Rightarrow F_s\,\{V(x, 0)\} = 0 \Rightarrow \overline{V}_s(p, 0) = 0 \Rightarrow A = 0$, by (iii).

In this event (ii) becomes

$$\overline{V}_s(p, t) = \frac{ac\omega \sin cpt}{\omega^2 - c^2p^2} + \frac{ac^2 p \sin \omega t}{c^2p^2 - \omega^2}.$$

Taking inverse finite sine transform,

$$V(x, t) = \frac{2}{\pi} \sum_{p=1}^{\infty} \left[\frac{ac\omega \sin cpt}{\omega^2 - c^2p^2} + \frac{ac^2 p \sin \omega t}{c^2p^2 - \omega^2}\right] \sin px$$

or $$V(x, t) = \frac{2a \sin \omega t}{\pi} \sum_{p=1}^{\infty} \frac{p}{p^2 - \dfrac{\omega^2}{c^2}} \sin px + \frac{2ac\omega}{\pi} \sum_{p=1}^{\infty} \frac{\sin cpt \sin px}{\omega^2 - c^2p^2} \qquad \ldots(v)$$

Observe that $F_s\left\{\sin \dfrac{\omega(\pi - x)}{c}\right\}$

$$= \int_0^{\pi} \sin \frac{\omega(\pi - x)}{c} \sin px\, dx$$

$$= \frac{1}{2}\int_0^{\pi} \left[\cos\left\{\frac{\omega(\pi - x)}{c} - px\right\} - \cos\left\{\frac{\omega(\pi - x)}{c} - px\right\}\right] dx$$

$$= \frac{1}{2}\left[\frac{\sin\left\{\dfrac{\omega}{c}(\pi - x) - px\right\}}{-\dfrac{\omega}{c} - p}\right]_{x=0}^{\pi} - \frac{1}{2}\left[\frac{\sin\left\{\dfrac{\omega}{c}(\pi - x) + px\right\}}{-\dfrac{\omega}{c} + p}\right]_{x=0}^{\pi}$$

$$= \frac{1}{2\left(\dfrac{\omega}{c} + p\right)}\left[\sin \frac{\omega\pi}{c} - 0\right] + \frac{1}{2\left(\dfrac{\omega}{c} - p\right)}\left[-\sin \frac{\omega\pi}{c}\right].$$

$$= \frac{1}{2} \sin \frac{\omega\pi}{c}\left[\frac{1}{\dfrac{\omega}{c} + p} - \frac{1}{\dfrac{\omega}{c} - p}\right]$$

$$= \frac{\sin\left(\frac{\omega\pi}{c}\right)}{\frac{\omega^2}{c^s} - p^2} \cdot (-p) = p\frac{\sin\left(\frac{\omega\pi}{c}\right)}{p^2 - \frac{\omega^2}{c^2}}.$$

Finally, $F_s\left\{\sin\frac{\omega(\pi - x)}{c}\right\} = \dfrac{p\sin\left(\frac{\omega\pi}{c}\right)}{p^2 - \frac{\omega^2}{c^2}}$

or $$\sin\omega\left(\frac{\pi - x}{c}\right) = F_s^{-1}\left\{\frac{p\sin\left(\frac{\omega\pi}{c}\right)}{p^2 - \frac{\omega^2}{c^2}}\right\}$$

$$= \frac{2}{\pi}\sum_{p=1}^{\infty}\frac{p\sin\left(\frac{\omega\pi}{c}\right)\sin px}{p^2 - \frac{\omega^2}{c^2}}$$

or $$\frac{\sin\omega\left(\frac{\pi - x}{c}\right)}{\sin\left(\frac{\omega\pi}{c}\right)} = \frac{2}{\pi}\sum_{p=1}^{\infty}\frac{p\sin(px)}{p^2 - \frac{\omega^2}{c^2}}.$$

Using this in (v),

$$V(x, t) = a\sin\omega t, \sin\omega\left(\frac{\pi - x}{c}\right)\operatorname{cosec}\left(\frac{\pi\omega}{c}\right) + \frac{2ac\omega}{\pi}\sum_{p=1}^{\infty}\frac{\sin cpt \cdot \sin px}{\omega^2 - c^2p^2}.$$

Example 3. *Suppose $V(x, y)$ denotes electrostatic potential in region bounded by the planes $x = 0$, $x = \pi$ and $y = 0$ in which there is a uniform distribution of space charge of density $h/4\pi$. If the planes $x = 0$ and $y = 0$ are kept at potential zero, the plane $x = \pi$ at another fixed potential $V = 1$ and V is finite as $y \to \infty$, determine V.*

Solution. Since $V(x, y)$ is a kind of potential and therefore it must satisfy Poisson's equation

$$\nabla^2 V = -4\pi\rho, \qquad \ldots(i)$$

where ρ is the density of charge.

Here $\rho = \frac{h}{4\pi}$, h being constant.

Boundary conditions are

(i) $V(0, y) = 0, y > 0$

(ii) $V(x, 0) = 0, 0 < x < \pi$

(iii) $V(\pi, y) = 1, y > 0.$

(iv) $\lim_{y \to \infty} V(x, y) =$ finite, $0 < x < \pi.$

(1) is equivalent to

$$\frac{\partial^2 V}{\partial x^2} + \frac{\partial^2 V}{\partial y^2} = -h. \qquad \text{...(ii)}$$

Since $(V)_{x=0}$ is given and so we shall apply finite sine transform to (ii) so that

$$\int_0^\pi \frac{\partial^2 V}{\partial x^2} \sin px\, dx + \int_0^\pi \frac{\partial^2 V}{\partial y^2} \sin px\, dx = -h \int_0^\pi \sin px\, dx$$

or $$\left(\frac{\partial V}{\partial x} \sin px\right)_0^\pi - p \int_0^\pi \frac{\partial V}{\partial x} \cos px\, dx + \frac{\partial^2}{\partial y^2} \int_0^\pi V \sin px\, dx$$

$$= -h \left(\frac{-\cos px}{p}\right)_0^\pi$$

or $$0 - p \left\{ (V \cos px)_0^\pi + p \int_0^\pi V \sin px\, dx \right\} + \frac{d^2 \overline{V}_s}{dy^2}$$

$$= \frac{h(\cos p\pi - 1)}{p}$$

or $$\frac{d^2 \overline{V}_s}{dy^2} - p^2 \overline{V}_s - p\,[V(\pi, y) \cos p\pi - V(0, y)]$$

$$= \frac{h}{p} (\cos p\pi - 1)$$

By virtue of (i) and (iii), thus becomes

$$\frac{d^2 \overline{V}_s}{dy^2} - p^2 \overline{V}_s - p \cos p\pi = \frac{h}{p} (\cos p\pi - 1)$$

or $$\frac{d^2 \overline{V}_s}{dy^2} - p^2 \overline{V}_s = p \cos p\pi - hF_s \{1\}$$

or $$\frac{d^2\overline{V}_s}{dy^2} - p^2\overline{V}_s = sp(-1)p - h F_s\{1\}$$

This solution of this is

$$\overline{V}_s = Ae^{-py} + Be^{py} + [p(-1)^p - h F_s\{1\}] \cdot \frac{1}{D^2 - p^2} e^{0y}$$

or $$\overline{V}_s = Ae^{-py} + Be^{py} + \frac{[p(-1)^p - h F_s\{1\}]}{-p^2}$$

Since V is finite and so $\overline{V}$ is finite, $B = 0$, otherwise $\overline{V}_s$ becomes infinite as $y \to \infty$.

$\therefore$ $$\overline{V}_s = Ae^{-py} + \frac{h F_s\{1\} - p(-1)p}{p^2} \qquad \ldots\text{(iii)}$$

This $$\Rightarrow \overline{V}_s(p, 0) = A + \frac{h F_s\{1\} - p(-1)^s}{p^2} \qquad \ldots\text{(iv)}$$

(ii) $\Rightarrow F_s\{V(x, 0)\} = 0 \Rightarrow V_s(p, 0) = 0.$ $\qquad \ldots$(v)

From (iv) and (v),

$$A + \frac{h F_s\{1\} - p(-1)^p}{p^2} = 0$$

or $$A = \frac{p(-1)^p - h F_s\{1\}}{p^2}.$$

Using this in (iii),

$$\overline{V}_s = \frac{[h F_s\{1\} - p' - 1)p]}{p^2}(1 - e^{-py})$$

Applying inverse finite sine transform,

$$V(x, y) = \frac{2}{\pi} \sum_{p=1}^{\infty} \frac{[h F_s\{1\} - p(-1)p](1 - e^{-py}) \sin px}{p^2}$$

Example 4. *Solve the differential equation*

$$\Delta^2 V = 0,$$

with boundary conditions

$$V = V_0 \text{ when } y = \pi$$

$$V = 0 \begin{cases} \text{when } x = 0, x = \pi \\ \text{when } y = 0 \\ \text{also when } z = 0 \text{ and } z = \pi \end{cases}$$

or

Find the steady temperature in a cube of side π when one face is kept at constant temperature and the other faces are at zero temperature.

Solution. The steady temperature $V(x, y, z)$ at any point (x, y, z) inside the cube is governed by the equation

$$\frac{\partial^2 V}{\partial x^2} + \frac{\partial^2 V}{\partial y^2} + \frac{\partial^2 V}{\partial z^2} = 0. \qquad \text{...(i)}$$

Boundary conditions are:

(i) $V(0, y, z) = 0 = V(\pi, y, z)$.

(ii) $V(x, 0, z) = 0$, $V(x, \pi, z) = V_0$.

(iii) $V(x, y, 0) = 0 = V(x, y, \pi)$.

Since $(V)_{x=0}$ is given and hence we shall apply finite sine transform. Taking finite sine transform of (1),

$$\int_0^\pi \frac{\partial^2 V}{\partial x^2} \sin px\, dx + \int_0^\pi \frac{\partial^2 V}{\partial y^2} \sin px\, dx + \int_0^\pi \frac{\partial^2 V}{\partial z^2} \sin px\, dx = 0$$

or

$$\left(\frac{\partial V}{\partial x} \sin px\right)_0^\pi - p\int_0^\pi \frac{\partial V}{\partial x} \cos px\, dx + \frac{\partial^2}{\partial y^2}\int_0^\pi V \sin px\, dx + \frac{\partial^2}{\partial z^2}\int_0^\pi \sin px\, dx = 0$$

or

$$-p\left[(V \cos px)_0^\pi + p\int_0^\pi V \sin px\, dx\right] + \frac{\partial^2 \overline{V}_s}{\partial y^2} + \frac{\partial^2 \overline{V}_s}{\partial z^2} = 0$$

or

$$\frac{\partial^2 \overline{V}_s}{\partial y^2} + \frac{\partial^2 \overline{V}_s}{\partial z^2} - p^2 \overline{V}_s - p\,[V(\pi, y, z) \cos s\pi - V(0, y, z)] = 0.$$

By virtue of (i), this becomes

$$\frac{\partial^2 \overline{V}_s}{\partial y^2} + \frac{\partial^2 \overline{V}_s}{\partial z^2} - p^2 \overline{V}_s = 0. \qquad \text{...(ii)}$$

Taking finite sine transform of boundary conditions, we get

(i)′ $\overline{V}_s = 0$ at $x = 0$ and $x = \pi$ both,

(ii)′ $\overline{V}_s = 0$ at $y = 0$

and $$(\overline{V}_s)_{y=\pi} = V_0\left(\frac{-\cos px}{p}\right)_0^{\pi} = V_0\left(\frac{1-\cos p\pi}{p}\right)$$

i.e., $$(\overline{V}_s)_{y=\pi} = \begin{cases} 0 & \text{if } p \text{ is even} \\ \dfrac{2V_0}{p} & \text{if } p \text{ is odd} \end{cases} \qquad \text{...(iii)}$$

(iii)′ $\overline{V}_s = 0$ at $z = 0$ and $z = \pi$ both.

From (ii), $$\int_0^{\pi} \frac{\partial^2 \overline{f}_s}{\partial y^2}\sin sz\, dx + \int_0^{\pi}\frac{\partial^2 \overline{V}_s}{\partial z^2}\sin sz\, dz - p^2\int_0^{\pi}\overline{V}_s \sin sz\, dz = 0$$

Taking $F_s\{\overline{V}_s\} = \overline{V}_s'$, we get

$$\frac{d^2\overline{V}'_s}{dy^2} - p^2\overline{V}'_s + \left(\frac{\partial \overline{V}_s}{\partial z}\sin sz\right)_0^{\pi} - s\int_0^{\pi}\frac{\partial \overline{V}_s}{\partial z}\cos sz\, dz = 0$$

or $$\frac{d^2\overline{V}'_s}{dy^2} - p^2\overline{V}'_s - s\left[\left(\overline{V}_s\cos sz\right)_0^{\pi} + s\int_0^{\pi}\overline{V}_s\sin sz\, dz\right] = 0$$

or $$\frac{d^2\overline{V}'_s}{dy^2} - p^2\overline{V}'_s - s^2\overline{V}'_s - s\,[\overline{V}_s(p, y, \pi)\cos s\pi - \overline{V}_s(p, y, 0)] = 0.$$

By virtue of (iii)′, this becomes

$$\frac{d^2\overline{V}'_s}{dy^2} - (s^2 + p^2)\,\overline{V}'_s = 0.$$

The solution of this is

$$\overline{V}'_s = A\cosh y\sqrt{(s^2+p^2)} + B\sinh y\sqrt{(s^n+p^2)} \qquad \text{...(iii)}$$

Again taking finite sine transform of boundary conditions (ii)′, (iii)′, we get

(ii)″ $\overline{V}'_s = 0$ at $y = 0$

and at $$y = \pi,\ \overline{V}'_s = \begin{cases} 0, & \text{if } p \text{ is even} \\ \dfrac{2V_0}{p}\displaystyle\int_0^{\pi}\sin sz\, dz = \dfrac{2V_0}{sp}(1-\cos sz)_0^{\pi} \end{cases}$$

i.e., at $y = \pi$,

$$\overline{V}'_s = \begin{cases} 0 & \text{if } s \text{ and } p \text{ both are even} \\ \dfrac{4V_0}{sp} & \text{if } s \text{ and } p \text{ both are odd} \end{cases}$$

(iii)" $\overline{V}'_s = 0$ at $z = 0$ and $z = \pi$ both, s, p both are even $\Rightarrow V'_s = 0, \Rightarrow V = 0.$

Hence we need not consider the case in which s and p both are even. Next we consider the case in which s and p both are odd. Now (3) says that $A = 0$.

Consequently (iii) becomes

$$\overline{V}'_s = B \sinh y \sqrt{(s^2 + p^2)}. \qquad \text{...(iv)}$$

At $y = \pi$, this becomes

$$\frac{4V_0}{sp} = B \sinh \pi \sqrt{(s^2 + p^2)}$$

or
$$B = \frac{4V_0}{sp} \operatorname{cosech} \pi \sqrt{(s^2 + p^2)}.$$

Using this in (4),

$$\overline{V}'_s = \frac{4V_0}{sp} \operatorname{cosech} \pi \sqrt{(s^2 + p^2)} \sinh y \sqrt{(s^2 + p^2)}$$

or
$$\overline{V}'_s = \frac{4V_0 \operatorname{cosech} \pi l}{(2n + 1)(2m + 1)} \sinh ly, \qquad \text{...(v)}$$

where $s = 2n + 1, p = 2m + 1,$

$$s^2 + p^2 = (2n + 1)^2 + (2m + 1)^2 = l^2.$$

Taking inverse finite Fourier sine transform of (v),

$$\overline{V}_s = \frac{4V_0}{(2n + 1)} \cdot \frac{2}{\pi} \sum_{m=0}^{\infty} \frac{\operatorname{cosech} l\pi \sinh ly \sin (2m + 1) z}{(2m + 1)}$$

Again taking inverse finite sine transform,

$$V = \frac{8V_0}{\pi} \cdot \frac{2}{\pi} \sum_{n=0}^{\infty} \sum_{m=0}^{\infty} \frac{\operatorname{cosech} l\pi \sinh ly \sin (2m + 1) z}{(2n + 1)(2m + 1)} \sin (2n + 1) x.$$

Finally, $$V = \frac{16V_0}{\pi^2} \sum_{n, m=0}^{\infty} \frac{\sin ly}{\sinh l\pi} \frac{\sin (2m + 1) z}{2m + 1} \cdot \frac{\sin (2n + 1) x}{2n + 1}.$$

Example 5. *Use finite Fourier transforms to solve*

$$\frac{\partial V}{\partial t} = \frac{\partial^2 V}{\partial x^2},$$

$$V(0, t) = 0, V(4, t) = 0, V(x, 0) = 2x,$$

where $0 < x < 4, t > 0.$

Give the physical interpretation of the problem.

Problem. The boundary conditions are

(i) $V(0, t) = 0,$

(ii) $V(4, t) = 0,$

(iii) $V(x, 0) = 2x, 0 < x < n$

Since $(V)_{x=0}$ is given and so we shall apply finite Fourier sine transforms.

Taking finite Fourier sine transform of

$$\frac{\partial V}{\partial t} = \frac{\partial^2 V}{\partial x^2},$$

we get $$\int_0^4 \frac{\partial V}{\partial t} \sin \frac{p\pi x}{4}\, dx = \int_0^4 \frac{\partial^2 V}{\partial x^2} \sin \frac{p\pi x}{4}\, dx$$

or $$\frac{\partial}{\partial t}\int_0^4 V \sin \frac{p\pi x}{4}\, dx = \left(\frac{\partial V}{\partial x} \sin \frac{p\pi x}{4}\right)_0^4 - \frac{p\pi}{4}\int_0^4 \frac{\partial V}{\partial x} \cos \frac{p\pi x}{4}\, dx$$

or $$\frac{d\overline{V}_s}{dt} = \frac{p\pi}{4}\left[\left(V \cos \frac{p\pi x}{4}\right)_0^4 + \frac{p\pi}{4}\int_0^4 V \sin \frac{p\pi x}{4}\, dx\right]$$

or $$\frac{d\overline{V}_s}{dt} = -\frac{p^2\pi^2}{16}\overline{V}_s - \frac{p\pi}{4}[V(4, t) \cos p\pi - V(0, t)].$$

By virtue of (i) and (ii), this takes the form

$$\frac{d\overline{V}_s}{dt} = -\frac{p^2\pi^2}{16}\overline{V}_s.$$

The solution of this is

$$\overline{V}_s(p, t) = A e^{\frac{-p^2\pi^2 t}{16}} \qquad \ldots(i)$$

From which, we get

$$\overline{V}_s(p, 0) = A$$

or $$A = F_s\{V(x, 0)\} = F_s\{2x\}, \text{ by (iii)}$$

or $$A = \int_0^4 2x \sin\frac{p\pi x}{4}\, dx$$

$$= 2\left[\left(-\frac{x.4}{p\pi}\cdot\cos\frac{p\pi x}{4}\right)_0^4 + \frac{4}{p\pi}\int_0^4 \cos\frac{p\pi x}{4}\, dx\right]$$

$$= 2\left[-\frac{16}{p\pi}\cos p\pi + \frac{16}{p^2\pi^2}\left(\sin\frac{p\pi x}{4}\right)_0^4\right] = -\frac{32(-1)^s}{p\pi}$$

Now (i) becomes

$$\overline{V}_s = -\frac{32(-1)^s}{p\pi} e^{-p^2\pi^2 t/16}$$

Applying inverse finite transform,

$$V = \frac{2}{4}\sum_{p=1}^{\infty} \frac{(-32)(-1)^s}{p\pi} e^{-p^2\pi^2 t/16} \sin\frac{p\pi x}{4}$$

$$V = -\frac{16}{\pi}\sum_{p=1}^{\infty} \frac{(-1)^s}{p} \cdot e^{-p^2\pi^2 t/16} \sin\frac{p\pi x}{4}.$$

Physical Interpretation. $V(x, t)$ represents temperature at any point x at any time t in a bar lying along x-axis whose ends are $x = 0$ and $x = 4$. The conditions $V(0, t) = 0$ and $V(x, t)$ show that the temperature at the ends $x = 0$ and $x = 4$ are zero, while $V(x, 0) = 2x$ shows that at $t = 0$, the temperature is a function of x.

EXERCISE

1. Solve $\dfrac{\partial V}{\partial t} = \dfrac{\partial^2 V}{\partial x^2}$, $0 < x < 6$, $t > 0$ with the conditions $V(0, t) = 0$, $V(6, t) = 0$, $V(x, 0) = \begin{cases} 1, & 0 < x < 3 \\ 0, & 3 < x < 6 \end{cases}$.

2. Use finite Fourier transform to solve $\dfrac{\partial V}{\partial t} = \dfrac{\partial^2 V}{\partial x^2}$, $0 < x < 6$, $t > 0$ where $V_x(0, t) = 0$, $V_x(6, t) = 0$, $V(x, 0) = 2x$.

3. Solve $\dfrac{\partial V}{\partial t} = \dfrac{\partial^2 V}{\partial x^2}$ if $V_x(0, t) = 0$, $V(x, 0) = \begin{cases} x, & 0 \le x \le 1 \\ 0, & x > 1 \end{cases}$ and $V(x, t)$ is bounded $\forall x > 0$ and $\forall t > 0$.

4. Solve the boundary value problem

$$\frac{\partial U}{\partial t} = \frac{\partial^2 U}{\partial x^2},\ U(0, t) = 1,\ U(\pi, t) = 3,\ U(x, 0) = 1, \text{ where } 0 < x < \pi,\ t > 0.$$

ANSWERS

1. $V(x, t) = \dfrac{2}{\pi} \displaystyle\sum_{p=1}^{\infty} \dfrac{1}{p}\left(1 - \cos \dfrac{p\pi}{2}\right) e^{-p^2\pi^2 t/36} \sin \dfrac{p\pi x}{6}.$

2. $V = 6 + \dfrac{24}{\pi^2} \displaystyle\sum_{s=1}^{\infty} \left(\dfrac{\cos p\pi - 1}{p^2}\right) e^{-p^2\pi^2 t/36} \cos \dfrac{p\pi x}{6}.$

3. $\dfrac{2}{\pi} \displaystyle\int_0^{\infty} \left(\dfrac{\sin p}{p} + \dfrac{\cos p - 1}{p^2}\right) e^{-p^2 t} \cdot \cos px \, dp.$

4. $U = \dfrac{4}{\pi} \displaystyle\sum_{p=1}^{\infty} \dfrac{\cos p\pi}{p} e^{-p^2 t} \sin px + 1 + \dfrac{2x}{\pi}.$

9

Hankel Transform and Mellin Transform

(A) THE INFINITE HAKEL TRANSFORM

9.0 DEFINITION

The infinite Hankel transform of a function $f(x)$, $0 < x < \infty$, is defined as

$$H\{f(x)\} = \bar{f}(p) = \int_0^\infty f(x)\, x\, J_n(px)\, dx \qquad \ldots(i)$$

where $J_n(px)$ is the Bessel function of the first kind of order n. Also here $\bar{f}(p)$ is defined as *Hankel transform of order* n of the function $f(x)$.

If $\bar{f}(p)$ is Hankel transform of order n of the function $f(x)$, then $\bar{f}(p)$ is denoted by $\bar{f}_n(p)$. Thus

$$\int_0^\infty x f(x)\, J_n(px)\, dx = \bar{f}_n(p) = H\{f(x), n\}.$$

Remark. In the integral (1), $x\, J_n(px)$ is called the *Kernel* of transformation.

9.1 DEFINITION

If $\bar{f}(p)$ is the (infinite) Hankel transform of order n of the function $f(x)$, then we write

$$H\{f(x)\} = \bar{f}(p) = \int_0^\infty f(x)\, x\, J_n(px)\, dx.$$

Here $f(x)$ is called the *inverse transform* of the function $\bar{f}(p)$ and we write

$$f(x) = H^{-1}\{\bar{f}(p)\}.$$

The *inverse formula for Hankel transform* is

$$f(x) = H^{-1}\{\bar{f}(p)\} = \int_0^\infty \bar{f}(p)\, p_n(px)\, dp$$

9.2 SOME IMPORTANT RESULTS ON BESSEL FUNCTIONS

I. Bessel function of first kind

$$J_n(x) = \sum_{r=0}^{\infty} \frac{(-1)^p}{r!\,\Gamma(n+r+1)} \left(\frac{x}{2}\right)^{n+2r}$$

II. Recurrence formula for $J_n(x)$

(1) $xJ'_n(x) = nJ_n(x) - xJ_{n+1}(x)$.

(2) $xJ'_n(x) = -nJ_n(x) + xJ_{n-1}(x)$.

(3) $2J'_n(x) = J_{n-1}(x) - J_{n+1}(x)$.

(4) $2nJ_n(x) = x\,[J_{n-1}(x) + J_{n+1}(x)]$.

(5) $\frac{d}{dx}[x^{-n} J_n(x)] = -x^{-n} J_{n+1}(x)$,

(6) $\frac{d}{dx}[x^n J_n(x)] = x^n J_{n-1}(x)$.

III. Infinite integrals Involving Bessel Functions

(1) $\int_0^{\infty} e^{-ax} J_0(sx)\,dx = (a^2+s^2)^{-1/2}$.

(2) $\int_0^{\infty} e^{-ax} J_1(sx)\,dx = \frac{1}{s} - \frac{a}{s(a^2+s^2)^{1/2}}$.

(3) $\int_0^{\infty} xe^{-ax} J_0(sx)\,dx = a(a^2+s^2)^{-3/2}$.

(4) $\int_0^{\infty} xe^{-ax} J_1(sx)\,dx = s(a^2+s^2)^{-3/2}$.

(5) $\int_0^{\infty} \frac{e^{-ax}}{x} J_1(sx)\,dx = \frac{(a^2+s^2)^{1/2} - a}{s}$.

9.3 LINEARITY PROPERTY

If $f(x)$ and $g(x)$ are two functions and a, b two constants, then

$$H\{af(x) + bg(x)\} = aH\{f(x)\} + bH\{g(x)\}.$$

Proof. $H\{af(x) + bg(x)\}$

$$= \int_0^{\infty} x\,[af(x) + bg(x)]\,J_n(sx)\,dx$$

$$\int_0^\infty x\,(afx)\,J_n(sx)\,dx + b\int_0^\infty xg(x)\,J_n(sx)\,dx$$

$$= aH\{xf(x)\} + bH\{g(x)\}.$$

9.4 CHANGE OF SCALE PROPERTY

If $H\{f(x)\} = \bar{f}(s)$, then $H\{f(ax)\} = \dfrac{1}{a^2}\bar{f}\left(\dfrac{s}{a}\right)$, a being a constant.

Proof. Let $H\{f(x)\} = \bar{f}(s)$.

$$H\{f(ax)\} = \int_0^\infty xf(ax)\,J_n(sx)\,dx$$

$$= \int_0^\infty \frac{y}{a}\cdot f(y)\cdot J_n\left(\frac{sy}{a}\right)\frac{dy}{a}, \text{ where } ax = y$$

$$= \frac{1}{a^2}\int_0^\infty y\cdot f(y)\cdot J_n\left(\frac{s}{a}\cdot y\right)dy$$

$$= \frac{1}{a^2}\bar{f}\left(\frac{s}{a}\right).$$

Example. *Find the Hankel transform of* $\dfrac{e^{-ax}}{x}$, *taking* $xJ_0(sx)$ *as the kernel of the transform.*

Solution. $H\left\{\dfrac{e^{-ax}}{x}\right\}$

$$= \int_0^\infty \frac{e^{-ax}}{x}\,xJ_0(sx)\,dx = \int_0^\infty e^{-ax}\cdot J_0(sx)\,dx$$

$$= (a^2 + s^2)^{-1/2}.$$

9.5 HANKEL TRANSFORM OF THE DERIVATIVES OF A FUNCTION

Let $\bar{f}_n(s)$ be the Hankel transform of order n of the function $f(x)$ and $\bar{f}'_n(s)$ is the transform of $f'(x)$. Then

$$\bar{f}'_n(s) = -\frac{s}{2n}\left[(n+1)\bar{f}_{n-1}(s) - (n-1)\bar{f}_{n+1}(s)\right].$$

Proof. $\bar{f}_n(s) = \int_0^\infty x f(x) J_n(sx)\, dx,$

$$\bar{f}'_n(s) = \int_0^\infty x \frac{df}{dx} J_n(sx)\, dx$$

$$= \int_0^\infty \frac{df}{dx} [x J_n(sx)]\, dx$$

Integrating by parts and assuming that $xf(x) \to 0$ as $x \to 0$ and $xf(x) \to 0$ as $x \to \infty$, we obtain

$$\bar{f}'_n(s) = \Big[f(x)\, x J_n(sx)\Big]_0^\infty - \int_0^\infty f(x) \frac{d}{dx}[x J_n(sx)]\, dx$$

$$= 0 - \int_0^\infty f(x)\, [J_n(sx) + sx J'_n(sx)]\, dx \qquad \ldots \text{(i)}$$

But $\quad x J'_n(x) = -n J_n(x) + x J_{n-1}(x).$

Replacing x by px, we get

$$px J'_n(px) = -n J_n(px) + px J_{n-1}(px)$$

or $\quad px J'_n(px) + J_n(px) = (1 - n) J_n(px) + px J_{n-1}(px).$

Using this in (i),

$$\bar{f}'_n(p) = -\int_0^\infty f(x)\, [(1 - n) J_n(px) + px J_{n-1}(px)]\, dx$$

$$= -(1 - n) \int_0^\infty f(x) J_n(px)\, dx - p \int_0^\infty x f(x) J_{n-1}(px)\, dx$$

or $\quad \bar{f}'_n(p) = -(1 - n) \int_0^\infty f(x) J_n(px)\, dx - p\bar{f}_{n-1}(p). \qquad \ldots \text{(ii)}$

We know from Recurrence formula for $J_n(x)$, that

$$2n J_n(x) = x\, [J_{n-1}(x) + J_{n+1}(x)].$$

Replacing x by sx,

$$2n J_n(px) = px\, [J_{n+1}(px) + J_{n-1}(px)].$$

Multiplying this by $f(x)$ and then integrating,

$$2n \int_0^\infty f(x) J_n(px)\, dx$$

$$= s\left[\int_0^\infty xf(x)\,J_{n-1}(px)\,dx + \int_0^\infty xf(x)\,J_{n+1}(px)\,dx\right]$$

$$= p\,[\bar{f}_{n-1}(p) + \bar{f}_{n+1}(p)]$$

or $$\int_0^\infty f(x)\,J_n(px)\,dx = \frac{p}{2n}\,[\bar{f}_{n-1}(p) + \bar{f}_{n+1}(p)].$$

In this event (ii) becomes

$$\bar{f}_n(p) = -\frac{(1-n)\,p}{2n}\,[\bar{f}_{n-1}(p) + \bar{f}_{n+1}(p)] - pf_{n-1}(p)$$

$$= \frac{p}{2n}\,[(n-1)\bar{f}_{n-1}(p) + (n-1)\bar{f}_{n+1}(p) - 2n\bar{f}_{n-1}(p)]$$

$$= \frac{p}{2n}\,[-(n+1)\bar{f}_{n-1}(p) + (n-1)\bar{f}_{n+1}(p)]$$

or $$\bar{f}'_n(p) = -\frac{p}{2n}\,[(n+1)\bar{f}_{n-1}(p) - (n-1)\bar{f}_{n+1}(p)] \qquad \text{...(iii)}$$

Corollary 1. When $n = 1$,

$$\bar{f}'_1(p) = -p\bar{f}_0(p)$$

or $$H\{f(x),\ n = 1\} = -pH\{f(x),\ n = 0\}.$$

This is obtained by putting $n = 1$ in (iii).

Corollary 2. When $n = 2$.
Putting $n = 2$ in equation (iii)

$$\bar{f}'_2(p) = -\frac{p}{4}\left[3\bar{f}_1(p) - \bar{f}_3(p)\right].$$

Corollary 3. When $n = 3$.
Putting $n = 3$, in equation (iii),

$$\bar{f}'_3(p) = -\frac{p}{6}\left[4f_2(p) - 2\bar{f}_4(p)\right].$$

Corollary 4. To prove that

$$\bar{f}'_n(p) = \frac{p^2}{4}\left[\left(\frac{n+1}{n-1}\right)\bar{f}_{n-2}(p) - 2\left(\frac{n^2-3}{n^2-1}\right)\bar{f}_n(p) + \left(\frac{n-1}{n+1}\right)\bar{f}_{n+1}(p)\right].$$

Proof. From (iii),

$$\bar{f}'_n(p) = -p\left[\left(\frac{n+1}{2n}\right)\bar{f}_{n-1}(p) - \left(\frac{n-1}{2n}\right)\bar{f}_{n+1}(p)\right] \qquad \text{iv)}$$

Replacing f by f', we get

$$\bar{f}''_v(p) = -p\left[\left(\frac{n+1}{2n}\right)\bar{f}'_{n-1}(p) - \left(\frac{n-1}{2n}\right)\bar{f}'_{n+1}(p)\right] \qquad \ldots(v)$$

Replacing n by $n-1$, and $n+1$ respectively in Eq. (iv), we get

$$\bar{f}'_{n-1}(p) = -p\left[\frac{n}{2n-2}\bar{f}_{n-2}(p) - \frac{n-2}{2(n-1)}\bar{f}_n(p)\right]$$

$$\bar{f}'_{n+1}(p) = -p\left[\frac{n+2}{2(n+1)}\bar{f}_n(p) - \frac{n}{2(n+1)}\bar{f}_{n+2}(p)\right]$$

Writing (v) with the help of these two equations,

$$\bar{f}''_v(p) = \frac{p^2}{4}\left[\left(\frac{n+1}{n}\right)\left\{\frac{n}{n-1}\bar{f}_{n-2}(p) - \left(\frac{n-2}{n-1}\right)\bar{f}_n(p)\right\}\right.$$

$$\left. - \left(\frac{n-1}{n}\right)\left\{\left(\frac{n+2}{n+1}\right)\bar{f}_n(p) - \left(\frac{n}{n+1}\right)\bar{f}_{n+2}(p)\right\}\right]$$

$$= \frac{p^2}{4}\left[\left(\frac{n+1}{n-1}\right)\bar{f}_{n-2}(p) + \left(\frac{n-1}{n+1}\right)\bar{f}_{n+2}(p) - \frac{2(n^2-3)}{n^2-1}\bar{f}_n(p)\right]$$

Example. *Find the Hankel transform of* $\frac{df}{dx}$, *when* $f = \frac{e^{-ax}}{x}$ *and* $n = 1$.

Solution. Let $f(x) = \frac{e^{-ax}}{x}$.

To determine $H\left\{\frac{df}{dx}, \; n = 1\right\} = \bar{f}'_1(p)$.

We know that

$$\bar{f}'_1(p) = -p\bar{f}_0(p)$$

$$= -p\int_0^{\infty} xf(x)\,J_0(px)\,dx$$

$$= -p\int_0^{\infty} x\,e^{\frac{-ax}{x}}\,J_0(px)\,dx$$

$$= -p\int_0^\infty e^{-ax} J_0(px)\, dx$$

$$= -p\,(a^2 + p^2)^{-1/2}.$$

9.6 TO FIND THE HANKEL TRANSFORM OF

$$\frac{d^2f}{dx^2} + \frac{1}{x}\frac{df}{dx} - \frac{n^2}{x^2}f.$$

Proof. $H\left(\frac{df}{dx^2}\right) = \int_0^\infty \frac{d^2f}{dx^2} xJ_n(px)\, dx$

$$= \left[\frac{df}{dx} xJ_n(px)\right]_0^\infty$$

$$- \int_0^\infty \frac{df}{dx}[J_n(px) + pxJ'_n(px)]\, dx$$

Supposing $xf'(x) \to 0$ as $x \to 0$ or $x \to \infty$, we get

$$H\left(\frac{d^2f}{dx^2}\right) + \int_0^\infty \frac{f'(x)}{x} xJ_n(px)\, dx = -s\int_0^\infty xf(x)\, J'_n(px)\, dx$$

or $$H\left(\frac{d^2f}{dx^2} + \frac{f'}{x}\right) = -s\left[xf(x)\, J'_n(px)\right]_0^\infty + \int_0^\infty f(x)\frac{d}{dx}[xJ'_x(px)]\, dx$$

Again taking $xf(x) \to 0$ as $x \to 0$ or $x \to \infty$, we obtain

$$H\left(\frac{d^2f}{dx^2} + \frac{f'}{x}\right) = p\int_0^\infty f\frac{d}{dx}[xJ'_n(px)]\, dx \qquad \ldots(i)$$

Since Bessel's function $J_n(x)$ satisfies the differential equation,

$$\frac{d}{dx}\left\{x\frac{dy}{dx}\right\} + \left(1 - \frac{n^2}{x^2}\right)xy = 0$$

This gives

$$\frac{d}{dx}\{xJ'_n(x)\} = -\left(1 - \frac{n^2}{x^2}\right)xJ_n(x).$$

Replacing x by sx, we get

$$\frac{d}{sdx}\{px\, J'_n(sx)\} = \left(\frac{n^2}{p^2x^2} - 1\right)px\, J_n(px)$$

or $$\frac{d}{dx}\{x J'_n(px)\} = \frac{n^2}{sx} J_n(px) - px\, J_n(px).$$

Using this in equation (i), we get

$$H\left(\frac{d^2f}{dx^2} + \frac{f'(x)}{x}\right) = p\int_0^\infty f\frac{n^2}{px} J_n(px)\, dx - p\int_0^\infty f(px)\, J_n(px)\, dx$$

$$= \int_0^\infty \left(\frac{n^2 f}{x^2}\right) x\, J_n(px)\, dx - p^2 \int_0^\infty f(x)\, J_n(px)\, dx$$

or $$H\left(\frac{d^2f}{dx^2} + \frac{f'}{x} - \frac{n^2}{x^2} f\right) = -p^2 \bar{f}_n(p)$$

Finally,

$$\int_0^\infty \left[\frac{d^2f}{dx^2} + \frac{1}{x}\frac{df}{dx} - \frac{n^2}{x^2} f\right] x\, J_n(px)\, dx = -p^2 \bar{f}_n(p).$$

Corollary (i). When $n = 0$,

$$\int_0^\infty \left(\frac{d_2 f}{dx^2} + \frac{1}{x}\cdot\frac{df}{dx}\right) x\, J_0(px)\, dx = -p^2 \bar{f}_0(p)$$

where $\bar{f}_0(p)$ is the Hankel transform of $f(x)$ of order zero, *i.e.*,

$H\{f(x),\ n = 0\} = \bar{f}_0(p)$.

If we write $H\{f(x),\ n = 0\} = \bar{f}(p)$, then

$$H\left\{\frac{d^2f}{dx^2} + \frac{1}{x}\frac{df}{dx}\right\} = -p\bar{f}(p).$$

(ii) When $n = 1$,

$$\int_0^\infty \left(\frac{d^2f}{dx^2} + \frac{1}{x}\frac{df}{dx} - \frac{1}{x^2} f\right) xJ_1(px)\, dx = -p^2 \bar{f}_1(p).$$

9.7 PARSEVAL'S THEOREM

If $\bar{f}(s)$ and $\bar{g}(s)$ be the Hankel transforms of the function $f(x)$ and $g(x)$ respectively, then

$$\int_0^\infty x f(x)\, g(x)\, dx = \int_0^\infty p\bar{f}(p)\, \bar{g}(p)\, dp$$

Proof. We have $\bar{f}(p) = \int_0^\infty f(x)\, x\, J_n(x)\, dx$,

$$\bar{g}(p) = \int_0^\infty g(x)\, x\, J_n(px)\, dx,$$

$$\int_0^\infty p\bar{f}(p)\, \bar{g}(p)\, dp$$

$$= \int_0^\infty p\bar{f}(p) \left[\int_0^\infty g(x)\, xJ_n(px)\, dx \right] dp$$

$$= \int_0^\infty p\bar{f}(p)\, dp \int_0^\infty g(x)\, xJ_n(px)\, dx$$

$$= \int_0^\infty xg(x)\, dx \int_0^\infty p\bar{f}(p)\, J_n(px)\, dp$$

(on interchanging order of integration)

$$= \int_0^\infty xg(x)\, dx\, f(x). \text{ For } f(x) = \int_0^\infty \bar{f}(p)\, pJ_n(px)\, dp$$

$$= \int_0^\infty xf(x)\, g(x)\, dx. \qquad \text{(This is inversion formula).}$$

ILLUSTRATIVE EXAMPLES

E mple 1. *Find the Hankel transform of $x^{-2}e^{-x}$ of order one.*

or

Find the Hankel transform of $x^{-2}e^{-x}$, taking $xJ_1(sx)$ as the kernel.

Solution. $H\{x^{-2}e^{-x},\ n = 1\}$

$$= \int_0^\infty x^{-2}e^{-x}\, xJ_1(px)\, dx$$

$$= \int_0^\infty \frac{e^{-x}}{x} J_1(px)\, dx$$

$$= \frac{(1+p^2)^{1/2} - 1}{p}.$$

Example 2. *Evaluate:*

(i) $H\left\{\dfrac{e^{-5x}}{x},\ n = 0\right\}$,

(ii) $H\left\{\dfrac{e^{-ax}}{x},\ n = 1\right\}$.

Solution. $H\left\{\dfrac{e^{-5x}}{x},\ n=0\right\}$

$$= \int_0^\infty \frac{e^{-5x}}{x}\, xJ_0(px)\, dx$$

$$= \int_0^\infty e^{-5x} J_0(px)\, dx$$

$$= (5^2 + p^2)^{-1/2} = (25 + p^2)^{-1/2},$$

(ii) $$H\left\{\frac{e^{-ax}}{x},\ n=1\right\} = \int_0^\infty \frac{e^{-ax}}{x}\, xJ_1(px)\, dx$$

$$= \int_0^\infty e^{-ax} J_1(px)\, dx$$

$$= \frac{1}{p} - \frac{a}{p(a^2+p^2)^{1/2}}.$$

Example 3. *Find* $H\{e^{-ax},\ n=0\}$.

or

Find the Hankel transform of e^{-ax} *taking* $xJ_0(px)$ *as the kernel of the transform.*

Solution. $$H\{e^{-ax},\ n=0\} = \int_0^\infty e^{-ax} xJ_0(px)\, dx$$

$$= a(a^2+p^2)^{-3/2}$$

Example 4. *Find* $H\{e^{-ax},\ n=1\}$.

or

Find the Hankel transform of e^{-ax} *taking* $xJ_1(px)$ *as the kernel of the transform.*

Solution. $$H\{e^{-ax},\ n=1\} = \int_0^\infty e^{-ax} xJ_1(px)\, dx$$

$$= p(a^2+p^2)^{-3/2}.$$

Example 5. *Obtain the inverse Hankel transform of* e^{-ap} *of order zero.*

Or

Evaluate $H^{-1}\{e^{-ap},\ n=0\}$.

Solution. $H^{-1}\{e^{-ap},\ n=0\} = \int_0^\infty e^{-ap}\, pJ_0(px)\, dp$

$$= a(a^2+x^2)^{-3/2}.$$

Example 6. *Evaluate* $H^{-1}\left\{\dfrac{e^{-ap}}{p},\ n=0\right\}$.

Solution. $H^{-1}\left\{\dfrac{e^{-ap}}{p},\ n=0\right\} = \int_0^\infty \dfrac{e^{-ap}}{p}\, pJ_0(px)\, dp$

$$= \int_0^\infty e^{-ap} J_0(sx)\, dp$$

$$= (a^2+x^2)^{-1/2}.$$

Example 7. *Find the Hankel transform of*

$$f(x) = \begin{cases} 1, & 0 < x < a,\ n=0, \\ 0, & x > a\ \ n=0 \end{cases}.$$

Solution. $H\{f(x),\ n=0\}$

$$= \int_0^\infty f(x)\, xJ_0(px)\, dx$$

$$= \int_0^a f(x)\, xJ_0(px)\, dx + \int_0^\infty f(x)\, xJ_0(px)\, dx$$

$$= \int_0^a 1\cdot xJ_0(px)\, dx + \int_0^\infty 0\cdot xJ_0(px)\, dx$$

$$= \int_0^a xJ_0(px)\, dx + 0. \qquad \ldots(\text{i})$$

By Recurrence formula for Bessel's function,

$$\frac{d}{dx}\{x^n J_n(x)\} = x^n J_{n-1}(x)$$

Replacing n by x by 1 and sx respectively,

$$\frac{d}{x\,dx}\{pxJ_1(px)\} = pxJ_0(px)$$

or $$\frac{d}{dx}\{xj_1(px)\} = pxJ_0(px).$$

Integrating this from $x = 0$ to $x = a$,

$$\left[xJ_1(px)\right]_0^a = p\int_0^a xJ_0(px)\,dx$$

or
$$\int_0^a xJ_0(px)\,dx = \frac{a}{p}J_1(pa). \qquad \ldots\text{(ii)}$$

Now (i) becomes

$$H\{f(x),\ n = 0\} = \frac{a}{p}J_1(pa).$$

Example 8. *To show that the Hankel transform of order zero is*

$$\{f(x) = \begin{cases} a^2 - x^2, & 0 < x < a \\ 0, & x > a \end{cases}$$

$$\frac{4a}{p^3}J_1(pa) - \frac{2a^2}{p^2}J_0(pa).$$

Solution. Prove as in Problem 9 that

$$H\{f(x),\ n = 0\} = \frac{2a^2}{p^2}J_2(pa). \qquad \ldots\text{(vi)}$$

By Recurrence formula No. 4,

$$2nJ_n(x) = x\,[J_{n-1}(x) + J_{n+1}(x)].$$

Putting $n = 1$,

$$2J_1(x) = x\,[J_0(x) + J_2(x)].$$

Replacing x by *sa*, we get

$$2J_1(pa) = pa\,[J_0(pa) + J_2(pa)].$$

or
$$\frac{2}{pa}J_1(pa) - J_0(pa) = J_2(pa).$$

Multiplying this by $\frac{2a^2}{p^2}$,

$$\frac{4a}{p^3}J_1(pa) - \frac{2a^2}{p^2}J_0(pa) = \frac{2a^2}{p^2}J_2(pa).$$

Using this in (vi),

$$H\{f(x),\ n = 0\} = \frac{4a}{p^3}J_1(pa) - \frac{2a^2}{p^2}J_0(pa).$$

Example 9. *Find the Hankel transform of order zero of $1/x$ and then apply the inversion formula to get the original function.*

Solution. Let $f(x) = \frac{1}{x}$.

$$H\{f(x),\ n = 0\} = \int_0^\infty \frac{1}{x} xJ_0(px)\,dx$$

$$= \int_0^\infty J_0(px)\,dx$$

$$= \int_0^\infty e^{-0x} J_0(px)\,dx$$

$$= (0^2 + p^2)^{-1/2} = \frac{1}{p}$$

or $$\bar{f}_0(s) = \frac{1}{p}.$$

Now we apply the inversion formula

$$f(x) = \int_0^\infty \bar{f}_0(p)\,pJ_0(px)\,dp$$

$$= \int_0^\infty \frac{1}{p} pJ_0(px)\,dp = \int_0^\infty J_0(px)\,dp$$

$$= \int_0^\infty e^{-0x} J_0(px)\,dp = (0^2 + x^2)^{-1/2} = \frac{1}{x}$$

This concludes the problem.

Example 10. *Find the Hankel transform of order zero of the function* $\frac{d^2f}{dx^2} + \frac{1}{x}\frac{df}{dx}$, *where* $f(x) = \frac{e^{-ax}}{x}$.

Solution. We know that

$$\int_0^\infty \left(\frac{d^2f}{dx^2} + \frac{1}{x}\frac{df}{dx} - \frac{n^2 f}{x^2}\right) xJ_n(px)\,dx = -p^2 \bar{f}_n(p), \text{ by § 9.6}$$

For $n = 0$, this gives

$$\int_0^\infty \left(\frac{d^2f}{dx^2} + \frac{1}{x}\frac{df}{dx}\right) xJ_0(px)\,dx = -p^2 \bar{f}_0(p)$$

or
$$H\left\{\frac{d^2f}{dx^2}+\frac{1}{x}\frac{df}{dx},\ n=0\right\} = -p^2\bar{f}_0(p)$$
$$= -p^2\int_0^\infty f(x)\,xJ_0(px)\,dx$$
$$= -p^2\int_0^\infty \frac{e^{-ax}}{x}\,xJ_0(px)\,dx$$
$$= -p^2\int_0^\infty e^{-ax}J_0(px)\,dx$$
$$= -p^2(a^2+p^2)^{-1/2}.$$

Example 4. *Find the Hankel transform of* $\cos ax/x$ *taking* $xJ_0(px)$ *as the kernel.*

Solution.
$$H\left\{\frac{\cos ax}{x}\right\} = \int_0^\infty \frac{\cos ax}{x}\,xJ_0(px)\,dx$$
$$= \int_0^\infty \cos ax\,J_0(px)\,dx$$
$$= \text{R.P. of}\int_0^\infty e^{-iax}J_0(px)\,dx$$
$$= \text{R.P. of}\,(i^2a^2+p^2)^{-1/2}$$
$$= \text{R.P. of}\,(p^2-a^2)^{-1/2}$$
$$= \begin{cases}(p^2-a^2)^{-1/2} & \text{if } \quad p>a\\ 0, & \text{if } \; 0<p<a\end{cases}$$

Problem. Find $H\left(\frac{\sin ax}{x}\right)$.

Example 5. *Find the Hankel transform of order n of the function* $\frac{\partial^2 f}{\partial t^2}$ *where f is a function of x and t.*

Solution.
$$H\left\{\frac{\partial^2 f}{\partial t^2},\ n\right\} = \int_0^\infty x\frac{\partial^2 f}{\partial t^2}J_n(px)\,dx$$

$$= \frac{\partial^2}{\partial t^2}\int_0^\infty f(x, t)\, xJ_n(px)\, dx$$

$$= \frac{d^2\bar{f}_n(p)}{dt^2}$$

where $\bar{f}_n(p)$ is the Hankel transform of order n of $f(x)$.

9.8 APPLICATION OF HANKEL TRANSFORM TO BOUNDARY VALUE PROBLEMS

ILLUSTRATIVE EXAMPLES

Example 1. *Find Hankel transform of*

$$f(x) = \begin{cases} x^n, & 0 < x < a \\ , & x > a \end{cases} \quad n > -1,$$

taking $xJ_n(px)$ as kernel.

Solution. $H\{f(x)\} = \int_0^\infty f(x)\, xJ_n(px)\, dx$

$$= \int_0^\infty f(x)\, xJ_n(px)\, dx + \int_a^\infty f(x)\, xJ_n(px)\, dx$$

$$= \int_0^a x^n \cdot xJ_n(px)\, dx + \int_0^\infty 0 \cdot xJ_n(px)\, dx$$

or $$\bar{f}_n(p) = \int_0^a x^{n+1} J_n(px)\, dx \qquad \ldots(i)$$

By Recurrence formula No. (6),

$$\frac{d}{dx}\{x^n J_n(x)\} = x^n J_{n-1}(x).$$

Replacing x by px,

$$\frac{d}{p\, dx}\{x^n J_n(px)\} = x^n J_{n-1}(px)$$

Replacing n by $n + 1$,

$$\frac{d}{p\, dx}\{x^{n+1} J_{n+1}(px)\} = x^{n+1} J_n(px)$$

Using this in (i),

$$\bar{f}_n(p) = \int_0^a \frac{1}{p}\frac{d}{dx}\{x^{n+1} J_{n+1}(px)\}\, dx$$

$$= \frac{1}{s}\left[x^{n+1} J_{n+1}(px)\right]_0^a$$

$$= \frac{a^{n+1}}{p} J_{n+1}(pa).$$

Example 2. *The magnetic potential V for a circular disc of radius a and strength ω, magnetised parallel to its axis, satisfies Laplace's equations is equal to 2πω on the disc itself and vanishes at exterior points in the plane of the disc, show that at the point (r, z), z > 0.*

$$V = 2\pi\omega a \int_0^\infty e^{-pz} J_0(rp) J_1(ap)\, dp.$$

Solution. The magnetic potential V satisfies the Laplace's equation

$$\frac{\partial^2 V}{\partial r^2} + \frac{1}{r}\frac{\partial V}{\partial r} + \frac{\partial^2 V}{\partial z^2} = 0 \qquad \ldots(i)$$

where $0 < r < \infty$

with the boundary conditions.

(i) $V = 2\pi\omega,\ 0 \le r \le a,\ z = 0$

(ii) $V = 0,\ r > a,\ z = 0.$

Taking the Hankel transform of order zero of equation (i),

$$\int_0^\infty \left(\frac{\partial^2 V}{\partial r^2} + \frac{1}{r}\frac{\partial V}{\partial r}\right) rJ_0(pr)\, dr + \int_0^\infty \frac{\partial^2 V}{\partial z^2} rJ_0(pr)\, dr = 0$$

or $$-p^2\bar{V} + \frac{d^2\bar{V}}{dz^2} = 0$$

where $$\bar{V} = H\{V,\ n = 0\} = \int_0^\infty V \cdot rJ_0(pr)\, dr \qquad \text{[by 9.6]} \quad \ldots(ii)$$

The solution of (ii) is

$$\bar{V} = Ae^{pz} + Be^{-pz}.$$

But V is bounded and so $\bar{V}$ is bounded.

Consequently $A = 0$, otherwise $\bar{V} \to \infty$ as $z \to \infty$.

$$\overline{V} = Be^{-pz} \quad \text{...(iii)}$$

To find B. For this we put $z = 0$. Then we have

$$B = [\overline{V}]_{z=0} \quad \text{...(iv)}$$

$$\overline{V} = \int_0^\infty V \cdot rJ_0(pr)\, dr$$

or,

$$B = (\overline{V})_{z=0} = \int_0^\infty (V)_{z=0}\, rJ_0(pr)\, dr$$

$$= \int_0^a (V)_{z=0}\, rJ_0(pr)\, dr + \int_a^\infty (V)_{z=0}\, rJ_0(pr)\, dr$$

$$= \int_0^a 2\pi\omega J_0(pr)\, dr + \int_a^\infty 0\, rJ_0(pr)\, dr$$

$$= 2\pi\omega \int_0^a rJ_0(pr)\, dr + 0$$

$$= 2\pi\omega \int_0^a \frac{1}{p}\frac{d}{dr}[rJ_1(pr)]\, dr$$

or,

$$B = \frac{2\pi\omega}{p} aJ_1(pa). \quad \text{...(v)}$$

Now (iii) becomes

$$\overline{V} = \frac{2\pi\omega a}{p} J_1(pa)\, e^{-pz}.$$

Applying inversion formula of the Hankel transformation of zero order,

$$V = \int_0^\infty \overline{V} \cdot pJ_0(pr)\, dp$$

$$= \int_0^\infty \frac{2\pi\omega a}{p} J_1(pa)\, se^{-pz}\, J_0(pr)\, dp$$

or

$$V(r, z) = 2\pi\omega a \int_0^\infty e^{-pz} \cdot J_1(pa)\, J_0(pr)\, dp.$$

Example 3. *Heat is supplied at a constant rate Q per unit area per unit time over a circular area of radius a in the plane z = 0 to an infinite solid of conductivity k. Show that the steady temperature at a distant r from the axis of circular area and distant z from the plate z = 0 is given by*

$$\frac{Qa}{2k}\int_0^\infty e^{-pz}\, J_0(pr)\, J_1(pa)\, p^{-1}\, dp.$$

Solution. Let $V(r, z)$ denote temperature at a point (r, z), then it is governed by the equation

$$\frac{\partial V}{\partial t} = k\left[\frac{\partial^2 V}{\partial r^2} + \frac{1}{r}\frac{\partial V}{\partial r} + \frac{\partial^2 V}{\partial z^2}\right]$$

Since the surface is circular and therefore we have taken cylindrical coordinates (r, θ, z). Here temperature is steady and so $\frac{\partial V}{\partial t} = 0$. Hence

$$\frac{\partial^2 V}{\partial r^2} + \frac{1}{r}\frac{\partial V}{\partial r} + \frac{\partial^2 V}{\partial z^2} = 0$$

Taking Hankel transform of order zero, *i.e.*, $n = 0$

$$\int_0^\infty \left(\frac{\partial^2 V}{\partial r^2} + \frac{1}{r}\frac{\partial V}{\partial r}\right) r J_0(pr)\, dr + \int_0^\infty \frac{\partial^2 V}{\partial z^2} r J_0(pr)\, dr = 0$$

Writing $H(V,\ n = 0) = \int_0^\infty V r J_0(pr)\, dr = \overline{V}$,

we get $\quad -p^2\overline{V} + \frac{d^2\overline{V}}{dz^2} = 0 \quad \text{or} \quad (D^2 - p^2)\,\overline{V} = 0$

Its solution is $\overline{V} = Ae^{pz} + Be^{-pz}$

But $\overline{V}$ must tend to zero as $z \to \infty$ so that $A = 0$.

$$\therefore \quad \overline{V} = Be^{-pz} \qquad \ldots\text{(i)}$$

$$\text{This} \Rightarrow \frac{d\overline{V}}{dz} = -Bpe^{-pz} \Rightarrow \frac{d\overline{V}}{dz} = -Bp \text{ at } z = 0 \qquad \ldots\text{(ii)}$$

The boundary conditions are

(i) $2\left(-k\frac{\partial V}{\partial z}\right) = Q,\ 0 \le r < a,\ z = 0$

(ii) $2\left(-k\frac{\partial V}{\partial z}\right) = 0,\ r > a,\ z = 0$

(i) $\Rightarrow \frac{\partial V}{\partial z} = -\frac{Q}{2k},\ 0 \le r < a,\ z = 0.$

$$\text{Also} \quad \frac{\partial V}{\partial z} = 0,\ r > a. \qquad \ldots\text{(iii)}$$

Consider the case when $z = 0$

$$\frac{d\overline{V}}{dz} = H\left\{\frac{\partial V}{\partial z}\right\} = \int_0^\infty \frac{\partial V}{\partial z} r J_n(pr)\, dr$$

$$= \int_0^a \frac{\partial V}{\partial z} r J_0(pr)\, dr + \int_a^\infty \frac{\partial V}{\partial z} r J_0(pr)\, dr$$

Using (iii), $\dfrac{d\overline{V}}{dz} = \int_0^a \left(-\dfrac{Q}{2k}\right) r J_0(pr)\, dr + \int_0^\infty 0\, r J_0(pr)\, dr$

or, $$\frac{d\overline{V}}{\partial z} = -\frac{Q}{2k} \int_0^a r J_0(pr)\, dr \qquad \text{...(iv)}$$

Since $\dfrac{d}{dx}[x^n J_n(x)] = x^n J^{n-1}(x)$

But $n = 1$ and replace x by pr,

$$\frac{d}{p\, dr}[(pr)^1 J_1(pr)] = (pr)^1 J_0(pr)$$

or, $$\frac{d}{dr}[r J_1(pr)] = pr J_0(pr)$$

Using this in (iv),

$$\frac{d\overline{V}}{dz} = -\frac{Q}{2k} \int_0^a \frac{1}{p} \frac{d}{dr}[r J(pr)]\, dr$$

or, $$\frac{d\overline{V}}{dz} = \frac{Q}{2kp}\left[rJ_1(pr)\right]_{r=0}^a = -\frac{Qa}{2kp} J_1(pa)$$

Equating this to (ii)

$$Bp = \frac{Qa}{2kp} J_1(pa)'$$

or $$B = \frac{Qa}{2kp^2} J_1(pa)$$

Putting this in (i),

$$\overline{V} = \frac{Qa}{2kp^2} J_1(pa)\, e^{-pz}$$

Applying inversion formula of Hankel transform,

$$V(r, z) = \int_0^\infty \left[\frac{Qa}{2kp^2} J_1(pa)\, e^{-pz}\right] pJ_0(pr)\, dp$$

or $$V(r, z) = \frac{Qa}{2k} \int_0^\infty p^{-1} J_1(pa) J_0(pr)\, e^{-pz}\, dp.$$

Example 4. *The vibrations of a very large membrane are governed by the equation*

$$\frac{\partial^2 U}{\partial r^2} + \frac{1}{r}\frac{\partial U}{\partial r} = \frac{1}{c^2}\frac{\partial^2 U}{\partial t^2},\ r \geq 0, t \geq 0$$

with $U = f(r), \dfrac{\partial U}{\partial t} = g(r)$, *when* $t = 0$.

Show that, for $t > 0$,

$$U(r, t) = \int_0^\infty p\bar{f}(p) \cos(pct) J_0(pr)\, dp + \frac{1}{c}\int_0^\infty \bar{g}(p) \sin(pct) J_0(pr)\, dp,$$

where $\bar{f}(p)$ *and* $\bar{g}(p)$ *are the zero order Hankel transform of* $f(r)$, $g(r)$ *respectively.*

Solution. Taking Hankel transform of zero order of the given equation,

$$\int_0^\infty \left(\frac{\partial^2 U}{\partial r^2} + \frac{1}{r}\frac{\partial U}{\partial r}\right) rJ_0(pr)\, dr = \frac{1}{c^2}\int_0^\infty \frac{\partial^2 U}{\partial t^2} rJ_0(pr)\, dr$$

or $$-p^2\bar{U} = \frac{1}{c^2}\frac{d^2\bar{U}}{dt^2} \text{ or } [D^2 + (pc)^2]\,\bar{U} = 0$$

Its solution is

$$\bar{U} = A \cos pct + B \sin pct \qquad \text{...(i)}$$

$$\frac{d\bar{U}}{dt} = cp\,[-A \sin pct + B \cos pct]$$

At $$t = 0, \frac{d\bar{U}}{dt} = Bcp \qquad \text{...(ii)}$$

$$U = f(r), t = 0 \Rightarrow \bar{U} = \int_0^\infty f(r)\, rJ_0(pr)\, dr = \bar{f}(p)$$

$\therefore$ $$\bar{U} = \bar{f}(p) \text{ at } t = 0 \qquad \text{...(iii)}$$

$$H\left(\frac{\partial U}{\partial t}\right) = H\{g(r)\} \Rightarrow \frac{d\bar{U}}{dt} = \bar{g}(p) \text{ at } t = 0 \qquad \text{...(iv)}$$

By (i) and (iii), $\bar{f}(p) = A$

By (ii) and (iv), $Bcp = \bar{g}(p)$

Using these values in (i),

$$\bar{U} = \bar{f}(p) \cos pct + \frac{1}{cp}\bar{g}(p) \sin pct$$

Applying inversion formula,

$$U(r,t) = \int_0^\infty \left[\bar{f}(p)\cos(pct)\right] pJ_0(pr)\,dp + \int_0^\infty \left[\frac{1}{cp}\bar{g}(p)\sin(pct)\right] pJ_0(pr)\,dp$$

From this the required result follows.

Example 5. *Find the potential V (r, z) of a field due to a flat circular disc with its centre at the origin and radius equal to one. The axis of the disc is along z-*axis and it satisfies the differential equation

$$\frac{\partial^2 V}{\partial r^2} + \frac{1}{r}\frac{\partial V}{\partial t} + \frac{\partial^2 V}{\sigma z^2} = 0,\ 0 \le r < \infty,\ z \ge 0$$

and the boundary conditions:

$$V = V_0 \text{ when } z = 0,\ 0 \le r < 1$$

$$\frac{\partial V}{\partial z} = 0, \text{ when } z = 0,\ r > 1.$$

Solution. Taking the Hankel transform of the differential equation for $n = 0$, we get

$$\int_0^\infty \left(\frac{\partial^2 V}{\partial r^2} + \frac{1}{r}\frac{\partial V}{\partial r}\right) rJ_0(pr)\,dr + \int_0^\infty \frac{\partial^2 V}{\partial z^2} rJ_0(pr)\,dr = 0$$

or $$-p^2\bar{V} + \frac{d^2\bar{V}}{dz^2} = 0, \text{ where } \bar{V} = \int_0^\infty VrJ_0(pr)\,dr$$

The solution of it is,

$$\bar{V} = Ae^{pz} + Be^{-pz},$$

V is finite and so $\bar{V}$ is finite as $z \to \infty$.

Consequently $A = 0$, otherwise $\bar{V}$ becomes infinite as $z \to \infty$.

Now we have $\bar{V} = Be^{-pz}$.

Applying inversion formula,

$$V(r,z) = \int_0^\infty Be^{-pz} pJ_0(pr)\,dp. \qquad \ldots\text{(i)}$$

Here $B = B(p)$.

This $$\Rightarrow \frac{\partial V}{\partial z} = \int_0^\infty Be^{-pz}(-p^2)J_0(pr)\,dp. \qquad \ldots\text{(ii)}$$

Putting $z = 0$ in (i) and (ii), we get

$$\int_0^\infty pBJ_0(pr)\,dp = (V)_{z=0} = V_0,\ 0 \le r < 1.$$

$$\int_0^\infty -p^2BJ_0(pr)\,dp = \left(\frac{\partial V}{\partial z}\right)_{z=0} = 0,\ r > 1,$$

or
$$\left.\begin{aligned}&\int_0^\infty pBJ_0(pr)\,dp = V_0,\ 0 \le r < 1,\\&\int_0^\infty p^2BJ_0(pr)\,dp = 0,\ r > 1.\end{aligned}\right\} \quad \ldots\text{(iii)}$$

Comparing (iii) with the well known integrals,

$$\int_0^\infty \frac{\sin p}{p} J_0(pr)\,dp = \frac{\pi}{2},\ 0 \le r < 1,$$

$$\int_0^\infty \sin p \cdot J_0(pr)\,dp = 0,\ r > 1.$$

We obtain

$$B = \frac{2}{\pi} V_0 \frac{\sin p}{p^2}.$$

Putting this in equation (i),

$$V(r, z) = \frac{2V_0}{\pi} \int_0^\infty e^{-pz} \frac{\sin p}{p} J_0(pr)\,dp.$$

Example 6. *Applying Hankel transform to solve the differential equation* $\frac{\partial^2 V}{\partial r^2} + \frac{1}{r}\frac{\partial V}{\partial r} + \frac{\partial^2 V}{\partial z^2} = 0$ *for the region* $r \ge 0,\ z \ge 0$ *satisfying the following conditions:*

$$V \to 0 \text{ as } z \to \infty \text{ and } r \to \infty,\ V = f(r) \text{ on } z = 0,\ r \ge 0.$$

Solution. Prove as in Problem 18 that

$$\bar{V} = Be^{-sz} \quad \ldots\text{(i)}$$

At $z = 0,\ V = f(r) \Rightarrow \bar{V} = \bar{f}(p) = \int_0^\infty f(r)\, rJ_0(pr)\,dr$

$\therefore$ $\bar{V}(p, 0) = \bar{f}(p)$. Using this in (i), $\bar{f}(p) = B$

or $\bar{V} = \bar{f}(p)\, e^{-sz}$

Using inversion formula,

$$V = \int_0^\infty \bar{V}\, s J_0(sr)\, ds$$

$$= \int_0^\infty \bar{f}(p)\, e^{-sz}\, s J_0(sr)\, ds.$$

EXERCISE 9(A)

1. Find the Hankel transform of

$$f(x) = \begin{cases} 1, & 0 < x < a \\ 0, & x > a \end{cases}$$

taking $xJ_0(px)$ as the kernel.

2. Find $H\left\{\dfrac{e^{-7x}}{x},\ n = 0\right\}$.

3. Find the Hankel transform of order zero of

$$f(x) = \begin{cases} 1 - x^2, & 0 < x < 1 \\ 0, & x > 1 \end{cases}.$$

4. Find the Hankel transform of

$$\frac{\partial^2 f(x, t)}{\partial t^3}.$$

5. Find Hankel transform of $\dfrac{\sin ax}{x}$ taking $xJ_0(px)$ as the kernel.

ANSWERS

1. $\dfrac{a}{p} J_1(ap)$.

2. $(49 + p^2)^{-1/2}$.

3. $\dfrac{2}{p^2} J_2(p)$.

4. $\dfrac{d^3 \bar{f}(p, t)}{dt^3}$.

5. $\begin{cases} 0, & \text{if } p > a \\ -(p^2 - a^2)^{-1/2}, & \text{if } 0 < p < a \end{cases}$.

(B) THE FINITE HANKEL TRANSFORM

9.9 FINITE HANKEL TRANSFORM

If $f(x)$ satisfies Dirichlet's conditions in the closed interval $[0, a]$, then its *finite Hankel transform* $\bar{f}(p_i)$, of order n is given by

$$\bar{f}(s_i) = \int_0^a f(x) \cdot xJ_n(xp_i)\, dx, \qquad \ldots\text{(i)}$$

where a is positive root of the transcendental equation

$$J_n(ap_i) = 0. \qquad \ldots\text{(ii)}$$

If the function $f(x)$ is continuous at any point of the interval $[0, a]$, then the inversion formula for $\bar{f}(p_1)$ is

$$f(x) = \frac{2}{a^2} \sum_i f(p_i) \frac{J_n(xp_i)}{[J'_n(ap_i)]^2}. \qquad \ldots\text{(iii)}$$

where the sum is taken over all the positive roots of the equation (ii).

If $f(x)$ is represented by generalised Fourier Bessel series

$$f(x) = \sum_i c_i J_n(xp_i),\ 0 \le x \le a,$$

then the coefficient c_i is given by

$$c_i = \frac{2}{a^2 J^2_{n+1}(ap_4)} \int_0^a f(x) \cdot xJ_n(xp_i)\, dx$$

$$= \frac{2\bar{f}(p_i)}{a^2 [J_{n+1}(ap_i)]^2}$$

$$= \frac{2\bar{f}(p_i)}{a^2 [J'_n(ap_i)]^2}.$$

This follows from (iv).

The recurrence formula,

$$xJ'_n(x) = nJ_n(x) - xJ_{n+1}(x)$$

Replacing x by as_i,

$$ap_i J'_n(ap_i) = nJ_n(ap_i) - ap_i J_{n+1}(ap_i),$$

Using (ii), we get

$$ap_i J'_n(ap_i) = -ap_i J_{n+1}(ap_i)$$

or
$$J'_a(ap_i) = -J_{n+1}(ap_i) \qquad \ldots \text{(iv)}$$

Consequently, $f(x) = \dfrac{2}{a^2} \sum\limits_i \bar{f}(p_i) \dfrac{J_n(xp_i)}{[J'_n(ap_i)]^2}$.

Remark. It has been found in practice that the choice of unity as the upper limit of the integral defining the transform is more convenient. Therefore the definition of finite Hankel transform becomes

$$\bar{f}(s_i) = \int_0^1 f(x), xJ_n(xp_i)\, dx.$$

9.10 FINITE HANKEL TRANSFORM OF $\dfrac{df}{dx}$

i.e., $$H_n\left\{\frac{df}{dx}\right\} = \int_0^p \frac{df}{dx} xJ_n(px)\, dx,$$

where s is any root of $J_n(pa) = 0$.

To show that

$$\bar{f}_n = \frac{p}{2n}\left[(n-1)\bar{f}_{n+1} - (n+1)\bar{f}_{n-1}\right], \text{ i.e.,}$$

To show that

$$H_n\left\{\frac{df}{dx}\right\} = \frac{p}{2n}[(n-1)H_{n+1}\{f(x)\} - (n+1)H_{n-1}\{f(x)\}],$$

where s is a root of the equation $J_n(pa) = 0$.

Proof. The finite Hankel transform of $\dfrac{df}{dx}$ of order n is denoted by

$$H_n\left\{\frac{df}{dx}\right\}.$$

$$H_n\left\{\frac{df}{dx}\right\} = \int_0^a \frac{df}{dx} xJ_n(px)\, dx, \text{ where } p \text{ is a root of } J_n(pa) = 0$$

integrating by parts

$$= \left[f(x) \cdot xJ_n(px)\right]_{x=0}^a - \int_0^a f(x) \frac{d}{dx}\{xJ_n(px)\}\, dx$$

$$= -\int_0^a f(x) \frac{d}{dx} \{xJ_n(px)\}\, dx \qquad \ldots\text{(i)}$$

For $\quad J_n(pa) = 0.$

By Recurrence formula,

$$2J'_n(x) = J_{n-1}(x) - J_{n+1}(x)$$

and $\quad 2n\, J_n(x) = x\, [J_{n-1}(x) + J_{n+1}(x)]$

Replacing x by px in both equations,

$$2J'_n(px) = J_{n-1}(px) - J_{n+1}(px) \qquad \ldots\text{(i)}$$

and $\quad 2n\, J_n(px) = px\, [J_{n-1}(px) + J_{n+1}(px)]. \qquad \ldots\text{(ii)}$

Now $\quad \frac{d}{dx}\{x\, J_n(px)\}$

$$= J_n(px) + px\, J'_n(px)$$

$$= \frac{px}{2n}[J_{n-1}(px) + J_{n+1}(px)] + \frac{px}{2}[J_{n-1}\, px) - J_{n+1}(px)]$$

[This follows from (i) and (ii)].

$$= \frac{px}{2n}[J_{n-1}(px) \cdot (1+n) + (1-n)\, J_{n+1}(px)]$$

Now (i) becomes

$$H_n\left\{\frac{df}{dx}\right\} = -\int_0^a f(x) \cdot \frac{px}{2n}[J_{n-1}(px) \cdot (1+n) + (i-n)\, J_{n+1}(px)]\, dx$$

$$= \frac{p}{2n}\int_0^a [f(x) \cdot x\, J_{n-1}(px) \cdot (1+n) - (n-1)\, f(x)\, x\, J_{n+1}(px)]\, dx$$

$$= \frac{p}{2n}[(1+n)\, H_{n-1}\{f\} - (n-1)\, H_{n-1}\{f\}]$$

$$= \frac{p}{2n}[(n-1)\, H_{n+1}\{f(x)\} - (1+n)\, H_{n-1}\{f\}].$$

Corollary. If $n = 1$, then the last gives

$$H_1\left\{\frac{df}{dx}\right\} = \frac{p}{2}[0 - 2H_0\{f(x)\}] = -p\, H_0\{f(x)\}.$$

9.11 TO FIND TRANSFORM OF

$$\frac{d^2f}{dx^2} + \frac{1}{x}\frac{df}{dx}$$

where s is a root of the equation $J_n(pa) = 0$.

Proof. We know that

$$H_n\left\{\frac{df}{dx}\right\} = \frac{p}{2n}(-n+1)\,H_{n-1}(f) + (n-1)\,H_{n+1}(f)].$$

Replacing f by $\frac{df}{dx}$,

$$H_n\left\{\frac{d^2f}{dx^2}\right\} = \frac{p}{2n}\left[-(n+1)\,H_{n-1}\left(\frac{df}{dx}\right) + (n-1)\,H_{n+1}\left\{\frac{df}{dx}\right\}\right] \quad \ldots\text{(i)}$$

$$H_n\left\{\frac{1}{x}\frac{df}{dx}\right\} = \int_0^a \frac{1}{x}\frac{df}{dx}\cdot x\,J_n(px)\,dx = \int_0^a \frac{df}{dx}\,J_n(px)\,dx \quad \ldots\text{(ii)}$$

By Recurrence formula,

$$2n\,J_n(x) = x\,[J_{n-1}(x) + J_{n+1}(x)]$$

Replacing x by sx,

$$2n\,J_n(px) = px\,[J_{n-1}(px) + J_{n+1}(px)]$$

or

$$J_n(px) = \frac{px}{2n}[J_{n-1}(px) + J_{n+1}(px)].$$

Multiplying by $\frac{df}{dx}$ and then integrating,

$$\int_0^a \frac{df}{dx}\cdot J_n(px)\,dx = \frac{p}{2n}\int_0^a\left[\frac{df}{dx}\cdot x\,J_{n+1}(px) + \frac{df}{dx}\cdot x\,J_{n+1}(px)\right]dx$$

$$= \frac{p}{2n}\left[H_{n-1}\left\{\frac{df}{dx}\right\} + H_{n+1}\left\{\frac{df}{dx}\right\}\right].$$

Using this in (ii),

$$H_n\left\{\frac{1}{x}\frac{df}{dx}\right\} = \frac{p}{2n}\left[H_{n-1}\left\{\frac{df}{dx}\right\} + H_{n+1}\left\{\frac{df}{dx}\right\}\right]. \quad \ldots\text{(iii)}$$

Adding (i) and (iii),

$$H_n\left\{\frac{d^2f}{dx^2} + \frac{1}{x}\frac{df}{dx}\right\}$$

$$= \frac{p}{2n}\left[(-n-1+1)\,H_{n-1}\left\{\frac{df}{dx}\right\} + (n-1+1)\,H_{n+1}\left\{\frac{df}{dx}\right\}\right]$$

$$= \frac{p}{2n}\left[-n\,H_{n-1}\left\{\frac{df}{dx}\right\} + n\,H_{n+1}\left\{\frac{df}{dx}\right\}\right]$$

$$= \frac{p}{2n}\left[-H_{n-1}\left\{\frac{df}{dx}\right\} + H_{n+1}\left\{\frac{df}{dx}\right\}\right].$$

9.12 TO FIND THE HANKEL TRANSFORM OF

$$\frac{d^2f}{dx^2} + \frac{1}{x}\frac{df}{dx} - \frac{n^2}{x^2}f(x)$$

when p is a root of the equation $J_n(ap) = 0$.

Proof. $H_n\left\{\dfrac{d^2f}{dx^2} + \dfrac{1}{x}\dfrac{df}{dx} - \dfrac{n^2}{x^2}f\right\}$

$$= \int_0^a \left(\frac{d^2f}{dx^2} + \frac{1}{x}\frac{df}{dx} - \frac{n^2}{x^2}x\right)\cdot x\cdot J_n(px)\,dx$$

$$= \int_0^a \frac{d^2f}{dx^2}\cdot x\,J_n(px)\,dx + \int_0^a \frac{df}{dx}\cdot J_n(px)\,dx - n^2\int_0^a \frac{f}{x}\cdot J_n(px)\,dx$$

(Integrating first integral by parts)

$$= \left[\frac{df}{dx}xJ_n(px)\right]_0^a - \int_0^a \frac{df}{dx}\cdot\frac{d}{dx}[xJ_n(px)]\,dx + \int_0^a \frac{df}{dx}\cdot J_n(px)\,dx$$

$$- n^2\int_0^a \frac{f}{x}\cdot J_n(px)\,dx$$

$$= 0 - \int_0^a \frac{df}{dx}\cdot[J_n(px) + pxJ_n'(px)]\,dx + \int_0^a \frac{df}{dx}\cdot J_n(px)\,dx - n^2\int_0^a \frac{f}{x}\cdot J_n(px)\,dx.$$

For $\quad J_n(pa) = 0$

$$= -p\int_0^a \frac{df}{dx}\cdot xJ_n'(px)\,dx - n^2\int_0^a \frac{f}{x}\cdot J_n(px)\,dx$$

(Integrating the first integral by parts)

$$= -p\left[f(x)\cdot xJ_n'(px)\right]_0^a + p\int_0^a f(x)\cdot\frac{d}{dx}[xJ_n'(px)]\,dx - n^2\int_0^a \frac{f}{x}\cdot J_n(px)\,dx$$

$$= pf(a) \cdot aJ_n(pa) + p\int_0^a f(x) \cdot [J_n'(px) + pxJ_n''(px)]\, dx - n^2 \int_0^a \frac{f}{dx} \cdot J_n(px)\, dx \quad \ldots \text{(i)}$$

$J_n(x)$ is solution of Bessel differential equation

$$x^2 \frac{d^2y}{dx^2} + x\frac{dy}{dx} + (x^2 - n^2)\, y = 0$$

$$x^2 \frac{d^2 J_n(x)}{dx^2} + x\frac{dJ_n(x)}{dx} + (x^2 - n^2)\, J_n(x) = 0$$

or $$x^2 J_n''(x) + xJ_n'(x) + (x^2 - n^2)\, J_n(x) = 0.$$

Replacing x by sx, we get

$$p^2x^2 J_n''(px) + pxJ_n'(px) + (p^2x^2 - n^2)\, J_n(px) = 0$$

or $$pxJ_n''(px) + J_n'(px) = \left(-px + \frac{n^2}{px}\right) J_n(px).$$

Using this in (i),

$$H_n\left\{\frac{d^2f}{dx^2} + \frac{1}{x}\frac{df}{dx} - \frac{n^2}{x^2}f\right\}$$

$$= -paf(a) \cdot J_n'(pa) + p\int_0^a f(x) \cdot \left[-px + \frac{n^2}{px}\right] J_n(px)\, dx - n^2 \int_0^a \frac{f}{x} \cdot J_n(px)\, dx$$

$$= -paf(a) \cdot J_n'(pa) + p\int_0^a - px \cdot f(x)\, J_n(px)\, dx$$

$$= -paf(a) \cdot J_n'(pa) - p^2 H_n\{f\}.$$

Finally,

$$H_n\left\{\frac{d^2f}{dx^2} + \frac{1}{x}\frac{df}{dx} - \frac{n^2}{x^2}f\right\} = -paf(a)\, J_n'(pa) - p^2 H_n\{f\}.$$

Corollary 1. If $a = 1$, then the last gives

$$H_n\left\{\frac{d^2f}{dx^2} + \frac{1}{x}\frac{df}{dx} - \frac{n^2}{x^2}f\right\} = -pf(1)\, J_n'(p) - p^2 H\{f\}$$

Again if $n = 0$, then the last gives

$$H_n\left\{\frac{d^2f}{dx^2} + \frac{1}{x}\frac{df}{dx}\right\} = -pf(1)\, J_0'(p) - p^2 H_0\{f\}$$

$$= pf(1) \cdot J_1(p) - p^2 H_0 \{f\}.$$

For $\quad \dfrac{d}{dx}\{x^{-n} J_n(x)\} = -x^{-n} J_{n+1}(x).$

ILLUSTRATIVE EXAMPLES

Example 1. *To show that*

$$H_0(c) = \frac{ca}{p} J_1(ap)$$

c being a constant.

or $\quad$ *To show that* $\displaystyle\int_0^a cxJ_0(px)\,dx = \frac{ca}{p} J_1(ap).$

Solution. $\displaystyle H_0\{c\} = \int_0^a cxJ_0(px)\,dx$

$$= c\int_0^a xJ_0(px)\,dx \qquad \ldots \text{(i)}$$

By recurrence formula No. 6,

$$\frac{d}{dx}[x^n J_n(x)] = x^n J_{n-1}(x).$$

Putting $n = 1$, $\dfrac{d}{dx}[xJ_1(x)] = xJ_0(x)$.

Replacing x by px,

$$\frac{d}{pdx}[pxJ_1(px)] = pxJ_0(px)$$

or
$$\frac{d}{dx}\{xJ_1(px)\} = pxJ_0(px).$$

Using this in (i), we get

$$H_0\{c\} = \frac{c}{p}\int_0^a \frac{d}{dx}\{xJ_1(px)\}\,dx = \frac{c}{p}\Big[xJ_1(px)\Big]_0^a$$

$$= \frac{ca}{p} J_1(pa).$$

Example 2. *Find the Hankel transform of x^2 if $xJ_0(px)$ is the kernel of the transform.*

Solution. By recurrence formulae No. (4) and (6),

$$2nJ_n(x) = x\,[J_{n-1}(x) + J_{n+1}(x)],$$

$$\frac{d}{dx}[x^n J_n(x)] = x^n J_{n-1}(x).$$

Replacing x by sx,

$$2nJ_n(px) = px\,[J_{n-1}(px) + J_{n+1}(px)] \qquad \ldots\text{(i)}$$

$$\frac{d}{pdx}[x^n J_n(px)] = x^n J_{n-1}(px). \qquad \ldots\text{(ii)}$$

$$H_0\{x^2\} = \int_0^a x^2 \cdot xJ_0(px)\,dx$$

$$= \int_0^a x^2 \cdot \frac{d}{pdx}\{xJ_1(px)\}\,dx, \text{ according to (ii)}$$

Integrating by parts

$$= \frac{1}{p}\left[x^2 \cdot xJ_1(px)\right]_0^a - \frac{1}{p}\int_0^a 2x \cdot xJ_1(px)\,dx$$

$$= \frac{a^3}{p}J_1(pa) - \frac{2}{p}\int_0^a x^2 J_1(px)\,dx$$

$$= \frac{a^3}{p}J_1(pa) - \frac{2}{p}\int_0^a \frac{d}{pdx}[x^2 J_2(px)]\,dx, \text{ according to (ii)}$$

$$= \frac{a^3}{s}J_1(pa) - \frac{2}{p^2}\left[x^2 J_2(px)\right]_0^a$$

or,

$$H_0\{x^2\} = \frac{a^3}{p}J_1(pa) - \frac{2a^2}{p^2}J_2(pa). \qquad \ldots\text{(iii)}$$

Putting $n = 1$, $x = a$ in (i),

$$2J_1(pa) = pa\,[J_0(pa) + J_2(pa)]$$

or

$$\frac{2}{pa}J_1(pa) - J_0(pa) = J_2(pa).$$

Putting this in (iii),

$$H_0\{x^2\} = \frac{a^3}{p}J_1(pa) - \frac{2a^2}{p^2}\left[\frac{2}{pa}J_1(pa) - J_0(pa)\right]$$

$$= \frac{a^3}{p} J_1(pa) - \frac{4a^2}{p^3 a} J_1(pa) + \frac{2a^2}{p^2} J_0(pa)$$

$$= \frac{a^2}{p^2}\left[\left(ap - \frac{4}{ap}\right) J_1(pa) + 2J_0(pa)\right].$$

Example 3. *Find the finite Hankel transform of x^n, $(n > -1)$ if $xJ_n(sx)$ is the Kernel of the transform.*

Solution. $H_n\{x^n\} = \int_0^a x^n \cdot xJ_n(px)\,dx$

or $$H_n\{x^n\} = \int_0^a x^{n+1} J_n(px)\,dx \qquad \ldots \text{(i)}$$

By Recurrence formula No. (6),

$$\frac{d}{dx}\{x^n J_n(x)\} = x^n J_{n-1}(px)$$

Replacing x by px,

$$\frac{d}{pdx}\{x^n J_n(px)\} = x^n J_{n-1}(px)$$

Replacing n by $n + 1$,

$$\frac{d}{pdx}\{x^{n+1} J_{n+1}(px)\} = x^{n+1} J_n(px).$$

Using this in (i),

$$H_n\{x^n\} = \int_0^a \frac{1}{p}\frac{d}{dx}\{x^{n+1} J_{n+1}(px)\}\,dx$$

$$= \frac{1}{p}\left[x^{n+1} J_{n+1}(px)\right]_0^a$$

$$= \frac{a^{n+1}}{p} J_{n+1}(pa).$$

Example 4. *Show that*

$$\int_0^1 \frac{J_n(ax)}{J_n(a)} \cdot xJ_n(px)\,dx = \frac{p}{a^2 - p^2} J'(p)$$

or

Show that the Hankel transform of

$$\frac{J_n(ax)}{J_n(a)} \text{ of order } n \text{ is } \frac{p}{a^2 - p^2} J_n'(p),$$

where $J_n(p) = 0.$

Solution. Here we take the limit $x = 0$ to $x = 1$ in place of $x = 0$ to $x = a$.

$$H_n\left\{\frac{J_n(ax)}{J_n(a)}\right\} = \int_0^1 \frac{J_n(ax)}{J_n(a)} \cdot x \cdot J_n(px)\, dx. \qquad \ldots(i)$$

$J_n(x)$ is the solution of Bessel differential equation

$$x^2 \frac{d^2y}{dx^2} + x\frac{dy}{dx} + (x^2 - n^2)\, y = 0.$$

$$\therefore \quad x^2 \frac{d^2 J_n(x)}{dx^2} + x\frac{d\, J_n(x)}{dx} + (x^2 - n^2)\, J_n(x) = 0.$$

Replacing x by px,

$$x^2 \frac{d^2}{dx^2} J_n(px) + x\frac{d}{dx} J_n(px) + (p^2x^2 - n^2)\, J_n(px) = 0. \qquad \ldots(ii)$$

Similarly,

$$x^2 \frac{d^2}{dx^2} J_n(ax) + x\frac{d}{dx} J_n(ax) + (a^2x^2 - n^2)\, J_n(ax) = 0. \qquad \ldots(iii)$$

Multiplying (ii) and (iii) by $J_n(ax)$ and $J_n(ax)$ respectively and then subtracting,

$$x^2\left[J_n(ax)\frac{d^2}{dx^2}J_n(px) - J_n(px)\frac{d^2}{dx^2}J_n(ax) + x\, J_n(ax)\frac{d}{dx}J_n(px) - J_n(px)\frac{d}{dx}J_n(ax)\right] + x^2(p^2 - a^2)\, J_n(px)\cdot J_n(ax) = 0$$

or

$$x\,(p^2 - a^2)\, J_n(px)\cdot J_n(ax)$$

$$= x\left[-J_n(ax)\cdot\frac{d^2}{dx^2}J_n(px) + J_n(px)\frac{d^2}{dx^2}J_n(ax)\right] + \left[-J_n(ax)\cdot\frac{d}{dx}J_n(px) + J_n(px)\cdot\frac{d}{dx}J_n(ax)\right]$$

Integrating this from $x = 0$ to $x = 1$, we get

$$\int_0^1 xJ_n(px) \cdot J_n(ax)\, dx$$

$$= \frac{1}{a^2 - p^2} \cdot \left[x\left\{J_n(ax) \cdot \frac{d}{dx} J_n(px) - J_n(px) \cdot \frac{d}{dx} J_n(ax)\right\}\right]_0^1$$

$$= \frac{1}{a^2 - p^2}\left[x\left\{J_n(ax) \cdot pJ_n'(px) - J_n(px)\, aJ_n(ax)\right\}\right]_0^1$$

$$= \frac{1}{a^2 - p^2}[J_n(a) \cdot pJ_n'(p) - J_n(p) \cdot aJ_n'(a)]$$

$$= \frac{p}{a^2 - p^2} J_n(a) \cdot J_n'(p).$$

For $\quad J_n(p) = 0$

or
$$\int_0^1 \frac{xJ_n(px) \cdot J_n(ax)}{J_n(a)}\, dx = \frac{p}{a^2 - p^2} J_n'(p).$$

Using (i), we

$$H_n\left\{\frac{J_n(ax)}{J_n(a)}\right\} = \frac{p}{a^2 - p^2} J_n'(p).$$

Example 5. *Find the finite Hankel transform of* $(1 - x^2)$, *taking* $xJ_0(sx)$ *as the kernel.*

Solution. Here p is a root of $J_0(ap) = 0$.

$$H_0\{(1 - x^2)\} = \int_0^a (1 - x^2)\, xJ_0(px)\, dx$$

$$= \int_0^a [xJ_0(px) - x^3 J_0(px)]\, dx$$

$$= I_1 - I_2 \qquad \ldots(\text{i})$$

where $\quad I_1 = \int_0^a xJ_0(px)\, dx = \int_0^a \frac{1}{p}\frac{d}{dx}[xJ_1(px)]\, dx$

$$\left[\text{For } \frac{d}{dx}[x^n J_n(x)] = x^n J_{n-1}(x)\right]$$

$$= \frac{1}{p}\Big[xJ_1(px)\Big]_0^a = \frac{a}{p}J_1(ap) \qquad \text{...(ii)}$$

$$I_1 = \int_0^a x^3 J_0(px)\,dx = H_0\{x^2\}$$

$$= \frac{a^2}{p^2}\left[\left(ap - \frac{4}{ap}\right)J_1(pa) + 2\cdot J_0(pa)\right] \qquad \text{...(iii)}$$

Writing (i) with the help of (ii) and (iii),

$$H_0\{1 - x^2\} = \frac{a}{p}J_1(ap) - \frac{a^2}{p^2}\left[\left(ap - \frac{4}{as}\right)J_1(pa) + 2J_0(pa)\right]$$

Note. If we take the limit from $x = 0$ to $x = 1$ in place of $x = 0$ and $x = a$, then

$$H_0\{1 - x^2\} = \frac{4}{p^3}J_1(p).$$

This is obtained by putting $a = 1$.

Example 6. *Find the finite Hankel transform of*

$$\frac{1}{r}\cdot\frac{\partial}{\partial r}\left(r\frac{\partial V}{\partial r}\right) - \frac{n^2V}{r^2},$$

where $$V = \begin{cases} 0 & \text{when } r = 0 \\ V_1 & \text{when } r = 1 \end{cases}$$

Solution. From the problem it is clear that we should take the limits $x = 0$ and $x = 1$ of the transform.

Let $$f(r) = \frac{1}{r}\cdot\frac{\partial}{\partial r}\left(r\frac{\partial V}{\partial r}\right) - \frac{n^2V}{r^2}.$$

Then $f(r)$ is expressible as

$$f(r) = \frac{1}{r}\left(\frac{\partial V}{\partial r} + r\frac{\partial^2 V}{\partial r^2}\right) - \frac{n^2V}{r^2}$$

$$= \frac{\partial V}{\partial r^2} + \frac{1}{r}\cdot\frac{\partial V}{\partial r} - \frac{n^2V}{r^2}.$$

By corollary of § 9.12

$$H_n\{f(r)\} = pf(1)\cdot J_1'(p) - p^2 H_n\{f\}$$

$$= pV_1 \cdot J_1'(p) - p^2 H_n\{f\}.$$

Example 7. *Prove that the finite Hankel transform of* $f(x)$, $0 \le x \le 1$ *is* $p^{n-m} J_m(p)$, *where*

$$f(x) = \frac{2^{1+n-m}}{\Gamma(m-n)} \cdot x^n (1+x^2)^{m-n-1}.$$

Solution. $H_n\{f(x)\}$

$$= \int_0^1 f(x) \cdot xJ_n(px)\, dx$$

$$= \int_0^1 \frac{2^{1+n-m}}{\Gamma(m-n)} x^n (1-x^2)^{m-n-1} \cdot xJ_n(px)\, dx$$

$$= \frac{2^{1+n-m}}{\Gamma(m-n)} \int_0^1 x^{n+1} (1-x^2)^{m-n-1} \sum_{r=0}^{\infty} \frac{(-1)^r}{r!\,\Gamma(n+r+1)} \left(\frac{sx}{2}\right)^{n+2r} dx$$

$$= \frac{1}{\Gamma(m-n)} \sum_{r=0}^{\infty} \frac{(-1)^r \cdot p^{n+2r}}{r!\,\Gamma(n+r+1)\cdot 2^{-1+m+2r}} \int_0^1 x^{2(n+r)} (1-x^2)^{m-1-1}\, x\, dx.$$

Putting $x^2 = y$ so that $2x\, dx = dy$

$$= \frac{1}{\Gamma(m-n)} \sum_{r=0}^{\infty} \frac{(-1)^r \cdot p^{n+2r}}{r!\,\Gamma(n+r+1)\cdot 2^{m+2r}} \int_0^1 y^{(n+r+1)^{-1}} (1-y)^{(m-n)^{-1}}\, dy$$

$$= \frac{1}{\Gamma(m-n)} \sum_{r=0}^{\infty} \frac{(-1)^s p^{n+2r}}{r!\,\Gamma(n+r+1)\cdot 2^{m+2r}} B(n+r+1, m-n)$$

$$= \frac{1}{\Gamma(m-n)} \sum_{r=0}^{\infty} \frac{(-1)^r p^{n+2r}}{r!\,\Gamma(n+r+1)\cdot 2^{m+2r}} \cdot \frac{\Gamma(n+r+1)\cdot\Gamma(m-n)}{\Gamma(n+r+1+m-n)}$$

$$= \sum_{r=0}^{\infty} \frac{(-1)^r p^{n+2r}}{r!\cdot 2^{m+2r}\cdot\Gamma(m+r+1)}$$

$$= s^{n-m} \sum_{r=0}^{\infty} \frac{(-1)^r}{r!\,\Gamma(m+r+1)} \cdot \left(\frac{p}{2}\right)^{m+2r}$$

$$= s^{n-m} J_m(p).$$

Example 8. *Use the Hankel transform to solve the differential equation*

$$\frac{\partial^2 V}{\partial r^2} + \frac{1}{r}\frac{\partial V}{\partial r} = \frac{1}{k}\frac{\partial V}{\partial t}, \quad 0 \le r < 1, \quad t > 0$$

where $\dfrac{\partial V}{\partial r} + hV = 0$ *when* $r = 1, t > 0$; $V = 1$ *when* $t = 0, 0 \le r < 1$.

Solution. Let $\bar{V} = \int_0^1 V_r J_0(pr)\,dr$, choosing p as a positive root of the equation

$$pJ'_0(p) + hJ_0(p) = 0.$$

Taking finite Hankel transform of

$$\frac{\partial^2 V}{\partial r^2} + \frac{1}{r}\frac{\partial V}{\partial r} = \frac{1}{k}\frac{\partial V}{\partial t},$$

we get
$$\int_0^1 \frac{\partial^2 V}{\partial r^2} \cdot rJ_0(pr)\,dr + \int_0^1 \frac{1}{r}\frac{\partial V}{\partial r} rJ_0(pr)\,dr = \int_0^1 \frac{1}{k}\frac{\partial V}{\partial t} r \cdot J_0(pr)\,dr \quad \ldots(i)$$

L.H.S. of (i)

$$= \left[\frac{\partial V}{\partial r} rJ_0(pr)\right]_{r=1}^{1} - \int_0^1 \frac{\partial V}{\partial r} \cdot [J_0(pr) + rp\,J_0'(pr)]\,dr + \int_0^1 \frac{\partial V}{\partial r} J_0(pr)\,dr$$

$$= \left[\frac{\partial V}{\partial r} J_0(p)\right]_{r=0}^{1} - \int_0^1 \frac{\partial V}{\partial r} \cdot rp\,J_0'(pr)\,dr \qquad \left[\because\ \frac{\partial V}{\partial r} + hV = 0 \text{ when } r = 1\right]$$

$$= -hJ_0(p)\,V_{r=1} - p\left[\left\{Vr\,J_0'(pr)\right\}_0^1 - \int_0^1 V\,[J'_0(pr) + pr\,J''_0(pr)]\right] dr$$

$$= pJ'_0(p)\,(V)_{r=1} - pJ'_0(p)\,(V)_{r=1} + p\int_0^1 V\,[J'_0(pr) + prJ''_0(pr)]\,dr$$

$$= 0 + p\int_0^1 V[J'_0(pr) + pr\,J''_0(pr)]\,dr.$$

Finally, L.H.S. of (i)

$$= p\int_0^1 V[pr\,J''_0(pr) + J'_0(pr)]\,dr. \qquad \ldots(ii)$$

$J_n(x)$ is the solution of Bessel's equation

$$x^2\frac{d^2y}{dx^2} + x\frac{dy}{dx} + (x^2 - n^2)\,y = 0.$$

$\therefore$ $J_0(x)$ is the solution of

$$x^2\frac{d^2y}{dx^2} + x\frac{dy}{dx} + x^2y = 0,$$

i.e. of $$x\frac{d^2y}{dx^2} + \frac{dy}{dx} + xy = 0.$$

This $$\Rightarrow x\frac{d^2J_0(x)}{dx^2} + \frac{d}{dx}J_0(x) + x\,J_0(x) = 0$$

$$\Rightarrow x\,J''_0(x) + J'_0(px) + x\,J_0(x) = 0$$

Replacing x by sx,

$$px\,J''_0(px) + J'_0(px) + px\,J_0(px) = 0$$

or $$pr\,J''_0(pr) + J'_0(pr) + pr\,J_0(pr) = 0$$

or $$pr\,J''_0(pr) + J'_0(pr) = -pr\,J_0(pr).$$

In this event (ii) becomes

$$\text{L.H.S. of (i)} = p\int_0^1 V[-pr\,J_0(pr)]\,dr$$

$$= -p^2\int_0^1 Vr\,J_0(pr)\,dr = -p^2\overline{V}.$$

Now (i) becomes

$$-p^2\overline{V} = \int_0^1 \frac{1}{k}\frac{\partial V}{\partial t}\cdot r\cdot J_0(pr)\,dr = \frac{1}{k}\frac{d\overline{V}}{dt}$$

or $$\frac{d\overline{V}}{dt} = -kp^2\,\overline{V}$$

The solution of this is

$$\overline{V} = Ae^{-kp^2t} \quad \text{(iii)}$$

or $$\overline{V}(s, t) = Ae^{-kp^2t}$$

This $\Rightarrow (\overline{V})_{t=0} = A$

$$\Rightarrow \int_0^1 (V)_{t=0}\, r J_0(pr)\, dr = A$$

$$\Rightarrow \int_0^1 r J_0(pr)\, dr = A$$

$$\Rightarrow A = \frac{1}{p} J_1(p).$$

Now (iii) becomes

$$\overline{V} = \frac{1}{p} J_1(p)\, e^{-kp^2t}.$$

Applying inversion formula,

$$V = 2 \sum_s e^{-kp^2t} \cdot \frac{p^2}{h^2 + p^2} \cdot \frac{J_1(p)}{p} \cdot \frac{J_0(pr)}{J_0^2(p)}$$

or $$V = 2 \sum_s e^{-kp^2t} \cdot \frac{pJ_1(p)}{h^2 + p^2} \cdot \frac{J_0(pr)}{J_0^2(p)}$$

where the summation is taken over all the positive roots of

$$pJ'_0(p) + hJ_0(p) = 0.$$

Example 9. *Use the Hankel transform to solve the differential equation*

$$\frac{\partial^2 V}{\partial r^2} + \frac{1}{r}\frac{\partial V}{\partial r} = \frac{1}{k}\frac{\partial V}{\partial t},\ 0 \le r < 1,\ t > 0.$$

When $V = V_0$ (constant) when $r = 1$, $t > 0$ and $V = 0$ when $t = 0$, $0 \le r < 1$.

Solution. Let $\overline{V} = \int_0^1 V \cdot rJ_0(pr)\, dr$, where s is a positive root of $J_0(p) = 0$.

Taking the finite Hankel transform of the given differential equation

$$\int_0^1 \frac{\partial^2 V}{\partial r^2} \cdot rJ_0(pr)\, dr + \int_0^1 \frac{1}{r}\frac{\partial V}{\partial r} \cdot J_0(pr)\, dr = \int_0^1 \frac{1}{k}\frac{\partial V}{\partial t} \cdot rJ_0(pr)\, dr.$$

or $$\frac{1}{k}\frac{d\bar{V}}{dt} = \int_0^1 \frac{\partial^2 V}{\partial r^2}\, rJ_0(pr)\, dr + \int_0^1 \frac{\partial V}{\partial r}\cdot J_0(pr)\, dr$$

Integrating first integral by parts

$$= \left[\frac{\partial V}{\partial r}\cdot rJ_0(pr)\right]_0^1 - \int_0^1 \frac{\partial V}{\partial r}\,[J_0(pr)^{-1}\, rpJ_0(pr)]\, dr + \int_0^1 \frac{\partial V}{\partial r}\cdot J_0(pr)\, dr$$

$$= \left(\frac{\partial V}{\partial r}\right)_{r=1} J_0(p) - p\int_0^1 \frac{\partial V}{\partial r}\cdot rJ_0(pr)\, dr$$

$$= 0 - p\left[\left\{VrJ'_0(pr)\right\}_0^1 - \int_0^1 V\,\{J'_0(pr) + rpJ''(pr)\}\, dr\right]$$

For $J_0(p) = 0$

$$= -pV_0J'_0(p) + p\int_0^1 V\,[J'_0(pr) + prJ''(pr)]\, dr. \qquad \ldots(i)$$

$J_n(x)$ is the solution of the Bessel's equation,

$$x^2\frac{d^2y}{dx^2} + x\frac{dy}{dx} + (x^2 - n^2)\, y = 0.$$

$\therefore$ $J_0(x)$ is the solution of

$$x^2\frac{d^2y}{dx^2} + x\frac{dy}{dx} + x^2y = 0$$

or $J_0(x)$ is the solution of

$$x\frac{d^2y}{dx^2} + \frac{dy}{dx} + xy = 0$$

or $$x\frac{d^2}{x^2}J_0(x) + \frac{d}{dx}J_0(x) + x\,J_0(x) = 0$$

or $$x\,J''_0(x) + J'_0(x) + x\,J_0(x) = 0$$

or $$x\,J''_0(x) + J'_0(x) + x\,J_0(x) = 0.$$

Replacing x by px,

$$px\,J''_0(px) + J'_0(px) = -\,px\,J_0(px).$$

Now (i) becomes

$$\frac{1}{k}\frac{d\bar{V}}{dt} = p\,V_0 J_0(p) + p\int_0^1 - pr J_0(pr)\cdot V\,dr$$

$$= -pV_0 J_0(p) - p^2\,\bar{V}$$

or $$\frac{d\bar{V}}{dt} + kp^2\bar{V} = -pV_0 J'_0(p)\cdot k. \qquad \ldots(ii)$$

It is a linear equation

$$\text{I.F.} = e^{\int kp^2\,dt} = e^{ktp^2}$$

Hence the solution of (ii) is

$$\bar{V}\cdot e^{ktp^2} = c - pV_0 J_0(p)\cdot k\int e^{ktp^2}\,dt$$

or $$\bar{V}\cdot e^{ktp^2} = c - \frac{pk\,V_0}{kp^2}J_0(p)\cdot e^{ktp^2}$$

or $$\bar{V} = ce^{-ktp^2} - \frac{V_0}{p}J_0(p). \qquad \ldots(iii)$$

This $\Rightarrow$ $$(\bar{V})_{t=0} = c - \frac{V_0}{p}J_0(p)$$

$$\Rightarrow \int_0^1 (V)_{t=0}\cdot rJ_0(pr)\,dr = c - \frac{V_0}{p}J_0(p)$$

$$\Rightarrow \int_0^1 0\cdot rJ_0(pr)\,dr = c - \frac{V_0}{p}J_0(p)$$

$$\Rightarrow c - \frac{V_0}{p}\cdot J_0(p) = 0 \Rightarrow c = \frac{V_0}{p}J_0(p).$$

Now (iii) becomes

$$\bar{V} = \frac{V_0}{p}\cdot J_0(p)\cdot(e^{-ktp^2} - 1).$$

Applying inversion formula,

$$V = 2\sum_p \frac{V_0}{p}\cdot J_0(p)\cdot(e^{-ktp^2} - 1)\cdot\frac{J_0(pr)}{[J'_0(p)]^2}$$

$$= 2\sum_p \frac{V_0}{p}(e^{-kts^2} - 1)\frac{J_0(pr)}{J_1(p)}$$

For $J_1(p) = -J'_0(p)$

where the summation is taken over all positive roots of

Example 10. *Show that*

$$\int_0^a r^3 J_0(pr)\, dr = \frac{a^2}{p^2}\left[2J_0(pa) + \left(ap - \frac{4}{ap}\right) J_1(pa)\right]$$

Solution. Prove it as in Example 2.

EXERCISE 9(b)

1. Show that $H_0(c) = \frac{ac}{p} J_1(ap)$, c being a constant.

2. Use the Hankel transform to solve the differential equation

$$\frac{\partial^2 F}{\partial r^2} + \frac{1}{r}\frac{\partial F}{\partial r} = \frac{1}{k}\frac{\partial F}{\partial t}, \quad 0 \le r < 1,\ t > 0$$

with $F = F_0$ (constant) when $r = 1$, $t > 0$

and $F = 0$ when $t = 0$, $0 \le r < 1$.

3. Show that

$$\int_0^a r^3 J_0(pr)\, dr = \frac{a^2}{p^2}\left[2J_0(pa) + \left(ap - \frac{4}{ad}\right) J_1(pa)\right]$$

4. (a) Find the finite Hankel transform of

$$\frac{1}{r}\cdot\frac{\partial}{\partial r}\left(r\frac{\partial V}{\partial r}\right) - \frac{n^2 V}{r^2},$$ where $V = 0$, when $r = 0$ and $V = V_1$

when $r = 1$.

(b) Find the Hankel transform of $\frac{\partial^2 f}{\partial t^2}$, where f is a function of x and t.

9.13 MELLIN TRANSFORM

The Mellin transform $f(p)$ of the function $F(x)$ is defined by the equation

$$f(p) = \int_0^\infty F(x)\, x^{s-1}\, dx. \qquad \ldots(i)$$

Putting $\xi = e^x$ and $s = c - i\alpha$ in

$$f(\alpha) = \frac{1}{\sqrt{(2\pi)}} \int_0^{\infty} e^{-t\alpha x} F(x)\, dx, \text{ we obtain}$$

$$f\left(\frac{-p+c}{i}\right) = \frac{1}{\sqrt{(2\pi)}} \int_0^{\infty} \xi^{-c} F(\log \xi)\, \xi^{s-1}\, d\xi. \qquad \ldots\text{(ii)}$$

The same substitutions in

$$F(x) = \frac{1}{\sqrt{(2\pi)}} \int_{-\infty}^{\infty} e^{i\alpha x} f(\alpha)\, d\alpha \text{ yield}$$

$$F(log\ \xi) = \frac{i}{i \cdot \sqrt{(2\pi)}} \int_{c-i\infty}^{c+i\infty} \xi^{i\alpha} f\left(\frac{c-p}{i}\right) ds$$

$$= \frac{1}{[\sqrt{(2\pi)}] \cdot i} \int_{c-i\infty}^{c+i\infty} \xi^{c-p} f\left(\frac{c-p}{i}\right) dp \qquad \ldots\text{(iii)}$$

Now, we assume $g(p) = f\left(\frac{c-p}{i}\right)$

$$= \frac{1}{\sqrt{(2\pi)}} \xi^{-c} F(\log \xi), \text{ so that equations (ii) and (iii) imply}$$

$$g(s) = \int_0^{\infty} G(\xi)\, \xi^{s-1}\, d\xi \qquad \ldots\text{(iv)}$$

and $$G(\xi) = \frac{1}{2\pi i} \int_{c-i\infty}^{c+i\infty} g(p)\, \xi^{-s}\, dp \qquad \ldots\text{(v)}$$

Equations (iv) and (v) give the Mellin-inversion formula and can be stated as follows:

If the integral $\int_0^{\infty} \xi^{k-1} |G(\xi)|\, d\xi$ is bounded for some $k > 0$ and if $g(s) = \int_0^{\infty} G(\xi)\, \xi^{s-1}\, d\xi$ then $G(\zeta) = \frac{1}{2\pi i} \int_{c-i\infty}^{c+i\infty} g(s)\, \zeta^{-s}\, ds$ where $c > k$.

9.14 MELLIN TRANSFORM OF THE DERIVATIVE ($d^r F/dx^r$).

Let M be the Mellin transform operator, then we have

$$M(d^r F/dx^r) = \int_0^{\infty} (d^r F/dx^r)\, x^{p-1}\, dx$$

$$= \left[\left(d^{r-1} F/dx^{r-1}\right) x^{s-1}\right]_0^{\infty} - (p-1) \int_0^{\infty} (d^{r-1} F/dx^{r-1})\, x^{s-2}\, dx$$

$$= -(p-1)\int_0^\infty (d^{r-1}F/dx^{r-1})\,x^{s-1-1}\,dx, \qquad \ldots(i)$$

if F is of such a nature that the square bracket vanishes. This implies $f^r(p) = -(p-1)f^{r-1}(p-1)\ldots$ (i), where $f^r(p)$ denotes the Mellin transform of the derivative $d^r F/dx^r$). Continuing this process until we reach $f^\circ(p)$, we find that

$$f^r(p) = (-1)^r \frac{\Gamma(p)}{\Gamma(p-r)} f(p-r) \qquad \ldots(ii)$$

9.15 FALTUNG THEOREMS FOR MELLIN TRANSFORMS

We have $M\{F(x)\,G(x)\} = \int_0^\infty F(x)\,G(x)\,x^{p-1}\,dx$

$$= \int_0^\infty G(x)\,dx\,x^{p-1}\cdot\frac{1}{2\pi i}\int_{c-i\infty}^{c+i\infty} f(u)\,x^{-u}\,du$$

$$= \frac{1}{2\pi i}\int_{c-i\infty}^{c+i\infty} f(u)\,du\int_0^\infty G(x)\,x^{s-u-1}\,dx$$

(changing the order of integration)

$$= \frac{1}{2\pi i}\int_{c-i\infty}^{c+i\infty} f(u)\,g(p-u)\,du \qquad \ldots(i)$$

putting $p = 1$ in this result, we obtain

$$\int_0^\infty F(x)\,G(x)\,dx = \frac{1}{2\pi i}\int_{c-i\infty}^{c+i\infty} f(u)\,g(1-u)\,du$$

$$= \frac{1}{2\pi i}\int_{c-i\infty}^{c+i\infty} f(p)\,g(1-p)\,dp \qquad \ldots(ii)$$

Again, we also have

$$M\{f(p)\,g(p)\} = \frac{1}{2\pi i}\int_{c-i\infty}^{c+i\infty} f(p)\,g(p)\,x^{-p}\,dp$$

$$= \frac{1}{2\pi i}\int_{c-i\infty}^{c+i\infty} f(p)\,x^{-p}\,ds\int_0^\infty G(\upsilon)\,\upsilon^{s-1}\,d\upsilon$$

$$= \int_0^\infty G(\upsilon)\frac{d\upsilon}{\upsilon}\cdot\frac{1}{2\pi i}\int_{c-i\infty}^{c+i\infty} f(p)\left(\frac{x}{\upsilon}\right)^{-p} dp$$

$$= \int_0^\infty F(x/\upsilon)\,G(\upsilon)\frac{d\upsilon}{\upsilon} \qquad \ldots(iii)$$

In, particular we have

$$\frac{1}{2\pi i}\int_{c-i\infty}^{c+i\infty} f(p)\,g(p)\,dp = \frac{1}{2\pi i}\int_{c-i\infty}^{c+i\infty} f(p)\,dp \int_0^\infty G(\upsilon)\,\upsilon^{s-1}\,d\upsilon$$

$$= \int_0^\infty G(\upsilon)\frac{d\upsilon}{\upsilon}\cdot\frac{1}{2\pi i}\int_{c-i\infty}^{c+i\infty} f(p)\,(1/\upsilon)^{-s}\,dp = \int_0^\infty F(1/\upsilon)\,G(\upsilon)\frac{d\upsilon}{\upsilon} \qquad \ldots\text{(iv)}$$

10

Complex Inversion Integral for Laplace Transforms

10.1 INTRODUCTION

If $L\{F(t)\} = f(p)$ or $\bar{F}(p)$, then

$$L^{-1}\{f(p)\} = F(t) = \frac{1}{2\pi i}\int_{\gamma - i\infty}^{\gamma + i\infty} f(p)\, e^{st}\, dp,\ t > 0 \qquad \ldots\text{(i)}$$

and $F(t) = 0$ for $t < 0$. This result is usually called the *complex inversion integral or formula.* It is also known as *Bromwich's integral formula.* This formula provides a direct means for obtaining the inverse Laplace Transform of a given function $f(s)$. The integration in (i) is to be carried out along the line $s = \gamma + iy$ in the complex plane where $s = x + iy$ and the real number γ is chosen in such a way that $s = \gamma$ always lies to the right of all the singularities (poles, branch points or essential singularities).

As a matter of fact the integral in (i) is evaluated by considering the contour integral $\frac{1}{2\pi i}\int_R e^{pt} f(p)\, dp$ $\qquad \ldots$(ii)

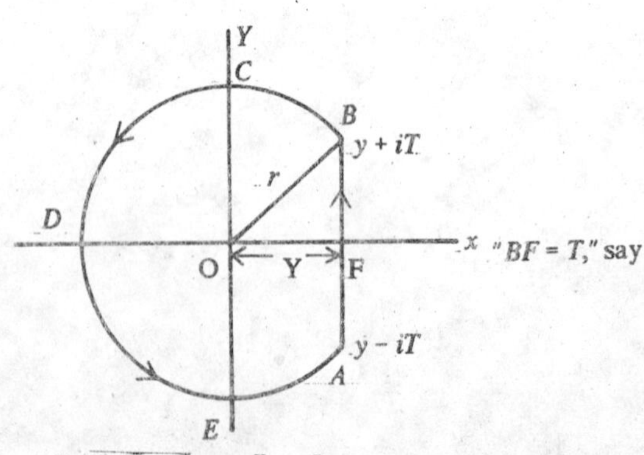

as shown in the diagram. The contour R is known as *Bromwich contour,* and consists of:

(i) a line AB. (ii) are $BCDEA$ of a circle of radius r with centre at the origin O.

Now, let the arc $BCDEA$ be denoted by Γ, then we have

$$F(t) = \lim_{r \to \infty} \frac{1}{2\pi i} \int_{\gamma - iT}^{\gamma + iT} e^{pt} f(p)\, dp$$

$$[\because (r^2 - \gamma^2) = BF^2 = T^2 \text{ say}] \qquad \ldots \text{(iii)}$$

$$= \lim_{r \to \infty} \left\{ \frac{1}{2\pi i} \int_R e^{pt} f(p)\, dp - \frac{1}{2\pi i} \int_\Gamma e^{pt} f(p)\, dp \right\} \qquad \ldots \text{(iii')}$$

10.2 THEOREM

Let Γ denote the curved portion "BCDEFA" of the Bromwich contour with equation $s = re^{i\theta}$, $\theta_0 \le \theta \le 2\pi - \theta_0$ and let on Γ, we have

$$^{*}|f(p)| < (M/r^k),$$

were $k > 0$ and M are constant. Prove that

$$\lim_{r \to \infty} \int_\Gamma e^{pt} f(p)\, dp = 0.$$

Proof. Let Γ_1, Γ_2, Γ_3 and Γ_4 represent arcs BC, CDE, EF and FA respectively. Then we have

$$\int_\Gamma e^{pt} f(p)\, dp = \int_{\Gamma_1} e^{pt} f(p)\, dp + \int_{\Gamma_2} e^{pt} f(p)\, dp$$

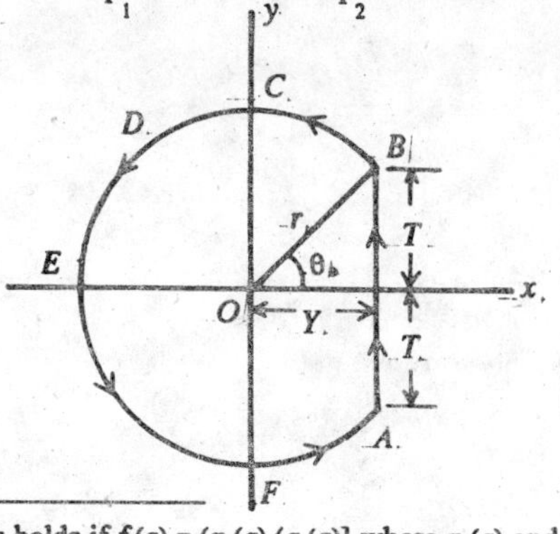

* This condition always holds if $f(s) = (p(s)/q(s)]$ where $p(s)$ and $q(s)$ are polynomials and degree of $p(s)$ <degree of $q(s)$.

$$+\int_{\Gamma_3} e^{pt} f(p)\, dp + \int_{\Gamma_4} e^{pt} f(p)\, dp \qquad \ldots \text{(i)}$$

Now $\displaystyle\int_{\Gamma_1} e^{pt} f(p)\, dp = \int_{\theta_0}^{\pi/2} e^{(r e\, \theta t)} f(re^{\theta i})\, (i\, re^{\theta i}\, d\theta$

$$\Rightarrow \quad \left| \int_{\Gamma_1} e^{pt} f(p)\, dp \right| \le \int_{\theta_0}^{\pi/2} e^{r \cos \theta t} \,\|\, e^{ir \sin \theta t} \,\|f(re^{\theta i})\,\|\, ire^{\theta i} \,|\, d\theta$$

$$\le \int_{\theta_0}^{\pi/2} e^{r \cos \theta t}\, |f(re^{\theta i})|\, r\, d\theta$$

$$\le \frac{M}{r^{k-1}} \int_{\theta_0}^{\pi/2} e^{r \cos \theta t}\, d\theta, \text{ i.e., } \le \frac{M}{r^{k-1}} \int_0^{\phi_0} e^{(r \sin \phi)\, t}\, d\phi \qquad \ldots \text{(A)}$$

[using the given condition $|f(s)| \le (M/r^k)$ on Γ_1 and the transformation $\theta = \frac{\pi}{2} - \phi$ where $\phi_0 = \frac{\pi}{2} - \theta_0 = \sin^{-1}(\gamma/r)$]

Again $\sin \phi \le \sin \phi_0 \le \cos \theta_0 = (\gamma/r)$.

Hence $\displaystyle\frac{M}{r^{k-1}} \int_0^{\phi_0} e^{r \sin \phi t}\, d\phi \le \frac{M}{r^{k-1}} \int_0^{\phi_0} e^{\gamma t}\, d\phi$

$$= \frac{Me^{\gamma t}\, \phi_0}{r^{k-1}} = \frac{Me^{\gamma t}}{r^{k-1}} \sin^{-1}(\gamma/r),$$

and $\displaystyle\left| \int_{\Gamma_1} e^{pt} f(p)\, dp \right| \le \frac{Me^{\gamma t}}{r^{k-1}} \sin^{-1}(\gamma/r)$, which tends to zero as $r \to \infty$.

This implies that $\displaystyle\lim_{r \to \infty} \int_{\Gamma_1} e^{pt} f(p)\, dp = 0.$ $\qquad \ldots$(i)

Also $\displaystyle\int_{\Gamma_2} e^{pt} f(p)\, dp = \int_{\pi/2}^{\pi} re^{\theta i t} f(re^{\theta i})\, (ire^{\theta i})\, d\theta$

$$\left(\because\ p = re^{\theta i},\ \frac{\pi}{2} \le \theta \le \pi\right)$$

Then proceeding as before, we get

$$\left| \int_{\Gamma_2} e^{pt} f(p)\, dp \right| \le \frac{M}{r^{k-1}} \int_{\pi/2}^{\pi} e^{(r \cos \theta)\, t}\, d\theta \le \frac{M}{r^{k-1}} \int_0^{\pi/2} e^{-r \sin \phi t}\, d\phi$$

$$\left[\text{choosing } \theta = \frac{\pi}{2} + \phi\right]$$

But $\sin\phi \geq (2\phi/\pi)$ for $0 \leq \phi \leq \frac{\pi}{2}$, so we have

$$\left|\int_{\Gamma_2} e^{pt} f(p)\, dp\right| \leq \frac{M}{r^{k-1}} \int_0^{\pi/2} e^{-2t\phi(t/\pi)}\, d\phi = \frac{\pi M}{2tr^k}(1 - e^{-rt}), \quad \ldots\text{(ii)}$$

which tends to zero as r tends to infinity.

Similarly, proceeding as for Γ_2, we prove that

$$\left|\int_{\Gamma_3} e^{pt} f(p)\, dp\right| \to 0 \quad \text{as} \quad r \to \infty. \quad \ldots\text{(iii)}$$

Finally, we have

$$\left|\int_{\Gamma_4} e^{pt} f(p)\, dp\right| \to 0 \text{ as } r \to \infty.$$

[Proceeding as for Γ_1] ...(iv)

Combining (i), (ii), (iii) and (iv), we say that

$$\lim_{r \to \infty} \int_{\Gamma} e^{pt} f(p)\, dp = 0.$$

10.3 USE OF RESIDUE THEOREM IN OBTAINING INVERSE LAPLACE TRANSFORMS

Theorem. *Assume that the only singularities of $f(p)$ are poles which all lie to the left of the line $x = \gamma$ for some real constant γ. Assume further that $f(p)$ satisfies the condition given in § 10.2.*

Prove that the inverse Laplace transform of $f(p)$ is given by $F(t)$ = Sum of residues of $e^{pt} f(p)$ at all the poles of $f(p)$.

Proof. We have

$$\frac{1}{2\pi i}\int_R e^{pt} f(p)\, dp = \frac{1}{2\pi i}\int_{\gamma - iT}^{\gamma + iT} e^{pt} f(p)\, dp + \frac{1}{2\pi i}\int_\Gamma e^{pt} f(p)\, dp$$

where R is the Bromwich contour [see figure art 10.1 "ABCDEA" Γ is the circular arc "BCDEA".

By residue theorem, we have

$$\frac{1}{2\pi i}\int_R e^{pt} f(p)\, ds = \Sigma \text{ [residues inside } R]$$

$$= \text{Sum of residues of } e^{pt} f(p) \text{ at all poles of } f(p) \text{ inside } R \quad \ldots\text{(ii)}$$

Using (ii), equation (i) implies

$$\frac{1}{2\pi i}\int_{\Gamma} e^{pt} f(p)\, dp = \Sigma \text{ [residues inside } R] - \frac{1}{2\pi i}\int_{\gamma - iT}^{\gamma + iT} e^{pt} f(p)\, dp$$

or $$\frac{1}{2\pi i}\int_{\gamma - iT}^{\gamma + iT} e^{pt} f(p)\, dp = \Sigma \text{ (residues inside } R) - \frac{1}{2\pi i}\int_{\Gamma} e^{pt} f(p)\, dp \quad \ldots\text{(iii)}$$

Taking limit of (iii) as $r \to \infty$, we obtain

$$\lim_{r \to \infty}\left[\frac{1}{2\pi i}\int_{\gamma - iT}^{\gamma + iT} e^{pt} f(p)\, dp\right]$$

$$= \Sigma \text{ [residues inside } R] - \lim_{r \to \infty}\left[\frac{1}{2\pi i}\int_{\Gamma} e^{pt} f(p)\, dp\right]$$

$$= \Sigma \text{ [residues inside } R] - 0 \qquad \text{[using § 10.2]}$$

i.e. $$F(t) = \Sigma \text{ [residues inside } R] \qquad \textit{[using (iii) of § 10.1]}$$

or $${}^{*}F(t) = \text{Sum of residues of } e^{st} f(s) \text{ at all the poles of } f(s) \quad \ldots\text{(iv)}$$

Note. When $r \to \infty$, T also tends to infinity implying

$$\frac{1}{2\pi i}\int_{\gamma - i\infty}^{\gamma + i\infty} e^{st} f(s)\, ds = F(t).$$

ILLUSTRATIVE EXAMPLES

Example 1. *Prove that* $\sin\theta \geq (2\theta/\pi)$ *for* $0 \leq \theta \leq (\pi/2)$.

Solution. Let $$G(\theta) = \frac{\sin\theta}{\theta} \quad \ldots\text{(i)}$$

$$\Rightarrow \quad \frac{dG}{d\theta} = G'(\theta) = \frac{\theta\cos\theta - \sin\theta}{\theta^2}. \quad \ldots\text{(ii)}$$

Now assume that $\theta\cos\theta - \sin\theta = H(\theta)$, then equation (ii) implies that
$$\frac{dH}{d\theta} = H'(\theta) = -\theta\sin\theta. \quad \ldots\text{(iii)}$$

This shows that $H'(\theta) \leq 0$ for $0 \leq \theta < \frac{\pi}{2}$

i.e. $H'(\theta)$ is negative. ...(iv)

Also $H(\theta)$ is a decreasing function, and

* This result is valid even if $f(s)$ has other singularities besides poles.

$H(0) = 0$, so we have $H(\theta) \leq 0$.

Again from (2), we have $G'(\theta) \leq 0$ or $G(\theta)$ is a decreasing function.

Now defining $G(0) = \lim_{\theta \to 0} G(\theta) = 1$, we see that $G(\theta)$ decreases from 1 to $(2/\pi)$ as θ varies from O to $\frac{\pi}{2}$ implying $1 \geq \frac{\sin\theta}{\theta} \leq \frac{2}{\pi}$.

Aliter.

Geometrical Proof. The curve OBA represents an arc of the sine curve $y = \sin\theta$ and $y = (2\theta/\pi)$ represents the line OB. Then by geometry of the figure it is obvious that $\sin\theta \geq (2\theta/\pi)$ for $O \leq \theta \leq (\pi/2)$.

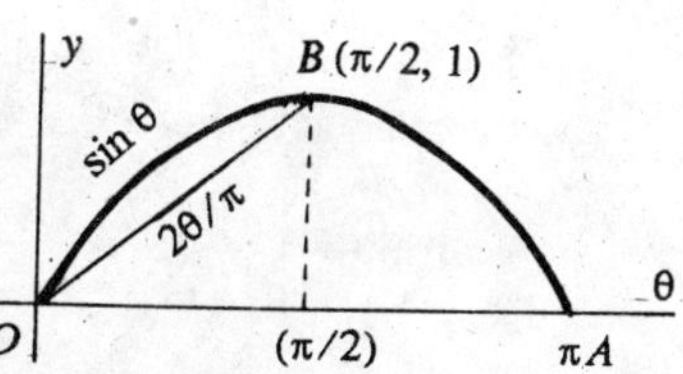

Example 2. *Evaluate* $L^{-1}\left\{\frac{1}{p-2}\right\}$ *by using the complex inversion formula.*

Solution First of all, we shall prove that $f(p) = \frac{1}{p-2}$ satisfies the condition of *Theorem* art 10.1.

$$\left|\frac{1}{p-2}\right| = \left|\frac{1}{re^{\theta i}-2}\right| \leq^{*} \frac{1}{|re^{\theta i}|-2} = \frac{1}{r-2} < \frac{2}{r}$$

for larger values of r $[k = 1, M = 2]$

Secondly, we shall obtain the residue of $e^{it} \cdot \frac{1}{p-2}$ at the pole $p = 2$.

$\therefore$ residue of $e^{pt} \cdot \left(\frac{1}{p-2}\right)$ at the simple pole $(s = 2)$ is

$$\lim_{s \to 2} (s-2) \cdot \frac{e^{pt}}{(p-2)} = e^{2t}$$

Now using *Theorem* art 10.2, we have

$$F(t) = L^{-1}\{f(p)\} = \text{Residue of } e^{pt}\left(\frac{1}{p-2}\right) = e^{2t}.$$

$* \; |a+b| \leq |a| + |b|$

Putting $a = z_1 - z_2$ and $b = z_2$, we get $|z_1| \leq |z_1 - z_2| + |z_2|$

i.e., $|z_1 - z_2| \geq |z_1| - |z_2|$ where z_1 and z_2 are complex quantities.

Example 3. *Evaluate* $L^{-1}\left\{\dfrac{1}{(p^2+1)^2}\right\}$.

Solution. The function $f(p)$ satisfies the conditions of *Theorem* art 10.1.

Now $f(p)=\dfrac{1}{(p^2+1)^2}=\dfrac{1}{[(p+i)(p-i)]^2}=\dfrac{1}{(p+i)^2(p-i)^2}$. Hence the required inverse is the sum of the residues of $\dfrac{e^{st}}{(p+i)^2(p-i)^2}$ ...(I)

at the poles $p=i$ and $p=-i$ which are of order two each.

Now the residue at the pole $p=i$ (of order two) is

$$\lim_{p\to i}\frac{d}{dp}\left[(p-i)^2\frac{e^{pt}}{(p+i)^2(p-i)^2}\right]=-\frac{1}{4}te^{-it}+\frac{1}{4}ie^{it} \quad \text{...(i)}$$

and the residue at the pole $s=-i$ (of order two) is

$$p\to\frac{d}{-idp}\left[(p+i)^2\frac{e^{pt}}{(p+i)^2(p-i)^2}\right]=-\frac{1}{4}te^{-it}+\frac{1}{4}ie^{-it} \quad \text{...(ii)}$$

$$\therefore \quad \Sigma\text{ residues}=-\frac{1}{4}t(e^{it}+e^{-it})-\frac{1}{4}i(e^{ti}-e^{-it})$$

$$=-\frac{1}{2}t\cos t+\frac{1}{2}\sin t=\frac{1}{2}(\sin t-t\cos t)$$

$$\Rightarrow \quad F(t)=L^{-1}\{f(p)\}=\Sigma\text{ residues}=\frac{1}{2}(\sin t-t\cos t).$$

Example 4. *Evaluate* $L^{-1}\left\{\dfrac{1}{(p+1)(p-2)^2}\right\}$ *by using the method of residues.*

Solution. Obviously the function $f(p)=(p+1)^{-1}(p-2)^{-2}$ satisfies the condition of Theorem art 10.1, so we have

$$L^{-1}\left\{\frac{1}{(p+1)(p-2)^2}\right\}=\frac{1}{2\pi i}\int_{\gamma-i\infty}^{\gamma+i\infty}\frac{e^{pt}\,ds}{(p+1)(p-2)^2}$$

$$=\frac{1}{2\pi i}\int_R\frac{e^{pt}\,ds}{(p+1)(p-2)^2}$$

$$=\sum\left[\text{residues of}\left\{\frac{e^{pt}}{(p+1)(p-2)^2}\right\}\text{ at poles }p=-1\text{ and }p=2\right] \quad \text{...(i)}$$

Now the residue at simple pole $p = -1$ is given by

$$\lim_{p \to -1} (p+1) \left\{ \frac{e^{pt}}{(p+1)(p-2)^2} \right\} = \frac{1}{9} e^{-t} \qquad \ldots \text{(i)}$$

and the residue at the double pole $s = 2$ is given by

$$\lim_{p \to 2} \frac{1}{1!} \frac{d}{dp} \left\{ (p-2)^2 \left(\frac{e^{pt}}{(p+1)(p-2)^2} \right) \right\} = \lim_{p \to 2} \frac{d}{dp} \left\{ \frac{e^{pt}}{p+1} \right\}$$

$$= \lim_{p \to 2} \left\{ \frac{(p+1)\, te^{pt} - e^{pt}}{(p+1)^2} \right\} = \left[\frac{1}{3} te^{2t} - \frac{1}{9} e^{2t} \right] \qquad \ldots \text{(ii)}$$

$$\therefore \quad L^{-1} \left\{ \frac{1}{(p+1)(p-2)^2} \right\} = \sum \text{residues} = \frac{1}{9} e^{-t} + \left[\frac{1}{3} te^{2t} - \frac{1}{9} e^{2t} \right].$$

Example 5. *Evaluate* $L^{-1} \left\{ \dfrac{s}{(p+1)^3 (p-1)^2} \right\}$.

Solution. Obviously the function $f(p) = p(p+1)^{-3}(p-1)^{-2}$ satisfies the condition of § 10.2, so we have

$$L^{-1} \left\{ \frac{p}{(p+1)^3 (p-1)^2} \right\} = \frac{1}{2\pi i} \int_{\gamma - i\infty}^{\gamma + i\infty} \frac{pe^{pt}\, dp}{(p+1)^3 (p-1)^2}$$

$$= \frac{1}{2\pi i} \int_R \frac{pe^{pt}\, dp}{(p+1)^3 (p-1)^2}$$

$= \Sigma$ [residues of $\{e^{pt} f(p)\}$ at poles $p = -1$ and $p = 1$ which are of orders three and two respectively].

Now the residue at $p = -1$ is given by ...(i)

$$\lim_{s \to -1} \frac{1}{2!} \left[\frac{d^2}{dp^2} \left\{ (p+1)^3 \frac{pe^{pt}}{(p+1)^3 (p-1)^2} \right\} \right] = \lim_{p \to -1} \frac{1}{2} \left[\frac{d^2}{dp^2} \left\{ \frac{pe^{pt}}{(p-1)^2} \right\} \right]$$

$$= \frac{1}{16} e^{-t} (1 - 2t^2) \qquad \ldots \text{(i)}$$

and the residue at $p = 1$ is given by

$$\lim_{s \to 1} \frac{1}{1!} \left[\frac{d}{dp} \left\{ (p-1)^2 \frac{pe^{pt}}{(p+1)^3 (p-1)^2} \right\} \right] = \lim_{p \to 1} \left[\frac{d}{dp} \left\{ \frac{pe^{pt}}{(p+1)^3} \right\} \right]$$

$$= \frac{1}{16} e^{t} (2t - 1) \qquad \ldots \text{(ii)}$$

$$\Rightarrow \quad F(t) = L^{-1}\left\{\frac{p}{(p+1)^3(p-1)^2}\right\} = \Sigma \text{ [residues]}$$

$$= \frac{1}{16}e^{-t}(1-2t^2) + \frac{1}{16}e^{t}(2t-1).$$

Example 6. *Find the Laplace Transform of the function*

$$F(t) = \frac{e^{at}-1}{a}.$$

Prove, by the method of contour integration that $F(t)$ *is itself the Inverse Laplace Transform of the function arrived at.*

Solution. Let $L\{F(t)\} = \dfrac{1}{p(p-a)} = f(p)$, say.

$$\Rightarrow \quad L^{-1}\{f(p)\} = \frac{1}{2\pi i}\int_{\gamma - i\infty}^{\gamma + i\infty} e^{pt} f(p)\, dp$$

$$= \frac{1}{2\pi i}\int_{\gamma - i\infty}^{\gamma + i\infty} \frac{e^{pt}}{p}\,\frac{dp}{(p-a)}$$

$$= \int_C \frac{e^{pt}\, dp}{p(p-a)}$$

$= $ Sum of residues of $\dfrac{e^{pt}}{p(p-a)}$ at simple poles $p = 0$ and $p = a$

$$= \lim_{p \to 0} \frac{e^{pt}}{p-a} + \lim_{p \to a} \frac{e^{pt}}{p} = -\frac{1}{a} + \frac{e^{at}}{a}$$

$$= \frac{e^{at}-1}{a} = F(t).$$

Example 7. *Use inversion theorem of Laplace transform to solve* $(D^2 + a^2)^2 x = \cos at$ *if* x, Dx, D^2x, D^3x *are zero when* $t = 0$.

Solution. Taking Laplace transform of both sides of the given equation, we get

$$L\{x^{(4)}\} + 2a^2 L\{x''\} + a^4 L\{x\} = L\{\cos at\}$$

$$\Rightarrow \quad p^4 L\{x\} - p^3 x(0) - p^2 x'(0) - px''(0) - x'''(0)$$

$$+ 2a^2 [p^2 L\{x\} - px(0) - x'(0)] + a^4 L\{x\} = \frac{p}{p^2 + a^2}$$

$$\Rightarrow \quad (p^4 + 2a^2 p^2 + a^4)\, L\{x\} = \frac{p}{p^2 + a^2}$$

$$\Rightarrow \quad L\{x\} = \frac{p}{(p^2 + a^2)^3}.$$

$$\Rightarrow \quad x = L^{-1}\left\{\frac{p}{(p^2 + a^2)^3}\right\}$$

$$\Rightarrow \quad x = \frac{1}{2\pi i}\int_{\gamma - i\infty}^{\gamma + i\infty} \frac{pe^{pt}\,dp}{(p^2 + a^2)^3}$$

= Sum of residues of $\dfrac{pe^{pt}}{(p^2 + a^2)^3}$ at the pole $p = ai$ of third order

+ " " " " $p = -ai$ of third order.

$$= \lim_{s \to ai} \frac{1}{2!}\frac{d^2}{dp^2}\left[\frac{pe^{pt}}{(p + ai)^3}\right] + \lim_{p \to -ai} \frac{1}{2!}\frac{d^2}{ds^2}\left[\frac{pe^{pt}}{(p - ai)^3}\right]$$

$$= \lim_{p \to ai} \frac{[-pt + ait - 2 + t(1 + pt)(p + ai)]\,(p + ai) - 4[(1 + pt)(p + ai) - 3p]}{2!\,(p + ai)^5}\, e^{pt}$$

$$+ \lim_{p \to -ai} \frac{[-pt + ait - 2 + t(1 + pt)(p + ai)]\,(p + ai) - 4[(1 + pt)(p - ai) - 3p]}{2!\,(p - ai)^5}\, e^{pt}$$

$$= \frac{[-ait + ait - 2 + t(1 + ait)(2ai)]\,(2ai) - 4[(1 + ait)(2ai) - 3ai]}{2!\,(2ai)^5}\, e^{ait}$$

$$+ \frac{[ait - ait - 2 + t(1 - ait)(-2ai)]\,(-2ai) - 4[(1 - ait)(-2ai) + 3ai]}{2!\,(-2ai)^5}\, e^{-ait}$$

$$= [-2 + t(1 + ait)(2ai) - 2\{2(1 + at) - 3\}]\, e^{ait}$$

$$+ \frac{[-2 + t(1 - ait)(-2ai)\, 2 - \{2(1 - ait) - 3\}]}{2!\,(2ai)^4}\, e^{-ait}$$

$$= \frac{[2ai(t + ait^2) - 4ait]\, e^{ait} + [-2ai(t - ait^2) + 4ait]\, e^{-ait}}{32a^4}$$

$$= \frac{-it \cdot 2i \sin at - at^2 \cdot 2\cos at}{16a^3}$$

$$= \frac{t \sin at - at^2 \cos at}{8a^3}.$$

10.4 INVERSE LAPLACE TRANSFORM OF FUNCTIONS WITH BRANCH POINTS

If $f(s)$ has branch points then *Bromwich contour* (R) is suitably modified, *viz*. if $f(p)$ has only one branch point at the point $p = 0$, then the contour given in the above figure can be used. Here BCD and GHA are the arcs of the circle of radius "r" with centre at O while EKF is the arc of a small circle centred at O of radius $\in$. The procedure will be best understood by studying the following examples.

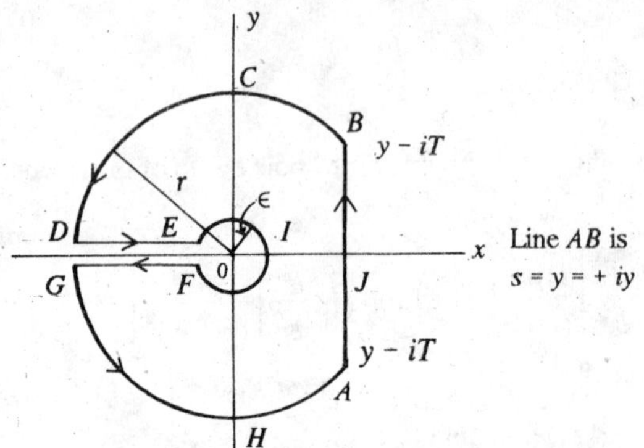

ILLUSTRATIVE EXAMPLES

Example 1. *Evaluate* $L^{-1}\{e^{-a\sqrt{(p)}}/p\}$ *by use of the complex inversion formula.*

Solution. Using complex inversion formula, we have

$$F(t) = \frac{1}{2\pi i}\int_{\gamma + i\infty}^{\gamma + i\infty} \frac{e^{st - a\sqrt{p}}}{p}\,dp \qquad \ldots(i)$$

But the point $p = 0$ is a branch point of $[e^{pt - a\sqrt{p}/p}]$, so modifying the *Bromwich contour* "R", we have

$$\frac{1}{2\pi i}\int_R \frac{e^{pt - a\sqrt{p}}}{p}\,dp = (2\pi i)^{-1}\int_{AB} \frac{e^{pt - a\sqrt{p}}}{p}\,dp + \frac{1}{2\pi i}\int_{BCD} \frac{e^{pt - a\sqrt{p}}}{p}\,dp$$

$$+ \frac{1}{2\pi i}\int_{DE} \frac{e^{pt - a\sqrt{p}}}{p}\,dp + \frac{1}{2\pi i}\int_{EKF} \frac{e^{pt - a\sqrt{p}}}{p}\,dp$$

$$+ \frac{1}{2\pi i}\int_{FG} \frac{e^{pt - a\sqrt{p}}}{p}\,ds + \frac{1}{2\pi i}\int_{GHA} \frac{e^{pt - a\sqrt{p}}}{p}\,dp \qquad \ldots(i)$$

where R is the contour, consisting of the line AB, the arcs BCD and GHA of a circle of radius r and centre at O, and the arc EIF of a circle of radius $\in$ with centre at O. As a matter of fact, the singularity $p = 0$ is not inside R, so $(2\pi i)^{-1} \int_R [e^{pt - a\sqrt{p}}/p]\, dp$ vanishes, by Couchy's residue theorem.

$$\text{Hence}^* \; F(t) = \lim_{\substack{r \to \infty \\ \epsilon \to 0}} \left[\frac{1}{2\pi i} \int_{AB} \frac{e^{pt - a\sqrt{p}}}{p}\, dp\right] = \left[\frac{1}{2\pi i} \int_{\gamma - i\infty}^{\gamma + i\infty} \frac{e^{pt - a\sqrt{p}}}{p}\, dp\right]$$

$$= -\lim_{\substack{r \to \infty \\ \epsilon \to 0}} \frac{1}{2\pi i}\left[\left\{\underbrace{\int_{DE} \frac{e^{pt - a\sqrt{p}}}{p}\, ds}_{\leftarrow \dots I_1 \rightarrow} + \underbrace{\int_{EKF} \frac{e^{pt - a\sqrt{p}}}{p}\, dp}_{\leftarrow \dots I_2 \rightarrow} + \underbrace{\int_{FG} \frac{e^{t - a\sqrt{p}}}{p}\, dp}_{\leftarrow \dots I_4 \rightarrow}\right\}\right] \quad \dots\text{(ii)}$$

Now along DE, $p = xe^{\pi i}$, $\sqrt{p} = \sqrt{xe^{\pi i/2}} = i\sqrt{x}$ and as p goes from $-r$ to $-\varepsilon$, x goes from r to ε.

$$\therefore \quad I_1 = \int_{DE} \frac{e^{pt - a\sqrt{p}}}{p}\, dp = \int_{-r}^{-\varepsilon} \frac{e^{pt - a\sqrt{p}}}{p}\, dp = \int_{r}^{\varepsilon} \frac{e^{-pt - at\sqrt{p}}}{x}\, dp \quad \dots\text{(i)}$$

Along $FG, p = xe^{-\pi i}, \sqrt{p} = \sqrt{xe^{-\pi i/2}} = -i\sqrt{x}$ and as p goes from $-\varepsilon$ to $-r$, x goes from ε to r.

$$\therefore \quad I_3 = \int_{FG} \frac{e^{pt - a\sqrt{p}}}{p}\, dp = \int_{-\varepsilon}^{-r} \frac{e^{pt - a\sqrt{p}}}{p}\, dp = \int_{\varepsilon}^{r} \frac{e^{-xt + ai\sqrt{x}}}{x}\, dx \quad \dots\text{(ii)}$$

Along EKT, $s = \varepsilon e^{\theta i}$.

$$\therefore \quad I_2 = \int_{EKF} \frac{e^{pt - a\sqrt{p}}}{p}\, dp = \int_{\pi}^{-\pi} \frac{e^{\varepsilon e^{\theta i} t - a\sqrt{\varepsilon e^{i\theta/2}}}}{\varepsilon e^{i\theta}}\, i\varepsilon e^{i\theta}\, d\theta$$

$$= i\int_{\pi}^{-\pi} e^{\varepsilon e^{\theta i} t - a\sqrt{\varepsilon e^{i\theta/2}}}\, d\theta \quad \dots\text{(iii)}$$

Substituting these values in (ii), we get

$$F(t) = -\lim_{r \to \infty} \frac{1}{2\pi i}\left[\int_{r}^{\varepsilon} \frac{e^{-xt - ai\sqrt{x}}}{x}\, dx + \int_{\varepsilon}^{r} \frac{e^{-xt + ai\sqrt{x}}}{x}\, dx + i\int_{\pi}^{-\pi} e^{\varepsilon e^{\theta i} t - a\sqrt{\varepsilon e^{(\theta i/2)}}}\, d\theta\right]$$

---

* The integrand satisfies the condition of theorem [art. 10.1]. Further more as $r \to \infty$, the integrals along BCD and GHA tend to zero.

$$= -\lim_{\substack{r \to \infty \\ \epsilon \to 0}} \frac{1}{2\pi i}\left[\int_{\varepsilon}^{\pi} \frac{e^{-xt}(e^{ai\sqrt{x}} - e^{-ai\sqrt{x}}}{x}\,dx + i\int_{\pi}^{-\pi} e^{\varepsilon e^{i\theta} t - a\sqrt{\varepsilon e^{i\theta/2}}}\,d\theta\right]$$

$$= -\lim_{\substack{r \to \infty \\ \epsilon \to 0}} \frac{1}{2\pi i}\left[2i\int_{\varepsilon}^{r} \frac{e^{-xt}\sin a\sqrt{x}}{x}\,dx + i\int_{\pi}^{-\pi} e^{\varepsilon e^{i\theta} t - a\sqrt{\varepsilon e^{i\theta/2}}}\,d\theta\right] \qquad \ldots\text{(iii)}$$

But $$\lim_{\varepsilon \to 0} \int_{\pi}^{-\pi} e^{\varepsilon e^{\theta i} t - a\sqrt{\varepsilon e^{(i\theta/2)}}}\,d\theta = \int_{\pi}^{-\pi} 1\,d\theta = -2\pi, \qquad \ldots\text{(iv)}$$

$\therefore$ $$F(t) = 1 - \frac{1}{\pi}\int_{0}^{\infty} \frac{e^{-xt}\sin a\sqrt{x}}{x}\,dx \qquad \ldots\text{(v)}$$

or $$F(t) = 1 - \operatorname{erf}(a/2\sqrt{t}) = \operatorname{erfc}(a/2\sqrt{t}). \qquad \ldots\text{(vi)}$$

10.5 INVERSE LAPLACE TRANSFORMS OF FUNCTIONS WITH INFINITELY MANY SINGULARITIES

In this case, the curved portion of the *Bromwich contour* is chosen to be of radius r_m such that there exist only a finite number of the singularities inside it and the curved portion does not pass through any singularity. Then taking an appropriate limit as $m \to \infty$, we can find the required inverse "L.T". The procedure will be best understood by studying the following example.

ILLUSTRATIVE EXAMPLES

Example 1. *Evaluate*

$$L^{-1}\left[\frac{\cosh x\sqrt{p}}{p\cosh\sqrt{p}}\right], \text{ where } 0 < x < 1.$$

Solution. First of all, we shall obtain the singularities of $f(s) = \left[\dfrac{\cosh x\sqrt{p}}{p\cosh\sqrt{p}}\right]$, where $0 < x < 1$. $\qquad \ldots$(i)

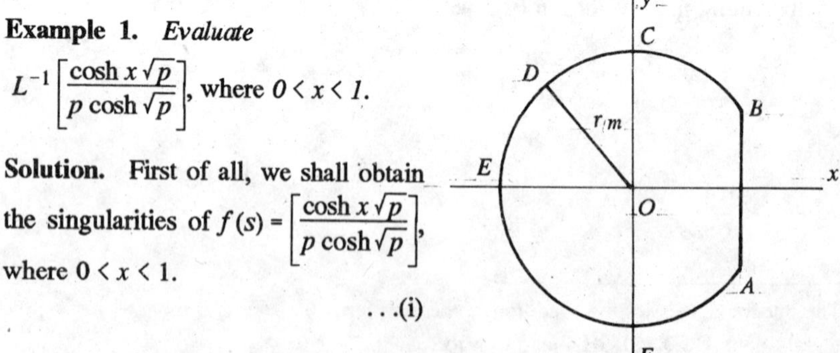

Now, we have

$$f(p) = \frac{\cosh x\sqrt{p}}{p\cosh\sqrt{p}}$$

$$= \frac{1 + [(x\sqrt{p})^2/2!] + [(x\sqrt{p})^4/4!] + \ldots}{p\,[1 + (\sqrt{p})^2/2!] + [(\sqrt{p})^4/4!] + \ldots}$$

$$= \frac{1 + (x^2 p/2!) + (x^4 p^2/4!) + \ldots}{p\,[1 + (p/2!) + (p^2/4!) + \ldots]} \qquad \ldots\text{(ii)}$$

Inspection of $f(p)$ shows that due to the presence of $\sqrt{p}$, there exists a branch point at $p = 0$. But this is not so, as is evident from (ii). However there exists a simple pole at $p = 0$. The function $f(p)$ has infinitely many poles obtained by the roots of the equation $\cosh\sqrt{p} = \frac{1}{2}\left[e^{\sqrt{p}} + e^{-\sqrt{p}}\right] = 0.$ ...(iii)

Equation (iii) implies that

$$e^{2\sqrt{p}} = -1 = e^{\pi i + 2n\pi i};\ n = 0; \pm 1, \pm 2, \ldots$$

i.e., $$\sqrt{p} = \left(n + \frac{1}{2}\right)\pi i \text{ or } p = -\left(n + \frac{1}{2}\right)^2 \pi^2$$

which are simple poles. Hence, we say that $f(s)$ has simple poles at $p = 0$ and $p = p_n$ where $p_n = -\left(n - \frac{1}{2}\right)^2 \pi^2,\ n = 1, 2, 3, \ldots$

Now $L^{-1}\{f(p)\}$ can be obtained by using the *Bromwich Contour.* The line AB is such that all the poles lie to the left of it. Again choose the *Bromwich Contour* so that the curved portion $BCDEFA$ is an arc of the circle Γ_m with centre at O and radius $r_m = m^2\pi^2$, where m is a positive integer. This choice implies that the contour does not pass through any of the poles.

We now find the residues of $e^{pt} f(p) = \dfrac{e^{pt}\cosh x\sqrt{p}}{p\cosh\sqrt{p}}$ at the poles.

Residue at $p = 0$ is, $\lim\limits_{p\to 0}(s - 0)\left\{\dfrac{e^{pt}\cosh x\sqrt{p}}{p\cosh\sqrt{p}}\right\} = 1.$

Residue at $p = -\left(n - \frac{1}{2}\right)^2\pi^2,\ n = 1, 2, 3, \ldots$ is given by

$$\lim_{p\to pn}(p - s_n)\left[\frac{e^{pt}\cosh x\sqrt{p}}{p\cosh\sqrt{p}}\right] = \lim_{p\to p_n}\left[\frac{p - p_n}{\cosh\sqrt{p}}\right] \times \lim_{p\to p_n}\left[\frac{e^{pt}\cosh x\sqrt{p}}{p}\right]$$

$$= \lim_{p \to p_n} \left[\frac{1}{(\sinh \sqrt{p})(1/2\sqrt{p})} \right] \lim_{p \to p_n} \left[\frac{e^{pt} \cosh x\sqrt{p}}{p} \right]$$

$$= \frac{4(-1)^n}{\pi(2n-1)} \left[e^{-\left(n-\frac{1}{2}\right)^2 \pi^2 t} \cos\left(n - \frac{1}{2}\right)\pi x \right]$$

Hence, if C_m denotes the contour of the given figure, then we have

$$\frac{1}{2\pi i} \int_{C_m} \left[\frac{e^{pt} \cosh x\sqrt{p}}{s \cosh \sqrt{p}} \right] dp = 1 + \frac{4}{\pi} \sum_{n=1}^{m} \frac{(-1)^n}{2n-1} e^{-\left(n-\frac{1}{2}\right)^2 \pi^2 t} \times \cos\left(n - \frac{1}{2}\right)\pi x.$$

Now taking the limit as $m \to \infty$ and remembering that the integral around Γ_m tends to zero, we get

$$L^{-1}\left[\frac{\cosh x\sqrt{p}}{p \cosh \sqrt{p}} \right] = 1 + \frac{4}{\pi} \sum_{n=1}^{\infty} \frac{(-1)^n}{2n-1} e^{-\left(n-\frac{1}{2}\right)^2 \pi^2 t} \cos\left(n - \frac{1}{2}\right)\pi x$$

$$= 1 + \frac{4}{\pi} \sum_{n=1}^{\infty} \frac{(-1)^n}{2n-1} e^{-(2n-1)^2 \pi^2 t/4} \cos \frac{(2n-1)\pi x}{2}$$

Example 2. *A semi-infinite beam which is initially at rest on the x axis is at time t = 0 given a transverse displacement h at its end x = 0. Determine the transverse displacement U (x, t) at any position x > 0 and at any time t > 0.*

Solution. The boundary-value problem is given by

$$\frac{\partial^2 U}{\partial t^2} + b^2 \frac{\partial^2 U}{\partial x^4} = 0, \; x > 0, \; t > 0 \qquad \ldots\text{(i)}$$

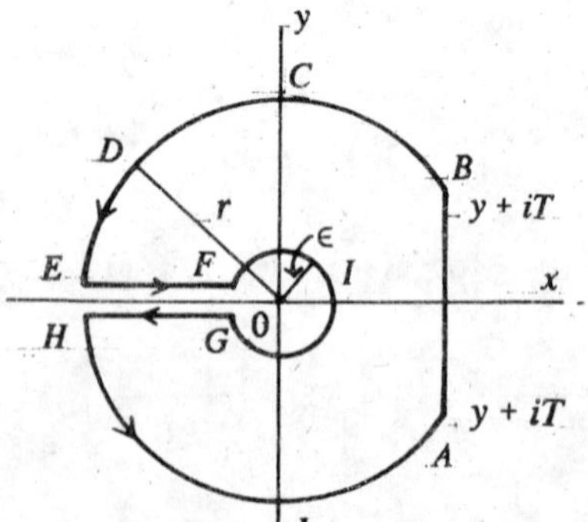

$U(x, 0) = 0.\ U_t(x, 0) = 0,\ U(0, t) = h,\ U_{xx}(0, t) = 0,\ |U(x, t)| < M.$ ...(ii)

Taking Laplace transforms, we obtain

$$p^2 u(x, p) - pU(x, 0) - U_t(x, 0) + b^2 \frac{d^4 u}{dx^4} = 0 \quad \text{or} \quad \frac{d^4 u}{dx^4} + \frac{p^2}{b^2} u = 0 \quad \text{...(iii)}$$

$$u(0, p) = (h/p),\ u_{xx}(0, p) = 0,\ u(x, p) \text{ is bounded.} \quad \text{...(iii)}$$

The general solution of the differential equation is given by

$$u(x, s) = e^{-\sqrt{(p/2b)}\,x} [c_1 \cos \sqrt{(p/2b)}\,x + c_2 \sin \sqrt{(p/2b)}\,x]$$

$$+ e^{-\sqrt{(p/2b)}\,x} [c_3 \cos \sqrt{(p/2b)}\,x + c_4 \sin \sqrt{(p/2b)}\,x$$

Equation (iii)′ $\Rightarrow c_1 = c_2 = 0$ so that

$$u(x, p) = e^{-\sqrt{(p/2b)}\,x} [c_3 \cos \sqrt{(p/2b)}\,x + c_4 \sin \sqrt{(p/2b)}\,x] \quad \text{...(iv)}$$

Using first and second boundary conditions in (iii)′ we find $c_4 = 0$ and $c_3 = (h/p)$

$$\therefore \quad u(x, p) = \frac{h}{p} e^{-\sqrt{(p/2b)}\,x} \cos \sqrt{(p/2b)}\,x \quad \text{...(v)}$$

Hence using complex inversion formula, the required inverse "L.T." is given by

$$U(x, t) = \frac{1}{2\pi i} \int_{\gamma - i\infty}^{\gamma + i\infty} \frac{he^{pt - \sqrt{[p/(2b)]}\,x} \cos \sqrt{(p/2b)}\,x}{p}\, dp \quad \text{...(vi)}$$

Here $p = 0$ is a branch point. Now proceeding as usual we find,

$$U(x, t) = -\lim_{\substack{r \to \infty \\ \epsilon \to 0}} \frac{1}{2\pi i} \left\{\int_{EF} + \int_{FIG} + \int_{GH}\right\} \quad \text{...(vii)}$$

Along $EF, p = pe^{\pi t}, \sqrt{p} = i = s$

$$\therefore \quad \int_{EF} = \int_r^{\varepsilon} \frac{he^{-st - i\sqrt{(s/2b)}\,x} \cosh \sqrt{(s/2b)}\,x}{s}\, ds \quad \text{...(i)}$$

Along $GH, p = se^{-\pi i}, \sqrt{s} = -i\sqrt{s}$

$$\therefore \quad \int_{GH} = \int_{\varepsilon}^{R} \frac{he^{-st + i\sqrt{(s/2b)}\,x} \cosh \sqrt{(s/2b)}\,x}{s}\, ds \quad \text{...(ii)}$$

Along $FIG, p = \varepsilon e^{i\theta}$,

$$\therefore \qquad \int_{FIG} = \int_{\pi}^{-\pi} he^{\varepsilon e^{i\theta} t} \sqrt{(\varepsilon e^{i\theta/2b})\, x} \cos \sqrt{(\varepsilon e^{i\theta}/2b)}\, x\, d\theta \qquad \ldots\text{(iii)}$$

Now equation (vii) implies,

$$U(x, t) = h\left[1 - \frac{1}{\pi}\int_0^{\infty} \frac{e^{-st} \sin \sqrt{(p/2b)}\, x \cosh \sqrt{(p/2b)}\, x}{s}\, ds\right] \quad \ldots\text{(viii)}$$

Putting $(s/2b) = q^2$, we have

$$U(x, t) = h\left[1 - \frac{2}{\pi}\int_0^{\infty} \frac{e^{-2bq^2t} \sin qx \cosh qx}{q}\, dq\right] \qquad \ldots\text{(ix)}$$

Example 3. *An infinitely long circular cylinder of unit radius has a constant initial temperature U_0. At $t = 0$ a temperature of 0°C is applied to the surface and is maintained. Find the temperature at any point of the cylinder at any later time t.*

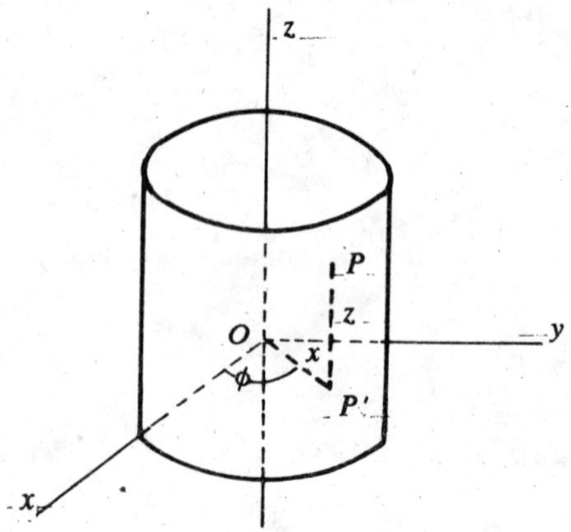

Solution. If (r, ϕ, z) are cylindrical coordinates of any point of the cylinder as shown in the figure, then it is clear the temperature is independent of ϕ and z and can therefore be denoted by $U(r, t)$. The boundary-value problem is

$$\frac{\partial U}{\partial t} = k\left(\frac{\partial^2 U}{\partial r^2} + \frac{1}{r}\frac{\partial U}{\partial r}\right), 0 < r < 1, t > 0 \qquad \ldots\text{(i)}$$

$$U(1, t) = 0,\ U(r, 0) = U_0,\ |U(r, t)| < M \qquad \ldots\text{(ii)}$$

First of all we shall solve

$$\frac{\partial U}{\partial t} = \frac{\partial^2 U}{\partial r^2} + \frac{1}{r}\frac{\partial U}{\partial r} \qquad \ldots\text{(iii)}$$

and then replace t by kt.

Taking Laplace transforms of (iii), we have

$$su - U(r, 0) = \frac{d^2u}{dr^2} + \frac{1}{r}\frac{du}{dr} \text{ or } \frac{d^2u}{dr^2} + \frac{1}{r}\frac{du}{dr} - su = -U_0 \qquad \text{...(iv)}$$

where $u(1, s) = 0$, $u(r, s)$ is bounded. ...(v)

Solving (iv), we get

$$u(r, s) = c_1 J_0(i\sqrt{sr}) + c_2 Y_0(i\sqrt{sr}) + \frac{U_0}{s} \qquad \text{...(vi)}$$

But $Y_0(i\sqrt{sr})$ is unbounded as $r \to 0$, so we chose $c_2 = 0$

$$\Rightarrow \quad u(r, s) = c_1 J_0(i\sqrt{sr}) + \frac{U_0}{s} \qquad \text{...(vii)}$$

Again $u(1, s) = 0$, implies

$$c_1 J_0(i\sqrt{s}) + \frac{U_0}{s} = 0, \text{ i.e. } c_1 = -\frac{U_0}{s J_0(i\sqrt{s})}$$

$$\Rightarrow \quad u(r, s) = \frac{U_0}{s} - \frac{U_0 J_0(i\sqrt{sr})}{s J_0(i\sqrt{s})} \qquad \text{...(viii)}$$

Now using complex inversion formula, we readily obtain

$$U(r, t) = U_0 - \frac{U_0}{2\pi i}\int_{\gamma - i\infty}^{\gamma + i\infty} \frac{e^{st} J_0(i\sqrt{sr})}{s J_0(i\sqrt{s})}\, ds \qquad \text{...(ix)}$$

The function $J_0(i\sqrt{s})$ has simple zeros, where $i\sqrt{s} = \lambda_1, \lambda_2, \ldots \lambda_n, \ldots$ *i.e.* where $s = -\lambda_n^2$, $n = 1, 2, 3, \ldots$

There also exists a pole at $s = 0$.

* Now residue of $e^{st} f(s)$ at $s = 0$ is given by

$$\lim_{s \to 0}\left[s \frac{e^{st} J_0(i\sqrt{sr})}{s J_0(i\sqrt{s})}\right] = 1$$

Also residue of $e^{st} f(s)$ at $s = -\lambda_n^2$ is given by

---

* The function $\frac{e^{st} J_0(i\sqrt{sr})}{s J_0(i\sqrt{s})} = e^{st} f(s)$ satisfies the condition of § 10. 2, hence the method of residues is applicable.

$$\underset{s \to -n^2}{\text{Lim}} \left[(s + \lambda_n{}^2) \frac{e^{st} J_0 (i \sqrt{sr})}{s J_0 (i \sqrt{s})} \right]$$

$$= \left[\underset{s \to -\lambda_n^2}{\text{Lim}} \frac{(s + \lambda_n^2)}{J_0 (i \sqrt{s})} \right] \left[\underset{s \to -\lambda_n^2}{\text{Lim}} \frac{e^{st} J_0 (i \sqrt{sr})}{s} \right]$$

$$= \left[\underset{s \to -\lambda_n^2}{\text{Lim}} \frac{1}{J'_0 (i \sqrt{s}) (i/2 \sqrt{s})} \right] \left[\frac{e^{-\lambda_n^2 t} J_0 (\lambda_n r)}{-\lambda_n^2} \right]$$

$$= \left[\frac{2e^{-\lambda_n^2 t} J_0 (\lambda_n r)}{\lambda_n J_1 (\lambda_n)} \right]$$

[using L'Hospital's rule and $J'_0 (u) = -J_1 (u)$]

$$\therefore \quad U (r, t) = U_0 - U_0 \left[1 - \sum_{n=1}^{\infty} \frac{2e^{-\lambda_n^2 t} J_0 (\lambda_n r)}{\lambda_n J_1 (\lambda_n)} \right]$$

$$= 2U_0 \sum_{n=1}^{\infty} \frac{e^{-k \lambda_n^2 t} J_0 (\lambda_n r)}{\lambda_n J_1 (\lambda_n)}$$

In the end replacing t by kt, we obtain the required solution of (i) as

$$U (r, t) = 2U_0 \left[\sum_{n=1}^{\infty} \frac{e^{-k\lambda_n^2 t} J_0 (\lambda_n r)}{\lambda_n J_1 (\lambda_n)} \right].$$

EXERCISE

1. Use the complex inversion formula to evaluate

   (i) $L^{-1} \left\{ \frac{s}{s^2 + a^2} \right\}$

   (ii) $L^{-1} \left\{ \frac{1}{s^2 + a^2} \right\}$.

2. Evaluate $L^{-1} \left\{ \frac{s^2}{(s^2 + 4)^2} \right\}$ justifying all steps.

3. Use the inversion formula to evaluate $L^{-1}\left\{\frac{s}{(s+a)(s-b)^2}\right\}$ where a and b are any positive constants.
4. Find $L^{-1}\{e^{-\sqrt{s}}\}$ using the complex inversion formula.
5. Find $L^{-1}\left\{\frac{1}{\sqrt{s}}\right\}$ by the inversion formula.
6. Find $L^{-1}\left\{\frac{1}{s(e^s+1)}\right\}$, using the complex inversion formula.
7. Find $L^{-1}\left\{\frac{1}{s^2 \sinh s}\right\}$.
8. A semi-infinite solid $x \geq 0$ is initially at temperature zero. At $t = 0$ the face $x = 0$ is suddenly raised to a constant temperature u_0 and kept at this temperature for a time t_0, after which the temperature is immediately produced to zero. Show that after an additional time t_0 has elapsed, the temperature is a maximum at a distance given by $x = 2\sqrt{(K_0^t \log 2)}$ where k the diffusivity, assumed constant.
9. A semi-infinite solid $x > 0$ has its initial temperature equal to zero. A constant heat flux A is applied at the face $x = 0$ so that $-Ku_x(0, t) = A$. Show that the temperature at the face after time t is $\frac{A}{K}\sqrt{\left(\frac{kt}{\pi}\right)}$
10. Solve the boundary-value problem

$$y_{tt} = y_{xx} + g \quad 0 < x < \pi,\ t > 0$$

$$y(0, t) = 0,\ y(\pi, 0),\ y(x, 0) = \mu x(\pi - x),\ y_t(x, 0) = 0$$

and interpret physically.

ANSWERS

1. (i) $\cos at$, (ii) $\frac{\cos at}{a}$.

2. $\frac{1}{4}\sin 2t + \frac{1}{2}t\cos 2t$.

7. $\frac{1}{2}t^2 + \frac{2}{\pi^2}\sum_{n=1}^{\infty}\frac{(-1)^n}{n^2}(1 - \cos n\pi t)$

10. $y(x, t) = \frac{1}{2}g\,x(\pi - x) + \frac{4}{\pi}(2\mu x - g) \times \sum_{n=1}^{\infty}\frac{\sin(2n-1)x\cos(2n-1)t}{(2n-1)^3}$.

11

Z-Transform

11.1 INTRODUCTION

In general, in communication branch, sampled data received by the control system is not continuous with respect to time but is in the form of pulses occurring at discrete instant of time. In discrete analysis Lapalace and Fourier transforms fail to provide any information. To study the discrete analysis a new transform is introduced, known as Z-transform.

Z-transform operates not on functions of continuous arguments but on sequences of the discrete integer valued arguments. i.e., $n = 0, \pm 1, \pm 2, \ldots$. Sequences that are to be Z-transformed must be defined for $n \geq 0$ and its values for $n < 0$, if any, do not effect the Z-transform .

11.2 Z-TRANSFORM (DEFINITION)

If the function u_n (or a sequence $f(n)$) defined for discrete values ($n = 0, 1, 2, \ldots$) and $u_n = 0$ for $n < 0$, then its Z-transform is defined to be

$$Z(u_n) = \bar{u}(z) = \sum_{n=0}^{\infty} u_n z^{-n}$$

whenever the infinite series converges.

or

$$Z[\{f(n)\}] = \sum_{n=0}^{\infty} f(n)\, z^{-n}$$

11.3 SOME STANDARD Z-TRANSFORMS

Z-transforms of some of the elementary functions can easily be found by the direct application of the definition. The process of finding these may be clear from following examples:

ILLUSTRATIVE EXAMPLES

Example 1: *Find the Z-transform of the sequence* (a^n), $n \geq 0$.

Solution: By Definition,

$$Z(a^n) = \sum_{n=0}^{\infty} a^n z^{-n}$$

$$= 1 + (a/z) + (a/z)^2 + \ldots \text{upto } \infty$$

$$= \frac{1}{1-(a/z)} \qquad \text{(Sum of infinite (G.P.)}$$

$$= \frac{z}{z-a}$$

Example 2: *If* $f(n) = \frac{1}{2n}$, $-4 \leq n < 3$, *then find* $Z|\{f(n)\}|$.

Solution: $= \sum_{n=-4}^{3} 2^{-n} z^{-n}$

$$= 16z^4 + 8z^3 + 4z^2 + 2z + 1 + \frac{1}{2z} + \frac{1}{4z^2} + \frac{1}{8z^3}.$$

Example 3: *Find the Z-transform of* $\{f(n)\}$, *where* $f(n) = \begin{bmatrix} 5^n, & n < 0 \\ 3^n, & n \geq 0 \end{bmatrix}$

Solution: $Z[\{f(n)\}] = \sum_{n=-\infty}^{-1} 5^n z^{-n} + \sum_{n=0}^{\infty} 3^n z^{-n}$

$$= [\ldots + 5^{-3}z^3 + 5^{-2}z^2 + 5^{-1}z^1] + \left[1 + \frac{3}{z} + \frac{9}{z^2} + \frac{27}{z^3} + \ldots\right]$$

$$= [5^{-1}z + 5^{-2}z^2 + 5^{-3}z^3 + \ldots + \text{upto } \infty] + \left[1 + \frac{3}{z} + \frac{3^2}{z^2} + \frac{3^3}{z^3} + \ldots + \text{upto } \infty\right]$$

$$= \frac{5^{-1}z}{1-5^{-1}z} + \frac{1}{1-\frac{3}{z}} = \frac{z}{5-z} + \frac{z}{z-3} \text{ because } \left[\frac{z}{5}\right] < 1, |3/z| < 1$$

$$= \frac{z^2 - 3z + 5z - z^2}{(5-z)(z-3)} = \frac{-2z}{z^2 - 2z + 15}$$

Example 4: *Find the Z-transform of cos (α n), n ≥ 0.*

Solution: $Z[\{\cos(\alpha n)\}] = \sum_{n=0}^{\infty} \cos(\alpha n).z^{-n}$

$$= \sum_{n=0}^{\infty} \left(\frac{e^{i\alpha n} + e^{-i\alpha n}}{2} \right) z^{-n}$$

$$= \frac{1}{2} \sum_{n=0}^{\infty} e^{i\alpha n} z^{-n} + \frac{1}{2} \sum_{n=0}^{\infty} e^{-i\alpha n} z^{-n}$$

$$= \frac{1}{2} \sum_{n=0}^{\infty} (e^{i\alpha} z^{-1})^n + \frac{1}{2} \sum_{n=1}^{\infty} (e^{-i\alpha} z^{-1})^n$$

$$= \frac{1}{2} [1 + (e^{i\alpha} z^{-1}) + (e^{i\alpha} z^{-1})^2 + \text{...upto } \infty]$$

$$+ \frac{1}{2} \{1 + (e^{-i\alpha} z^{-1}) + (e^{-i\alpha} z^{-1})^2 + \text{...upto } \infty]$$

$$= \frac{1}{2} \cdot \frac{1}{(1 - e^{i\alpha} z^{-1})} + \frac{1}{2} \cdot \frac{1}{(1 - e^{-i\alpha} z^{-1})} \qquad \text{(sum of two infinite G.P.)}$$

$$= \frac{1}{2} \cdot \frac{z}{(z - e^{i\alpha})} + \frac{1}{2} \cdot \frac{z}{(z - e^{-i\alpha})}$$

$$= \frac{z}{2} \left[\frac{z - e^{-i\alpha} + z - e^{i\alpha}}{z^2 - z(e^{i\alpha} + e^{-i\alpha}) + 1} \right]$$

$$= \frac{z}{2} \left[\frac{2z - (e^{-i\alpha} + z - e^{-i\alpha})}{z^2 - z(e^{i\alpha} + e^{-i\alpha}) + 1} \right]$$

$$= \frac{z(z - \cos\alpha)}{z^2 - 2z\cos\alpha + 1}$$

Example 5: *Find the Z-transform of sin (α n), n ≥ 0.*

Solution: $Z[\{\sin(\alpha n)\}] = \sum_{n=0}^{\infty} \sin(\alpha n).z^{-n}$

$$= \sum_{n=0}^{\infty}\left(\frac{e^{i\alpha n} - e^{-i\alpha n}}{2i}\right) z^{-n}$$

$$= \frac{1}{2i}\sum_{n=0}^{\infty} e^{i\alpha n} z^{-n} + \frac{1}{2i}\sum_{n=0}^{\infty} e^{-i\alpha n} z^{-n}$$

$$= \frac{1}{2}[1 + (e^{i\alpha}z^{-1}) + (e^{i\alpha}z^{-1})^2 + ...]$$

$$- \frac{1}{2i}\{1 + (e^{-i\alpha}z^{-1}) + (e^{-i\alpha}z^{-1})^2 + ...]$$

$$= \frac{1}{2i} \cdot \frac{1}{(1 - e^{i\alpha}z^{-1})} - \frac{1}{2i} \cdot \frac{1}{(1 - e^{-i\alpha}z^{-1})}$$

$$= \frac{1}{2\mathrm{i}} \cdot \frac{z}{z - e^{i\alpha}} - \frac{1}{2i} \cdot \frac{z}{z - e^{-i\alpha}}$$

$$= \frac{1}{2i}\left[\frac{z(z - e^{-i\alpha}) - z(z - e^{i\alpha})}{(z - e^{i\alpha})(z - e^{-i\alpha})}\right]$$

$$= \frac{1}{2i} \frac{z(e^{i\alpha} - e^{-i\alpha})}{z^2 - z(e^{i\alpha} + e^{-i\alpha}) + 1}$$

$$= \frac{z \sin \alpha}{z^2 - 2z \cos \alpha + 1}$$

Example 6: *Find the* Z [{cosh (α *n*)}].

Solution: $Z[\{\cosh(\alpha n)\}] = \sum_{n=0}^{\infty} \cosh(\alpha n)\, z^{-n}$

$$= \sum_{n=0}^{\infty} \frac{e^{\alpha n} + e^{-\alpha n}}{2} .z^{-n}$$

$$= \frac{1}{2}\sum_{n=0}^{\infty} e^{\alpha n} z^{-n} + \frac{1}{2}\sum_{n=1}^{\infty} e^{-\alpha n} z^{-n}$$

$$= \frac{1}{2}[1 + e^{\alpha}z^{-1} + (e^{\alpha}z^{-1})^2 + ...]$$

$$+ \frac{1}{2}\{1 + e^{-\alpha}z^{-1} + (e^{-\alpha}z^{-1})^2 + ...]$$

$$= \frac{1}{2} \cdot \frac{1}{1 - e^{\alpha} z^{-1}} + \frac{1}{2} \cdot \frac{1}{1 - e^{-\alpha} z^{-1}}$$

$$= \frac{1}{2}\left[\frac{z}{z - e^{\alpha}} + \frac{z}{z - e^{-\alpha}}\right]$$

$$= \frac{z}{2}\left[\frac{z - e^{-\alpha} + z - e^{\alpha}}{z^2 - z(e^{\alpha} + e^{-\alpha})}\right]$$

$$= \frac{z}{2}\left[\frac{2z - (e^{\alpha} + e^{-\alpha})}{z^2 - z(e^{\alpha} + e^{-\alpha}) + 1}\right]$$

$$= \frac{z(z - \cosh \alpha)}{z^2 - 2z \cosh \alpha + 1}$$

Note: Similarly, we can find $Z[\{\sinh(\alpha n)\}] = \dfrac{z \sinh \alpha}{z^2 - 2z \cosh \alpha - 1}$

Example 7: *Find the Z-transform of* $C^n \cos(\alpha n), n > 0$.

Solution: We have $Z\left[\{C^n \cos(\alpha n)\}\right] = \sum_{n=0}^{\infty} [C^n \cos \alpha n]\, z^{-n}$

$$= \sum_{n=0}^{\infty} C^n \left[\frac{e^{i\alpha n} + e^{-i\alpha n}}{2}\right] z^{-n}$$

$$= \sum_{n=0}^{\infty} \left(\frac{1}{2} C^n e^{i\alpha n}\right) z^{-n} + \sum_{n=1}^{\infty} \left(\frac{1}{2} C^n e^{-i\alpha n}\right) z^{-n}$$

$$= \frac{1}{2} \sum_{n=0}^{\infty} (Ce^{i\alpha} z^{-1})^n + \frac{1}{2} \sum_{n=1}^{\infty} (Ce^{-i\alpha} z^{-1})^n$$

$$= \frac{1}{2}\left[1 + (Ce^{i\alpha} z^{-1}) + (Ce^{i\alpha} z^{-1})^2 + \ldots\right]$$

$$+ \frac{1}{2}\left[1 + (Ce^{-i\alpha} z^{-1}) + (Ce^{-i\alpha} z^{-1})^2 + \ldots\right]$$

$$= \frac{1}{2}\left[\frac{1}{1 - Ce^{i\alpha} z^{-1}}\right] + \frac{1}{2}\left[\frac{1}{1 - Ce^{-i\alpha} z^{-1}}\right], |z| > |c|$$

$$= \frac{1}{2}\left[\frac{1 - Ce^{-i\alpha}z^{-1} - Ce^{i\alpha}z^{-1}}{(1 - Ce^{i\alpha}z^{-1})(1 - Ce^{-i\alpha}z^{-1})}\right]$$

$$= \frac{1}{2}\frac{2 - c\,(e^{i\alpha} + e^{-i\alpha})\,z^{-1}}{(1 - Ce^{i\alpha}z^{-1} - Cei\alpha z^{-1} + c^2z^{-2}}$$

$$= \frac{1 - c\cos\alpha\,.\,z^{-1}}{1 - 2cz^{-1}\cos\alpha + c^2z^{-2}}$$

$$= \frac{z^2 - cz\cos\alpha}{z^2 - 2cz\cos\alpha + c^2}$$

Note: Similarly, we can find $Z[\{C^n \sin(\alpha\, n)\}] = \dfrac{c\,z\sin\alpha}{z^2 - 2cz\cos\alpha + c^2}$

Example 8: *Find the value of* $Z[\{C^n \cosh \alpha\, n\}]$ $(n > 0)$.

Solution: $Z[\{c^n \cosh(\alpha\, n)\}] = \sum_{n=0}^{\infty} [c^n \cosh \alpha\, n]\, z^{-n}$

$$= \sum_{n=0}^{\infty} \frac{c^n}{2}(e^{\alpha n} + e^{-\alpha n})\,z^{-n}$$

$$= \frac{1}{2}\sum_{n=0}^{\infty}(ce^{\alpha}z^{-1})^n + \frac{1}{2}\sum_{n=1}^{\infty}(ce^{-\alpha}z^{-1})^n$$

$$= \frac{1}{2}[1 + (ce^{\alpha}z^{-1}) + (ce^{\alpha}z^{-1})^2 + ...]$$

$$+ \frac{1}{2}[1 + (ce^{-\alpha}z^{-1}) + (ce^{-\alpha}z^{-1})^2 + ...]$$

where $|z| > |ce^{\alpha}|, |z| > |ce^{-\alpha}|$

$$= \frac{1}{2}\cdot\frac{1}{1 - ce^{\alpha}z^{-1}} + \frac{1}{2}\frac{1}{1 - ce^{-\alpha}z^{-1}}$$

$$= \frac{1}{2}\cdot\frac{1 - ce^{-\alpha}z^{-1} + 1 - ce^{\alpha}z^{-1}}{(1 - ce^{\alpha}z^{-1})(1 - ce^{-\alpha}z^{-1})}$$

$$= \frac{1}{2}\cdot\frac{2 - c\,(e^{\alpha} + e^{\alpha})\,z^{-1}}{1 + c^2z^{-2} - cz^{-1}(e^{\alpha} + e^{-\alpha})}$$

$$= \frac{1 - (c \cosh \alpha) z^{-1}}{1 - c^2 z^{-2} - 2cz^{-1} \cosh \alpha}$$

$$= \frac{z(z - c \cosh \alpha)}{z^2 + c^2 - 2cz \cosh \alpha}$$

Note: Similarly, $Z[\{C^n \sinh (\alpha n)\}] = \dfrac{c\, z \sinh \alpha}{z^2 + c^2 - 2cz \cosh \alpha}$

Example 9: *Find* $z[\{a^{|n|}\}]$.

Solution:

$$Z[\{a^{|n|}\}] = \sum_{n=-\infty}^{\infty} a^{|n|} z^{-n}$$

$$= \sum_{n=-\infty}^{-1} a^{-n} z^{-n} + \sum_{n=0}^{\infty} a^n z^{-n}$$

$$= [... + a^3 z^3 + a^2 z^2 + az] + [1 + az^{-1} + a^2 z^{-2} + a^3 z^{-3} + ...]$$

$$= [az + a^2 z^2 + a^3 z^3 + ...] + [1 + az^{-1} + a^2 z^{-2} + ...]$$

$$= \frac{az}{1 - az} + \frac{1}{1 - az^{-1}}, \text{ where } |az| < 1 \text{ and } |az^{-1}| < 1$$

$$= \frac{az}{1 - az} + \frac{z}{z - a} = \frac{az^2 - a^2 z + z - az^2}{(1 - az)(z - a)}$$

$$= \frac{z - a^2 z}{(1 - az)(z - a)}$$

Example 10: *Find Z-transform of unit impulse.*

$$\delta(n) = \begin{cases} 1, n = 0 \\ 0, n \neq 0 \end{cases}$$

Solution: $Z[\{\delta(n)\}] = \sum_{n=-\infty}^{\infty} \delta(n) z^{-n}$

$$= [... + 0 + 0 + 1 + 0 + 0 + ...] = 1.$$

Example 11: *Find the Z-transform of discrete unit step function*

$$U(n) = \begin{cases} 0, n < 0 \\ 1, n \geq 0 \end{cases}$$

Solution: $Z[\{U(n)\}] = \sum_{n=-\infty}^{\infty} U(n) z^{-n}$

$$= [1 + z^{-1} + z^{-2} + z^{-3} + ...]$$

$$\frac{1}{1 - z^{-1}} = \frac{z}{1 - z}$$

Example 12: *Find the Z-transform of* $\{^kC_n\}$

Solution: $Z[\{^kC_n\}] = \sum_{n=0}^{\infty} {}^kC_n z^{-n}$

$$= 1 + {}^kC_1 z^{-1} + {}^kC_2 z^{-2} + {}^kC_3 z^{-3} + ... + {}^kC_k z^{-k}$$

$$= (1 + z^{-1})^k$$

Some important result of the above cases can be tabulated as given below:

S.N.	$\{f(n)\}$	$Z\{f(n)\}$
1.	a^n	$(1 - az^{-1})^{-1}$, $\lvert z \rvert > \lvert a \rvert$
2.	$a^{\lvert n \rvert}$	$(1 - a^2)(1 - az)(1 - az^{-1})^{-1}$
3.	$\sin \alpha n$	$\dfrac{z \sin \alpha}{z^2 - 2z \cos \alpha + 1}$, $n \geq 0$
4.	$\cos \alpha n$	$\dfrac{z^2 - z \cos \alpha}{z^2 - 2z \cos \alpha + 1}$, $n \geq 0$
5.	$c^n \sin \alpha n$	$\dfrac{cz \cos \alpha}{z2 - 2cz \cos \alpha + 1}$, $n \geq 0$
6.	$c^n \cos \alpha\, n$	$\dfrac{z^2 - cz \cos \alpha}{z^2 - 2cz \cos \alpha + c^2}$, $n \geq 0$
7.	$\cosh \alpha n$	$\dfrac{z^2 - z \cosh \alpha}{z^2 - 2z \cosh \alpha + 1}$, $n \geq 0$
8.	$\sinh \alpha n$	$\dfrac{z \sinh \alpha}{z^2 - 2z \cosh \alpha + 1}$, $n \geq 0$

9.	$c^n \cosh \alpha n$	$\dfrac{z^2 - cz\cosh\alpha}{z^2 - 2cz\cosh\alpha + c^2}$, $n \geq 0$
10.	${}^kc_n$	$(1 - z^{-1})^k$, $\mid z \mid > 0, 0 \leq n \leq k$
11.	${}^nc_k$	$z^{-k}(1 - z^{-1})^{k+1}$, $\mid z \mid > 1$
12.	$U(n)$ or 1	$(1 - z^{-1})^{-1}$

SOME MORE EXAMPLES

Example 1: *Find Z-transform of* sin $(an + b)$.

Solution: We have

$$Z[\{\sin(an + b)\}] = \sum_{n=0}^{\infty} \sin(an + b)z^{-n}$$

$$= \sum_{n=0}^{\infty} \frac{e^{i(an+b)} - e^{-i(an+b)}}{2i} z^{-n}$$

$$= \frac{1}{2i}\sum_{n=0}^{\infty} e^{i(an+b)}z^{-n} - \frac{1}{2i}\sum_{n=0}^{\infty} - e^{-i(an+b)}z^{-n}$$

$$= \frac{1}{2i} e^{bi}\sum_{n=0}^{\infty}(e^{ai}z^{-1})^n - \frac{1}{2i} e^{-bi}\sum(e^{-ai}z^{-1})^n$$

$$= \frac{1}{2i} e^{bi}[1 + (e^{ai}z^{-1}) + (e^{ai}z^{-1})^2 + ...]$$

$$- \frac{1}{2i} e^{-bi}[1 + (e^{-ai}z^{-1}) + (e^{-ai}z^{-1})^2 + ...]$$

$$= \frac{e^{bi}}{2i} \cdot \frac{1}{1 - e^{ai}z^{-1}} - \frac{1}{2i} e^{-bi} \frac{1}{1 - e^{-ai}z^{-1}}$$

$$= \frac{1}{2i} \cdot \frac{e^{bi}(1 - e^{-ai}z^{-1}) - e^{-bi}(1 - e^{ai}z^{-1})}{(1 - e^{ai}z^{-1})(1 - e^{-ai}z^{-1})}$$

$$= \frac{\dfrac{e^{bi} - e^{-bi}}{2i} - z^{-1}\dfrac{e^{(b-a)i} - e^{-(b-a)i}}{2i}}{1 - (e^{ai} + e^{-ai})z^{-1} + z^{-2}}$$

$$= \frac{\sin b - z^{-1}\sin(b-a)}{1 - (2\cos a)z^{-1} + z^{-2}}$$

$$= \frac{z^2 \sin b - z\sin(b-a)}{z^2 - 2z\cos a + 1}, \quad \text{where } |z| > 1$$

Example 2: *Find the Z-transform of* $\left\{\sin\left(\frac{n\pi}{2} + \alpha\right)\right\}$.

Solution:

$$Z\left\{\sin\left(\frac{n\pi}{2} + \alpha\right)\right\} = \sum_{n=0}^{\infty} \sin\left(\frac{n\pi}{2} + \alpha\right) z^{-n}$$

$$= \sum_{n=0}^{\infty}\left\{\sin\frac{n\pi}{2}\cos\alpha + \cos\frac{n\pi}{2}\sin\alpha\right\} z^{-n}$$

$$= \sum \sin\frac{n\pi}{2}\cos\alpha\, z^{-n} + \sum \cos\frac{n\pi}{2}\sin\alpha\, z^{-n}$$

$$= \cos\alpha \sum \sin\frac{n\pi}{2} z^{-n} + \sin\alpha \sum \cos\frac{n\pi}{2} z^{-n}$$

$$= \cos\alpha \frac{z\sin\dfrac{\pi}{2}}{z^2 - 2z\cos\dfrac{\pi}{2} + 1} + \sin\alpha \frac{z^2 - z\cos\dfrac{\pi}{2}}{z^2 - 2z\cos\dfrac{\pi}{2} + 1}$$

$$= \frac{z\cos\alpha}{z^2 + 1} + \frac{z^2\sin\alpha}{z^2 + 1}$$

$$= \frac{z^2\sin\alpha + z\cos\alpha}{z^2 + 1}$$

Example 3: *Find the Z-transform of* $\sinh\left(\frac{n\pi}{2} + \alpha\right)$.

Solution: We have $Z\left[\left\{\sinh\left(\frac{n\pi}{2} + \alpha\right)\right\}\right] = \sum_{n=0}^{\infty} \sinh\left(\frac{n\pi}{2} + \alpha\right) z^{-n}$

$$= \sum_{n=0}^{\infty} \frac{e^{n\pi/2+\alpha} - e^{-(n\pi/2+\alpha)}}{2} z^{-n}$$

$$= \frac{1}{2}\sum_{n=0}^{\infty} e^{n\pi/2+\alpha} z^{-n} - \frac{1}{2}\sum_{n=0}^{\infty} - e^{-(n\pi/2+\alpha)} z^{-n}$$

$$= \frac{1}{2} e^{\alpha} \sum_{n=0}^{\infty} (e^{\pi/2} z^{-1})^n - \frac{1}{2} e^{-\alpha} \sum_{n=0}^{\infty} (e^{-\pi/2} z^{-1})^n$$

$$= \frac{1}{2} e^{\alpha} [1 + (e^{\pi/2} z^{-1}) + (e^{-\pi/2} z^{-1})^2 + ...]$$

$$- \frac{1}{2} e^{-\alpha} [1 + (e^{-\pi/2} z^{-1}) + (e^{-\pi/2} z^{-1})^2 + ...]$$

$$= \frac{1}{2} e^{\alpha} . \frac{1}{1 - e^{\pi/2} z^{-1}} - \frac{1}{2} e^{-\alpha} \frac{1}{1 - e^{-\pi/2} z^{-1}}$$

$$= \frac{1}{2} \frac{e^{\alpha}(1 - e^{-\pi/2} z^{-1}) - e^{-\alpha}(1 - e^{\pi/2} z^{-1})}{(1 - e^{\pi/2} z^{-1})(1 - e^{-\pi/2} z^{-1})}$$

$$= \frac{\dfrac{e^{\alpha} - e^{-\alpha}}{2} + \dfrac{e^{(\pi/2-\alpha)} - e^{-(\pi/2-\alpha)}}{2} . z^{-1}}{1 - e^{-\pi/2} . z^{-1} - e^{-\pi/2} . z^{-1} + z^{-2}}$$

$$= \frac{\sinh \alpha + \sinh (\pi / 2 - \alpha) z^{-1}}{1 - 2 \cosh (\pi / 2) z^{-1} + z^{-2}}$$

$$= \frac{z^2 \sinh \alpha + z \sinh (\pi / 2 - \alpha)}{z^2 - 2z \cosh (\pi / 2) + 1}$$

Example 4: *Find the Z-transform of* $\left\{\dfrac{a^n}{n!}\right\}, (n \geq 0)$

Solution: We have $Z\left[\left\{\dfrac{a^n}{n!}\right\}\right] = \displaystyle\sum_{n=0}^{\infty} \frac{a^n}{n!} z^{-n}$

$$= \sum_{n=0}^{\infty} \frac{(az^{-1})^n}{n!} = 1 + \frac{az^{-1}}{1!} + \frac{(az^{-1})^2}{2!} + \frac{(az^{-1})^3}{3!} + ... = e^{a/z}$$

Example 5: *Find Z-transform of* ${}^{n+r}C_r$

Solution: We have $Z[\{{}^{n+r}C_r\}] = \sum_{n=0}^{\infty} \{{}^{n+r}C_r\, z^{-n}\}$

$$= \sum_{n=0}^{\infty} {}^{n+r}C_n\, z^{-n} \qquad \left({}^{n}C_r = {}^{n}C_{n-r}\right)$$

$$= 1 + {}^{n+1}C_1\, z^{-1} + {}^{n+2}C_2\, z^{-2} + {}^{n+3}C_3\, z^{-3} + \ldots$$

$$= 1 + (n+1)\, z^{-1} + \frac{(n+2)(n+1)}{2!} z^{-2} + \frac{(n+3)(n+2)(n+1)}{3!} (z^{-3}) + \ldots$$

$$= 1 + (-n-1)(-z^{-1}) + \frac{(-n-1)(-n-2)}{2!}(-z^{-1})^2$$

$$+ \frac{(-n-1)(-n-2)(-n-3)}{3!}(-z^{-1})^3 + \ldots$$

$$= (1-z^{-1})^{-n-1} = (1-z^{-1})^{-(n+1)}$$

EXERCISE 11 (A)

Find the Z-transform of the following for (n > 0)

1. 2^n
2. $\left(\frac{1}{2}\right)^{|n|}$
3. $\sin(3n+5)$
4. $\text{Sinh}\, \frac{n\pi}{2}$
5. $\cos\left(\frac{n\pi}{8} + \alpha\right)$
6. $\cosh\left(\frac{n\pi}{2} + \alpha\right)$
7. $\cos\left(\frac{n\pi}{8} + \frac{\pi}{4}\right)$
8. ${}^{n+r}C_r a^n$

ANSWERS

1. $\frac{z}{z-2};\ |z| > 2$
2. $\frac{3z}{5z - 2 - 2z^2};\ \left|\frac{1}{2}\right| < |z| < 2$
3. $\frac{z^2 \sin 5 - z \sin 2}{z^2 - 2z\cos 3 + 1},\ |z| > 2$
4. $\frac{z \sinh \pi/2}{z^2 - 2z\cosh \pi/2 + 1}$
5. $\frac{z^2 \cos\alpha - z\cos(\pi/8 - \alpha)}{z^2 - 2z\cos \pi/8 + 1}$
6. $\frac{z^2 \cosh\alpha - z\cosh(\pi/2 - \alpha)}{z^2 - 2z\cosh \pi/2 + 1}$
7. $\frac{z^2 - z}{\sqrt{2}(z^2+1)}$
8. $(1 - az^{-1})^{-(n+1)}$

11.4 LINEARITY PROPERTY

If a, b, c be any constants and u_n, v_n, w_n be any discrete functions, then

$$Z(au_n + bv_n - cw_n) = aZ(u_n) + bZ(v_n) - cZ(w_n)$$

By definition,

$$Z(au_n + bv_n - cw_n) = \sum_{n=0}^{\infty} (au_n + bv_n - cw_n) z^{-n}$$

$$= a\sum_{n=0}^{\infty} u_n z^{-n} + b\sum_{n=0}^{\infty} v_n z^{-n} - c\sum_{n=0}^{\infty} w_n z^{-n}$$

$$= aZ(u_n) + bZ(v_n) - cZ(w_n).$$

11.5 CHANGE OF SCALE

If $Z[\{f(n)\}] = F(z)$, then $Z[\{a^n f(n)\}] = F\left(\frac{z}{a}\right)$.

We have $\quad F(z) = Z[\{f(n)\}] = \sum_{n=-\infty}^{\infty} f(n) z^{-n}$

$$\Rightarrow \quad F\left(\frac{z}{a}\right) = \sum_{n=-\infty}^{\infty} f(n)\left(\frac{z}{a}\right)^{-n} \qquad ...(1)$$

Again $\quad Z[\{a^n f(n)\}] = \sum_{n=-\infty}^{\infty} a^n f(n) z^{-n}$

$$= \sum_{n=-\infty}^{\infty} a^n f(n)\left(\frac{z}{a}\right)^{-n} \qquad ...(2)$$

Then from (1) and (2), we have

$$Z[\{a^n f(n)\}] = F\left(\frac{z}{a}\right).$$

11.6 DAMPING RULE

If $Z[\{f(n)\}] = F(z)$, then $Z[\{a^{-n} f(n)\}] = F(az)$.

By definition, $\quad Z[\{a^{-n} f(n)\}] = \sum_{n=0}^{\infty} a^{-n} f(n) z^{-n}$

$$= \sum_{n=0}^{\infty} f(n).(az)^{-n} = F(az).$$

Note: The geometric factor a^{-n} when $|a| < 1$, damps the function $f(n)$, hence, the name damping rule.

11.7 SHIFTING PROPERTY

If $Z[\{f(n)\}] = F(z)$, *then* $Z[\{f(n \pm a)\}] = z^{\pm a} F(z)$.

We have,
$$Z[\{f(n \pm a)\}] = \sum_{n=-\infty}^{\infty} f(n \pm a)\, z^{-n}$$

$$= z^{\pm a} \sum_{n=-\infty}^{\infty} f(n \pm a)\, z^{-(a \pm n)}$$

Putting $r = n \pm a$, we have

$$= z^{\pm a} \sum_{r=-\infty}^{\infty} f(r)\, z^{-r} = z^{\pm a} F(z)$$

11.8 MULTIPLICATION BY *n*.

$$Z[\{f(n)\}] = F(z),$$

$$\Rightarrow \quad Z[\{nF(n)\}] = z \frac{d}{dz} F(z).$$

We have,
$$Z[\{n\, F(n)\}] = \sum_{n=-\infty}^{\infty} n\, f(n)\, z^{-n}$$

$$= -z \sum_{n=-\infty}^{\infty} -n\, f(n)\, z^{-n-1}$$

$$= -z \sum_{n=-\infty}^{\infty} f(n)\, (-nz^{-n-1})$$

$$= -z \sum_{n=-\infty}^{\infty} f(n) \frac{d}{dz} (z^{-n})$$

$$= -z \frac{d}{dz} \sum_{n=-\infty}^{\infty} f(n) z^{-n} = -z \frac{d}{dz} F(z)$$

$$Z[\{n^r f(n)\}] = \left(-z \frac{d}{dz}\right)^r F(z) \qquad \text{[in general]}$$

Cor. 1. If $f(n) = 1$, then

$$Z[\{1\}] = (1 - z^{-1})^{-1}, \; n \geq 0$$

Putting these values in the above theorem (for $n = 1$)

$$Z[\{n\}] = z \frac{d}{dz} (1 - z^{-1})^{-1}$$

$$= z(1 - z^{-1})^{-2} \left(+ \frac{1}{z^2} \right) = z^{-1} (1 - z^{-1})^{-2}.$$

Cor. 2. If $f(n) = 1$, then

$$Z[\{1\}] = (1 - z^{-1})^{-1} = \frac{z}{z - 1}$$

Then for $r = 2$, we have

$$Z[\{n^2\}] = \left(-z \frac{d}{dz} \right)^2 \cdot \frac{z}{z-1}$$

$$= \left(-z \frac{d}{dz} \right) \left(-z \frac{d}{dz} \right) \cdot \frac{z}{z-1}$$

$$= -z \frac{d}{dz} \left[-z \frac{(z-1).1 - z.1}{(z-1)^2} \right]$$

$$= -z \frac{d}{dz} \left[\frac{z}{(z-1)^2} \right]$$

$$= \frac{z(z+1)}{(z-1)^3}.$$

11.9 DIVISION BY *n*.

$$Z[\{f(n)\}] = F(z)$$

$$\Rightarrow \qquad \left[\left\{ \frac{f(n)}{n} \right\} \right] = \int^{z} z^{-1} f(z) \, dz$$

We have,

$$Z \left[\left\{ \frac{f(n)}{n} \right\} \right] = \sum_{n=-\infty}^{\infty} \frac{f(n)}{n} z^{-n}$$

$$= \sum_{n=-\infty}^{\infty} f(n) \left(\frac{1}{n} z^{-n} \right)$$

$$= -\sum_{n=-\infty}^{\infty} f(n)\left\{\int^{z} z^{-n-1}\, dz\right\}$$

$$= \int^{z} \sum_{n=-\infty}^{\infty} f(n)\, z^{-n}\, dz$$

$$= \int^{z} z^{-1} \sum_{n=-\infty}^{\infty} f(n)\, z^{-n}\, dz$$

$$= \int^{z} z^{-1} F(z)\, dz$$

$$\Rightarrow \qquad Z\left[\left\{\frac{f(n)}{n}\right\}\right] = \int^{z} z^{-1} F(z)\, dz.$$

11.10 INITIAL VALUE THEOREM

$$Z\,[\{f(n)\}] = F(z),\ n \geq 0$$

$$\Rightarrow \qquad f(0) = \lim_{z\to\infty} F(z).$$

We have,

$$Z[\{f(n)\}] = \sum_{n=0}^{\infty} f(n)\, z^{-n} = F(z)$$

$$\Rightarrow \qquad f(0) + f(1)\, z^{-1} + f(2)\, z^{-2} + \ldots = F(z)$$

Taking the lim z $\to \infty$, we get

$$f(0) = \lim_{z\to\infty} F(z).$$

11.11 FINAL VALUE THEOREM

$$\lim_{z\to\infty} f(n) = \lim_{z\to 1} (z-1)\, F(z)$$

We have

$$Z\,[\{f(n+1) - f(n)\}] = \sum_{n=0}^{\infty} [f(n+1) - f(n)]\, z^{-n}$$

$$\Rightarrow \quad = z\,F(z) - f(0) - F(x)$$

$$= \lim_{n\to\infty} \sum_{n=0}^{\infty} [f(n+1) - f(n)]\, z^{-n}$$

$$= \lim_{n\to\infty} [(z-1)\,F(z)]$$

$$= f(0)\ \lim_{z\to\infty}\left[\lim_{n\to\infty} \sum [f(n+1) - f(n)]\, z^{-n}\right]$$

By changing the order of limits, we get

$$= \lim_{z\to 1}[(z-1)F(z)]$$

$$= f(0) + \lim_{n\to\infty} \sum_{n=0}^{n} \lim_{z\to 1} [f(n+1) - f(n)]\, z^{-n}$$

$$= \lim_{n\to\infty}\left[f(0) + \sum_{n=0}^{n} [f(n+1) - f(n)]\right]$$

$$= \lim_{n\to 0}[f(0) - f(0) + f(1) + f(2) + \ldots + f(n+1) - f(n)]$$

$$= \lim_{n\to\infty} f(n+1) = \lim_{n\to\infty} f(n).$$

11.12 CONVOLUTION OF TWO SEQUENCES

Let the two sequences be $\{f(n)\}$ and $\{g(n)\}$ and let the convolution of {f(n)} and $\{g(n)\}$ be $\{h(n)\}$; where

$$\{h(n)\} = \{f(n)\} * \{g(n)\}$$

$$= \textit{convolution of } \{f(n)\}, \{g(n)\}$$

$$= \sum_{m=-\infty}^{\infty} f(m)\, g(n-m)$$

$$= \sum_{m=-\infty}^{\infty} g(m)\, f(n-m) = \{g(n)\} * \{f(n)\}$$

$$= \textit{Convolution of } \{g(n)\}, \{f(n)\}$$

Then $\quad Z\{h(n)\} = Z\{f(n)\}.\, Z\{g(n)\}$

We have

$$Z\{h(n)\} = \sum_{n=-\infty}^{\infty}\left(\sum_{m=-\infty}^{\infty} f(m)\, g(n-m)\right) z^{-n}$$

$$= \sum_{m=-\infty}^{\infty}\sum_{n=-\infty}^{\infty} f(m)\, g(n-m)\, z^{-n}$$

$$= \sum_{m=-\infty}^{\infty} f(m)\, z^{-m} \sum_{n=-\infty}^{\infty} g(n-m)\, z^{-(n-m)}$$

$$= \left[\sum_{m=-\infty}^{\infty} f(m)\, z^{-m}\right] G(z)$$

$$= F(z)\, G(z)$$

i.e., $$Z\{h(x)\} = Z\{f(n)\} . Z\{g(n)\}$$

where the region of convergence of $H(z)$ is the common region of convergence of $F(z)$ and $G(z)$.

ILLUSTRATIVE EXAMPLES

Example 1: *Find the Z-transform of a^n, $n \geq 0$.*

Solution: We know that

$$Z[\{1\}] = \frac{z}{z-1}$$

$$Z[\{a^n . 1\}] = \frac{z/a}{z/a-1} = \frac{z}{z-a}$$

Example 2: *Find the Z-transform of c^n, $\cos \alpha n$, $n \geq 0$.*

Solution: We know that $Z[\{\cos\alpha\, n\}] = \dfrac{z^2 - z\cos\alpha}{z^2 - 2z\cos\alpha + 1}$

Then by change of scale property

$$Z\{[c^n \cos\alpha\, n]\} = \frac{\left(\frac{z}{c}\right)^2 - \left(\frac{z}{c}\right)\cos\alpha}{\left(\frac{z}{c}\right)^2 - \left(\frac{z}{c}\right)\cos\alpha + 1}$$

$$= 1 + \frac{z^2 - cz\cos\alpha}{z^2 - 2cz\cos\alpha + c^2}, \qquad k \geq 0$$

Example 3: *Show that* $Z\left[\frac{1}{n!}\right] = e^{1/z}$. *Hence, evaluate* $Z[1/n+1)!]$ *and* $Z[1/n+2)!]$.

Solution: We have

$$Z\left[\frac{1}{n!}\right] = \sum_{n=0}^{\infty} \frac{1}{n!} z^{-n}$$

$$= 1 + \frac{z^{-1}}{1!} + \frac{z^{-2}}{2!} + \frac{z^{-3}}{3!} + \ldots = e^{1/z}$$

Shifting (1/*n*!) one unit to the left, we get

$$Z\left[\frac{1}{(n+1)!}\right] = Z\left[\left(Z\left(\frac{1}{n!}\right) - 1\right)\right]$$

$$= z(e^{1/z} - 1)$$

Similarly, shifting (1/*n*!) two units to the left, we get

$$Z\left[\frac{1}{(n+2)!}\right] = z(e^{1/3} - 1 - z^{-1}).$$

Example 4: *If* $Z[\{f(n)\}] = \frac{2z^2 + 5z + 14}{(z-1)^4}$ *evaluate* $Z\{f(2)\}$ *and* $\{f(3)\}$.

Solution: We have

$$Z[\{f(n)\}] = \frac{2 + 5z^{-1} + 14z^{-2}}{(1 - z^{-1})^4}$$

By initial value theorem.

$$f(0) = \lim_{n\to\infty} Z[\{f(n)\}] = 0$$

Similarly $$f(1) = \lim_{n\to\infty} [z\{Z[f(n)] - f(0)\}] = 0$$

Now, $$f(2) = \lim_{n\to\infty} [z^2 \{Z[f(n)] - f(0) - f(1)z^{-1}\}]$$

$$= 2 - 0 - 0 = 2.$$

and $$f(3) = \lim_{n\to\infty} [z^3 \{Z[f(n)] - f(0) - f(1)z^{-1} - f(2)z^{-2}\}]$$

$$= \lim_{n\to\infty} z^3 [\{Z\{f(n)\} - 0 - 0 - 2z^{-2}]$$

$$= \lim_{n\to\infty} z^3 \left[\frac{2z^2+5z+14}{(z-1)^4} - \frac{2}{z2}\right]$$

$$= \lim_{n\to\infty} z^3 \left[\frac{13z^3+2z^2+8z-2}{z^2\,(z-1)^4}\right] = 13.$$

Example 5: *Evaluate the Z-transform of the sequence*

$$\{f(n)\} = \sum_{n=0}^{\infty} 2^n \sum_{n=0}^{\infty} 3^n$$

Solution: We have

$$Z[\{2^n\}] = 1 + 2z^{-1} + 2^2\, z^{-2} + 2^3\, z^{-3} + ...$$

$$= \frac{1}{1-2z^{-1}}$$

$$Z[\{3^n\}] = \frac{1}{1-3z^{-1}}$$

$$Z[\{f(n)\}] = Z\left(\sum_{n=0}^{\infty} 2^n\right)\left(\sum_{n=0}^{\infty} 3^n\right)$$

$$= Z\,\{2^n\}\,.\,Z\,\{3^n\}$$

$$= \frac{1}{(1-2z^{-1})}\,.\,\frac{1}{(1-3z^{-1})}$$

$$= \frac{1}{(1-2z^{-1})\,(1-3z^{-1})}$$

EXERCISE 11(B)

Find the Z-transform of the following for (n > 0)

1. $\cos 3n$
2. $\sin 5n$
3. $\sin (5n + 3)$
4. $e^{\alpha n}$
5. $3^n \cos 5n$
6. $\cos\left(\frac{n\pi}{5} + 6\right)$

ANSWERS

1. $\dfrac{z(z-\cos 3)}{z^2 - 2z\cos 3 + 1}$ 2. $\dfrac{z\sin 5}{z^2 - 2z\cos 5 + 1}$

3. $\dfrac{z^2 \sin 3 + z\sin 2}{z^2 - 2z\cos 5 + 1}$ 4. $\dfrac{1}{1 - z^{-1} e^{\alpha n}}$

5. $\dfrac{z(z - 3\cosh 5)}{z^2 - 2z\cosh 5 + 9}$ 6. $\dfrac{z^2 \cos 6 - z\cosh(\pi/5 - 6)}{z^2 - 2z\cosh \pi/5 + 1}$

11.13 TABLE OF Z-TRANSFER THEOREM

S. No.	Operation	$f(n)$	$Z\{f(n)\}=F(z)$
1.	Linearity Property	$a f(n) + b g(n)$	$a F(z) + b G(z)$
2.	Change of Scale	$a^n f(n)$	$F(z/a)$
3.	Damping Rule	$a^{-n} f(n)$	$F(az)$
4.	Shifting Property	$f(n \pm a)$	$z^{\pm a} F(z)$
5.	Multiplication by *n*	$n f(n)$	$-z\dfrac{d}{dz}F(z)$
		$n^r f(n)$	$\left(-z\dfrac{d}{dz}\right)^r F(z)$
6.	Division by *n*	$\dfrac{f(n)}{n}$	$-\int^z z^{-1} f(z)\,dz$
7.	Initial Value Theorem	—	$f(0) = \lim\limits_{z\to\infty} F(z)$
8.	Final Value Theorem	—	$\lim\limits_{n\to\infty} f(n) = \lim\limits_{z\to\infty} (z-1) f(z)$

INVERSE OF Z-TRANFORM

11.14 EVALUATION OF INVERSE Z-TRANSFORMS

For inverting $F(z)$, we apply reverse the methods of evaluating $F(z)$. These methods include use of standard formulae and operations rules. Some operational rules of inversion are:

(a) Linearity Property

$$\begin{aligned} Z^{1}[aF(z)+bG(z)] &= \{af(n)+bg(n)\} \\ &= a\{f(n)\}+b\{g(n)\} \\ &= aZ^{-1}\{f(n)\}+bZ^{-1}\{g(n)\} \end{aligned}$$

(b) Change of Scale

$$Z^{-1}F(z/a)=\{a^{n}f(n)\}$$

(c) Shifting Property

$$\begin{aligned} Z^{-1}[z^{\pm a}F(z)] &= f(n\pm a) \\ Z^{-1}[z^{-1}F(z)] &= f(n-1) \\ Z^{-1}[zF(z)-zf(0)] &= f(n+1) \\ Z^{-1}\{z^{2}F(z)-z^{2}f(0)-zf(1)] &= f(n+2) \end{aligned}$$

(d) $Z^{-1}\left[z\frac{d}{dz}F(z)\right]=-\{f(n)\}$

$$Z^{-1}\left(-z\frac{d}{dz}\right)^{r}F(z)=\{n^{r}f(n)\}$$

$$Z^{-1}\left[\int^{z}z^{-1}F(z)\,dz\right]=\left\{\frac{f(n)}{n}\right\}$$

In addition of these methods of long division and power series expansion are used. The method for inverting rational transforms consists of decomposing $F(z)/z$ into partial fractions, multiplying the resulting expansion by z and then inverting the expansion.

1. Division Method

Example 1: *Find* $Z^{-1}\left\{\frac{1}{z-3}\right\}$

Solution: **Case I.** $|z|>3$

$$\frac{1}{3}+\frac{3}{z^2}+\frac{3}{z^3}$$

$$z-3\,\big)\,1$$

$$1-\frac{3}{z}$$

$$\frac{3}{z}$$

$$\frac{3}{z}-\frac{9}{z^2}$$

$$\frac{9}{z^2}$$

$$\frac{9}{z^2}-\frac{27}{z^3}$$

$$\frac{27}{z^3}$$

$$\Rightarrow \qquad \frac{1}{z-3}=\left(\frac{1}{z}+\frac{3}{z^2}+\frac{9}{z^3}\right)+\frac{27/z^3}{z-3}$$

$$=\left(\frac{1}{z}+\frac{3}{z^2}+\frac{9}{z^3}\right)+\frac{27}{z^4}\left(1-\frac{3}{z}\right)^{-1}$$

$$=\left(\frac{1}{z}+\frac{3}{z^2}+\frac{9}{z^3}\right)+\frac{27}{z^4}\left(1-\frac{3}{z}+\frac{9}{z^2}+\ldots\right)$$

$$=z^{-1}+3z^{-2}+9z^{-3}+27z^{-4}+\ldots$$

$$=(3^{n-1}z^{-n})$$

$$\Rightarrow \qquad Z^{-1}\left(\frac{1}{z-3}\right)=(3^{n-1})$$

Case II. $|z| < 3$

$$-\frac{1}{3}-\frac{z}{9}-\frac{z^2}{27}-\frac{z^3}{81}$$

$$-3+z \,\overline{)\,1\qquad\qquad}$$

$$1-\frac{z}{3}$$

$$\frac{z}{3}$$

$$\frac{z}{3}-\frac{z^2}{9}$$

$$-\frac{z^2}{9}$$

$$\frac{z^2}{9}-\frac{z^3}{27}$$

$$-\frac{z^3}{27}$$

$$-\frac{z^3}{27}-\frac{z^4}{81}$$

$$-\frac{z^4}{81}$$

$$\frac{1}{z-3} = -\frac{1}{3}-\frac{z}{9}-\frac{z^2}{27}-\frac{z^3}{81}+\frac{z^4/81}{z-3}$$

$$= -\frac{1}{3}-\frac{z}{9}-\frac{z^2}{27}-\frac{z^3}{81}+\frac{z^4}{243}\left(1+\frac{z}{3}+\frac{z^2}{3^2}+\frac{z^3}{3^3}+\ldots\right)$$

$$= -\frac{1}{3}\left[\left\{1+\frac{z}{3}+\frac{z^2}{3^2}+\frac{z^3}{3^3}+\ldots\right\}+\frac{z^4}{3^4}+\ldots\right]$$

$$= -\frac{1}{3}-\frac{z}{3}-\frac{z2}{32}-\frac{z3}{33}-\ldots-\frac{z^n}{3^{n+1}}-\ldots$$

$$= \{3^{-n-1}\}\, z^n$$

$$\Rightarrow \quad Z^{-1}\left[\frac{1}{z-3}\right] = \{3^{-n-1}\} \text{ for } |z| < 3.$$

BINOMIAL EXPANSION METHOD

Example 1: *Find the inverse z-transform of* $\frac{z}{z-1}$ *when* (*i*) $|z|>|a|$

(*ii*) $|z|<|a|$.

Solution: **Case I.** When $|z|>|a|$

We have $$\frac{z}{z-a} = \frac{z}{z}\left(1-\frac{a}{z}\right)^{-1}$$

$$= \left[1+\frac{a}{z}+\frac{a^2}{z^2}+\frac{z^3}{z^3}+ ....\right], \quad \text{when } \left|\frac{a}{z}\right|<1$$

$$= 1 + az^{-1} + a^2z^{-2} + a^3z^{-3} + ... + a^nz^{-n} + ...$$

$$= \left[a^n\right]z^{-n}$$

$$Z^{-1}\left[\frac{z}{z-a}\right] = \{a^n\}$$

Case II. When $|z|<|a|$

We have $$\frac{z}{z-a} = \frac{1}{a}\frac{z}{\left(1+\frac{z}{a}\right)}$$

$$= \frac{z}{a}\left(1-\frac{z}{a}\right)^{-1}$$

$$= \frac{z}{a}\left(1-\frac{z}{a}+\frac{z^2}{a^2}+...\right)$$

$$= \frac{z}{a}-\frac{z^2}{a^2}-\frac{z^3}{a^3}-\frac{z^4}{a^4}-...$$

$$\Rightarrow \quad f(n) = Z^{-1}\left(\frac{z}{z-a}\right) = \left\{...\frac{1}{a^4}, -\frac{1}{a^3}, -\frac{1}{a^2}, -\frac{1}{a}\right\} \quad \text{when } \left|\frac{z}{a}\right|<1$$

3. Partial Fractions

Given fraction is changed into simple fractions by the usual methods of partial Fractions. Then by linearity property the inverse Z-transform may be found as the sum or difference of the inverse Z-transforms of the simple fractions.

ILLUSTRATIVE EXAMPLES

Example 1: *Find the inverse Z-transform of* $\dfrac{1}{(z-3)(z-4)}$, *when (i)* $|z| < 3$ *(ii)* $3 < |z| < 4$ *(iii)* $|z| > 4$.

Solution:

$$F(z) = \frac{1}{(z-3)(z-4)} = \frac{A}{z-4} + \frac{B}{z-3}$$

$$\Rightarrow \qquad F(z) = \frac{1}{z-4} - \frac{1}{z-3}.$$

Case (i) When $|z| < 3$.

We have $$F(z) = -\frac{1}{4}\left(1-\frac{z}{4}\right)^{-1} + \frac{1}{3}\left(1-\frac{z}{3}\right)^{-1}$$

$$= -\frac{1}{4}\left[1+\frac{z}{4}+\frac{z^2}{4^3}+\frac{z^3}{4^3}+\ldots\right] + \frac{1}{3}\left[1+\frac{z}{3}+\frac{z^2}{3^3}+\frac{z^3}{3^3}+\ldots\right]$$

$$= \left[-\frac{1}{4}-\frac{z}{4^2}-\frac{z^2}{4^3}-\frac{z^3}{4^4}+\ldots\right] + \left[\frac{1}{3}+\frac{z}{3^2}+\frac{z^2}{3^3}+\frac{z^3}{3^4}+\ldots\right]$$

$$= \{-4^{-n-1}\}\,z^n + \{3^{-n-1}\}\,z^n$$

$$Z^{-1}[F(z)] = -\{4^{-n-1}\} + \{3^{-n-1}\}$$

Case (ii) When $3 < |z| < 4$.

$$F(z) = \frac{-1}{4}\,\frac{1}{\left(1-\frac{z}{4}\right)} - \frac{1}{z}\,\frac{1}{\left(1-\frac{3}{z}\right)}$$

$$= -\frac{1}{4}\left[1-\frac{z}{4}.\right]^{-1} - \frac{1}{z}\left[1-\frac{3}{z}\right]^{-1}$$

$$= -\frac{1}{4}\left(1+\frac{z}{4}+\frac{z^2}{4^2}+\frac{z^3}{4^3}+\ldots\right) - \frac{1}{2}\left(1+\frac{z}{z}+\frac{z^2}{z^2}+\frac{z^3}{z^3}+\ldots\right)$$

$$= \left(-\frac{1}{4}-\frac{z}{4^2}-\frac{z^2}{4^3}-\frac{z^3}{4^4}-\ldots\right) - \left(\frac{1}{z}+\frac{3}{z^2}+\frac{3^2}{z^3}+\frac{3^3}{z^4}+\ldots\right)$$

$$= \ldots - \frac{z^3}{4^4} - \frac{z^2}{4^3} - \frac{z}{4^2} - \frac{1}{4} - \frac{1}{z} - \frac{3}{z^2} - \frac{3^2}{z^3} - \frac{3^3}{z^4}\ldots$$

$$= \ldots - \frac{z^3}{4^4} - \frac{z^2}{4^3} - \frac{z}{4^2} - \frac{1}{4} - z^{-1} - 3z^{-2} - 3^2 z^{-3} - 3^3 z^{-4} - \ldots$$

$$= \{-3^{n-1}\} z^n, n > 0$$

$$= \{-4^{n-1}\} z^{-n}, \ n \leq 0$$

$$\therefore \quad Z^{-1}\{F(z)\} = \{-3^{n-1}\}, n > 0$$

$$= \{-4^{n-1}\}, n \leq 0.$$

Case (iii) $|z| < 4$.

We have $F(z) = \frac{1}{z} \cdot \frac{1}{1 - \frac{4}{z}} - \frac{1}{z} \cdot \frac{1}{1 - \frac{3}{z}}$

$$= \frac{1}{z}\left(1 - \frac{4}{z}\right)^{-1} - \frac{1}{z}\left(1 - \frac{3}{z}\right)^{-1}$$

$$= \frac{1}{z}\left(1 + \frac{4}{z} + \frac{4^2}{z^2} + \frac{4^3}{z^3} + \ldots\right) - \frac{1}{2}\left(1 + \frac{3}{z} + \frac{3^2}{z^2} + \frac{3^3}{z^3} + \ldots\right)$$

$$= \{4^{n-1} - 3^{n-1}\} z^{-k}, k > 0$$

$$= 0, \qquad n \leq 0$$

$$\therefore \quad Z^{-1}\{[F(z)]\} = 4^{n-1} - 3^{n-1}, \ n > 0$$

$$= 0, \qquad n \leq 0.$$

Example 2: *Obtain* $Z^{-1}\left\{\frac{1}{\left(z - \frac{1}{3}\right)\left(z - \frac{1}{4}\right)}\right\}$ *when* (*i*) $\frac{1}{4} < |z| < \frac{1}{3}$; (*ii*) $\frac{1}{3} < |z|$.

Solution: We have

$$F(z) = \frac{1}{\left(z - \frac{1}{3}\right)\left(z - \frac{1}{4}\right)} = 12\left[\frac{1}{\left(z - \frac{1}{3}\right)} \frac{1}{\left(z - \frac{1}{4}\right)}\right]$$

$$= \frac{12}{\left(z - \frac{1}{3}\right)} - \frac{12}{\left(z - \frac{1}{4}\right)}$$

Case (i).

$$F(z) = \frac{12}{-\frac{1}{3}(1-3z)} - \frac{1}{z}\frac{12}{\left(1-\frac{1}{4}z^{-1}\right)}$$

$$= 36\,(1-3z)^{-1} - \frac{12}{z}\left(1-\frac{1}{4}z^{-1}\right)$$

$$= -36\,[1 + 3z + 3^2z^2 + 3^3z^3 + \ldots + 3^nz^n + \ldots]$$

$$-\left(\frac{12}{z}\right)\left[1 + \frac{1}{4}z^{-1} + \frac{1}{4^2}z^{-2} + \frac{1}{4^3}z^{-3} + \ldots + \frac{1}{4^n}z^{-n} + \ldots\right]$$

where $|3z| < 1$ and $\left|\frac{1}{4z}\right| < 1$, *i.e.*, $\frac{1}{4} < |z| < \frac{1}{3}$.

$$Z^{-1}\{F(z)\} = -\frac{12}{4^{n-1}}, \text{ if } n > 0$$

$$= -36 \times 3^{-n}, \text{ if } n < 0.$$

Case (ii). $\frac{1}{3} < |z|$

$$F(z) = \frac{12}{z-\frac{1}{3}} - \frac{12}{z-\frac{1}{4}} = \frac{1}{z}\frac{12}{\left(1-\frac{1}{3z}\right)} - \frac{1}{z}\frac{12}{\left(1-\frac{1}{4z}\right)}$$

$$= 12z^{-1}\left(1-\frac{1}{3}z^{-1}\right)^{-1} - 12z^{-1}\left(1-\frac{1}{4}z^{-1}\right)^{-1}$$

$$= 12z^{-1}\left[1 + \frac{1}{3}z^{-1} + \left(\frac{1}{3}\right)^2 z^{-2} + \left(\frac{1}{3}\right)^3 z^{-3} + \ldots\right]$$

$$-12z^{-1}\left[1 + \frac{1}{4}z^{-1} + \left(\frac{1}{4}\right)^2 z^{-2} + \left(\frac{1}{4}\right)^3 z^{-3} + \ldots\right]$$

$$= 12\left[z^{-1} + \frac{1}{3}z^{-2} + \left(\frac{1}{3}\right)^2 z^{-3} + \left(\frac{1}{3}\right)^3 z^{-4} + \ldots\right]$$

$$-12\left[z^{-1} + \frac{1}{4}z^{-2} + \left(\frac{1}{4}\right)^2 z^{-3} + \left(\frac{1}{4}\right)^3 z^{-4} + \ldots\right]$$

$$= 12\left\{\frac{1}{3^{n-1}}\right\}z^{-n} - 12\left\{\frac{1}{4^{n-1}}\right\}z^{-n}$$

$$\therefore \quad Z^{-1}\{F(z)\} = 12\left\{\frac{1}{3^{n-1}} - \frac{1}{4^{n-1}}\right\},\ n \geq 1.$$

Example 3: *Obtain* $Z^{-1}\left\{\frac{2z^2 - 10z + 13}{(z-3)^2 (z-2)}\right\}$ *when* $2 < |z| < 3$.

Solution: We have

$$F(z) = \frac{2z^2 - 10z + 13}{(z-3)^2 (z-2)} = \frac{A}{(z-3)^2} + \frac{B}{z-3} + \frac{C}{z-2}$$

Converting it into partial fraction, we have

$$F(z) = \frac{1}{(z-3)^2} + \frac{1}{z-3} + \frac{1}{z-2}$$

$$= \frac{1}{9}\frac{1}{\left(1-\frac{z}{3}\right)^2} - \frac{1}{3}\frac{1}{\left(1-\frac{z}{3}\right)} + \frac{1}{2}\frac{1}{\left(1-\frac{2}{z}\right)}$$

$$= \frac{1}{9}\left(1-\frac{z}{3}\right)^{-2} - \frac{1}{3}\left(1-\frac{z}{3}\right)^{-1} + \frac{1}{z}\left(1-\frac{2}{z}\right)^{-1}$$

$$= \frac{1}{9}\left[1 + \frac{2z}{3} + 3.\frac{z^2}{9} + 4.\frac{z^3}{27} + \ldots\right] - \frac{1}{3}\left[1 + \frac{z}{3} + \frac{z^2}{9} + \frac{z^3}{27} + \ldots\right]$$

$$+ \frac{1}{z}\left[1 + \frac{2}{z} + \frac{4}{z^2} + \frac{8}{z^3} + \ldots\right]$$

where $|z/3| > 1, |2/z| < 1$, *i.e.*, $2 < |z| < 3$.

$$\text{Then, } F(z) = \left\{\frac{1}{3^2} + \frac{2z}{3^3} + 3.\frac{z^2}{3^4} + 4.\frac{z^3}{3^5} + \ldots\right\} - \left\{\frac{1}{3} + \frac{z}{3^2} + \frac{z^2}{3^3} + \frac{z^3}{3^4} + \ldots\right\}$$

$$+ \frac{1}{2}\left[\frac{1}{z} + \frac{2}{z^2} + \frac{4}{z^3} + \frac{8}{z^4} + \ldots\right]$$

$$= \{2^{n-1}\}z^{-n}, n \geq 1$$

$$= \left[\frac{n+1}{3^{n+2}} - \frac{1}{3^{n+1}}\right] z^n, n < 0$$

$$\therefore \quad Z^{-1}\{F(z)\} = 2^{n-1}, \text{ if } n \geq 1 \text{ and } -(n+2)\,3^{n-2}, \; n \leq 0$$

Example 4: *Find the inverse of Z-transform of* $\frac{1}{(z-4)^3}, |z|> 4.$

Solution: Let

$$F(z) = \frac{1}{z^3}(1 - 4z^{-1})^{-3}$$

$$= z^{-3}\left[1 + 12^{z-1} + 6(4z^{-1})^2 + 10(4z^{-1})^3 + \ldots + \frac{(n+1)(n+2)}{2}(4z^{-1})^n + \ldots\right]$$

where $|4z^{-1}| < 1$, *i.e.*, $|z| > 4$.

$$= z^{-3}\left\{\frac{(n+1)\;(n+2)}{2} 4^n\right\} z^{-n}$$

$$= \left\{\frac{(n+1)(n+2)}{2} 4^n\right\} z^{-n-3}$$

Replacing n by $n - 3$, we get

$$F(z) = \left\{\frac{(n-3+1)(n-3+2)}{2} 4^{n-3}\right\} z^{-n}$$

$$= \left\{\frac{(n-2)(n-1)}{2} 4^{n-3}\right\} z^{-n}$$

$$\therefore \quad Z^{-1}\{F(z)\} = \frac{(n-2)(n-1)}{2} 4^{n-3} \quad n \geq 3$$

and $\qquad = 0, \; n < 3.$

EXERCISE 11(C)

Find the inverse Z-transform of the following:

1. $\frac{1}{z-2}$
2. $\frac{4z}{z-a}$ (*i*) $|z| < |a|$, (*ii*) $|z| < |a|$
3. $\frac{z}{z-a}$ (*i*) $|z| > |a|$, (*ii*) $|z| < |a|$
4. $\frac{z}{3-z}$, $|z| < 3$

5. $\dfrac{z^3}{z^3 - 27}, |z| > 3$

6. $\dfrac{1}{(z-3)(z-2)}$ (*i*) $|z| < 2$ (*ii*) $2 < |z| < 3$ (*iii*) $|z| > 3$

7. $\dfrac{2z^2 - 5z}{(3-2)(z-3)}, |z| > 3$

8. $\dfrac{2z}{(z-2)^2}, |z| > 2$

9. $\dfrac{1}{\left(z-\frac{1}{2}\right)\left(z-\frac{1}{3}\right)}$ *when* (*i*) $\frac{1}{3} < |z| < \frac{1}{2}$; (*ii*) $\frac{1}{2} < |z|$

10. $\dfrac{1}{(z-5)^3}; |z| > 5$

11. $\dfrac{z(z^2 + 4z + 1)}{(z-1)^4}, |z| > 1$

12. $\dfrac{4z}{4z+1} + \dfrac{5z}{5z+1}; \frac{1}{5} < |z| < \frac{1}{4}$.

ANSWERS

1. $\{2^{n-1}\}$ when $|z| > 2$, $-\{2^{-n-1}\}$ when $|z| < 2$

2. (*i*) $\{4a^n\}$ (*ii*) $\left\{\ldots -\frac{4}{a^4}, -\frac{4}{a^3}, -\frac{4}{a^2}, \frac{4}{a}\right\}$

3. (*i*) $\{a^n\}$ (*ii*) $\left(-\frac{1}{a^n}\right)$

4. $\{3^n\}, n > 0$

5. $\{3^n\}$ for $n = 0, 3, 6, 9 = 0$

6. (*i*) $\left\{-\frac{1}{3^{n-1}} + \frac{1}{2^{n-1}},\right\}, n < 0$ (*ii*) $\{-2^{n-1}\}, n > 0; \{-3^{n-1}\}, n < 0$

   (*iii*) $\{3^{n-1} - 2^{n-1}\}\ k \geq 0,\ 0,\ n < 0$

7. $\{2^n + 3^n\},\ n \geq 0$
8. $\{n\,.\,2^n\}, n \geq 0$
9. (*i*) $\left\{-\dfrac{6}{3^{n-1}}\right\}$, if $n > 0$, -12×12^{-n}, if $n < 0$

   (*ii*) $6\left\{\dfrac{1}{2^{n-1}} - \dfrac{1}{3^{n-1}}\right\}, n \geq 1$
10. $\dfrac{(n-1)\ (n-1)}{2}\ 5^{\pi-3}, n \geq 3$ and $0,\ n < 3$
11. $\{n^3\}$
12. $\begin{cases} -\left(-\dfrac{1}{4}\right)^n, & n < 0 \\ \left(-\dfrac{1}{5}\right)^n, & n \geq 0 \end{cases}$

12

Applications of Z-transforms to Solve Difference Equations

12.1 INTRODUCTION

When we study mathematical models, in which a variable is assumed to have only discrete set of values, then we come across difference equations. Study of difference equations is so much useful in computer and social sciences that a detailed study of these equations becomes unavoidable.

12.2 DIFFERENCE EQUATIONS

Definition: *An equation relating the values of a function y and one or more of its differences* Δy, $\Delta^2 y$, ... *for each value of some set of number A for which each of these functions is defined is called a difference equations over the set A.*

Therefore a difference equation is a *relation involving differences.* If we consider functions y defined for all real number x, the following equations are examples of difference equations over the set of real number.

$$\Delta y(x) + 3y(x) = 0 \quad ...(i)$$

$$\Delta^2 y(x) - 2\Delta y(x) + 5y(x) = 7 \quad ...(ii)$$

$$\Delta^2 y(x) - xy(x) = 3x + 5 \quad ...(iii)$$

$$y(x) \cdot \Delta^3 y(x) = 8 \quad ...(iv)$$

$$[\Delta y(x)]^2 + [y(x)]^2 = 6 \quad ...(v)$$

Note 1: It is not necessary that the difference equations are defined over the set of all real numbers. They can be considered as difference equations over some other set.

Note 2: We can not tell by merely looking at equations (i) to (v) whether they are difference equations over the set of all real numbers or over the set of positive integers, or some other set. This information must clearly be given separately.

Note 3: To emphasize the restriction of the set to consecutive integers, we shall use the symbol h rather than x to denote a number in the domain of the functions related by the difference equation, and write y_h rather than $y(h)$ for the value of y at h.

All difference operators are taken with a difference interval equal to 1 since we have a consecutive value of h. Now equations (i) to (v) can be written as follows:

$$\Delta y_h + 3y_h = 0 \qquad \text{...(vi)}$$

$$\Delta^2 y_h - 2\,\Delta y_h + 5y_h = 7 \qquad \text{...(vii)}$$

$$\Delta^2 y_h - hy_h = 3h + 5 \qquad \text{...(viii)}$$

$$y_h \Delta^3 y_h = 8 \qquad \text{...(ix)}$$

$$(\Delta y_h)^2 + (y_h)^2 = 6 \qquad \text{...(x)}$$

In each case we must specify the range of values of the integer h.

12.3 DIFFERENCES AND OPERATORS

Forward Difference: Consider the function $y = f(x)$. Let this function is defined for a set of values (x_0, y_0), (x_1, y_1), $(x_2\, y_2)$, ..., (x_n, y_n), then the differences

$$\Delta y_0 = y_1 - y_0 \text{ or } \Delta f(x) = f(x + h) - f(x),$$

where h is the interval of differencing.

$$\Delta y_1 = y_2 - y_1$$

$$\Delta y_2 = y_3 - y_2$$

- - - - - - - - - - -

- - - - - - - - - - -

$$\Delta y_n = y_{n-1} - y_n$$

are called the first forward differences, where Δ is the *forward difference operator.*

Similarly, 2nd, 3rd, ... nth forward differences can be defined as

$$\Delta^2 y_r = \Delta y_{r+1} - \Delta y_r,\ \Delta^3 y_r = \Delta^2 y_{r+1} - \Delta^2 y_r,\ ....,$$

$$\Delta^n y_r = \Delta^{n-1} y_{r+1} - D^{n-1} y_r.$$

Backward differences: Backward differences are defined as

$$\Delta y_r = y_r - y_{r-1},\ \Delta^2 y_r = \Delta y_r - \Delta y_{r-1} \text{ ... etc.}$$

Here Δ is the *backward difference operator.*

Shift Operator E: If $y = f(x)$ is any function then operation of E on $f(x)$ implies that given an increment to the value of x in the function. If this increment is of quantity h, then the operation of E means to put $(x + h)$ in the function whenever there is x, i.e.,

$$E f(x) = f(x+h)$$

$E f(x)$ does not mean that E is multiplied to $f(x)$ but this means that E is operated on $f(x)$ and as such it is only a symbol and not an algebraic number. E is known as *shift operator*.

Similarly,

$$E^2 f(x) = f(x+2h),\ E^3 f(x) = f(x+3h) \ldots,$$

$$E^n f(x) = f(x+nh).$$

Note (i) $E \equiv 1 + \Delta$ or $\Delta \equiv E - 1$

(ii) $\Delta \equiv 1 - E^{-1}$ or $E^{-1} \equiv 1 - \Delta$

12.4 TO WRITE A DIFFERENCE EQUATION AS A RELATION AMONG THE VALUES OF *y*

We know the relation between E and Δ as

$$E = 1 + \Delta \quad \text{or} \quad \Delta = E - 1$$

Hence,

$$\Delta y_h = Ey_h - y_h \qquad \ldots\text{(i)}$$

$$\Delta^2 y_h = E^2 y_h - 2Ey_h + y_h \qquad \ldots\text{(ii)}$$

$$\Delta^3 y_h = E^3 y_h - 3E^2 y_h + 3Ey_h - y_h \qquad \ldots\text{(iii)}$$

We also know that

$$E^n y(x) = y(x+nk)$$

$$\ldots \quad E^n y_h = y(h+nk)$$

$$= y_{h+n}, \text{ if } k = 1 \qquad \ldots\text{(iv)}$$

Therefore the equations (vi) to (x) of § 12.2 can be written as

$$y_{h+1} + 2y_h = 0 \qquad \ldots\text{(v)}$$

$$y_{h+2} - 4y_{h+1} + 7y_h = 7 \qquad \ldots\text{(vi)}$$

$$y_{h+2} - 2y_{h+1} + (1-h)\, y_h = 3h + 5 \qquad \ldots\text{(vii)}$$

$$y_h y_{h+2} - 3y_h y_{h+2} + 3y_h y_{h+1} - y^2_h = 8 \qquad \ldots\text{(viii)}$$

$$(y_{h+1} - y_h)^2 + y^2_h = 6 \qquad \ldots\text{(ix)}$$

12.5 LINEAR DIFFERENCE EQUATION

Definition: *A difference equation over a set A is linear over A if it can be written in the form* $f_0(h)\, y_{h+n} + f_1(h)\, y_{h+n-1} + \ldots + f_n(h)\, y(h) = g(h)$, ...(i)

where $f_0, f_1, \ldots, f_{n-1}, f_n$ *and g are each functions of h only, defined for all values of h in the set A.*

The equation (v), (vi) and (vii) come under this category.

Since in equations (v), (vi) and (vii) the coefficients are constant functions, hence this type of equations are called the *linear difference equations with constant coefficients.*

Equations (viii) and (ix) are *non-linear difference equations.*

If the right side of (i) is replaced by zero, *i.e.,* if $f(h) = 0$ then we obtain

$$f_0(h)\, y_{h+1} + f_1(h)\, y_{h+n-1} + \ldots + f_n(h)\, y_h = 0,$$

which is called the *homogeneous linear difference equation* corresponding to (i).

If $g(h) \neq 0$, the equation (i) is called the *non-homogenous linear difference equation.*

12.6 ORDER OF A LINEAR DIFFERENCE EQUATION

The order of a linear difference equation defined over the set A and written in the form of equation (i) of § 12.5 is n if both f_0 *and* f_n *are difference from zero at each point of the set A.*

In other words the order of a linear difference equation is the *difference between the largest and smallest arguments* for the function *y* involved in the equation.

For example:

$$y_{h+2} + 3y_{h+1} - 8y_h = 3 \qquad \text{order} = 2$$

$$y_{h+2} + 4y_{h+1} = 2^h \qquad \text{order} = 1$$

$$hy_{h+2} + y_{h+1} - 3y_h = 0 \qquad \text{order} = 2$$

$$2^h y_{h+3} - y_{h+2} + 3^h y_{h+1} - y_h = 6 \qquad \text{order} = 3$$

12.7 SOLUTION OF A DIFFERENCE EQUATION

A solution of a difference equation is a relation between the independent variable and the dependent variable which satisfies the equation. Substituting such a relation in the equation the left hand and right hand members become identically equal.

A solution which involves n arbitrary periodic constants is called a *general solution* of a difference equation of order n.

A solution obtained from the general solution by assiging particular periodic constants is called a *particular solution.*

Let us consider the difference equation

$$y_{h+1} - 3y_h = 0, h = 0, 1, 2, \ldots \quad \ldots\text{(i)}$$

Let

$$y_h = 3^h, h = 0, 1, 2, \ldots \quad \ldots\text{(ii)}$$

The function y defined by (ii) satisfies the difference equation (i). So it is said to be a solution of (i) in general, (i) is satisfied by

$$y_h = c.3^h \quad \ldots\text{(iii)}$$

for any constant c.

The function y given by (ii), is the *particular solution* of (i) while the function y in (iii) containing the arbitrary constant c, is the *general solution* of (i).

A difference equation may have no solution just as in the case of algebraic equations, i.g.,

$$(y_{h+1} - y_h)^2 + y^2_h = -1$$

is satisfied for no real-valued function y.

12.8 SOLUTION OF DIFFERENCE EQUATION BY Z-TRANSFORMS

Z-transforms play the same role in discrete analysis as Laplace and Fourier transforms in continuous systems. Communication branch is the field whose development is based on discrete analysis. Difference equations are formed in discrete systems and their solutions and analysis are carried out by Z-transforms. The method of solving differences equation by Z-transform method will be clear by following illustrative examples.

ILLUSTRATIVE EXAMPLES

Example 1: *Solve the difference equation*

$$6y_{k+2} - 7y_{k+1} + y_k = 0,$$

$y(0), y(1) = 1$ *by Z-transforms.*

Solution: We have

$$6y_{k+2} - 7y_{k+1} + y_k = 0 \quad \ldots\text{(i)}$$

Taking Z-transform of both sides of (i), we get

$$Z[6y_{k+2} - 7y_{k+1} + y_k] = 0$$

$$\Rightarrow \quad 6\,Z(y_{k+2}) - 7\,Z(y_{k+1}) + Z(y_k) = 0$$

$$\Rightarrow \quad 6\,[z^3\,Y(z) - z^3\,y(0) - 3y(1)]$$

$$-7\,[z\,Y(z) - z\,y(0)] + Y(z) = 0 \qquad \text{...(ii)}$$

By putting the value of y (0) and y (1) in (ii), we get

$$6z^2\,Y(z) - 6z - z\,Y(z) + Y(z) = 0$$

$$\Rightarrow \quad (6z^2 - 3 + 1)\,Y(z) = 6$$

$$\Rightarrow \quad Y(z) = \frac{6z}{6z^2 - z + 1} = \frac{6z}{(3z+1)(2z-1)}$$

$$= \frac{z^{-1}}{\left(1 + \frac{z^{-1}}{3}\right)\left(1 - \frac{z^{-1}}{2}\right)}$$

$$= \frac{6/5}{\left(1 - \frac{z^{-1}}{2}\right)\left(1 + \frac{z^{-1}}{3}\right)}$$

Taking inverse *Z*-transform, we get

$$y_k = Z^{-1}\left[\frac{\frac{6}{5}}{\left(1 - \frac{z^{-1}}{2}\right)}\right] - Z^{-1}\left[\frac{\frac{6}{5}}{\left(1 + \frac{z^{-1}}{3}\right)}\right]$$

$$= \frac{6}{5}\left(\frac{1}{2}\right)^k - \frac{6}{5}\left(-\frac{1}{3}\right)^k$$

$$= \frac{6}{5}\left[\left(\frac{1}{2}\right)^k - \left(-\frac{1}{3}\right)^k\right]$$

Example 2: *Solve the following difference equation by Z-transform:*

$$y_{k+2} - 2\cos\alpha\; y_{k+1} + y_k = 0,$$

$y_0 = 0,\ y_1 = 1.$

Solution: We have

$$y_{k+2} - 2\cos\alpha\; y_{k+1} + y_k = 0$$

Taking Z-transform on both sides

$$Z\,[y_{k+2} - 2\cos\alpha\, y_{k+1} + y_k] = 0$$

$$\Rightarrow \quad Z\,(y_{k+2}) - 2\cos\alpha\, Z\,(y_{k+1}) + Z\,(y_k) = 0$$

$$\Rightarrow \quad [z^2\, Y(z) - z^2\, y\,(0) - 3y\,(1)] - 2\cos\alpha\,[z\, Y(z) - z\, y\,(0)] + Y(z) = 0$$

By putting the value of y (0) and y (1), we get

$$[z^2\, Y(z) - z] - 2\cos a\, z\, Y(z) + Y(z) = 0$$

$$\Rightarrow \quad [z^2 - 2z\cos\alpha + 1]\, Y(z) = z$$

$$\Rightarrow \quad Y(z) = \frac{z}{z^2 - 2z\cos\alpha + 1}$$

$$= \frac{z}{z^2 - (e^{i\alpha} + e^{-i\alpha})\, z + 1}$$

$$= \frac{z}{(z - e^{i\alpha})(z - e^{-i\alpha})}$$

$$= -\frac{i}{2\sin\alpha}\left(\frac{z}{z - e^{i\alpha}}\right) + \frac{i}{2\sin\alpha}\left(\frac{z}{z - e^{-i\alpha}}\right)$$

Taking inverse Z - transform, we get

$$y_k = -\frac{i}{2\sin\alpha}\left[(e^{i\alpha})^k - (e^{-i\alpha})^k\right]$$

$$= -\frac{i}{2\sin\alpha}[\cos\alpha\, k + i\sin\alpha\, k - \cos\alpha\, k + i\sin\alpha\, k]$$

$$= \frac{-i}{2\sin\alpha}[2i\sin\alpha\, k] = \frac{\sin\alpha\, k}{\sin\alpha}.$$

Example 3: *Solve by Z-transform* $y_{k+1} + \frac{1}{4} y_k = \left(\frac{1}{4}\right)^k \; (k \geq 0),\; y(0) = 0$

Solution: We have

$$y_{k+1} + \frac{1}{4} y_k = \left(\frac{1}{4}\right)^k$$

Taking Z-transform of both sides, we get

$$Z\left[y_{k+1} + \frac{1}{4} y_k\right] = Z\left[\left(\frac{1}{4}\right)^k\right]$$

$$\Rightarrow \quad Z\,[y_{k+1}] + Z\left[\frac{1}{4} y_k\right] = Z\left[\left(\frac{1}{4}\right)^k\right]$$

$$zY(z) - z\,y(0) + \frac{1}{4}Y(z) = \frac{1}{1-\frac{1}{4}z^{-1}} \qquad \textit{where } |z| > \frac{1}{4}.$$

$$\Rightarrow \qquad zY(z) - 0 + \frac{1}{4}Y(z) = \frac{1}{1-\frac{1}{4}z^{-1}}$$

$$\Rightarrow \qquad \left(z+\frac{1}{4}\right)Y(z) = \frac{1}{1-\frac{1}{4}z^{-1}}$$

$$\Rightarrow \qquad Y(z) = \frac{1}{\left(z+\frac{1}{4}\right)} \times \frac{1}{\left(1-\frac{1}{4}z^{-1}\right)}$$

$$= \frac{z^{-1}}{\left(1+\frac{1}{4}z^{-1}\right)\left(1-\frac{1}{4}z^{-1}\right)}$$

$$= \frac{-2}{\left(1+\frac{1}{4}z^{-1}\right)} + \frac{2}{\left(1-\frac{1}{4}z^{-1}\right)}$$

Taking inverse Z-transform, we get

$$y(k) = Z^{-1}\frac{2}{\left(1+\frac{1}{4}z^{-1}\right)} + Z^{-1}\left[\frac{2}{1-\frac{1}{4}z^{-1}}\right]$$

$$= Z^{-1}\left[-2\left(1+\frac{1}{4}z^{-1}\right)^{-1}\right] + Z^{-1}\left[2\left(1-\frac{1}{4}z^{-1}\right)^{-1}\right]$$

$$= -2\left(-\frac{1}{4}\right)^{k} + 2\left(\frac{1}{4}\right)^{k}$$

Example 4: *Use Z-transform to solve the difference equation:*

$$y_{n+2} - 2\,y_{n+1} + y_n = 3n + 5$$

Solution: We have

$$y_{n+2} - 2\,y_{n+1} + y_n = 3n + 5$$

Taking the Z-transform of both sides, we get

$$[z^2 Y(z) - z^2 y(0) - z\,y(1)] - 2[z\,Y(z) - z\,y(0)] + Y(z)$$

$$= 3.\frac{z}{(z-1)^2} + 5.\frac{z}{z-1}$$

or $$Y(z)(z^2 - 2z + 1) = \frac{5z^2 - 2z}{(z-1)^2} + y_0(z^2 - 2z) + y_1 z$$

or $$r(z) = \frac{5z^2 - 2z}{(z-1)^4} + y_0\frac{z^2 - 2z}{(z-1)^2} + y_1\frac{z}{(z-1)^2}$$

on inversion, we get

$$y_n = Z^{-1}\left[\frac{5z^2 - 2z}{(z-1)^4}\right] + y_0 Z^{-1}\left[\frac{z^2 - 2z}{(z-1)^2}\right] + y_1 Z^{-1}\left[\frac{z}{(z-1)^2}\right]$$

Noting that

$$Z(1) = \frac{z}{z-1},\ Z(n) = \frac{z}{(z-1)^2},$$

$$Z(n^2) = \frac{z^2 + z}{(z-1)^3},\ Z(n^3) = \frac{z^2 + 4z^2 + z}{(z-1)^4}$$

$$\therefore \quad \frac{5z^2 - 2z}{(z-1)^4} = A.\frac{z^3 + 4z^2 + z}{(z-1)^4} + B.\frac{z^2 + z}{(z-1)^3} + C.\frac{z}{(z-1)^2} + D.\frac{z}{z-1}$$

Equating coefficients of like power of z we get

$$A = \frac{1}{2},\ B = 1,\ C = -\frac{3}{2},\ D = 0$$

$$\therefore \quad Z^{-1}\left[\frac{5z^2 - 2z}{(z-1)^4}\right] = \frac{1}{2}n^3 + n^2 - \frac{3}{2}n$$

$$= \frac{1}{2}n(n-1)(n+3)$$

$$Z^{-1}\left[\frac{z^2 - 2z}{(z-1)^2}\right] = Z^{-1}\left[\frac{z}{z-1}\right] - Z^{-1}\left[\frac{z}{(z-1)^2}\right]$$

$$= 1 - n$$

and $$Z^{-1}\left[\frac{z}{(z-1)^2}\right] = n$$

Substituting these values, we get

$$\begin{aligned} y_n &= \frac{1}{2} n(n-1)(n+3) + y_0(1-n) + y_1 n \\ &= \frac{1}{2} n(n-1)(n+3) + y_0 + (y_1 - y_0)_n \\ &= \frac{1}{2} n(n-1)(n+3) + C_0 + C_1 n, \end{aligned}$$

where $C_0 = y_0,\quad C_1 = y_1 - y_0.$

Example 5: *Solve by Z-transform the difference equation*

$$y_{k+2} + 6y_{k+1} + 9y_k = 2^k,\ (y_0 = y_1 = 0)$$

Solution: We have

$$y_{k+2} + 6y_{k+1} + 9y_k = 2^k \qquad \text{...(i)}$$

Taking Z-transform of both sides of (i), we get

$$Z[y_{k+2}] + 6Z[y_{k+1}] + 9Z[yk] = Z[2^k]$$

$$\Rightarrow\ z^2 Y(z) - z^2 y(0) - 3y(1) + 6z\,Y(z) - 6zy(0) + 9Y(z) = \frac{1}{(1-2z^{-1})}$$

$$\Rightarrow\ z^2 Y(z) + 6z\,Y(z) + 9Y(z) = \frac{z}{(z-2)}$$

$$\Rightarrow\ (z^2 + 6z + 9)\,Y(z) = \frac{z}{(z-2)}$$

$$\therefore\qquad Y(z) = \frac{z}{(z-2)(z+3)^2}$$

Taking Z-inverse

$$Z^{-1}[Y(z)] = Z^{-1}\left[\frac{z}{(z-2)(z+3)^2}\right]$$

It has one pole of second order at $z = -3$ and a single pole at $z = 2$.

Residue at $z = 2$ is

$$= \left[(z-2)\,.\,z^{k-1} \frac{z}{(z-2)(z+3)^2} \right]$$

$$= \left[\frac{z^k}{(z+3)^2} \right]_{z=2} = \frac{2^k}{25}.$$

Residue at $z = -3$ is

$$= \frac{\mathrm{d}}{\mathrm{dz}} \left[(z+3)^2\, z^{k-1} \frac{z}{(z-2)(z+3)^2} \right]_{z=-3}$$

$$= \frac{d}{dz} \left[\frac{z^k}{z-2} \right]_{z=-3}$$

$$= \left[\frac{(z-2)\,.\,kz^{k-1} - zk}{(z-2)^2} \right]_{z=-3}$$

$$= \left[\frac{z^k}{(z-2)^2} \left\{ \frac{(z-2)\,k}{z} - 1 \right\} \right]_{z=-3}$$

$$= \frac{(-3)^k}{25} \left[\frac{-5k}{-3} - 1 \right]$$

$$= \frac{(-3)^k}{25} \left[\frac{5k}{3} - 1 \right]$$

$$y_k = \frac{2^k}{25} + \frac{(-3)^k}{25} \left(\frac{5k}{3} - 1 \right).$$

Example 6: *Solve by Z-transform*

$$yk + \frac{1}{25}\, yk - 2 = \left(\frac{1}{5} \right)^k \cos \frac{k\pi}{2}, \ (k \geq 0) \ \textit{using residue method.}$$

Solution: We have

$$yk + \frac{1}{25}\, yk - 2 = \left(\frac{1}{5} \right)^k \cos \frac{k\pi}{2}$$

Taking z-transform of both sides of (i), we get

$$Z\left[y_k + \frac{1}{25} y_{k-2}\right] = Z\left(\frac{1}{5}\right)^k \cos\frac{k\pi}{2}$$

$$\Rightarrow \quad Y(z) + \frac{1}{25} z^{-2} Y(z) = \frac{z^2}{z^2 + \frac{1}{25}}$$

$$\Rightarrow \quad \left[1 + \frac{1}{25} z^{-2}\right] Y(z) = \frac{z^2}{z^2 + \frac{1}{25}}$$

$$\Rightarrow \quad Y(z) = \frac{z^2}{\left(1 + \frac{1}{25} z^{-2}\right)\left(z^2 + \frac{1}{25}\right)}$$

$$= \frac{z^4}{\left(z^2 + \frac{1}{25}\right)\left(z^2 + \frac{1}{25}\right)} = \frac{z^4}{\left(z^2 + \frac{1}{25}\right)^2}$$

Here, we have two poles of second order at $z = \frac{i}{5}$ and $z = -\frac{i}{5}$ respectively.

Residue at $z = \frac{i}{5}$

$$= \left[\frac{d}{dz}\left(z - \frac{i}{5}\right)^2 \frac{z^{k-1} z^4}{\left(z^2 + \frac{1}{25}\right)^2}\right]_{z=\frac{i}{5}}$$

$$= \left[\frac{d}{dz} \frac{z^{k-1} z^4}{\left(z + \frac{i}{5}\right)^2}\right]_{z=\frac{i}{5}}$$

$$= \left[\frac{\left(z + \frac{i}{5}\right)^2 (k+3) z^{k+2} - z^{k+3} 2\left(z + \frac{i}{5}\right)}{\left(z + \frac{i}{5}\right)^4}\right]_{z=\frac{i}{5}}$$

$$= \left[\frac{\left(z + \frac{i}{5}\right)(k+3)\, z^{k+2} - z^{k+3}}{\left(z + \frac{i}{5}\right)^3} \right]_{z=\frac{i}{5}}$$

$$= \frac{\left(\frac{2i}{5}\right)(k+3)\left(\frac{i}{5}\right)^{k+2} - 2\left(\frac{i}{5}\right)^{k+3}}{\left(\frac{2i}{5}\right)^3}$$

$$= \left(\frac{5}{2i}\right)^3 (2k+4)\left(\frac{i}{5}\right)^{k+3} = \left(\frac{1}{g}\right)(2k+4)\left(\frac{i}{5}\right)^k$$

$$= \frac{1}{4}(k+2)\left(\frac{1}{5}\right)^k \left[\cos\frac{\pi}{2} + i\sin\frac{\pi}{2}\right]^k$$

$$= \frac{1}{4}(k+2)\left(\frac{1}{5}\right)^k \left[\cos\frac{k\pi}{2} + i\sin\frac{k\pi}{2}\right]$$

and residue at $\left(z = \frac{i}{5}\right)$

$$= \frac{1}{4}(k+2)\left(\frac{1}{5}\right)^k \left[\cos\frac{k\pi}{2} + i\sin\frac{k\pi}{2}\right]$$

$\therefore \quad y_k$ = Sum of the residues

$$= \frac{1}{2}(k+2)\frac{1}{5k}\cos\frac{k\pi}{2}.$$

Example 7: *Using Z-transform, solve the following difference equation:*

$$y_{k+2} + 4y_{k+1} + 3y_k = 3^k,$$

given $y_0 = 0$ *and* $y_1 = 1$.

Solution: Taking Z-transform of both sides, we get

$$Z[y_{k+2}] + 4Z[y_{k+1}] + 3Z[y_k] = Z[3^k]$$

$$\Rightarrow \quad z^2 Y(z) - z^2 y(0) - zy(1) + 4z\,Y(z) - 4zy(0) + 3Y(z) = \frac{z}{z-3}$$

$$\Rightarrow \quad (z^2 + 4z + 3)\,Y(z) - z = \frac{z}{z-3} \qquad [\because y_0 = 0 \text{ and } y_1 = 1]$$

$$\Rightarrow \qquad y(z) = \frac{z}{(z-3)(z+1)(z+3)} + \frac{z}{(z+1)(z+3)}$$

Taking inverse Z-transform

$$y_k = Z^{-1}\left[\frac{z}{(z-3)(z+1)(z+3)}\right] + Z^{-1}\left[\frac{z}{(z+1)(z+3)}\right]$$

$$= Z^{-1}[P(z)] + Z^{-1}[Q(z)]$$

Consider the region $|z| = 4$

$$\text{Residue of } P(z) \text{ at } z = 3 = \lim_{z\to 3}(z-3)\,z^{k-1}\frac{z}{(z-3)(z+1)(z+2)}$$

$$= \frac{3^k}{24}$$

$$\text{Residue of } P(z) \text{ at } (z = -1) = \lim_{z\to -1}(z+1)\,z^{k-1}\frac{z}{(z-3)(z+1)(z+3)}$$

$$= \frac{(-1)^k}{-8}$$

$$\text{Residue of } P(z) \text{ at } (z = -3) = \lim_{z\to -3}(z+3)\,z^{k-1}\frac{z}{(z-3)(z+1)(z+3)}$$

$$= \frac{(-3)^k}{12}$$

$$\text{Residue of } Q(z) \text{ at } (z = -1) = \lim_{z\to -1}(z+1)\,z^{k-1}\frac{z}{(z+1)(z+3)}$$

$$= \frac{(-1)^k}{2}$$

$$\text{Residue of } Q(z) \text{ at } (z = -3) = \lim_{z\to -3}(z+3)\,z^{k-1}\frac{z}{(z+1)(z+3)}$$

$$= \frac{(-3)^k}{-2}$$

$$\therefore \; y_k = \text{Sum of residues} = \left[\frac{3^k}{24} - \frac{(-1)^k}{8} + \frac{(-3)^k}{12}\right] + \left[\frac{(-1)^k}{-2} - \frac{(-3)^k}{2}\right]$$

$$= \left[\frac{3^k}{24} + \frac{3}{8} + (-1)^k - \frac{5}{12}(-3)^k\right]$$

EXERCISE 12

Solve the difference equation by Z-transform:

1. $2y_{k+2} - 5y_{k+1} + 3y_k = 0;\ y_0 = 0$ and $y_1 = 1$
2. $9y_{k+2} - 6y_{k+1} + y_k = 0;\ y_0 = 0$ and $y_1 = 1$
3. $y_{k+1} - 2y_k + y_{k-1} = a^k,\ a \neq 1$
4. $y_k + \frac{1}{9} y_{k-2} = \left(\frac{1}{3}\right)^k \cos\frac{k\pi}{2},\ (k \geq 0)$

ANSWERS

1. $y_k = -\frac{2}{3}\left(\frac{1}{2}\right)^k + \frac{2}{3}.2^k$
2. $y_k = 3k\left(\frac{1}{3}\right)^k$
3. $y_k = \frac{1}{a}(k+1)\,U(k) - \frac{a}{(a-1)^2}U(k) + \frac{a}{(a-1)^2}a^k\,U(k) + \frac{1}{1-a}k\,U(k-1)$
4. $y_k = \left(\frac{k+2}{2}\right)\left(\frac{1}{3}\right)^k \cos\frac{k\pi}{2}\,U(k).$